REFUGE
MUST BE GIVEN

REFUGE
MUST BE GIVEN

*Eleanor Roosevelt, the Jewish Plight,
and the Founding of Israel*

John F. Sears

Purdue University Press | West Lafayette, Indiana

Copyright 2021 by Purdue University. All rights reserved.
Printed in the United States of America.

Cataloging-in-Publication data is on file at the Library of Congress.
ISBN: 978-1-61249-659-7 (hardcover)
ISBN: 978-1-61249-633-7 (paperback)
ISBN: 978-1-61249-634-4 (epub)
ISBN: 978-1-61249-635-1 (epdf)

Cover artwork: ER with Moroccan Jewish children at a Youth Aliyah transit camp in Cambous, France, March 1955. Courtesy of the FDR Library.

For Jane

For lo, the winter is past,
*   The rain is over and gone.*
The blossoms appear in the land,
*   The time of singing has come.*

The Song of Songs

Whatever one's philosophy may be, one has to face the stark realities affecting the Jewish people of Europe. Refuge must be given them wherever possible.
                        ROSE SCHNEIDERMAN TO ELEANOR ROOSEVELT, APRIL 14, 1938

———•———

One of the most compelling reasons for the existence of Israel is the fact that it is the only sure haven for the Jewish people. In troubled times, when they are the first to suffer, it is essential for them to have their own country of refuge.
                        ELEANOR ROOSEVELT, MY DAY, DECEMBER 7, 1956

———•———

Here in Israel the twenty-fifth Jubilee of Youth Aliyah is being celebrated, and the name of Eleanor Roosevelt appears again and again like a silver thread in the weaving of this particular piece of history.
                        JOSEPH BARATZ TO ELEANOR ROOSEVELT,
                        KIBBUTZ DEGANIA A, FEBRUARY 23, 1959

CONTENTS

	Introduction	1
1.	A Cautious Response to Nazi Germany	7
2.	Partnering with Clarence Pickett	19
3.	Responding to the Threat of War and the Nazi Assault on the Jews	32
4.	Antisemitism and *The Moral Basis of Democracy*	40
5.	The Wagner-Rogers Bill	49
6.	The United States Committee for the Care of European Children	60
7.	The Emergency Rescue Committee, Sumner Welles, and the Obstacles to Rescue	72
8.	Continuing the Fight on Behalf of Visa Applicants	93
9.	Combating Anti-Immigrant Sentiment and Antisemitism on the Home Front	107
10.	A Failed Attempt at Rescue	116
11.	Responding to News of the Extermination Camps, 1942–45	127
12.	A March to a Better Life	140
13.	The Postwar Refugee Crisis and the Future of Palestine	156
14.	Committing to the Establishment of a Jewish State	176
15.	Visiting Israel as World Patron of Youth Aliyah	194
16.	Immigrant Children and the Task of Cultural Integration	214
17.	American Policy toward Israel in the 1950s	223
18.	A Special Bond with Israel	235
	Conclusion	246
	Acknowledgments	*251*
	Notes	*255*
	Bibliography	*303*
	Index	*309*
	About the Author	*329*

INTRODUCTION

MUCH HAS BEEN written and debated about the failure of President Franklin D. Roosevelt (FDR) and his State Department to do more to rescue Jews before and during the Holocaust. The lack of effective leadership on the part of many Jewish leaders in pressuring the Roosevelt administration to act and the opposition of Congress and the American people to admitting refugees, particularly Jews, have also been thoroughly analyzed.[1] Much less has been written about the role Eleanor Roosevelt (ER) played during the European refugee crisis and the Holocaust;[2] even less about her role in the postwar refugee crisis and the founding of Israel. In many ways she was unique among the central players in the drama. Not only was she a woman, while most of her colleagues were male, she was perhaps the most influential woman in American public life between 1933 and her death in 1962. From 1933 until 1945, she was the most effective First Lady in American history, constricted in some ways by the role she had to play but also politically powerful in her own right. She had to find indirect ways of exercising her influence, however, since she did not hold elected or appointed public office for much of the time period during which she was active.

ER's role was unique in another way as well. She was near the center of American power over a longer period than the other players involved in these affairs. She was active from the advent of Hitler's persecution of the Jews in 1933, through World War II and the Holocaust, during the debate over the future of Palestine, on through the establishment of Israel, and up to the point where Israel was a well-established state. We can see how these events in the history of the Jewish people changed her views and stimulated her to action.

She was also unusual in the way she approached human problems. The humanitarian impulses at the core of her being set her apart from most of her male contemporaries in the political and diplomatic worlds. Although she operated on the national stage, and later, on the world stage as a politician and stateswoman, the impetus for her actions was often the distress of individuals or groups of people she met in her travels, such as out-of-work coal miners in West Virginia, refugees from persecution in Germany and Eastern Europe who arrived in the United States, and survivors of the Holocaust and immigrant Jews from the Middle East who found a haven in Palestine and, later, Israel. The journalist Doris Fleeson remarked on this element of ER's character when she wrote: "I get so impatient with individuals and then I see you in operation and remind myself that that is the real achievement—to care for the individuals as well as for social justice. That is why you are so strong."[3]

It is also important to keep in mind that ER cared deeply not just about the rescue of people in distress but about their rehabilitation—about how to restore people to normal living who had, in many cases, lost everything. She and her colleagues sought ways to care for refugees once they arrived in the United States, to find them homes and jobs, fight prejudice against them, and make them feel welcome. She admired the way the American Friends Service Committee restored the spirits of displaced persons and provided them with the tools to make a new start and become self-sustaining. Later she supported the similar work that Youth Aliyah carried out in Israel with children rescued from Europe, Africa, and the Middle East.

Looking at the response of the Roosevelt administration to the persecution of the Jews through the lens of Eleanor Roosevelt shifts the discussion from those who failed to facilitate or obstructed the admission of refugees to the United States to those organizations and individuals who pushed hard, in the face of many barriers, to admit them. Today, Holocaust historians focus on why the Roosevelt administration and the American people did not do more to rescue the Jews. ER recognized that the Jews were the principal target of Nazi cruelty, but she also knew that many non-Jews were also in grave danger. From her perspective at the time, the question was: Why did the United States government and her fellow Americans resist admitting the victims of Nazi persecution, whoever they were, and what could be done to change American attitudes toward immigration? ER knew that most American Christians failed not only to demand the admittance of Jewish refugees to the United States but failed to demand the rescue of their fellow Christians. In the visa cases in which she intervened, she did not find it any easier for a non-Jew to get a visa than for a Jew to do so. Some of the cases she brought to the attention of the State Department involved Jews, some non-Jews. Although antisemitism was clearly a major factor in America's opposition to immigration, most of the obstacles ER tried to overcome applied to both groups.

In her efforts to assist refugees seeking to immigrate to America, ER served as a liaison between the President's Committee on Political Refugees, the Emergency Rescue Committee, and the United States Committee for the Care of European Children on the one hand and the president and the State Department on the other. She helped James McDonald, Marshall Field III, Clarence Pickett, and other leaders of rescue efforts to gain access to the president and the State Department. She advised them, encouraged them, and advocated on their behalf. The story of Pickett, executive director of the American Friends Service Committee, who was ER's closest partner in refugee work, has been almost completely neglected by historians. In addition, an examination of ER's persistent appeals to Undersecretary of State Sumner Welles on behalf of visa applicants and his response throws new light on Welles's enigmatic record during the refugee crisis and the Holocaust.

ELEANOR ROOSEVELT'S EXTRAORDINARY CAPACITY to grow as a person was rooted in her warm sympathy for other people, her interest in the special circumstances of their lives, and her desire to help when needed. Having felt unloved and excluded as a child, she identified with minorities and other outsiders.[4] Her openness to experience and her capacity to reach out beyond the privileged and circumscribed world in which she grew up to connect personally with people from other racial, ethnic, religious, and economic backgrounds helped make her one of the great humanitarians of the twentieth century.

Although she was still expressing antisemitic attitudes she had acquired as a child to a member of her family in 1918 when she was in her mid-thirties, ER became a crusader against antisemitism and other forms of prejudice during the New Deal and World War II. She argued that mere tolerance of other religions and races was not sufficient; people had to fight for the basic rights of all people. Paradoxically, she still occasionally repeated cultural stereotypes of Jews in her writing. In addition, as a way she and others believed would reduce prejudice, she favored policies that would distribute Jews more widely among the professions and throughout the nation. In her political work, however, Jews were among her most valued colleagues. She continued to advocate for the admission of more Jewish refugees to the United States after World War II, and she became a strong supporter of the United Nations plan to partition Palestine into a Jewish and an Arab state. After Israel's founding, she became Israel's most prominent Gentile champion in the United States and worked closely with Hadassah, the American women's Zionist organization, to assist Youth Aliyah in bringing Jewish children to the new nation and train them to become productive citizens—a largely untold part of her story.[5]

In 1903, when Eleanor Roosevelt was being courted by her cousin, Franklin Roosevelt, she was doing volunteer work at Rivington Street Settlement on the Lower East Side where many of the settlement's clients were Jews. ER taught calisthenics and dance, and on one occasion took FDR with her when she visited a family in the dark and crowded tenement where they lived. He had no idea that people lived under such appalling conditions. That visit inaugurated the role she would later play in bringing social problems, including the plight of refugees, to his attention. Her experience at Rivington Street stimulated an interest in addressing the needs of immigrants and the poor. It had no effect on the kind of antisemitism she had acquired from members of her family and friends, however. When FDR began law school at Columbia in 1904, ER wrote to him, "I am anxious to hear about your first day and whether you found any old acquaintances or had only Jew Gentlemen to work with." Much later, in 1918, when she attended a party in honor of Bernard Baruch for his contributions to the war effort during World War I, she wrote her mother-in-law, Sara: "The Jew party [was] appalling. I never wish to hear money, jewels and . . . sables mentioned again."[6]

This form of antisemitism was of a different character from the surge of paranoid antisemitism abetted by Henry Ford and others in the 1920s. Ford inaugurated a series of articles in his newspaper, the *Dearborn Independent*, called "The International Jew: The World's Problem," which repeated the substance of *The Protocols of the Elders of Zion*, a document forged by the Russian secret police around 1900. The *Protocols* purported to reveal a secret Jewish conspiracy to bring about the destruction of Christian civilization by controlling the world economy. The newspaper carried the series for ninety-one weeks straight. The circulation of the *Independent* increased from 72,000 in 1920 to 700,000 in 1924, exposing hundreds of thousands of Americans to these accusations.[7] Another series of articles, written by Kenneth Roberts for the *Saturday Evening Post* in 1920–21, described Polish Jews as "human parasites" who were "unassimilatable [*sic*]" and "incapable of grasping American ideals."[8]

These and other antisemitic writings helped create the atmosphere that led to the passage of restrictive immigration laws in 1921 and 1924. The laws, which established quotas for the number of immigrants admitted from each country, created the "paper walls" that would keep out so many refugees in the 1930s and 1940s. Although the campaign against the Jews initiated by Ford subsided after 1927, antisemitism persisted, and the nation became still more antisemitic over the course of the following decade as Americans faced the devastating effects of the Great Depression and the fear of another world war. Antisemitism would reach its peak in the late 1930s and early 1940s, just at the time when European Jews desperately needed America's help.[9]

While many Americans remained deeply antisemitic during the 1920s and 1930s, ER moved in the opposite direction. The main motivator of this change was her active participation in progressive politics and her growing embrace of America's diversity that went with it. Her decision to stay with her husband in 1918 after his affair with Lucy Mercer, her social secretary, and commit herself to an independent life of public service brought her into contact with an ever-growing number of people from different backgrounds. She developed a network of allies among progressive activists, including Jews who were active in the Democratic Party, the labor movement, social welfare organizations, and other areas of public life. Among these colleagues were Lillian Wald, pioneering public health nurse and founder of Henry Street Settlement, with whom ER worked on child welfare, health, and labor issues; Rose Schneiderman, union organizer and president of the Women's Trade Union League, which ER joined in 1922; and Belle Moskowitz, Governor Al Smith's key political adviser, with whom she worked on passing progressive legislation in New York State and organizing Smith's gubernatorial and presidential campaigns. ER and FDR also became friends with Herbert Lehman and his wife Edith. Lehman was a leading philanthropist and supporter of progressive causes, including Henry Street Settlement. He served as FDR's lieutenant governor, his successor as governor of New York, and, later, as a senator. ER came to depend greatly on her Jewish colleagues, whom she found unusually responsive to appeals for assistance in meeting human needs.

ER's closest Jewish friend was Elinor Morgenthau, wife of Henry Morgenthau Jr. Unlike Rose Schneiderman and Belle Moskowitz, who were from recently immigrated Eastern European families, the Morgenthaus were from German-Jewish families who had been in the United States for several generations and become highly assimilated. The Morgenthaus were the married couple with whom Franklin and Eleanor Roosevelt maintained the closest friendship. The fact that the Morgenthaus were Jewish made this unusual. "[The Roosevelts] would not have been part of a normal friendship and social circle that my family moved in," recalled Henry Morgenthau III many years later. But the Morgenthaus, like the Roosevelts, owned a farm in Dutchess County, New York, and Henry and Franklin were drawn together by their common passion for agriculture and public service. When FDR became governor of New York in 1928, he appointed Morgenthau chair of the New York State Agricultural Advisory Committee and later to the state Conservation Commission. In 1933, when he was president, FDR appointed Morgenthau secretary of the Treasury, a position Morgenthau held throughout the rest of FDR's presidency. Eleanor Roosevelt and Elinor Morgenthau began working closely together as leaders in the Women's Division of the Democratic Party in the 1920s and remained close friends and political allies until Elinor's death in 1949.

Despite the friendship and close working relationships established between the Roosevelts and Morgenthaus, however, there remained some distance between them as a result of their different religious backgrounds. "[T]here was a separation between

Jewish families and Christian families," Henry Morgenthau III remembered. He could not have gone to the same schools the Roosevelt children attended, for example. "And you didn't talk about it."[10]

Like the Morgenthaus, who did not observe Jewish holy days, most of ER's Jewish friends were secular and, as a result, ER had scant familiarity with Jewish religious practices. When asked what ER learned from his parents about being a Jew in America, Henry Morgenthau III said, "Nothing."[11] This was not entirely true, however. ER was aware of how antisemitism sometimes affected the lives of the highly assimilated Jews whom she knew. In 1937, when ER proposed Elinor Morgenthau for membership in the Colony Club, the most prestigious women's club in New York, which ER had helped found, the club refused to admit her because it did not accept Jews as members. The rejection offended both women deeply, and ER quietly resigned from the club. Although deeply hurt by the rejection, Elinor Morgenthau did not want ER to protest publicly.[12]

Henry and Elinor Morgenthau, like many of the prominent Jewish families in the United States, saw themselves as Americans first and foremost. But this did not mean they wished to lose their Jewish identity or advocate that American Jews abandon their traditions. In a 1936 speech to the Federation of Brotherhoods of the Temples and Synagogues of Baltimore on the need to defend American democracy against the fierce challenges it faced from within and without, Henry Morgenthau told the audience that "each minority group through its unique contributions serves to enrich the whole of American life." Jews brought to America "the song and the art, the belief and the morality, the poetry and the literature of our four thousand year old tradition." This heritage was "no little thing" that the Jews had to offer for it embraced "the attitude of an Amos, the dream of an Isaiah, the gentle humanity of a Hillel, the philosophy of a Maimonides." Jews could therefore best serve America "not by abandoning our Jewish tradition but by maintaining it." The only way to preserve their tradition was to strengthen democracy, whose essence was its "assumption of the equality of all human beings" and whose goal was to provide every individual with "an opportunity to attain to the fullness of life."[13]

As ER's activities brought her into contact with people from varied backgrounds, she too became committed to promoting a society that nurtured the welfare of all Americans. Her changing view of Jews went along with this larger conception of what America could become. The close relationships that Eleanor Roosevelt developed with Jews while working for progressive causes laid the groundwork for the key role she played in efforts to admit more European refugees to the United States, her leadership in combating antisemitism, and, ultimately, her strong support for the new state of Israel. Initially, however, she responded very cautiously to the persecution of the Jews by Nazi Germany.

1

A CAUTIOUS RESPONSE TO NAZI GERMANY

*"The German news is horrible and
I don't wonder you feel as you do
for I feel much the same"*

ELEANOR ROOSEVELT BECAME acutely aware of the effect of Nazi ideology on German citizens and its special impact on Jews soon after FDR's inauguration as president on March 4, 1933.[1] After Hitler had been named chancellor of Germany in late January of that year, the Nazi Party immediately began a brutal campaign against German Jews, as well as socialists, Communists, and other opponents of the regime. The Nazis expelled Jews from the faculties of universities, forbade them from continuing to practice law and medicine, and excluded their children from schools and universities. Nazi storm troopers insulted, robbed, and terrorized Jews on the streets. These violations of the rights of Jewish citizens in Germany were well publicized, yet ER's public statements before 1938 are remarkable for the near absence of reference to these events. Her silence did not reflect a lack of knowledge or concern, however. She was eager to hear accounts of events in Germany and acted behind the scenes to make sure that her husband was as aware of the situation as she was. Her informants were friends and colleagues whose opinions she highly valued and who actively opposed Hitler's policies or tried to mitigate their effects. Their activities, statements, and relationship to ER provide insight into how ER felt about the Nazi assault on Germany's Jewish citizens in these early years.

In April 1933, ER heard a disturbing report on the persecution of Jews in Germany from James G. McDonald, who had recently met face to face with Adolf Hitler. McDonald was head of the Foreign Policy Association (FPA), which sought to keep Americans informed of events abroad, especially in Europe. McDonald was a spokesman for the internationalist viewpoint shared by Franklin and Eleanor Roosevelt and he knew them both. FDR had addressed the FPA in 1919 and ER served on the organization's nominating committee from 1927 to 1929.

No one could have provided ER with a more intimate portrait of the attitudes and policies of the new regime in Germany than McDonald. Fluent in German and on good terms with many people in the German government, particularly in the Foreign Office, McDonald had access at the highest levels of power. Partly because he was tall, fair-haired, and fair-skinned—close to the Nazis' Aryan ideal—and had written sympathetically about Germany after World War I, the Nazis accorded him an unusual degree of trust. They hoped he would take their side: "My Nazi friends believe that I am not completely lost," he wrote in April 1933.[2]

The man who arranged McDonald's interview with Hitler was Ernst "Putzi" Hanfstaengl, Hitler's foreign press chief. When McDonald challenged him about the April 1 boycott of Jewish businesses organized by the Nazis, Hanfstaengl told him: "The boycott is only a beginning. It can be made to strangle all Jewish business." When McDonald suggested that such a course could endanger Germany economically by provoking reaction abroad, Hanfstaengl laughed. "The Jews are the vampire sucking German blood. We shall not be strong until we have freed ourselves of them."[3] When McDonald raised the issue of the treatment of the Jews with Hitler himself in their meeting on April 7, Hitler retorted: "I will do the thing that the rest of the world would like to do. It doesn't know how to get rid of the Jews. I will show them."[4]

After McDonald returned to the United States, he wrote to ER, telling her of his disturbing conversations in Germany. The next day he received a telegram from ER's secretary asking him to spend the night of May 1 at the White House: "President most anxious to hear your impressions."[5] As a result, just three weeks after his interview with Hitler, McDonald went to the White House to report about his trip to ER and to spend two hours alone with the president, informing him about the nature of Hitler's regime and discussing its implications for international affairs. Thus began a partnership between McDonald and ER that would last until Hitler's defeat at the end of World War II. McDonald kept ER informed of the situation in Europe and of his efforts to aid refugees (both Jewish and non-Jewish); ER provided moral support and assisted him when she could, most often by helping him gain access to the president and the State Department.

On May 4, after his discussion with FDR about his experiences in Germany, McDonald wrote to ER expressing his thanks for the chance to talk at such length with the president: "His grasp of the underlying elements in the present complicated international situation was very reassuring. I was deeply touched, too, by his willingness to talk to me so frankly."[6]

Accounts of the persecution of Jews in Germany also appeared in the American press in the spring and summer of 1933, where ER would have read them. The *New*

York Times, normally cautious in calling attention to Jewish issues, condemned "the Nazi scheme of wholesale oppression" by which Jews would be deprived of a livelihood and their children of access to education. In response to the threat by the Nazi regime to hold German Jews hostage until foreign governments silenced the criticism of Germany, the *Times* declared that the German government "cannot compel citizens of other nations to be dumb in the presence of what they consider an outrage upon the finer professions and ideals of modern states. If they keep silent, the very stones would cry out."[7]

Many groups that included both Jews and non-Jews expressed their disapproval of Nazi policies. Two of the most significant protests, however, involved Christians only because the signers believed it was important that the Nazis understand that American Christians as a group objected to the persecution of Jews. Twelve hundred Christian clergymen signed a letter declaring that "the endeavor of the German Nazis to humiliate a whole section of the human family threatens the civilized world with the return of medieval barbarity."[8]

Carrie Chapman Catt, one of ER's political mentors, organized the other significant protest involving Christians only. Catt, who had played a leading role in the suffragist movement and founded the League of Women Voters after the ratification of the Nineteenth Amendment, inspired ER's early work with the League and her participation in the women's international peace movement in the late 1920s and 1930s. Catt was so sickened by McDonald's description of Hitler's war against the Jews that she founded the Protest Committee of Non-Jewish Women Against the Persecution of Jews in Germany.[9] The group began circulating a letter of protest throughout the country seeking the signatures of five thousand Christian women who played important roles in their communities, including club presidents, businesswomen, and churchwomen.

The letter condemned "the German pogrom against the Jews," which "carries a Christian banner" but "is a subversion of all things Christian." Instead of adhering to "the highest ethics of modern international understanding" that make protecting "the lives, rights, and liberties" of national minorities "the sacred trust" of the national majority, the letter stated, the German majority has "threatened the destruction" of its 600,000 Jewish citizens.

The letter enacted an idea that was only beginning to gain currency in international affairs: that when a nation abuses its own citizens, the international community of nations and the citizens of other nations have a responsibility to do what they can to protect the human rights of the victims. "If the German majority is unwilling to protect the Jewish minority," the letter read, "it becomes the duty of the world's nations to assume this obligation."[10] The failure of the nations of the world to protect the European Jews would become one of the impetuses for the adoption of the Universal Declaration of Human Rights by the United Nations, which Eleanor Roosevelt would help draft after World War II as chair of the United Nations Human Rights Commission.

Beginning in June 1933, Catt's protest letter circulated among women throughout the country. By August 13, when Catt's committee released the letter to the press, it had far exceeded its goal, gathering 9,000 signatures from 753 towns in the 48 states, plus the District of Columbia.

FDR had also considered protesting the Nazi persecution of the Jews but received conflicting advice from his Jewish advisers and from Jewish leaders. Some of them, like Rabbi Stephen Wise, founder of the American Jewish Congress, and Harvard law professor Felix Frankfurter, who had become an influential adviser to FDR, wished him to speak out; others, including members of the American Jewish Committee, who feared that Germany would react by increasing restrictions on German Jews, wanted him to remain silent. FDR chose silence, but he appears to have urged the Senate majority leader, Joseph Robinson, to speak out. On June 4 Robinson gave a speech in the Senate condemning the "cruelty and inhumanity" of Germany's treatment of the Jews.[11]

In conformity with FDR's cautious approach to the issue, ER did not sign Catt's petition, but she did publicly recognize the contribution Catt had made. In November, when Catt received the American Hebrew Medal for her work in organizing the protest against the persecution of German Jews and for promoting better understanding between Christians and Jews in the United States, ER presented the award. She praised Catt's contributions to the struggle for women's suffrage and her leadership in the women's peace movement. She did not refer directly to Catt's petition campaign against Nazi persecution, leaving that part of the tribute to Rabbi Isaac Landman, editor of the *American Hebrew*, the weekly Jewish magazine that made the annual award. In accepting the award, Catt described the state of mind in Germany as a "psychosis" in whose "paroxysms" the Jews had tragically been caught up. Was "this disease curable or incurable, infectious or contagious?" she asked. "No one knows."[12] For diplomatic reasons, ER could not say such things, but she honored a woman who did.

MCDONALD WAS NOT THE ONLY person to furnish ER with firsthand reports of the persecution of Jews in Germany during the early months of Hitler's rule. In August 1933, ER and Elinor Morgenthau stayed overnight at Lillian Wald's Connecticut home. They spent an afternoon, an evening, and most of the following day talking with Jane Addams and Dr. Alice Hamilton, a professor at the Harvard School of Public Health. Addams, Hamilton, and Wald had all played prominent roles in the Progressive campaign for social reform in America and helped build the international women's peace movement. They had close relationships with their counterparts throughout Europe. Hamilton had just returned from a trip to Germany with Clara Landsberg, a rabbi's daughter. During six painful weeks in Germany, they had witnessed the devastating implementation of Nazi policies. As the Nazis moved to shut down women's organizations in Germany, many of the women with whom Hamilton and Landsberg had worked, including leaders of the Women's International League for Peace and Freedom that Addams and Wald helped found, sought refuge abroad or were at risk of being sent to a concentration camp. In a few short months, the Nazis wiped out all the advances in status that German women had struggled for years to achieve.

What ER learned about the swift, frightening reversal of progressive values in Germany—values that she herself had been working for in the United States for over a decade—shocked her. It prompted her to invite Hamilton to Hyde Park to give FDR a firsthand report on what she had observed and to express her outrage. Hamilton met privately with FDR, joined the Roosevelt family for dinner at ER's Val-Kill cottage, and breakfasted the following morning alone with ER.[13]

Despite the brutality Hamilton had witnessed and heard about—the ruined lives and fortunes, the suicides, the despair of the Jews she knew and admired—Hamilton believed that the economic crisis of the Great Depression made it impossible for the United States to rescue the Jews of Germany: "If only we could open our doors to these people, they are so fine, but of course we cannot," she wrote to Jane Addams as she traveled back to the United States.[14]

Catt, however, thought otherwise. ER had also invited her to visit Hyde Park in the spring of 1933 to speak to the president about the Nazi assault on the Jews, but she had declined, apparently feeling that she could have a greater effect by arousing public support for allowing more refugees to enter the United States.[15] In speeches to civic groups and at universities she called for the liberalization of America's immigration laws. Some other groups also urged a change in American policy. On September 10, 1933, thirty-six members of the American Civil Liberties Union (ACLU) urged the president to support a more open immigration policy in order to permit the admission of religious and political refugees, particularly from Germany. Such a policy, they told him, would be in keeping with the American "tradition of asylum for refugees from foreign tyrannies." Among those making the appeal were ER's friends Lillian Wald, Jane Addams, and Felix Frankfurter, one of the founders of the ACLU.[16]

During the first year or so after Hitler took control of the German government, the protests in the United States against his policies were vocal and widespread. They included petitions; statements by Jewish, Protestant, and Catholic religious and political leaders; and resolutions passed by professional organizations. On March 7, 1934, the American Jewish Congress, the American Federation of Labor, and nearly fifty other anti-Nazi groups organized a protest rally at Madison Square Garden in New York City. Twenty thousand people attended the rally. A series of speakers, including Rabbi Stephen Wise, Senator Millard Tydings of Maryland, former governor of New

York Al Smith, and Mayor Fiorello LaGuardia of New York City, acted as "witnesses" in a mock trial of Hitler's government. Catt told Rosa Manus that "Mrs. Roosevelt came to speak" at the rally, but it was only wishful thinking on her part because ER did not participate. Catt's mistake, however, suggests that she had heard very clearly in private where ER stood on the issue.[17]

The vehement protests against Hitler's policies that began in the spring of 1933 and lasted for about a year died down as it became clear that the Nazis were bent on imposing ever more restrictive measures against the Jews and threatening to impose more if foreign criticism continued. Efforts to liberalize American immigration policy continued, but not at the same level of energy. Catt, however, was not easily discouraged. The National Committee on the Cause and Cure of War, the women's peace organization that Catt had founded in 1924, was the only women's peace group that pressed throughout the 1930s for changes in the immigration laws so that more Jewish refugees could enter the United States.[18] ER did not publicly support Catt's campaign to change American immigration laws, probably because she did not wish to challenge the policies of her husband's administration on such a controversial issue.

LIKE CATT, ER'S FRIEND JAMES McDONALD persisted in his efforts to find a way to assist the refugees fleeing Germany. He worked successfully with colleagues from the Foreign Policy Association and others interested in the problem to persuade the League of Nations to establish the High Commission for Refugees (Jewish and Other) Coming from Germany.[19] On October 13, 1933, after having achieved this goal during a trip to Europe, McDonald met with Undersecretary of State William Phillips, Jay Pierrepont Moffat, chief of the Division of European Affairs in the State Department, and Secretary of State Cordell Hull to discuss America's relationship to the new agency and his possible appointment by the League as its high commissioner. At the State Department, McDonald encountered the two attitudes that would impede the efforts of Americans to assist European Jews from the beginning of the refuge crisis in the early 1930s until after World War II: antisemitism and resistance to immigration. Phillips expressed this bias in saying that if an American were placed in the position of high commissioner, he might become a tool for "'prying open' the floodgates of Jewish immigration into this country."[20]

The next day, over lunch with ER at the White House, McDonald reported to her on the dispiriting situation in Germany, the proposed plan for the high commission, and, no doubt, the response to the proposal by the State Department. He told her that FDR would need to act on the matter soon. ER asked him if he had seen the president, and when he said that no appointment had been scheduled, she turned to FDR's secretary, Marguerite "Missy" LeHand, who was also at the table, and asked her, why not?

LeHand said the reason was they were just too busy. McDonald concluded that ER's interest in what he had to say would help him get an appointment with the president, but he did not get that opportunity until several months later.

On October 26, 1933, the Council of the League of Nations selected McDonald to be the high commissioner for refugees. When McDonald heard the news, he "felt no exaltation—rather, a deep sense of the many things which had to be done at once."[21]

FOR THE NEXT TWO YEARS McDonald traveled from one European capital to another, to New York and Washington, and to South America, laboring to find countries in which the refugees from Germany could settle and urging nongovernmental organizations to raise the funds needed to assist the refugees. He experienced little success. He found from the outset that the governments who already had refugees on their soil "were anxious to be rid of them, and those who have none, anxious not to receive any."[22]

In December 1934 McDonald wrote to ER, asking her if he could see her to ask her counsel "about some of those aspects of my work abroad which are troubling me most just now."[23] When he arrived in Washington on December 17, he found a telephone message from ER's personal secretary, Malvina Thompson ("Tommy"), waiting for him, inviting him to a dinner with the family that evening. "I had not asked the President for an appointment," he wrote in his diary, "indeed, I had not communicated with him at all" but had simply told ER that he would like to see her if she were free. ER's initiative resulted in McDonald and FDR having a substantive discussion about the refugee problem. McDonald reported in his diary that the president "expressed vigorously his opposition to the anti-Semitic policy of the Reich." He impressed McDonald with his memory of the issues they had addressed in their conversation in April 1933 when McDonald had stayed overnight at the White House. "His fundamental opposition to the principles of the Third Reich, which he had shown at the very beginning and had indicated subsequently each time I had talked with him, were obviously as strong as ever."

Before he left the White House on December 17, ER asked McDonald to let her know if he were coming to Washington again before returning to Europe, and after the meeting McDonald sent ER a copy of the latest report of the High Commission's governing body.[24]

AS MCDONALD STRUGGLED TO ADDRESS the needs of the refugees who had already left Germany, the Nazis continued to tighten the restrictions placed on Germany's Jews and on those Christians it classified as "non-Aryan" because they had a Jewish grandparent or a Jewish spouse, even if the Jewish member of the family had converted to

Christianity. By the summer of 1935 McDonald believed the situation had reached another crisis. "I wish I might have now an opportunity to sit down and talk with you," McDonald wrote ER on July 24, 1935. "Not since my visit to Germany in March and April 1933—about which I told you and the President on my return home—have I had as deep a sense of impending tragedy as now." McDonald believed that the Nazis had adopted "a program of forcing gradually the Jews from Germany" by creating intolerable conditions for them. Hitler's announcement of the Nuremberg Laws, a new set of antisemitic restrictions, at the annual Nazi Party rally in September 1935 would confirm McDonald's fears. In his letter to ER, McDonald asked "how long" could "the Governments of the world . . . continue to act on the assumption that everything which is taking place in Germany, and the threat implicit in present developments, are matters purely of German domestic concern?" He wondered if "the time has not come when, in harmony with other precedents in American history,[25] the American Government should take the initiative in protesting against the prevailing violations of elementary civil and religious rights in Germany." From Campobello, where she had gone for vacation, ER immediately sent McDonald's letter on to the White House with a handwritten note: "Please give Miss LeHand for the President and tell her Mrs. R says it is important."[26]

But the American government made no official protest, even after Hitler's announcement of the Nuremberg Laws. FDR and the State Department continued to pursue a policy of noninterference in Germany's internal affairs for fear that official condemnation would make matters worse and disrupt the efforts of the democracies to keep the peace. Great Britain and France pursued the same course.

BY THE FALL OF 1935, the situation in Europe that he had described in his July 24 letter to ER left McDonald stymied. He concluded that the High Commission could not solve the underlying problem and that he had done as much as he could. On December 27 McDonald submitted his letter of resignation to the secretary-general of the League.

In the letter, McDonald noted that the German policies that generated refugees had evolved "catastrophically" since his appointment in 1933. He feared that Jews and non-Aryan Christians, having been stripped of their right to vote or hold public office, practice their professions, attend university, or participate in the cultural life of German society, and finding it increasingly difficult to support themselves, would, in their "utter anguish and despair, . . . burst the frontiers in fresh waves of refugees." Trying to meet the needs of these refugees would overwhelm private philanthropic organizations, whose financial resources were already overstretched, and the refugees would not be welcome in other nations because current economic conditions gave these nations "only a limited power" to absorb new immigrants. Therefore, an effort had to be made "to remove or mitigate the causes which create German refugees." This, he said, could not be the responsibility of the High Commission. "It is a political function, which properly belongs to the League itself." Drawing on its "moral authority," the League of Nations and its member states had to make "a determined appeal" to the German government to modify policies that were driving refugees into neighboring countries.[27]

Having issued a report on the refugee situation, as FDR had suggested he do if his mission were unsuccessful, McDonald hoped the impact of his resignation and statement would move the United States, Great Britain, and other nations to take action to bring about a change in German policies. The *New York Times* and the *London Times* ran the story on their front pages and published the full text of McDonald's letter of resignation.

On January 8, 1936, McDonald sent a copy of his statement to ER. Although he knew she had probably seen news reports of it, he thought she might discover in the complete text "something of interest" which she "might care to call to the attention of the President." McDonald expressed a desire to see ER the next time he visited Washington. When he visited the city in early February 1936, ER again invited him to dinner at the White House.[28] After dinner, ER arranged for McDonald to meet briefly with the president. The president "could not have been more cordial," McDonald reported, but he found the twenty minutes he spent discussing the situation in Germany "discouraging." The hope that he had once had that the president would listen to his appeal for a public protest faded as FDR remained characteristically indefinite about his intentions: "He doesn't seem to have become any more friendly to the regime. On the other hand, I had kind of an impression that he was not any more inclined to take an initiative in the matter than he had been previously." Apparently, FDR indicated an unwillingness to denounce publicly the Nazi persecution of its own people or even make a friendly appeal to the German government through private diplomatic channels, as McDonald proposed in a meeting with Undersecretary William Phillips at the State Department the following day.[29]

While ER encouraged McDonald behind the scenes in his valiant, though failed mission and helped honor Catt for organizing a group to protest the Nazi persecution of the Jews, she, like her husband, did not publicly protest Hitler's treatment of the Jews. She had no power herself to affect Hitler's policies beyond making sure that FDR had access to the most informed observers of events in Germany in the hope that he would find an effective way to respond. But ER's readiness to arrange for McDonald to meet with FDR, even when he did not request it, and his appreciation of her counsel indicate that she shared McDonald's alarm at the situation in Germany and wished that something could be done. The State Department remained opposed to confronting the Nazi government, however, even though German policies generated an increasing exodus of refugees from the country. While FDR himself expressed to McDonald his strong opposition to Hitler's policies, he did not deviate from the position taken by the State Department on how the United States should respond to the situation.

WHILE ER FOLLOWED THE POLICY OF FDR, the State Department, and some Jewish leaders of not condemning Hitler publicly, the events in Germany intensified her efforts to address prejudice in the United States, where she was in a position to make a difference. From 1933 onward, while Hitler destroyed the Jewish community in Germany with increasing brutality, both ER and FDR forged close bonds with the Jewish community in America. No president before FDR brought so many Jews into important positions in the American government.

FDR's inclusion of Jews in his administration sometimes provoked vitriolic attacks from American antisemites, who claimed that the Roosevelt administration was "Loaded with Jews," as well as from the Nazi press.[30] For American Jews, on the other hand, who rejoiced to find so many of their brethren in positions of power for the first time in American history, FDR's inclusive attitude toward Jews reinforced the other reasons most of them supported him. An editorial endorsing FDR in the *Washington Jewish Review* in 1936 praised him for restoring "confidence to a panic-stricken people" and addressing the needs of the forgotten man, as well as placing Jews in high positions. Most of the Jewish press supported FDR, the editorial concluded, "because his social outlook most closely approximates the transcendental ideals of Jewry."[31]

FDR's unprecedented inclusion of Jews in his administration reinforced ER's own growing acceptance of Jews and her appreciation for the contributions they were making to American society. With the encouragement of Elinor Morgenthau, she began to speak frequently to Jewish groups, particularly women's groups, and refuse to speak to groups that excluded Jews.[32] But when she spoke to Jewish groups, she did not allude to the persecution of Jews in Europe or address the problem of German refugees, or even focus on the problems of Jews in the United States. She spoke instead about the economic, educational, health, and other problems faced by every American. Her implicit and sometimes explicit message in speaking to Jewish groups was that Jews possessed the same rights and responsibilities as all Americans. In her first appearance before a Jewish group after FDR's election as president, ER spoke at the Hotel Commodore in New York to thousands of Jewish women from seven organizations. Florence Rothschild reported in the *Wisconsin Jewish Chronicle* in March 1934 that some members of the audience felt disappointed that "as she stood under the Zionist flag," ER did not refer to problems particular to Jews, but Rothschild took it as "an additional instance of her tact that at the very beginning of her address she emphasized that she was speaking not as a non-Jewess to Jewish women but as an American to fellow Americans." Her speech focused on the ways in which American women could contribute to solving the social problems caused by the economic depression facing the nation.³³

ER's avoidance of references to the persecution of Jews in Germany extended to her private correspondence even with her Jewish friends. Nevertheless, it is clear from ER's sympathetic support of McDonald's efforts and her frequent emphasis on the need for religious freedom in the United States that ER shared the pain that events in Germany caused her friends. When ER spoke to 4,000 women at the twentieth annual convention of Hadassah in October 1934, she focused on the poor health conditions she had observed in the United States, which she called "a disgrace to any country that calls itself civilized." She hoped that "every woman, regardless of religion or race, would make it her job to know the conditions of the community in which she lives" and then join with other women to "change unsuitable living conditions." If "we can forget ourselves as individuals and think of the objects we have to accomplish, we shall override pettynesses and meanesses, no matter what race we belong to."³⁴

While ER did not directly refer to the treatment of Germany's Jewish citizens, the subtext of her talk was that the United States must show that it was not like Nazi Germany, that in America people of all backgrounds worked together to solve the nation's problems. ER was also well aware from the speech Elinor Morgenthau gave at the same conference, and no doubt from private conversations with her, of the effect that the persecution of Jews abroad was having on American Jews: "Suffering and oppression always tie people together," Morgenthau said, "and the cruel misfortunes of Jews in certain parts of the world has made even those of us who were not primarily concerned with Jewish affairs eager to reaffirm our Jewishness." She urged Jews not to isolate themselves or let others segregate them, thus reinforcing ER's message.³⁵ In August 1935, in the most direct reference in her correspondence at this time to the Nazi persecution of the Jews, ER wrote to Morgenthau: "The German news is horrible and I don't wonder you feel as you do for I feel much the same."³⁶

ER's connection to the American Jewish community was also strengthened by her characteristic responsiveness to individuals in need. Usually her intervention involved putting the person in touch with a government or private agency or individual who could be of assistance, for example, in finding the person a job, but occasionally it led her to become deeply involved in the lives of particular people by supporting their efforts to improve their own lives. One of the people in whom she took a special interest was Bertha Brodsky, a fourteen-year-old Jewish girl who suffered from scoliosis, a spinal disease. Her family could not afford surgery to correct the problem and her brother appealed to ER for help. In response ER arranged for the operation at the New York Orthopedic Hospital. Her generosity to Brodsky was well enough known in the Jewish community for Florence Rothschild to mention it in her article on ER in the *Wisconsin Jewish Chronicle*.³⁷ For the rest of her life, ER continued to correspond with Brodsky, invite her for visits, help her and her brother get jobs, and counsel her about her marital problems.

The relationships ER developed with Jews were the most important influence on her changing attitude toward them. Her deepening commitment to a society in which people of all backgrounds respected each other's traditions shaped that change as well. Her growing ties to the American Jewish community and more inclusive vision of democracy advanced together and reinforced each other. The disturbing news about the growing repression of Jews, other minorities, and political opponents by the Nazi regime in Germany created an urgent need to address issues of inequality and intolerance in the United States. At the same time, Americans needed to find a way to assist the refugees fleeing Germany because of Nazi policies.

2

PARTNERING WITH CLARENCE PICKETT

"The spirit of social cooperation"

ONE OF THE PEOPLE who helped shape Eleanor Roosevelt's response to the problem of refugees from Germany and intolerance in the United States was Clarence E. Pickett, executive director of the American Friends Service Committee (AFSC), the public service agency of the American Quakers. ER's relationship with Pickett helps us to understand her reticence about the Nazi persecution of the Jews in the 1930s, the ways in which she responded to the refugee crisis behind the scenes, her efforts to combat antisemitism and anti-immigrant sentiment in the United States, and her later attachment to the cooperative communities and programs for immigrant children in Israel.

ER met Pickett through her friend Lorena Hickok. "Hick," as she was known, had covered ER for the Associated Press, but after she and ER developed an intimate friendship, she felt she could no longer write objectively about ER and consequently quit her job. She then took a job as chief field investigator with the Federal Emergency Relief Administration (FERA). Her job was to visit the areas most severely affected by the Depression and report to Harry Hopkins, the federal relief administrator, on the conditions she saw and on the effectiveness of New Deal programs. She also sent her sharply observed reports to ER, who read portions of them to FDR.

In August 1933 Hick sent a report on the conditions of unemployed coal miners and their families in West Virginia, one of the most distressed regions in the country, and urged ER to visit the state to see the scars of poverty for herself.[1] When ER arrived in Morgantown, West Virginia, she found the miners and their families living in houses that were little more than wooden tents with dirt floors, no running water, and no indoor plumbing. She observed the self-help projects established by the AFSC, which not only provided work but helped build morale. The AFSC had established a shop that employed miners in making furniture and gardens where families could grow some of their own food.[2] During her two-day visit, ER made an immediate personal connection with the people she met. In a few cases she provided concrete help after her visit, such as finding out where a child with a bad eye could go for treatment and offering to pay the expenses for the child's care.[3]

The problems of the Appalachian coal miners were severe and chronic. Because of new technologies, a shrinking demand for coal, and company failures, 300,000 miners found only temporary work and 200,000 would never work again, according to AFSC estimates. The coal miners were only one group of workers among many whose conditions at the time made them virtual refugees. There were tenant farmers from the South, farmers from the dust bowl, and unemployed factory and construction workers from the cities who, like the coal miners, had no jobs and lived in squalid conditions on relief or took to the road looking for new opportunities. Some gathered in temporary encampments called "Hoovervilles" that were essentially refugee camps. The desperate plight of these jobless, uprooted people was created by economic depression, however, not by government persecution as in Germany, and both FDR and ER believed that the American government should address the problem of massive unemployment aggressively and creatively. FDR imagined moving large portions of the population out of overcrowded cities into rural areas, establishing the migrants in inexpensive housing in small communities, and stimulating regional industrial and agricultural development. In August 1933, the month when ER visited Morgantown, he established the Subsistence Homestead Division within the Interior Department, and Interior secretary Harold Ickes appointed M. L. Wilson head of the agency. When ER sent Pickett to talk to Wilson about the work of the AFSC, Wilson took Pickett on as his assistant in charge of the settlement projects in the coal mining regions of West Virginia, Pennsylvania, Kentucky, and Illinois, although Pickett retained his position with the AFSC as well.[4]

ER's visit to the mining communities around Morgantown began a long association between her and the AFSC, whose approach to social and economic problems she greatly admired. She began supporting the AFSC's activities and working closely with Clarence Pickett on an experiment to establish a subsistence homestead near Reedsville, West Virginia, called Arthurdale. The Subsistence Homestead Division built houses for the displaced miners who settled there and provided a plot of land on which they could grow vegetables and raise a few animals for food. Handicraft projects, including furniture making, provided some employment, and ER sought to create more jobs by persuading a company to build a factory near the village.

In September 1934 Pickett reported in his journal that ER wanted to give the AFSC $3,000 for its overhead, plus $55 for scholarships for girls from the AFSC camps in

Kentucky and West Virginia.⁵ She also decided to give the AFSC the future income she received from her radio broadcasts, which in 1934 brought in $36,000 (equivalent to over $650,000 in 2020 purchasing power). Some of these contributions went to AFSC overhead and programs both in the United States and in Europe; some of it went into a special fund that Pickett set up for ER, which she controlled. When she wished to make a contribution to assist an organization or individual, she would write to Pickett and ask the AFSC to send the amount she specified to the organization or individual she desired to help. One of the recipients of the monetary gifts ER distributed from this fund was her young friend Bertha Brodsky.⁶

In 1935, as part of an AFSC message broadcast on CBS, ER explained why she contributed the income from her radio broadcasts to the Quaker organization. The AFSC was "doing work of the type which I was most interested in," she said:

> Their program of long-time rehabilitation seems to me to fit in with the philosophy which I have always held, namely, that while charity may be necessary, our aim should be to get people back to a point where they can look after themselves. I have never felt that people should be grateful for charity. They should be resentful, and so should we, of the circumstances which make charity a necessity. The American Friends Service Committee seems to me to work toward building up people's own initiative and security, and, therefore, I have been particularly happy to be able to work with them.⁷

To nurture the development of the community of out-of-work miners at Arthurdale, ER took Bernard Baruch to visit the new community and secured his financial assistance. It is one measure of ER's changing attitude toward Jews that Baruch, the man in whose honor the "Jew party" had been held back in 1918, now became her friend and someone she could turn to for advice and financial support for her project.

Although Arthurdale became the target of criticism because construction costs ran well over the government's budget for the project and the industries that tried to establish themselves in the community failed, the residents of the town felt the experiment had transformed their lives. ER never lost faith in the principles that drove the project. As ER put it in her radio talk in 1935, "like all experiments, there undoubtedly have been mistakes made," but "if through these mistakes we are able to acquire knowledge as to what can be done with people and for people who have been through the most disheartening conditions, . . . it may be of value not only to the government, but to many other people all over the country."⁸

The Quaker approach to rehabilitation, which ER helped to apply at Arthurdale, shaped her lifelong understanding of how best to address human problems caused by the collapse of an economic and social system or the displacement and resettlement of populations. In 1949, in recalling the work the AFSC did during the Depression, ER said that while the Quakers responded to the need to provide immediate "physical relief" in the form of food and clothing, they recognized that "personal rehabilitation" was "often much more complex." It required the satisfaction of "equally vital needs which could not be measured in terms of calories or shoes. These," she said, "were the needs of the spirit." To address the needs of the spirit, the Quakers worked from the beginning "to give these people a sense that they were truly helping to rebuild their own lives instead of merely receiving hand-outs."9

Years later, when ER made four visits to Israel beginning in 1952, the lessons she had learned from the Quakers prepared her to admire the cooperative spirit of community building and economic development she found in the youth villages, training centers, and kibbutzim designed to transform the lives of displaced Jews beginning their lives in a new land.

THERE WAS ANOTHER REASON THAT the AFSC was important to ER: it provided her with an indirect way to assist refugees seeking to leave Germany. In her radio talk in 1935, she said that because the AFSC programs in West Virginia embodied her philosophy of self-help and promised better living conditions and greater security, she felt "great confidence" in the AFSC's work "not only here but in European countries."10 Although she did not identify the nature of the AFSC's activities in Europe, she was referring to the AFSC's work in assisting Jewish, non-Aryan Christian, and political refugees in Germany where it had established itself in a unique position to act effectively, despite its small staff and limited financial resources. Some of the money ER contributed to the AFSC supported this work. Picket kept her informed of these efforts and tried to enlist her more publicly in German refugee issues.

After World War I, from the date of the armistice on November 11, 1918, until the signing of the Versailles Treaty on June 28, 1919, the victorious nations maintained a naval blockade of Germany, thus limiting the importation of food and causing widespread suffering. As many as 250,000 Germans died from starvation or disease during this eight-month period. To address this crisis the AFSC set up a relief program that provided food to thousands of people and won the gratitude of the German people. The AFSC continued to operate relief programs in Germany and elsewhere in Europe throughout the 1920s and into the 1930s. In 1932, the Quakers helped found the Entr'aide Européenne, an independent relief agency that opened first in Berlin and then moved to Paris after Hitler came to power. The AFSC worked closely with this organization in its efforts to assist German refugees in France. The organization helped refugees immigrate to France, learn new skills, and find work as craftsmen or in other manual jobs. It ran a kindergarten, provided health and social services, and offered opportunities for social activities. According to Grace Rhoads Jr., Pickett's assistant, it also offered "sympathy and a new orientation to people bewildered by their recent experiences."[11]

After Hitler came to power and the persecution of the Jews, non-Aryan Christians, and others began, the AFSC office in Berlin delivered relief to those deprived of a means of supporting themselves and, whenever possible, facilitated their emigration. By 1934, as Pickett later put it, the representatives of the AFSC in Berlin "became primarily emigration officers."[12] Because they had earned the trust of the Germans in the years immediately following the First World War, the AFSC was permitted to continue to operate in Germany until the outbreak of the Second World War. Although lack of funds hampered the AFSC's work, the Quakers made a significant contribution to addressing the needs of German and Austrian refugees, both Jewish and non-Jewish.

AFTER ER AND PICKETT BECAME partners in the Arthurdale experiment in 1933, Pickett began to consult regularly with ER, to visit the White House and Hyde Park, and to join in family meals. The commitments ER made to assist Pickett, some of which ER neglected to mention to her personal secretary, "Tommy" Thompson, became so frequent that in 1937 an exasperated Tommy asked Pickett to send her a memo whenever "Mrs. Roosevelt agrees to see any one for you or agrees to do anything you request." Pickett replied that he would be happy to do so.[13]

Pickett's relationship with ER provided him with occasional access to FDR, sometimes during informal meals. He discussed a range of issues with the president, including the prevention of war in Europe, German refugees, and the subsistence homestead program, in which FDR took a keen interest. FDR's interest in rural revitalization, together with his desire to understand what was happening in Germany, gave Pickett and the president much to talk about. At one point, they even contemplated using the subsistence homestead program to ease, if only slightly, the German refugee crisis.

In January 1934, recognizing that the German refugees the AFSC sought to bring to the United States, like the West Virginia coal miners, had been dispossessed of the means of earning a living and needed housing, jobs, and the support of a community in order to make a new start, Pickett proposed settling a number of German refugees on subsistence homesteads in the United States. The adoption of such a program would have enabled the refugees to grow much of their own food and create new industries or craft enterprises rather than compete with unemployed Americans for jobs. He told James McDonald, then serving as high commissioner for refugees, that ER was much interested in the idea and asked him if he thought it would be "a desirable gesture, for it could hardly be more than that." McDonald told him that "it would be an excellent move to make."[14]

In early March, after a meeting with ER and FDR, Pickett wrote to McDonald to tell him that ER wanted him to speak with the president "particularly on the matter of the admission of at least a few refugees to our Subsistence Homestead communities."[15] When neither Pickett nor ER succeeded in arranging a meeting between McDonald and FDR, McDonald sent Pickett a summary of the proposed plan.[16] He told Pickett:

> If it were possible to admit a few of these families and place them in some of the homesteads, this action would do more than relieve these particular exiles; it would be an unmistakable token of the interest of our Government in the refugees as a whole, and as such it would be an excellent example to hold up before other Governments.

He asked Pickett to let him know, after conferring with those in authority, if this "generous gesture can be taken."[17]

THE QUESTION OF PLACING REFUGEES in subsistence homesteads was still unanswered in May 1934, when Clarence and Lilly Pickett left for a five-week tour of Europe to meet with AFSC staff and determine how to strengthen the programs they ran. Their reports on their journey provided ER with more disturbing details of the cruel effect that Hitler's treatment of Germany's Jews was having. As Pickett and Lilly returned on board the *Aquitania*, Pickett wrote a confidential letter "To Our Friends," including ER, sharing his observations. He reported meeting a rabbi who told him that the synagogue in Worms had just celebrated its 900th anniversary. Now, having been excluded by their own government from schools and professions, the Jews had created four hundred small schools financed by contributions from the Jewish community and provided training in locksmithing and other manual occupations for lawyers and others who could no longer practice their professions. "The tragedy goes deep," Pickett noted, and gave an example of the effects that the persecution of Jews inflicted on a family he visited:

> The father, a distinguished lawyer, mother a German-American of wealth, four boys. The father defended two Jews against what was obviously a travesty against justice and decency. For this he lost his right to practice. He is bewildered—his old friends shun him as tho he were a leper. Meanwhile, all four sons are Nazi. They parade, greet each other when they arrive at home by "Heil Hitler!," spurn English (which they formerly prided themselves on being able to speak) because German is superior,

and youthfully hope for and believe in and work for the new Germany. The tragedy will kill the father and mother. What will it do to the boys?[18]

ER, whose heart went out to anyone in distress, must have been deeply moved by reading Pickett's account of this family's quandary.

In June 1934, soon after he and Lilly had returned from Europe, Pickett met with ER at the White House and reported to a colleague that he was "pressed so much by Mrs. Roosevelt to say all that was on my chest that I did so." After listening to him, she asked him to stay for dinner and repeat what he had said about Germany and Austria to the president.

Pickett also talked at length with FDR about the subsistence homestead program, and, encouraged by ER's support for the proposal, may have returned to the idea of placing some German refugees in subsistence homestead communities in the United States.[19] In any event, FDR did not discourage the plan because McDonald asked Cecilia Razovsky, executive director of the National Coordinating Committee for Aid to Refugees and Emigrants coming from Germany, to identify someone who could explore it further. McDonald reported to Pickett, however, that Max Blitzer, project manager for the Department of Interior Division of Subsistence Homesteads, had told him that "applications for homesteads on this and other projects will be approved only in the cases of United States citizens."[20] Since Blitzer turned out to be correct, nothing further came of an innovative idea that would have permitted more German refugees to enter the United States. ER's strong support for this initiative and effort to make sure that FDR had an opportunity to consider it was one of the first steps she took to assist German refugees. Regretfully, her support for the proposal ran up against the roadblock of government regulations, a problem she would face throughout the refugee crisis.

PICKETT TRIED TO INVOLVE ER in publicly supporting efforts to assist refugees by inviting her to speak at events sponsored by the American Christian Committee for German Refugees (ACCGR). The ACCGR was organized by a group of Protestants and Catholics in 1934 at the urging of James McDonald, who told the Federal Council of Churches and other Christian groups that the German refugee problem was not primarily a Jewish problem. It was a Christian one because the Nazis were carrying out the persecution of the Jews in the name of Christianity: "The Christians are the persecutors, and they are violating every principle of Christianity."[21] It was also a Christian problem because an increasing number of the refugees were non-Aryan Christians who were being persecuted along with the Jews and needed aid as much as they did. The ACCGR was formed to meet this need.[22]

In 1935, frustrated that Christians were not responding to funding appeals from the ACCGR as much as he had hoped, Frank Ritchie, executive director of the organization, suggested that Christians set a fundraising goal of $400,000 for German Christian refugees. Since the Quakers were the group best positioned on the ground to provide practical assistance for refugees, he proposed making the AFSC, through its offices in Berlin, Vienna, Prague, and Paris, the agent of the ACCGR for the distribution of the funds. Ritchie reported that German Christian refugees often fared worse than the Jewish refugees because they had no community to support them: "Since, in Germany, any attempt on the part of Christians to help their non-Aryan co-believers would be regarded as an act of hostility against the state, the non-Aryan Christians are entirely dependent on the help of their co-believers in other countries."[23]

As part of the effort to meet the $400,000 goal, Christian clergymen signed a letter appealing for contributions, and the ACCGR planned a fundraising dinner in New York for February 27, 1936.[24] It seemed like a perfect opportunity to draw ER into the work of the ACCGR, and Ritchie asked Pickett to urge ER to attend: "Her presence ought to bring a thousand people to the dinner."[25] Despite her sympathy for the plight of the refugees and her close relationship to Pickett, ER turned Pickett and the ACCGR down. By doing so she avoided being publicly identified with a campaign that implied a criticism of German policies and would provide aid to non-Americans at a time of economic hardship in the United States.

The following fall, sixty Protestant clergy and laymen gathered at Riverside Church in New York City where they issued an appeal to 100,000 clergymen requesting that they ask their congregations to support the effort to raise $400,000 to assist the 2,500 German refugees with the most urgent needs.[26] The ACCGR knew that it would greatly strengthen their effort if FDR issued a statement supporting their fundraising campaign after the 1936 presidential election and before the big drive by the Protestant churches. On November 7, 1936, a few days after the election, Pickett met with ER to enlist her help in persuading the president to do so. He also asked her to incorporate information on the campaign into her syndicated My Day column, which she began writing at the end of 1935. She agreed to ask the president if he would sign a letter to the Rev. Harry Emerson Fosdick, the eminent minister of Riverside Church, endorsing the campaign. The president agreed to do so, and ER assured Pickett that she would make sure he did.[27]

Despite FDR's assent, however, he never signed the letter. The State Department had advised against it, arguing that "it would not be appropriate for the President to support an appeal for assistance for one particular class of refugees or for refugees from one particular country."[28] If he endorsed this drive, primarily for Christian refugees, how could he refuse to support drives for Jewish refugees without appearing to discriminate? The State Department's caution may also have stemmed from excessive fear of upsetting relations with Germany, despite the fact that the refugees the fundraising drive would help had already left Germany. In thanking Pickett for his effort, Ritchie wrote: "I regret exceedingly that it did not materialize but one can readily understand the delicate position the President is in, and how he would hesitate to do anything that would seem to involve him in International complications."[29]

ER did keep her promise to promote the ACCGR campaign in her My Day column, however. My Day, which by November 1936 appeared in over sixty papers with a circulation of over four million, gave her direct access to a large national audience.[30] While many of her columns, especially in the early years of their publication, simply reported on her daily life—where she was, whom she met, what she read, and so on—she also used it to call attention to organizations or individuals she thought were doing constructive work. Over time, and as changing political circumstances allowed her to be more forthright, the column became a means of expressing her opinion on important matters. In her December 2, 1936, My Day column, drawing on background provided by Pickett,[31] she wrote:

> I was much interested this morning to find in my mail an account of the work done by the American Christian Committee for non-Jewish German refugees. During the past months, churches in this country have been raising a fund to take care of refugees who have come to this country and who are to be found in various European and South American countries in still larger numbers. The Jewish people have done a wonderful piece of work in caring for their own refugees and have generously contributed many thousands of dollars for the care of the non-Jewish refugees but there still seems to be a need for further assistance.[32]

Frank Ritchie greatly appreciated ER's column, although "there still seems to be a need for further assistance" hardly constituted a ringing appeal or conveyed a sense of urgency. Perhaps she felt she should not ask people too directly for money to help support foreign refugees when so many people in the United States continued to suffer economic hardship. Nevertheless, given the reticence of ER and FDR on this issue up to this point, her column represented a breakthrough for those seeking greater publicity for the refugee cause. "It was in response to my talk with her and also the material that I put in her hands that she wrote that paragraph," Pickett reported. "It was a little slow getting done, but I know she has been terribly crowded."[33]

Despite the efforts of the ACCGR, the response of American Christians to the persecution of non-Aryan Christians in Germany remained tepid.[34] In September 1937, as it continued its struggle to raise funds, the ACCGR tried once more to persuade ER to speak on behalf of Christian German refugees, this time at a luncheon in Cleveland, but again they failed. "She still feels that she cannot do it," Pickett reported to Ritchie:

"Relations with Germany are rather tense anyway and she does not want to do anything that will unduly jeopardize our relations with Germany. I am awfully sorry we can't use her, but I am sure that we all will want to respect her feeling about it."[35]

ER'S EXTREME CAUTION ABOUT MAKING any statement or even gesture that might disturb German-American relations reflected her unwillingness to undermine the Roosevelt administration's strict policy of noninterference in German affairs. FDR and State Department officials no doubt told her not to say anything that might upset diplomatic efforts the United States was making. ER herself understood the need for such limits, even when she chafed under them or disagreed with the policies FDR and the State Department pursued. But ER's silence also stemmed from her own idealistic hope that a nonconfrontational approach to Germany would help keep Europe and the United States out of war. Even speaking at a fundraising event for an organization that sought to assist Christian refugees, which would not require directly condemning German policies, seemed to her unwise. Keeping out of war, of course, would not ease the crisis faced by German Jews, but few Americans, including ER, would have been willing to risk war solely for humanitarian reasons, especially in light of the failure of World War I to open the way to a stable, democratic Europe.

While ER refrained from condemning Nazi policies or publicly supporting efforts to assist the refugees who were the victims of those policies, she played an important role as a speaker for the American peace movement in the 1930s. The brutality of World War I and its disillusioning aftermath had instilled in ER, along with many other Americans, a deep abhorrence of war. "Judged by the actual accomplishments of objectives," she wrote in an assessment of the achievements of the Great War, "these four years were absolutely wasted. Far from preventing future wars, the settlements arrived at have simply fostered hostilities."[36] After the war many Americans simply withdrew into isolationism, thinking that America could avoid involvement in overseas affairs altogether. Others, like ER and Carrie Chapman Catt, became ardent internationalists and pondered the question: if war were so evidently futile, what could replace it? Looking at war as a human disease, they tried to study its causes and propose ways of curing it. ER worked closely with her friends Esther Lape and Elizabeth Read in their campaign to secure entry of the United States into the World Court. In addition, she participated in the efforts of Catt, Jane Addams, and Lillian Wald to achieve a broad disarmament agreement and create international mechanisms for settling disputes among nations through mediation and the rule of law.[37] She also collaborated with Clarence Pickett in this search for a peaceful solution to the political crisis in Europe.

ER spoke at conferences of the Women's International League for Peace and Freedom and the Conference on the Cause and Cure of War and made "Peace" one of the principal topics of her paid lecture tours. In 1936 ER helped launch a two-year national emergency drive for peace, spearheaded by the peace section of the American Friends Service Committee.[38] In her speeches, ER denounced the glamorization of war and urged people to find alternatives to the excitement generated by war toys, the romance of "gorgeously dressed soldiers," and stories of military heroism by glorifying the deeds performed by "armies of foresters and farmers" instead.[39]

ER did not speak about anything at this time more passionately than she did when speaking out against war, but her denunciations of violence avoided specific criticism of other nations. Hamilton and Pickett had given her horrifying firsthand accounts of the Nazis' brutal treatment of the Jews, but she did not make use of this material in her writing or speeches. In the summer of 1934, after receiving Clarence and Lilly Pickett's "To Our Friends" letter reporting on their trip abroad, ER wrote in her column in the *Women's Democratic News* that the Picketts had provided a "most interesting" report on "conditions in Europe." The only part of their account she mentioned in her column, however, was their description of the "different methods which have been used in Germany, France and England in their subsistence homestead venture."[40] Having noted ER's omission of the Picketts' "presentation of fascist violence and repression," and the plight of Jews and refugees, the historian Blanche Cook asks, "How does one understand ER's failure to impart the Picketts' message to her readers?" As Cook says, her reticence conformed to the policy of her husband's administration. But that was not the main reason for ER's silence. In this case, she was following Pickett's explicit instructions not to publish the information he and Lilly provided in their report. Lilly and I "are writing this letter as a rather confidential note," he said: "what we say here is not for publication. Europe is so sensitive especially in spots that statements which are published should be given most careful thought. One may easily do more harm than good."[41]

ER was not just abiding by Pickett's request; she in fact shared Pickett's view and advocated a similar policy of restraint. In a speech at the Tenth Conference on the Cause and Cure of War in Washington, DC, in January 1935, she asked what women could do to eliminate the causes of war. In answer she proposed a gentle, Quaker-like approach to achieving peace. Especially in retrospect, her vision seems hopelessly naïve given the character of Nazi Germany:

> We can be courteous to other nations and to the inhabitants of other nations, and try to make people as a whole understand that every nation has pride just as we have pride; the first step toward understanding and good feeling is courtesy between nations. We cannot say to another nation, "We do not trust you"; we cannot say, "We think your motives are this or that," without making that nation feel resentful as we would feel resentful. And I think that we could have some influence on

the press, which occasionally forgets that there are newspapers which repeat unfortunate things beyond our own borders, just as the radio carries things beyond our own borders and makes for bad feeling.[42]

In the case of Germany, ER adhered to this prescription for tact and understanding, rather than public condemnation.

In her book *This Troubled World*, which ER wrote in September 1937, she kept her discussion of international problems and her prescriptions for peace on a general plane. When referring to the Spanish Civil War, the intervention by Germany and Italy in that conflict, and the Japanese assault on China, she avoided naming any of the countries involved:

> To me the whole situation seems intolerable. We face today a world filled with suspicion and hatred. We look at Europe and see a civil war going on, with other nations participating not only as individual volunteers, but obviously with the help and approval of their governments. We look at the Far East and see two nations, technically not at war, killing each other in great numbers.

That is as specific as she got in a book about the world's troubles. She was not much more specific about solutions. She called the League of Nations inadequate but said she was "not advocating any particular machinery" to replace it. She outlined, instead, a general framework for international peacekeeping. She argued that disputes "should automatically go before some body which will publish the facts to the world at large and give public opinion an opportunity to make a decision. Then, a group of world representatives will have to decide with whom the fault lies." If a nation used force, despite the decision of the world body, then the majority of nations would have to "resort to some method" to assert their will. Although she did not use the term "world court," the establishment of which she and her friends ardently supported, she said: "We need to have a tribunal where the facts in any case may be discussed, and the decision made before the world, as to whether a nation is an aggressor or not." Then there had to be sanctions such as withdrawal of trade, and, if that failed, the deployment of an international police force. Until such mechanisms were in place, however, she rejected a unilateral shrinking of America's army and navy. America had to be ready to defend itself militarily if attacked.[43]

The creation of an international police force and the maintenance of a strong national defense until international mechanisms became effective were not the prescriptions of a pacifist like Clarence Pickett. But in another respect ER continued to embrace the Quaker approach to healing a troubled world. After presenting her outline of an international system for settling conflict, ER said she doubted if any plans that anyone had devised for achieving peace would actually bring it about. She proposed instead a more utopian goal: "Our real ultimate objective must be a change in human nature for I have, as I said, yet to see a peace plan which is really practical and which has been thought through in every detail." Here she expressed an essentially Quaker view of conflict: only through inner change, not outward mechanisms, can human beings achieve peace. ER admitted that such a transformation of human nature would not be easy. It would mean reaching "a point where we can recognize the rights and needs of others, as well as our own rights and needs." Only when brotherly love "becomes our accepted way of life" would the nations of the world be able to create effective mechanisms for maintaining peace and actually make them work.[44]

Neither ER's dream of brotherly love nor her proposed mechanisms for maintaining peace addressed directly the difficult issue of how the international community could deal with a nation like Germany that was waging a campaign of repression against a group of its own citizens or how other nations should respond to the flood of refugees produced by such policies. The year 1938 would bring these problems sharply to the forefront and force ER to take a more active role in dealing with the issue of refugees seeking admission to the United States.

3

RESPONDING TO THE THREAT OF WAR AND THE NAZI ASSAULT ON THE JEWS

"This Troubled World"

*T*HIS *TROUBLED WORLD* appeared in January 1938. The year that followed marked a turning point in the political crisis in Europe and in ER's response to it. The Anschluss, Germany's absorption of Austria into the Third Reich, occurred in March. In October, after the Munich Agreement, Germany occupied the Sudetenland in Czechoslovakia, and in November mobs in Germany destroyed Jewish businesses and synagogues and attacked Jews on the streets. Over the course of 1938, aided by weapons and "volunteers" from Nazi Germany and Fascist Italy, General Francisco Franco's forces gained the upper hand in the civil war in Spain. After its defeat at the Battle of Ebro in July, the Republican army began to come apart, and by the end of the year only Madrid remained in Loyalist hands.

These devastating events made it tragically clear that the dream of a world at peace would not soon become a reality. While Eleanor Roosevelt never gave up her conviction that the world needed to develop adequate international machinery to resolve conflicts or altered her belief that in the long run peace required a profound change in human nature that could only come about through the education of individual people, she increasingly recognized that neither of these cures for the causes of war could be applied in time to arrest Hitler's assault on the world. As violence more and more came to rule European politics and the threat of war grew increasingly stronger, ER drew further away from the pacifism of her Quaker ally. Pulled toward the view that only force would halt the advance of Nazism in Europe, she became a reluctant and, eventually, firm supporter of FDR's defense buildup.

The war correspondent and novelist Martha Gellhorn was one of those whose perspective on the world moved ER toward a more realistic view of events. Harry Hopkins had hired Gellhorn in 1934 to travel around the United States as a field investigator for the Federal Emergency Relief Administration (FERA), documenting the conditions of workers hit hard by the Depression. Appalled by what she saw and disturbed by the failure of New Deal programs to meet the needs of distressed workers, Gellhorn returned to Washington and vented her frustration to Hopkins. Hopkins told her that he had been forwarding copies of her reports to ER and suggested she meet with ER to discuss her concerns. His suggestion led to an invitation to dine at the White House, where she described the conditions she had observed to both ER and FDR. ER persuaded her to stay with her job and the two began a friendship that would last until the end of ER's life. In 1935, however, Gellhorn encouraged a group of workers in Coeur d'Alene, Idaho, to protest against their exploitation by a corrupt contractor by breaking the windows of the local FERA offices. They did so, and Hopkins had to fire her.[1] ER then invited her to live in the White House while Gellhorn wrote a book of short stories (*The Trouble I've Seen*, 1936) based on her experiences. Later, as a war correspondent during the Spanish Civil War, Gellhorn sent ER vivid letters describing the situation in Spain, warning about the dangers of a Franco victory and criticizing American neutrality and the failure of Americans to recognize what was at stake. She also wrote about the absorption of Czechoslovakia by Nazi Germany and the refugee crisis.

Gellhorn, whose father was a German Jew who left Germany for the United States in 1900 because of antisemitism and whose mother was half-Jewish, was passionately outspoken, blunt, and partisan (the very opposite of Clarence Pickett). No one registered the emotional impact of the events of 1938 more intensely than she did. "It makes me helpless and crazy with anger to see how the world goes, to watch the next Great War hurtling toward us," Gellhorn told ER, while the leaders of the democracies failed to respond.[2] Gellhorn chafed at the ostrich-like behavior of the American people who clung to the illusion that the events happening thousands of miles away in Spain and Czechoslovakia could not touch them as long as the United States refused to become involved.

ER shared Gellhorn's dismay but tempered Gellhorn's outrage by recognizing that such shortsightedness manifested the sad reality of human nature. Very few people "look far into the future," she told Gellhorn, "... and you can't blame them, for we have been for years a country that felt secure in isolation.... I am afraid it is not human nature to be unselfish except in great crises. People look at things as individuals from an individual point of view, not from the point of view of history or the whole picture of the world."[3]

AFTER THE ANSCHLUSS, VIOLENCE BROKE OUT in Austria against Jews, non-Aryan Christians, and Nazi opponents. Hundreds of people crowded American consular offices seeking to leave the country. The situation focused renewed attention on refugees, and for the first time, FDR responded decisively, taking several steps to try to address the refugee crisis. Although, for various reasons, these initiatives had very limited effect, they did indicate his concern and represented his most concerted effort to deal with the problem prior to his establishment of the War Refugee Board in January 1944.

At a cabinet meeting on March 18, FDR asked his cabinet for advice on how the United States could assist Austrians seeking to flee their country. "After all," he said, according to Henry Morgenthau Jr., "America had been a place of refuge for so many fine Germans in the period of 1848 and why couldn't we offer them again a place of refuge at this time." He suggested merging the German and Austrian quotas and introducing a bill in Congress to expand the quotas. He was strongly advised not to pursue the second proposal because, as Vice President John Nance Garner put it, if Congress could act in secret, it would shut down immigration altogether. The German and Austrian quotas, however, were soon combined, allowing more Austrians to obtain visas since the German quota was not full at the time. In 1939 the combined German-Austrian quota of 27,370 was filled, resulting in a significantly larger number of Jewish immigrants entering the United States.[4]

FDR also asked Undersecretary of State Sumner Welles and Henry Morgenthau to draw up a plan for an international conference to discuss ways of meeting the refugee crisis, including the formation of an international committee to facilitate the immigration of political refugees from Germany and Austria. The conference to be held in Évian-les-Bains, France, to which Secretary of State Cordell Hull invited twenty Latin American and nine European nations, plus Canada, Australia, and New Zealand, had a fatal flaw, however: no country, the invitation stated, would be asked "to receive a greater number of emigrants than is permitted by its existing legislation."[5]

On April 13 FDR convened an interfaith White House conference on refugees to discuss how private organizations and individuals could support the work of the intergovernmental committee that he expected the conference to establish. Those invited included representatives of the State Department, Department of Labor, religious leaders, and other private persons active in refugee issues, including James McDonald, who had continued to speak out on the refugee issue after resigning his position as high commissioner for refugees. FDR told them that private organizations and individuals would have to raise funds to implement whatever plans for emigration emerged from the international conference, and he hoped the group whom he had invited to the White House would serve as a permanent advisory committee to act as an intermediary between the proposed international committee and the private organizations in charge of relief operations. After the meeting, the group established by the president as the President's Advisory Committee on Political Refugees (PACPR) chose James McDonald to chair the committee.[6] After McDonald became chairman, ER resumed her role as liaison between McDonald and the president and again provided McDonald with advice and moral support.

FDR's determination to set up an international mechanism for responding to the refugee crisis lifted the hopes of American Jews that something would be done for their brethren in Europe. "We all applaud most heartily the president's interest in the persecuted of Europe," Rose Schneiderman wrote to ER, "and we hope something will be worked out for their benefit."[7] But it was the impression of Joseph Hyman of the Joint Distribution Committee, who spoke with Clarence Pickett about German and Austrian refugees on April 14, that "the President talked in generalities" and "that the government is not likely to receive any great number of refugees." The following day ER told Pickett that in regard to the refugee problem "expectations beyond what is possible [have] been created."[8]

ER and Hyman were right. When the conference FDR had called met in Évian-les-Bains in July, almost every one of the thirty-two nations that attended refused to consider revising its immigration policy and opening its doors to German refugees. The only exception was the Dominican Republic, which offered to take in 100,000 refugees. The conference did establish the Intergovernmental Committee on Refugees (IGCR), whose purpose was to coordinate efforts to assist the refugees and, if possible, negotiate an agreement with Germany that would facilitate the exit of refugees from that country. It soon became clear, however, that the German government would not cooperate with the committee in devising a reasonable plan for the orderly emigration of Jews.

Nevertheless, somewhere for the refugees who managed to leave had to be found. FDR believed that they could be settled in unoccupied or lightly populated corners of the world, where they would not compete with anyone for jobs but contribute, instead, to the economic development of these areas. In October 1938 he asked Professor Isaiah Bowman, a professor at Johns Hopkins University and America's leading geographer, to identify undeveloped parts of the world for refugees to colonize. Little came of Bowman's efforts. With some exceptions, inhospitable conditions, the economic and logistical challenges of resettlement, and the resistance of other nations to such plans made FDR's dream unattainable. Antisemitism also played a role. Bowman's belief that Jews lacked the practical bent and physical stamina necessary to undertake the hard task of agricultural pioneering—a belief contradicted by the resilience of Jewish settlements in Palestine—colored his evaluation of potential sites for colonization.[9] When Sumner

Welles, who did succeed in persuading some Latin American nations to accept more refugees, looked back at the record of the Intergovernmental Committee on Refugees in 1946, he said that it had not succeeded in implementing a "single constructive plan" of resettlement, despite the existence of "vast unpopulated territories and great undeveloped natural resources."[10]

WHILE THE TRAGIC EVENTS OF 1938 UNFOLDED, and FDR made efforts to address the refugee crisis, ER continued to meet regularly with Clarence Pickett to discuss the refugee problem and other mutual concerns. In July, Pickett and his wife, Lilly, left on another trip to visit American Friends Service Committee (AFSC) service centers in Europe. Pickett again recorded his observations for his friends, as he had done in 1934.[11] In Berlin he discussed the refugee problem with Raymond Geist, the American consul. The Saturday before the Picketts' arrival, 3,000 people came to the consulate to apply for visas: "[Geist] was simply deluged with people who had heartrending tales of woe—Jews or non-Aryans. They could get no work—were thrown out of their apartments—had property confiscated—lawyers lost clients—doctors must all quit practice October first, etc."[12]

In Vienna the Picketts visited the AFSC's refugee center, the only center in the city that served non-Aryan Christians. Pickett reported that eight American and British workers were interviewing persons seeking to leave the country. In some cases, they helped them make arrangements to emigrate; in many cases they could only offer sympathy. "There are almost 100,000 non-Aryan people in Vienna," Pickett estimated, "and few of them eventually will be able to earn a living."[13]

On October 27, Pickett wrote to ER to tell her that he would like to speak to her about his European trip. ER replied by inviting Pickett to Hyde Park for lunch on November 9. At lunch Pickett sat next to the president, "had his full attention," and "reported quite fully to him as to what we saw in Prague and in Germany."[14] In his memoir, Pickett said that he urged the president to try to arrange a face-to-face meeting with Hitler to discuss disarmament and FDR said he had thought about that, but Pickett was dismayed that the president's immediate goal was to strengthen the American air force.[15] FDR continued to believe that his first responsibility was to make sure that America was prepared if events should draw it into war.

MARTHA GELLHORN, WHO WAS ALSO in Europe in October 1938, sent ER a passionate report from Prague on the plight of refugees in Czechoslovakia after the German occupation of the Sudetenland. Gellhorn said that the Czech government had no central agency to handle the refugees and that private charities were running out of resources to help them. The refugees themselves had no money, no visas, and no political support. At the end of her report, Gellhorn described a group of young refugees who were stranded in Prague. They were staring silently at a world map trying to find a country where a person "could keep his freedom of conscience and live." But they knew that the borders of the democracies were closed to them. Although they "had committed no crime," they knew that they "were welcome no place."

In replying to Gellhorn's report, ER wrote, "I hope the day will come when you can write something that will not make one feel ashamed to read it. The pity and horror of all these poor people—it is really appalling."[16] ER sent the report to Hick and to FDR, from whom it was returned with a note: "The President has read."

THE FOLLOWING MONTH, THE AGE turned darker still. On November 9 and 10, beginning the evening of the day Pickett reported to the president and ER about his trip to Germany, Nazi violence against the Jews erupted at a new level. Two days earlier, Herschel Grynszpan, a young Jew whose parents had been forced to leave Germany, together with thousands of other Jews holding Polish citizenship, assassinated Ernst vom Rath, an official at the German Embassy in Paris. In response, on what became known as Kristallnacht (the "night of broken glass"), Nazi party leaders, storm troopers, and members of Hitler Youth instigated riots in cities and towns across Germany. Crowds looted Jewish stores and homes, burned synagogues, desecrated cemeteries, dragged Jews out of their houses, beat them, and forced them to perform humiliating acts. The SS and Gestapo arrested as many as 30,000 Jewish men, sending most of them to concentration camps.

FDR responded by issuing a public statement condemning the atrocities: "The news of the past few days from Germany has deeply shocked public opinion in the United States," he said. "I myself could scarcely believe that such things could occur in a twentieth century civilization." He also ordered Hugh Wilson, the American ambassador to Berlin, to return to Washington. He was the only world leader to recall his nation's ambassador.[17]

Like the steps he took to address the refugee situation after the Anschluss, FDR's statement gave renewed hope to American Jews. "May I tell you at this time how deeply all of us appreciate the President's statement on the outrages in Germany," Rose Schneiderman wrote to ER. "He has done a lot to awaken our own people of the nation to an understanding of how dangerous it is to the cause of democracy to allow such cruel and heartless treatment to go unchallenged."[18]

ER too found some relief in FDR's response. At least the United States was now publicly condemning Germany's treatment of its Jewish citizens. "This German-Jewish business makes me sick," ER wrote to Hick on November 14, and "when F.D.R. called to-night I was glad to know Wilson was being recalled & we were protesting."[19] ER herself refrained from commenting immediately on Kristallnacht publicly, but she envied those who did speak out—unrestrained by diplomatic considerations. She had particularly high regard for Dorothy Thompson, one of the leading columnists of the day, the most outspoken American opponent of Hitler, and a constant defender of European Jews. As in the case of Martha Gellhorn, Thompson's blunt condemnation of the Nazis stood in sharp contrast to ER's cautious public statements on the international situation.

Thompson's column, On the Record, appeared for the first time in March 1936, not long after ER began My Day. At the pinnacle of Thompson's influence, in the late 1930s, an estimated eight to ten million people a day read her column. In 1939 she would appear on the cover of *Time* magazine, which ranked her second to Eleanor Roosevelt among "the most influential" women in America.

Thompson was an ardent advocate for refugees. Her plan for addressing the refugee problem, which she laid out in detail in an article in the April 1938 issue of *Foreign Affairs*, may have helped prompt FDR's proposal for the formation of the intergovernmental committee that was charged with facilitating the emigration of refugees from Germany.

On November 14, 1938, four days after Kristallnacht, Thompson published an open letter entitled "To a Jewish Friend" in her column. The letter expressed the need for Gentiles to recognize that a world in which one group of people could be so denigrated was a world in which everyone was in peril. As Peter Kurth, Thompson's biographer, notes, the letter was "unique at the time as an expression of solidarity" between Gentiles and Jews.[20]

Worried that the mob violence of Kristallnacht would spread, Thompson's friend had asked her, "What will become of my child if this goes on?" In her letter, Thompson replied, "What will become of my child?" Would her friend rather have her child brought up to become the persecutor instead of the persecuted: "Would you like him to be taught to burn, and beat, and steal? . . . Would you like him to be trained in prejudice and brutality and violence?" Thompson wished to protect her child from that fate as much as her friend wanted to shield her child from persecution. And so, they were, "as we always were, on the same side, standing for the same things." Her friend had told her, "I feel debased, degraded," but Thompson refused to accept such an idea of honor: "No one is debased by what is done to him. He is debased only by his own actions," and by that measure, Thompson as an "Aryan" in "the idiotic parlance of the day," had "more reason for furious protest" against "abasement" than her friend. Thompson begged her friend "to regard this horror as not more personal to you than it is to me" for the Nazi assault on the Jews "is not a Jewish crisis. It is a human crisis."[21]

After reading Thompson's column during a visit to Cincinnati, ER commented in My Day in the constricted, understated manner she sometimes employed when writing or speaking about sensitive topics:

> I cannot somehow believe that under any circumstances in any country it can be good for human nature to deal cruelly and oppressively with any group of people. It seems to me to show such a woeful lack of imagination not to be able to achieve legitimate objectives of orderly government without a procedure which in the end harms most those who carry it out. Dorothy Thompson is right, I think, what is done to people is never so harmful as what people do.[22]

This less-than-wholehearted endorsement of Thompson's column is ER's only reference to Kristallnacht in My Day during the weeks following the event. One wonders what "legitimate objectives of orderly government" ER could have supposed the Nazis were trying to achieve on Kristallnacht through violent means. She not only slights her subject, but quickly moves on to a lengthy description of the peaceful Ohio countryside and the beautiful décor of the old house she visits on the outskirts of Cincinnati that belonged to her cousin, Mrs. Nicholas Longworth. She retreats back into the world of privileged Americans in which she grew up and of which she was still a part, despite her distaste for its prejudices and intense engagement with social problems.

When Thompson sent a letter to ER and other journalists asking that they join a committee to defend Grynszpan or make a contribution to his defense, ER replied: "I should love to be as free as you are in the present situation but so many of you do a far finer job than I could probably do that I feel real gratitude for your work."[23] Deeply disturbed by Kristallnacht, and glad that people like Thompson were speaking out forcefully against Nazi violence against Jews, ER nevertheless operated under such constraint that all she felt she could do in response to Thompson's request was send a small personal contribution with a note asking that it remain anonymous. Later, in February 1939, she told Thompson, "I have ... great admiration for the courage which you have shown in your stand on the international situation."[24]

4

ANTISEMITISM AND *THE MORAL BASIS OF DEMOCRACY*

"Love thy neighbor as thyself"

THE VIOLENCE AGAINST Jews on Kristallnacht shocked people outside Germany and focused increased attention on the status of Jewish minorities in other countries. On December 24, 1938, a little over a month after Kristallnacht, *Liberty*, a popular illustrated weekly magazine, published an article by the British novelist H. G. Wells on "The Future of the Jews," followed a week later by "Mrs. Roosevelt Answers Mr. Wells on the Future of the Jews." While the events in Germany gave the topic its urgency, H. G. Wells and Eleanor Roosevelt focused on the way the issue manifested itself in each of their own countries.

Wells recognized that large numbers of Jews suffered extreme persecution in Germany and in other countries. But he argued that in the French- and English-speaking parts of the world, Jews remained "a peculiar people" mostly "by their own free choice." If the Jews had chosen to assimilate, the "Jewish Question" would have disappeared. Now, however, in Germany and other countries, "the doors of assimilation are being slammed upon him."

Wells did not regard the "intensification of the Jewish problem" as a separate issue, however. It was, instead, just one result of the "immense dismay" that overwhelmed the world following the economic collapse of the early Thirties and was driving a return to the "dwarfish politics of nationalism and imperialism." To counter this state of affairs, the world needed to evolve into a unified society in which national boundaries and identities disappeared.[1] The Jews, however, had "caught the fever of irrational nationalism" worse than any other people and had "intruded into an Arab country." In seeking to establish a homeland in Palestine, Wells charged, they had, in turn, inflamed Arab nationalism and created problems for an already unstable British Empire.

The only solution to the dilemma in which the world found itself, Wells insisted, was for Jews and Gentiles alike to join in an educational campaign to get rid of the "old legends that divide and antagonize and waste us." Jewish thinkers, writers, publishers, and capitalists could make a great contribution to this emancipating effort, "if only they would forget they are Jews and remember that they are men. The future of the Jews is like the future of the Irish, Scotch, Welsh, English, Germans, and Russians—and that is, common humanity in one large and varied world order, or death."[2]

Wells's article presented a narrative about the Jews that ER found unacceptable at its core but she did not absolve the Jews entirely of some responsibility for the prejudice against them. She wrote with far greater sympathy for the Jews, but less directly and forcefully than Wells. This may have resulted, in part, from the fact that she had not completely overcome her view of Jews as prone to exhibiting a characteristic set of unpleasant traits. In the United States, she wrote, "Many of us might say" that even Jews "who have the advantages of education and culture" possess "certain mannerisms or traits of character which rub us the wrong way." She quickly added that it was not these characteristics that led to the persecution of Jews, "for we feel that same way about other nations and we have no desire to wipe out any of them," but the implication of her words was that the more Jews (and other ethnic groups) behaved like mainstream Protestants, the better it would be for everyone.

Wells attacked Zionism because he rejected nationalism in any form and because his country had to deal with the consequences of Zionist activities in the British Mandate for Palestine, including the death of its soldiers. ER ignored the anti-Zionist part of Wells's argument, except to say that she thought Europeans and Americans "have pushed the Jewish race into Zionism and Palestine and into their nationalistic attitude." She focused instead on the issue of antisemitism, which, in the American context, presented the central problem. She began by recognizing that Wells was probably correct in his prediction that dire consequences would ensue if the human community permitted, in her words, "the kind of racial and religious intolerance which is sweeping the world today to keep merrily on its way." But by introducing the word "intolerance," a term Wells never used in his article, ER began shifting responsibility from the Jews to the people who harbored prejudice against them.

After altering the terms of the debate, ER continued, in her characteristically gentle, understated, yet piercing manner, by saying to Wells: "I cannot help wondering, however, if you are not aiding that lack of truth-telling just a little when you start your article by putting so much of the blame for the present situation on the shoulders of those Jews who are always conscious of their own race?" Having for a long time "lived in restricted areas and under restrictive laws" that, among other things, excluded them from certain businesses and professions, it seemed understandable to ER that Jews should feel separate. Even when most restrictions disappeared, she argued, assimilation takes time. Now, in the 1930s, the Jews in some nations faced a renewal of the kinds of restrictions prevalent in the Middle Ages. ER did not believe, as she put it, that "this is entirely because of anything which the Jewish people have done." One could take ER's "entirely" as ironic, it being so obvious that nothing justified the persecution the Nazis inflicted on the Jews and therefore blaming the Jews themselves for their troubles, as Wells did, was absurd. Possibly she meant it ironically (she was not without guile), but three paragraphs later she gingerly attributed a portion of the blame to the Jews for their failure to integrate themselves thoroughly enough into the societies of which they were a part: "It is true, perhaps, that on occasions the Jewish people haven't scattered themselves sufficiently through a wide area where they could be less concentrated in a racial group" and "have perhaps not grasped all the opportunities open to them to diversify their occupations," thus provoking resentment when they achieved "preponderance" in some professions.

ER herself believed in "the melting pot": America's ethnic, religious, and racial groups should adopt American ways, live among Americans from other backgrounds rather than in separate neighborhoods, and fully participate in American life as a whole. But her view that Jews should take some responsibility for distributing themselves more thinly throughout society and the professions reflected a special concern, shared at the time by some Jews as well as by Gentiles and satirized much later in Philip Roth's brilliant novel, *The Plot Against America* (2004). According to James McDonald, Max Warburg, a member of the powerful German Jewish banking family, who emigrated from Hamburg to New York in 1938, believed in "the necessity of Jewish committees everywhere deliberately redirecting the education of their children, so that in the course of time their professional, industrial and agricultural occupations might be so varied as to avoid giving the sort of excuse which had been so ruthlessly capitalized by the Nazis."[3] In 1934 Maier M. Levin, a fraternity brother in Phi Epsilon Pi, the Jewish national fraternity, told Louis Fushan, the fraternity's Grand Superior, that a fear was developing among Jews that "too many Jewish students are selecting the professions of Medicine and Law" and this overcrowding "might lead to similar results as we have in Germany." He suggested that the fraternity design a plan to encourage Jewish students to enter "less crowded fields." Fushan thought this an "excellent" idea.[4]

The lesson of Germany for Warburg and Levin was that Jews should actively avoid becoming too prominent to shield themselves from persecution. ER shared that belief, but she did not think that Jews should shed their religious identity. Wells urged Jews to abandon their religious traditions as superstitious baggage handed down from the distant past and join in building a secular world society. ER, on the other hand, argued that Jews derived their identity as a people from their religion: "It is their religion which seems to have made them conscious of themselves as a race[5] as well as a religious sect." And she did not believe that assimilation required any group to give up its religious beliefs.

Throughout her career, ER warned against the power of fear to distort reality, whether it was fear of Jews, African Americans, Communists, immigrants, or some other "Other." For ER, the root of antisemitism was not the assertiveness of Jews, but the fears of Gentiles. The real source of the hatred of Jews, she believed, was not their traits of character or their prominence but the suspicion of Jews harbored by Gentiles: "It is the secret fear that the Jewish people are stronger or more able than those who still wield superior physical power over them which brings about oppression." Those nations with confidence in their own standing in the world refrain from persecuting, she said. Although Jews "may be in part responsible for the present situation," the Jews were "not as responsible as the other races who need to examine themselves and grapple with their own fears."

In a passage that once again reflected her assumption that a "Jewish problem" existed, ER illustrated the way a confident nation might act, by asking her readers to imagine a situation in an American city whose government "had become too much ridden by politicians of one racial group." Americans, she said, would not kill the members of this group. They would, instead, "find some other way to bring in new blood; to restrict the number of high places which could be occupied by one racial strain. A little imagination would scatter and change this population without resorting to tyranny."[6] Religious and racial quotas, the strategy that American colleges and universities had begun using in the 1920s to limit the number of Jewish students they would admit, was a solution to the "Jewish problem" that ER found acceptable.

In conclusion, ER said that the future of the Jews "depends almost entirely on the course of the Gentiles." The Gentiles could choose "cooperative, mutual assistance, gradual slow assimilation, with justice and fair-mindedness" or they could choose "injustice, hatred, and death." Whichever they choose would determine their future as well.[7]

After the publication of her article in *Liberty*, ER's friend George Carlin, manager of the United Features Syndicate that handled the distribution of ER's My Day column, wrote to congratulate her: "I was afraid [your article] would be just conventionally flattering. Instead it was completely forthright and honestly met the issue."[8] But some Jews expressed concern about ER's assimilationist agenda. Rabbi Louis Swichkow of Milwaukee felt ER's article was "written in a fair-minded and unbiased manner," but he asked her to explain more fully what she meant by "gradual slow assimilation." Did she mean "intermarriage on the part of the Jew, with the Jew ultimately losing his identity as a 'Jew'"? ER replied that she did "not mean intermarriage or giving up religion. I mean becoming an active citizen with a feeling of being an American; for instance, in the same way people of other religions feel. Many people of Jewish faith whom I know think of themselves as Jews first and as nationals second."⁹ It is not clear whom she had in mind, for many of the Jews she knew, including the Morgenthaus, Lehmans, Frankfurters, and Bernard Baruch, were highly assimilated active citizens and strongly identified themselves as Americans. Despite ER's disclaimer, it is likely, considering her belief in assimilation, that she regarded the manner in which the Morgenthaus and Lehmans had integrated themselves into the society around them as the way she hoped Jews (and other minorities) would melt into American society. ER's belief in assimilation would later reinforce her enthusiastic support for Israel's program to thoroughly assimilate its immigrant population into a unified people.

HITLER'S PERSECUTION OF GERMAN JEWS led to heightened insecurity among American Jews who already suffered discrimination. The fact that the wife of the president publicly defended the Jews against charges that they were primarily responsible for the prejudice against them was, therefore, enormously important. After Kristallnacht, ER increased her efforts to combat religious intolerance. One of the ways she did so was through her support for the National Conference of Christians and Jews (NCCJ). Beginning in the winter of 1938, ER regularly praised the work of the NCCJ in My Day and sometimes participated in the organization's meetings.¹⁰ Sharing in its activities was another way in which ER joined forces with Jewish leaders and drew closer to the American Jewish community.

The NCCJ was formed in 1927 as the National Conference of Jews and Christians (its name was changed in 1938–39)¹¹ after Jewish leaders lost faith in earlier efforts at establishing respectful relations between Christians and Jews because of the announced intention of some Protestants to use the cloak of goodwill to ultimately convert the Jews to Christianity. The new organization, which included some Catholics as well as Protestants, attracted strong support from nine Jewish organizations that represented the full range of Jewish religious practice. The NCCJ gradually overcame Jewish concerns about its intentions under the able leadership of Rev. Everett R. Clinchy, a Presbyterian minister.¹²

The NCCJ had responded vigorously to Hitler's antisemitic program even before he came to power. Dr. S. Parkes Cadman, one of the founders of the NCCJ, wrote a widely syndicated article condemning Hitler entitled "The Jew's Lot in Germany," which first appeared in the *New York Herald Tribune* Sunday magazine in November 1932. In it, Cadman described the "tragic disease of hate" he had observed in Germany and warned that "unless something is done about it the contagion is liable to spread to other countries, perhaps to our own."¹³ After Hitler came to power, many other Protestant and Catholic leaders condemned Hitler's racial policies. In March 1933, the Federal Council of Churches' Executive Committee issued a statement prepared by Dr. Henry Smith Leiper, in cooperation with Clinchy, protesting the antisemitic policies of the new regime.[14]

Although these strong responses to Hitler's antisemitic program by some of America's Christian leaders did not translate into a liberalization of American immigration laws, they helped fuel a campaign to ensure that what was occurring in Germany did not happen in the United States. Hitler's policies challenged American Christians to examine their own treatment of Jews and to reaffirm the principle of freedom of worship embedded in the First Amendment. The NCCJ undertook a study of Sunday school textbooks to identify passages that could generate antisemitic attitudes and to make suggestions for revising them.[15] In 1933 the NCCJ sent a "pilgrimage team" composed of a Protestant minister, a priest, and a rabbi across the United States to promote understanding among Protestants, Catholics, and Jews. Among the topics they discussed in forums large and small were the lessons that religious conflict in Germany had to teach Americans.[16]

Striving to create amity among the three faiths and "immunize" Americans against antisemitism, the NCCJ created "Round Tables" in cities and towns throughout the nation, which brought together local Protestant, Catholic, and Jewish leaders to discuss their common values; instituted "Brotherhood Day," an annual celebration of the beliefs shared by people of all three faiths; and created programs in schools and colleges to combat intolerance.[17] By October 1938, Clinchy reported, the programs of the NCCJ reached 1,150 communities in the United States.[18]

In her My Day column, articles, and speeches, ER backed the efforts of the NCCJ to lead Americans in precisely the opposite direction from the direction in which the Nazis were leading the German people. "I have just received a most interesting release entitled 'Ten Commandments of Good Will,' issued for Brotherhood Day by the National Council of Jews and Christians," she wrote in My Day in February 1938. She then quoted several of the commandments, including, "I will do more than live and let live; I will live and help live." In February 1940 she called attention to the seventh annual celebration of Brotherhood Week and urged her readers to adopt the NCCJ's ten goodwill commandments. This time she published them in full in her column because she believed that they should "be kept in a place where all of us can look at them day by day."[19]

As ER had made plain in her essay on "The Future of Jews," she believed the root of intolerance was fear. "There is a growing wave in this country of fear, and of intolerance which springs from fear," she wrote in 1939 in her article "Keepers of Democracy." Propaganda about the dangers of Communism, she wrote, helped create a "fear complex." In one part of the country she was told that "the schools of the country are menaced because they are all under the influence of Jewish teachers and that the Jews, forsooth, are all Communists." Perhaps it was a measure of how much antisemitism had increased in the United States that in her essay "Intolerance," published in *Cosmopolitan* in 1940, ER identified "the wave of anti-Semitism" in America as "our greatest manifestation of intolerance." Considering the situation of African Americans in the United States at the time, that seems like an odd statement, but it is possible ER was placing religious intolerance in a different category from racial prejudice and discrimination. ER found the origin of the rise of antisemitism in the fear of war, in the economic situation, and the concern that other groups might fare better in the competition for jobs. Intolerance could not be eliminated unless people were economically secure and free from the fear of war.[20]

As she had made clear in her 1938 article on the future of the Jews, acceptance of others did not mean blurring distinctions. In April 1939, after attending a meeting of the NCCJ, ER wrote: "It is a fine ideal this, that each of us, Catholic, Jew or Protestant, preserving our individual differences of religion or race, should still join together to preserve democracy and a liberty which allows us to have our differences."[21]

ER's own religious beliefs were very much in keeping with the values of the NCCJ. She was not a strict adherent to a particular theology, but she was a deeply spiritual person. She belonged to the Episcopal Church in which she had been reared and to which FDR also belonged, and believed in attending church, but the church as an institution meant little to her. She regarded attending church as an outward symbol that should proclaim "inner growth." If people felt they could achieve that growth without church attendance, that was up to them to decide. The dour religious atmosphere in which she grew up may have soured her on theology, but it left her with a love of hymns and a religious cast of mind. When she was fifteen, she left home to attend the Allenswood School in England, a school headed by a French woman named Marie Souvestre. Although decidedly nonreligious, Souvestre possessed a strong social conscience and sought to instill in her students an interest in other human beings, the problems they faced, and the question of how to address those problems.

Souvestre's views stimulated ER's interest in social problems, but ER did not abandon her religious convictions. In her speech at Chautauqua in July 1933, she urged her audience to "make a vital, living thing of religion—not a theory, but a mode of living."[22] Later that fall, she told a gathering of Presbyterians that government programs aimed at bringing about economic recovery "can only do so much....[U]nless we have a great spiritual revival, a rededication to unselfishness, there is very little hope for a permanent change."[23] Over the course of the 1930s, ER frequently articulated and expanded on these views.

In an article in *Forum Magazine* in 1936 entitled "What Religion Means to Me," reprinted, significantly, the same year by the *Washington Jewish Review*, ER said, "To me religion has nothing to do with any specific creed or dogma." Religion meant living by the highest standard. For Christians "that standard is the life of Christ" but, whatever a person's religion, what really counted, ER felt, was caring unselfishly for others: "The fundamental, vital thing which must be alive in each human consciousness is the religious teaching that we cannot live for ourselves alone and that as long as we are here on this earth we are all of us brothers, regardless of race, creed or color."[24] Religion, she believed, was synonymous with "the spirit of social cooperation." People grew spiritually by actively participating in efforts to make sure that everyone had the opportunity to at least meet their own basic needs.[25] This view of religion broke down barriers among different faiths and formed a strong philosophical basis for her collaboration with the NCCJ and her Jewish colleagues who were also working to build a more inclusive and just society. The fact that she found Jews especially willing to assist her in addressing social problems reinforced this bond. When she was working on refugee issues in the late 1930s with her Jewish friend Justine Polier, she told Polier that "whenever I appealed for help for people whether they were sharecroppers, southern negroes, poor unemployed, Jews are among the first people in this country who come forward and offer to help."[26]

The American Friends Service Committee (AFSC) provided ER with a perfect partner for putting her religious beliefs into practice. Clarence Pickett shared her conviction that religious belief should express itself primarily in service to others, not in adherence to a church or synagogue: through action in the world, not through the observance of ritual. "Religion," Pickett wrote in "Christianity in Action: Experiments in Social Regeneration," "is a matter of the relation of men to each other and to their God, and not an affair of institutions."[27] An active Christianity, ER and Pickett believed, could transform society by helping people find ways to address their own problems.

During the 1930s ER traveled throughout the United States preaching the need for a revitalized democracy. In an article in the Richmond *Times-Dispatch* in May 1938, entitled "Mrs. Roosevelt Is on Stump for New Brand of Citizenship," Beth Campbell wrote: "Her subject may be peace, youth or prisons. Her listeners may be students, workers or congressmen's wives. But always she drives in with homely phrases and amusing experiences her theory that every individual must know conditions in his own community in order to make democracy work." Wherever ER went around the country she visited factories, mines, farms, and people's homes, taking in what she saw, asking questions, and collecting information and stories with which to educate her listeners about conditions in the country. The change that ER sought required an awakened democracy in which citizens became actively engaged in their communities and worked to better the lives of everyone. Greater justice and more equitable economic conditions would emerge from a participatory, more cooperative society.

Through her "sermons on citizenship," which Campbell estimated in 1938 were heard by more than 100,000 people, ER urged Americans to reject the brutal spirit of

Nazi Germany and other totalitarian regimes and to cultivate, instead, a caring spirit of love: "If human beings can be trained for cruelty and greed and a belief in power which comes through hate and fear and force," as the totalitarian regimes were doing, she wrote in 1940, "certainly we can train equally well for gentleness and mercy and the power of love."[28] In a democracy that worked for everyone—including workers, the unemployed, and minorities—the threat of totalitarian ideologies would subside, and prejudice abate.

In *The Moral Basis of Democracy* (1940), a book that expanded on the views ER had been preaching in her sermons on citizenship, she contrasted the Nazi and Communist forms of government in which individuals "merge their will in devotion and submission to the force of the state and of the man who is the symbol of power" to the democratic way of life in which "the individual controls his government through active participation in the processes of political Democratic government." She argued that as American democracy developed, people came to realize "that differences in religious belief are inherent in the spirit of true Democracy" and, therefore, individuals had the right to practice any religion or, if they wished, no religion. The religious idea "of the responsibility of the individual for the well-being of his neighbors," which is summed up in the New Testament dictum "Love thy neighbor as thyself," persisted, however, and distinguished democracy from every other form of government.[29] (ER might have added that this commandment originated in the Old Testament dictum "You shall love thy neighbor as yourself" [Leviticus 19:17] and is a basic tenet of Judaism.)

The Moral Basis of Democracy expressed the central idea that ER shared with Clarence Pickett and the Quakers: Christianity required action, not just prayer but deeds that built bridges of trust between people and achieved greater equality. Confirming the harmony of the book's viewpoint with Quaker philosophy, the AFSC publicized *The Moral Basis of Democracy* in its newsletter and in three Quaker periodicals. The AFSC received one-third of the price of each book ordered through its office and used these funds to carry out programs in keeping with the views ER espoused in the book.[30]

Although ER would come to firmly reject the pacifism of her Quaker ally, her ideal of citizenship in a democracy and belief in the "power of love" were in complete harmony with Clarence Pickett's vision of Christianity in action as expressed in the work of the AFSC. Both ER and Pickett formed strong relationships with Jewish leaders and organizations in seeking to achieve their vision of democracy, work for peace, fight antisemitism, and aid Jewish and non-Aryan Christian refugees.

5

THE WAGNER-ROGERS BILL

"The best propaganda for America
you could possibly have"

A FTER FDR BECAME president in 1933, the burden of responding to the national crisis brought on by the Great Depression occupied much of Eleanor Roosevelt's time. Hitler's persecution of the Jews and the refugee crisis created by his policies were not among the most pressing issues before her, and not the most accessible to her influence. The economic conditions during the Depression, the New Deal programs to remedy those conditions, the needs of youth who were disproportionately unemployed, public health (especially of women and children), workplace safety, unionization of American labor, women's employment, women's access to public office, civil rights, and other issues received ER's attention. In the case of civil rights, the Nazi assault on the rights of Germany's Jewish citizens and the violence directed against them brought home the need for Americans to address the way their nation treated African Americans, especially the practice of lynching—a practice unchecked by federal law.

ER knew that the practice of lynching made it hypocritical for Americans to denounce German persecution of its Jewish population unless Americans also acted to correct their own nation's shortcomings. Passing the federal antilynching bill that came before Congress in the 1930s became crucial. The matter seemed especially urgent because the number of lynchings in the United States had increased from seven in 1929 to twenty-one in 1930 and in each of the following two years and then to twenty-eight in 1933.[1] ER served as a liaison between Walter White, executive secretary of the NAACP, and FDR on this issue. In April 1934 White sent ER a memo reporting that several senators had told him that there were now "enough votes and to spare" to pass the Costigan-Wagner antilynching bill in the Senate if it were brought up for a vote, but only "insistence by the White House" would guarantee a Senate vote on it. White asked ER to discuss this development with the president.[2] ER did so, but, fearing that if he pressed for a vote on the antilynching bill, Southern committee chairs in the House and Senate would prevent the passage of New Deal legislation he deemed crucial to reviving the economy, FDR held back.

Pressure to pass the bill increased in October 1934 after the lynching of Claude Neal, one of the most horrific incidents in the history of lynching. In December nine governors, including Democrat Herbert Lehman of New York, wrote to the president supporting the bill's passage:

> The killing and burning alive of human beings by mobs in the United States is a reproach upon our nation throughout the civilized world. The recent shameful abduction of a prisoner and transportation across the State line from Alabama to Florida to be lynched, with the crime advertised throughout the nation twelve hours in advance, is a notorious example of the breakdown of the machinery of justice which has grown out of the lynching evil. Since 1882, 5,068 human beings have been lynched in the United States, with less than a dozen convictions; in each of these cases only nominal prison terms were given the lynchers.

The nine governors urged the president to put the antilynching bill on his "'must' program" in his opening address to Congress in 1935.[3] This time, FDR supported a vote on the bill, but he would not endorse it publicly or speak out against the Southern filibuster mounted against the bill's passage. The president continued to believe that he could not risk angering the Southern legislators whom he depended on to move other legislation through Congress. His fears were not without basis. When Southern senators threatened to filibuster as long as necessary to block the bill in the spring of 1935 and thus prevent passage of the Social Security bill, Costigan withdrew it.[4]

Nevertheless, ER continued to press for passage of an antilynching bill. The sooner Americans "unite to stamp out any such action," she said in a speech on December 12, 1935, "the better will we be able to face the other nations of the world and to uphold our real ideals here and abroad."[5] When the antilynching bill was reintroduced in 1937, ER once more pushed FDR to throw his support behind it.[6] But FDR again refused to press the issue.

Writing to FDR in December 1938, the month after Kristallnacht, Walter White noted that "Seven lynchings have taken place since the Congress adjourned. No member of any one of the seven mobs, which total more than 1000 in membership, has even been arrested, much less punished." White urged the president to appeal in the strongest terms in his opening message to the 76th Congress to speedily pass antilynching legislation: "A strong word is needed from you as the leader of the nation to the effect that while we rightly condemn racial persecution abroad we as Americans should at the same time clean up our own domain." To drive home the point, White enclosed a United Press report from Berlin "in which your own fine pronouncements against the horrible persecution of minorities in Germany is discounted by Germany's pointing to unpunished and unrebuked lynchings in America." After White sent a copy of his letter to ER, she replied: "There is a difference [between what is happening in Germany and America], which the south will of course point out, but I think there is enough similarity to make quite a good argument along these lines."[7] The fact that the president never publicly supported and Congress failed to enact an antilynching bill during his tenure placed the United States on morally indefensible ground and may have played a role in muting American criticism of Germany's policies toward its Jewish minority.

WHILE THE NAZI PERSECUTION of the Jews helped spur ER and others to fight for a federal antilynching law, she did not actively address the refugee crisis created by Hitler's policies until 1939, by which time it had become acute. The events of 1938 swelled the number of Jews, non-Aryan Christians, and political refugees applying for American visas. The barriers established by American immigration law and State Department regulations for obtaining an American visa were high, however, and the process of applying for a visa was time consuming. With the rising demand for visas after the Anschluss, the waiting list for visas grew and the length of time it took for visa applications to be reviewed greatly increased. In addition, consular officers often applied the immigration laws and regulations inconsistently. Other obstacles, such as the cost and availability of transportation, blocked immigration as well.

In 1939 an applicant for an American visa faced two hurdles. The first was the annual quota on German and Austrian immigration imposed by the immigration laws passed by Congress in the early 1920s that restricted the number of immigrants the United States could admit from each country every year. Although the German and Austrian quotas had not been filled in the years 1933–37, the combined German-Austrian quota was nearly filled in fiscal 1938, filled in 1939, and nearly filled again in 1940.[8] Since the quota was only filled completely in 1939, the immediate problem was not the quota itself, but the enormous demand for visas coupled with the long process of screening applications. That meant it could take years for an applicant's name to rise to the top of the quota list. Only then would the applicant be even considered for admission to the United States.

The second hurdle was the so-called LPC rule. LPC stood for "likely to become a public charge." From 1882 onward American immigration law excluded people who fell into that category. Originally the rule applied to people who did not have the mental or physical ability to do productive work and would therefore be dependent on others for support. In 1930, however, because of his concern that immigration would add still more people to the masses of unemployed during the deepening Great Depression, President Herbert Hoover instructed the State Department to apply the LPC rule more stringently in light of the fact that few immigrants would be able to obtain employment in Depression America. Those with independent resources or relatives with sufficient resources to support them were eligible for visas. But they were required to furnish proof of their financial status or submit affidavits from relatives guaranteeing the applicant's support and backed by bank statements, tax returns, and documents showing income. Largely as a result of Hoover's policy, the number of visas issued to German applicants between 1931 and 1933 dropped from 10,100 to 1,324. Although the number increased slightly during the early years of the Roosevelt administration to nearly 4,400 in the year ending June 30, 1934, that was still only slightly more than 17 percent of the German quota. A rise in the number of visa applicants, not a more liberal immigration policy accounted for much of the increase. After the 1936 election, the Roosevelt administration adopted a somewhat more liberal interpretation of the LPC rule and the number of German immigrants admitted into the United States increased significantly in the years immediately following, but the LPC rule remained a formidable barrier.[9] Those visa applicants with affidavits from nonrelatives and without independent resources failed the LPC test. Finding someone willing to furnish an affidavit and provide the necessary documentation was often a challenge to a would-be immigrant. Even when he or she succeeded, it was up to the consular officer to make a judgment about whether the financial information the visa applicant submitted was sufficient to ensure the applicant would not become a public charge. The LPC rule became a powerful device for American consular officials acting on behalf of the State Department to administratively limit immigration to the United States, and it was one of the obstacles that frustrated ER's efforts to assist refugees seeking visas.

GIVEN THE DEEP RESISTANCE TO immigration, Americans who wished to assist refugees sought ways of allowing more refugees into the country in ways that would cause less anxiety and circumvent the barriers thrown up by the long quota lists, the required affidavits, and the lengthy application process for immigrant visas. In 1939, in response to Kristallnacht, a group of ER's friends initiated an effort to secure the admission of 20,000 German children to the United States outside the normal German quota. This initiative would have bypassed the waiting list for visas and expanded the number of refugees entering the United States. Since children aroused the most sympathy and posed the least threat, the plan seemed the most promising way of persuading Congress and the American people to open America's doors a bit wider.

The group that organized the initiative began meeting regularly at the apartment of Dr. Marion Kenworthy, a psychiatrist and director of the Mental Hygiene Department of the New York School of Social Work, to plot strategy for achieving their goal. The group included Clarence Pickett; the philanthropists Marshall Field III and Adele Rosenwald Levy;[10] Dr. Viola W. Bernard, a child psychiatrist and child welfare advocate; and Benjamin Cohen, one of FDR's most influential domestic advisers, who was deeply concerned with the fate of German Jews. Levy, one of the heirs to the Sears, Roebuck fortune, remained a friend and ally of ER's in the field of child welfare throughout the rest of ER's life. Levy, Bernard, and Cohen were all Jews, as was another member of the group, Justine Polier. Polier, a domestic relations court judge in New York City, would develop a close working relationship with ER, especially in the fields of child welfare and civil rights. Bishop Bernard Sheil of Chicago, an expert on child welfare, represented the Catholics.[11]

When Polier wrote to ER about the plan, ER spoke to FDR about it. He encouraged it but recognized that the initiative had to come from Congress and that its success depended on bipartisan approval and wide support from the religious community that would put pressure on Congress to act. In early January 1939, ER wrote to Polier,

> My husband says that you had better go to work at once and get two people of opposite parties in the House and in the Senate and to have them jointly get agreement on the legislation which you want for bringing in children. The State Department is only afraid of what Congress will say to them and, therefore, if you remove that fear the State Department will make no objection. He advises that you choose your people rather carefully and if possible get all the Catholic support you can.[12]

On January 9, 1939 as a result of the group's efforts to solicit support for their plan from Protestant and Catholic leaders, a group of over fifty prominent Protestant and Catholic clergymen delivered a petition to the White House expressing their support for the plan:

> To us it seems that the duty of Americans in dealing with the youthful victims of a regime which punishes innocent and tender children as if they were offenders, is to remember the monition of Him who said, "Suffer little children to come unto me."[13]

Both John L. Lewis, head of the American Federation of Labor (AFL), and William Green, president of the CIO, whose unions normally opposed increasing immigration for fear that the immigrants would compete for American jobs in a depressed economy, endorsed the plan, as did former president Hoover.

While seeking support for the proposed bill, the organizers also made plans for the selection and reception of the children. They began identifying families willing to accept the children into their homes and raising private funds to cover the costs of transportation and the provision of health and other services to the children once they were in the United States.

By the time Senator Robert Wagner, Democrat of New York, and Representative Edith Nourse Rogers, Republican of Massachusetts, introduced the bill in February 1939, the organizers had a detailed plan in hand that they could use to persuade Congress and the American public that the children and foster families would be carefully selected and the continued welfare of the children ensured, all at no expense to the taxpayer. The bill provided for the admission of 10,000 German refugee children to the United States in 1939 and another 10,000 in 1940 above the usual German immigration quota. In a press release promoting the bill, ER's associates noted that the bill made no changes in current immigration laws. The committee emphasized that the children selected would come from various religious backgrounds:

> In Germany, Sudetenland and Austria there are to-day at least seventy thousand children, fourteen years of age and under, whose situation is desperate.... Many are without food, clothing or permanent homes because one or both parents are in concentration camps, or are no longer allowed to earn a living. This is not a racial problem. Thousands are of Catholic and Protestant parentage but classed as "Non-Aryan"; thousands are of families whose political beliefs have made them special outcasts.[14]

The committee reported that thousands of Americans had already volunteered to welcome refugee children into their homes.

ER herself was cautious about endorsing the bill publicly. She told Pickett that she would be glad to join the sponsoring group but that the announcement of her membership would have to be delayed until after passage of the bill.[15] Jay Pierrepont Moffat, one of Sumner Welles's colleagues at the State Department, told Welles that he found even such delayed support on ER's part worrisome, since "it will inevitably remain a controversial issue."[16] Nevertheless, when ER was asked about the bill at her weekly press conference on February 13, she said, "It seems to me to be a wise way to do a humanitarian thing. England, France and the Scandinavian countries are taking their share of these children, and I think we should."[17]

Many newspapers, including some in the South, endorsed the bill. An editorial in the Richmond, Virginia *Times Dispatch* observed that the children the bill was designed to assist were "treated as outcasts, scoffed at in public, and in many cases thrown out of orphan asylums and left on the verge of starvation. How can we, who profess to believe in democracy and human rights, sit idly by and allow such atrocities to be committed without raising a finger?"[18]

Despite this outpouring of support, the assurance that the program would cost taxpayers nothing, the existence of a detailed plan for the children's care, and the sense of relief it seemed to provide for many people that something meaningful would finally be done to address the refugee problem, the bill immediately ran into difficulty. Representative Rogers reported her alarm to Pickett that two-thirds of the letters she received on the issue expressed opposition to the bill.[19]

The anti-immigration sentiment was so strong in Congress and among a large portion of the public that those who favored the bill were reluctant to urge FDR to publicly support it for fear that Congress might react by tightening immigration restrictions rather than relaxing them.[20] ER reported to Justine Polier that when she spoke to James McDonald about it, he told her that while he personally supported the bill, he had been warned "that pressing the President at the present time may mean that the people in Congress who have bills to cut the quota will present them immediately and that might precipitate a difficult situation which would result in cutting the quota by ninety percent." Given that danger, McDonald's committee didn't feel it should advise the president to make a public statement urging passage of the bill. ER reported to Polier that Sumner Welles, who also personally favored the bill, agreed completely with McDonald "because his desk is flooded with protests accusing the State Department of conniving in allowing a great many more Jewish people than the quota permits to enter the country under various pretenses." When she cabled FDR about the matter, ER reported, he told her that she could publicly endorse the bill and tell Welles "he would be pleased to have the bill go through. But he did not want to say anything publicly at the present time."[21]

On March 2 the group that had initiated the Wagner-Rogers bill announced the formation of the Non-Sectarian Committee for German Refugee Children, with Clarence Pickett as its director. The AFSC agreed to select the children in Germany and the Non-Sectarian Committee planned to take responsibility for placing them in foster homes in the United States.[22]

Thorough planning and the establishment of a nongovernmental organization to implement the plan strengthened the argument in favor of the bill but proved insufficient to overcome the opposition. At joint hearings of the Senate and House subcommittees on immigration in April and at hearings before the House Committee on Immigration and Naturalization in May, the bill came under sharp attack from the American Legion, the Immigration Restriction League, various self-proclaimed patriotic societies, and individuals. The American Legion, which advocated halting immigration completely for ten years or until the millions of unemployed American citizens had found jobs, opposed any exceptions to the current immigration laws.

One argument against the bill was that it would lead inevitably to a greater and greater relaxation of the immigration laws. Another was that there were many children suffering throughout the world, including the United States. Why single out German children? And why admit foreign children to the United States when so many American children lacked the basic necessities of life? John Cecil, president of the American Immigration Conference Board, cited the "half-naked children" of tenant farmers who "eat thickened gravy and biscuits as a year-round diet" and lack medical care. "Shall we first take care of our own children," he asked, "or shall we bestow our charity on children imported from abroad?"

Some of the testimony was explicitly antisemitic or bore a subtext of antisemitism. When Dr. F. W. Buck, representing the Defenders of the Constitution, reported that there was no large city in the country where he had not been "importuned to work against the Jews," Representative Samuel Dickstein, chairman of the House Committee on Immigration and Naturalization, who had emigrated with his Jewish parents from what is now Lithuania as a child, cut him off. The committee, Dickstein informed him, had "tried as far as possible to keep those questions out of the discussion."[23]

The Non-Sectarian Committee rallied an impressive group of organizations and individuals to present opposing arguments. Dorothy Thompson, for example, testified that the Wagner-Rogers bill was "the first intelligently planned immigration bill" introduced into Congress: "it will be the best propaganda for America you could possibly have. The worst possible propaganda would be for the greatest democracy on earth to refuse to do anything about this terrific international problem."[24]

But opposition to the bill because of antisemitism and for economic reasons ran deep. One problem was that the supporters of the bill did not get the kind of Catholic support they hoped for. Cardinal Spellman of New York, the most powerful leader of the Catholic Church in America, refused to back the bill. Justine Polier, whose father was Rabbi Stephen Wise, attributed his refusal to religious intolerance: "I personally feel and I know my father felt that he was profoundly anti-Semitic."[25]

Most crucially, the prevailing sentiment in the nation, even in the wake of Kristallnacht, was against admitting refugees. A poll in *Fortune* magazine, published in its April 1939 issue and cited during the congressional testimony against the bill, found that the number of Americans opposed to admitting more European refugees above the current immigration quotas had actually risen from 67.4 percent in July 1938 to 83 percent in April 1939. The number of Americans who favored allowing more refugees into the country had also risen, but only slightly, from 4.9 percent in 1938 to 8.7 percent in 1939. The editors of *Fortune* wrote:

> There is about this answer a finality that seems to mean that the doors of this country should be virtually closed to refugees, and should stay closed to them, no matter

what their need or condition. The answer is the more decisive because it was made at a time when public sympathy for victims of European events was presumably at its highest.[26]

By May it appeared that the Wagner-Rogers bill might pass, but only in a form unacceptable to its sponsors. On June 30, when the Senate immigration committee finally voted to report favorably on the bill, it no longer fulfilled its original purpose. Although the 20,000 children would receive visas before anyone else on the quota list, they would be included within the normal German quota. Adult applicants who were in danger and had been waiting a long time for visas would be displaced and the number of refugees allowed to enter the United States would not increase. On July 3, Wagner announced that the altered bill was "wholly unacceptable" and he would rather "have no bill at all."[27]

The fate of the Wagner-Rogers bill goes to the very heart of why America did not respond adequately to the persecution of European Jews or other victims of the Nazis. If Congress did not see fit to make an exception to its immigration laws and admit to the United States 20,000 German children—a group who would not, in the short run at least, compete for American jobs and the least likely group to harbor subversives or criminals—then it was unthinkable that Congress would liberalize America's immigration laws in any other way. ER and her friends would continue to fight to bring refugee children to the United States, and have some modest successes, but they never again had an opportunity to rescue such a large group or receive such strong public and media support for their work.

ANOTHER, MORE SUCCESSFUL, THOUGH SMALL-SCALE, way of aiding a single category of refugees after Kristallnacht was initiated by a group of Harvard students who formed the Intercollegiate Committee to Aid Student Refugees (ICASR). The aim of the organization was to provide scholarships to American colleges and universities for outstanding students from Nazi-controlled central Europe who were being prohibited from pursuing their education in their native lands. Since the students would be admitted on student visas, they would not have to wait for immigrant visas or be counted in the German quota. The program would provide them with temporary refuge for the duration of the war. The presidents of Harvard, Vassar, and the University of Chicago signed on as sponsors of ICASR.[28] When Clarence Pickett approached ER about becoming a sponsor, she asked Tommy to get the advice of Sumner Welles. Welles, in turn, consulted George Messersmith, the former consul general in Berlin. Messersmith told Welles that he was worried that the State Department was already receiving criticism for "facilitating the admission of people in one way or another outside of the quotas."

He thought "it would be just as well if Mrs. Roosevelt did not permit the use of her name in this connection." But this was one of the few cases when Welles's sympathy with ER's efforts on behalf of refugees led him to overrule a State Department colleague. Finding Messersmith's reply unsatisfactory, Welles turned to Pierrepont Moffat, to whom he said: "it would seem to me rather difficult for me to express the opinion to Mrs. Roosevelt that she should not permit the use of her name on this committee which is apparently composed of some of the outstanding people in this country and which, at the same time, is headed by an individual [Clarence Pickett] who is in such close touch with the Advisory Committee [the President's Advisory Committee on Political Refugees] and with the Red Cross and who, I understand, is cooperating most effectively. I cannot see that a student scholarship project would be likely to create any particular ill will in this country—much less, in fact, than the proposal to admit a large number of children."

Moffat agreed. Since "the emphasis is on the scholarships rather than on the admission of refugee students," he told Welles, he did not think it would "give rise to misunderstanding." Reassured in his opinion by Moffat, Welles enthusiastically endorsed ER's sponsorship of the student program. He thought that "Mrs. Roosevelt's cooperation would in fact be desirable from any point of view."[29]

Despite Welles's approval, the student scholarship program ran into another State Department barrier. In letters to Secretary of State Cordell Hull and Secretary of Labor Frances Perkins, Pickett explained that students and faculty members at American colleges and universities had raised enough money to make it possible to offer 200 scholarships to both Jewish and non-Jewish students from the Nazi-controlled nations of Central Europe. But the State Department was blocking their entrance to the United States because the students could not demonstrate, as required by American immigration regulations, that they would be able to return to their native countries once they completed their studies. Pickett argued that since the students constituted a small, "highly specialized" group and American consuls would be assured that the students would leave the United States at the end of their studies (even if it were not to their native country), no one could say that issuing them student visas meant "a relaxation of existing immigration restrictions."

Another difficulty some of the students faced was that their passports would expire before they completed their studies. These students, Pickett told Hull, needed to be provided with some other travel document, such as the Nansen passports that were issued to Russian student refugees following the World War.

After Pickett sent a copy of his letter to Hull and Perkins to ER, who had accepted the honorary chairmanship of ICASR, ER sent Hull a note urging his "careful consideration" of Pickett's appeal.[30] Hull replied that he was "keenly sympathetic with and understanding of the unfortunate situation of these young people." The technical and legal officers of the State Department had carefully examined the issue, however, and concluded that the State Department could not "properly relax the requirements of the regulations in the absence of an amendment by Congress of the controlling provisions of law."[31]

Despite these obstacles, Catherine Doony, executive secretary of ICASR, was able to report by the end of June 1939 that "213 colleges, representing 39 states and the District of Columbia, have made a constructive contribution to the solution of the refugee problem through the establishment of approximately 300 scholarships for the best of those young students of Central Europe who have been barred from their own Universities by the inhumane decrees of a merciless Dictator." Because of State Department regulations, not all of the students offered scholarships were able to reach the United States. For those who did, however, the program saved their lives. In addition, Doony said, the program helped the more than 300,000 American students who contributed to the scholarship fund to recognize "that the denial of racial and religious freedom in Nazi Germany constituted a challenge to all of us who cherish the principles of Democracy and Christianity."[32]

During the summer of 1939, ICASR organized a monthlong Work Camp for Democracy at a site in the Hudson Valley. ER visited the camp just a few days before the German invasion of Poland and recorded her impressions in her My Day column of August 30. The purpose of the camp, she said, was to bring some American students together with a group of refugee students (including "Jews, Catholics and liberal Germans") to "study democracy theoretically and practically through work experiences together." The students engaged in four hours of manual labor each day—painting a house, repairing a road—and four hours of study.[33]

In September 1939, after the war began and no more students could leave Germany, ICASR merged with the International Student Service. ER's young friend Joseph Lash headed the combined organization, which continued to administer the program for students who had already left Germany and advocate for those still seeking visas.[34] Like the widespread, though insufficient, support for the Wagner-Rogers bill, the endorsement of the student refugee program by prominent educators and the contributions made to it by college and university faculty and students demonstrated that there was a pent-up desire among many Americans to do something to relieve the refugee crisis. Given the strong anti-immigrant and antisemitic sentiment in Congress, the State Department, and throughout the nation, however, this impulse found very few avenues for expression.

6

THE UNITED STATES COMMITTEE FOR THE CARE OF EUROPEAN CHILDREN

"Red tape ought not to be used to trip up little children on their way to safety"

IN SEPTEMBER 1939 after the outbreak of war in Europe, prospects for reviving the Wagner-Rogers bill grew dim. On September 14, Pickett met with Justine Polier and other members of the Non-Sectarian Committee for German Refugee Children to decide how to proceed. They concluded that they should not raise the issue of the German children at the beginning of the upcoming special session of Congress because the president wanted the session to focus on revising the Neutrality Act. He hoped a revised act would give him the flexibility to deny aid to aggressors without withholding aid to nations that resisted aggression. Polier, Pickett, and Louis Weiss, Marshall Field's attorney, were instead charged with finding alternative methods of meeting the committee's goals. When the members met again in November, they decided to concentrate on bringing into the United States as many refugee children as they could within the current quota.[1] They hoped to revive the bill in the future, if the time was ripe.

In March 1940, to implement the new plan, members of the Non-Sectarian Committee created the Non-Sectarian Foundation for Refugee Children. Eleanor Roosevelt agreed to serve as an honorary vice-president of the new organization, along with New York governor Herbert Lehman, and others. Pickett kept her up-to-date on its work. The foundation's purpose was to assist children who had become refugees because of war or religious or racial persecution and could be admitted by the United States within the quota. The foundation planned to work with existing organizations, including the American Friends Service Committee (AFSC), as a clearinghouse for placing refugee children of all religious faiths who arrived in the United States in private homes.²

When the Non-Sectarian Foundation Executive Committee met in mid-May 1940, however, the German invasion of the Low Countries and France had thrown the plans of the foundation into confusion. Then, when France fell in June 1940, the danger in which refugees found themselves intensified once again. Nevertheless, the crisis seemed to open a window of opportunity in which public pressure might move Congress to act: "The time seems to be ripe for aid and comfort to the refugees," ER's close friend and ally, Representative Caroline O'Day, wrote to her on June 14.³ Galvanized by the situation, ER entered into the period of her deepest involvement with the refugee crisis.

WITH GREAT BRITAIN NOW STANDING alone in resistance to Hitler and German warplanes able to reach the British coast in four minutes, the danger that English children faced disturbed many Americans. Clarence Pickett received phone calls from all over the country asking that large numbers of British children be brought to safety in the United States. This outpouring of sympathy did not signal a radical change in American public opinion toward immigration, but the emotional bond between the United States and Great Britain generated by the visit of the king and queen of England to the United States in June 1939, the outbreak of war in September, and the peril that Great Britain now faced increased public concern for the British people. Furthermore, antisemitism was not a factor, since most of the children who would come from Great Britain were not Jews. Even so, the resistance of the State Department to immigration of any kind proved daunting. At Pickett's request, ER chaired a meeting with representatives of all the groups interested in evacuating the children for a discussion of how to take action.⁴

At the meeting on June 20, 1940, ER, Clarence Pickett, Marshall Field, Frank Kingdon, Justine Polier, and other veterans of the Non-Sectarian Committee for German Refugee Children and the fight for the Wagner-Rogers bill, together with representatives of other child and social welfare groups, formed the United States Committee for the Care of European Children (USCCEC). The USCCEC was an umbrella organization set up to work out arrangements with the State Department for the admission of child refugees to the United States and to coordinate their reception, placement, and ongoing supervision. While the first group of children the USCCEC sought to help were largely Gentiles, the USCCEC would later turn its attention to Jews trapped in unoccupied France. ER, who was named honorary chairman of the administrative committee of the USCCEC, also chaired the subsequent organizational meetings of the group held in New York City on June 25 and 28. Marshall Field became chairman of the administrative committee and Agnes Inglis its secretary.⁵

During the week when the USCCEC was formed, the British government reinforced the hope that large numbers of children might be brought to the United States for safekeeping when Parliament adopted a plan for the evacuation of children from Britain to the United States and the British dominions. News accounts and editorials about the plans inspired thousands of Americans to flock to immigration and child care agencies and offer to care for British children in their homes. Thousands wrote letters to the committee, many directly to ER. ER also received unsolicited checks from individuals and organizations wishing to support the USCCEC's work.

The USCCEC's plans faced a major problem, however: the State Department's inflexible regulations regarding visas and affidavits. The first obstacle was that the State Department expected the children, like adult refugees, to apply for permanent admission to the United States. That meant that the committee would have to find someone to sign an affidavit pledging financial support for each child. It was obviously not a method suited to quickly evacuating a large number of children before German bombs endangered them.[6]

On July 3 Joseph Alsop, ER's second cousin, telegrammed her a memo drafted under his direction for Francis Biddle, the solicitor general at that time, to send to FDR. Biddle was in charge of the Immigration and Naturalization Service. The memo stated that State Department policy "imposes a series of elaborate restrictions, both as to the number of visas to be issued and the conditions of issuance, which make it impossible to plan any important refugee movement to this country." The result was that although the USCCEC reported receiving over 1,000 applications every day from Americans willing to care for English children trying to escape the bombing, "the present system followed by the Department of State permits the issuance of not more than 100 visas a day." The problem could be overcome, Alsop's memo asserted, if the State Department issued the children visitor visas, "on the understanding they would be returned to England when the danger ended," rather than require them to apply for admission as immigrants.

The second obstacle was the State Department's requirement of affidavits of support for each child. As Alsop summarized the problem: "All affidavits must be scrutinized by the consuls in England. Each affidavit must be made by an individual American citizen. And each maker of an affidavit must show, preferably by relationship but at least by friendship some reason for his interest in the child whose support he guarantees as well as evidence of his financial condition." Alsop proposed that this bottleneck could be cleared if the State Department centralized the examination of the affidavits in Washington and if it would accept corporate affidavits from organizations such as "Mrs. Roosevelt's Committee" (the USCCEC).

At the end of the telegram, Alsop added that Francis Biddle told him that the Justice Department saw absolutely no objection to making these changes to the handling of visas for the children, "And as they will save the lives of thousands, there is every reason on the other side." He thanked ER for her help, and ER replied, "[I want] to tell you how grand I think you have been about the refugee children."[7]

In a bold move to pressure the State Department to alter its visa policy for the British children, ER addressed the issue in her radio address on the evening of July 6, 1940. Reading from a script prepared by Alsop,[8] ER said that an administrative order could direct that English refugee children be allowed to come to the United States immediately on traveler or visitor visas for the duration of the war. Under the current State Department regulations, she said, the children not only needed to come as immigrants, they had to contend with "all sorts of thorny regulations":

> In truth, before they can reach their safe harbor in America, speaking very frankly, the children must find their way through a labyrinth of red tape. Red tape has its uses in government—for there are many times when it is better that the government move slowly and cautiously—but the red tape ought not to be used to trip up little children on their way to safety.

ER told her radio audience that the red tape "can all be swept aside, if you, and I, and every one else will only insist on it." By streamlining the application process, visas could "be issued freely" and the children could "come in, not in sad little bands, but as they ought to come, by the thousands." ER urged her audience to act:

> The time is very short. The Battle of England is at hand, and if the children are to be saved we must act now. Make it known you want the children in. If you are able to care for a child—but only if you are able—send your application to the Child Refugee Committee.[9]

In her My Day column for July 13, ER continued to press her case by venting her frustration at the "horrid legal details" choking the effort to bring the British children to the United States. She pressured the State Department by adopting a stance of naïve certainty that they would do what was right by making it possible for large numbers of children to enter the country: "Our responsibility is to see that we facilitate their coming in every possible way, which I am sure is being done."[10]

ER's speech put the State Department on the defensive. Caught off guard, State Department officials scrambled to figure out how to respond to requests for information from citizens prompted to action by ER's words. Sophonisba Breckinridge, prominent social reformer, professor of public welfare administration at the University of Chicago, and distant cousin of Assistant Secretary of State Breckinridge Long, telegrammed Secretary of State Hull asking for an explanation of ER's statement that by executive order the British children could be admitted to the country as visitors for the duration of the war. She also asked Hull to identify the "proper authorities" to whom she should communicate her wishes, as ER had suggested.[11] Richard Flournoy, the State Department official receiving the request, sent a memo to several of his colleagues saying that the question was "not easy to answer." He had not been able to obtain a copy of ER's speech but assumed that Dr. Breckinridge's summary of it was accurate. He thought it might be possible to revise the regulations to permit some children to enter the United States as visitors, but, at first, only for a two-year period. He was sympathetic to ER's idea, however. He assumed that "something will be done to carry out the humane proposal of Mrs. Roosevelt, although it may be found necessary to amend the existing law in order to admit the refugee children in large numbers."[12]

When Hull responded to Dr. Breckinridge, however, in a letter apparently drafted by Breckinridge Long, he ignored the issue of visitor visas entirely and claimed that the process of admitting British children to the United States was running smoothly. If a problem existed, it lay at the British end: "Officials of this Department have cooperated wholeheartedly and enthusiastically" with other government officials and with private organizations, including the USCCEC. Red tape had been cut and "all the nonessential requirements eliminated," he insisted. The American consuls had refused no visa to "a qualified child" and "no delay whatever exists." The United States was, in fact, ready to take more children than British authorities were ready to send.[13]

Three days after ER's radio address, Drew Pearson observed in his Washington Merry-Go-Round column: "There is something awfully strange about the way the State Department is functioning in regard to the admission of refugee children from war-bombed England. Although the sympathies of the entire country are strongly pro-Ally, although Mrs. Roosevelt is chairman of the Children's Refugee Committee, and although both Secretary Hull and Sumner Welles sympathize with the admission of refugee children, the career men in the State Department have turned thumbs down." He reported that Avra Warren had ruled that English children could not enter the United States on visitor visas—"given as a matter of routine to German and other European business men"—but had to wait weeks or months to obtain quota visas.[14]

Although the memo from Biddle to FDR that Alsop drafted with ER's encouragement furnished the president with a legal basis for ordering a dramatic change in American policy regarding refugee children, FDR was apparently assured by the State Department that American immigration policy was not the problem. Speaking at his press conference on July 9, he said that the delay in bringing children to the United States resulted from Great Britain's failure to provide the ships needed to transport them and not from American visa regulations. "Shipping is the bottleneck," he insisted.[15]

He was partly right. There were, in fact, two daunting obstacles to the plan to bring British children to the United States: the shortage of ships, cited by the president, and the danger from German submarines. On July 10, Joseph Kennedy, American Ambassador to Great Britain, informed FDR and Hull that he believed the proposed evacuation of British children to the United States would be a "colossal failure" because the British had not "given enough serious thought as to how they were going to get them there." There were no ships available to transport the children. German submarines were sinking more and more ships and the ports out of which ships would have to sail would soon come under air attack. Once the British realized the problem, they would try to blame the United States for the failure. "I hate to see Mrs. Roosevelt's name being used as chairman of a committee that I feel will turn out to be a bust and the idea of raising millions of dollars to take care of children who will never arrive just doesn't make any sense."

Kennedy said that the assertions made in the press that bureaucratic red tape was severely limiting the number of children who could reach America were simply untrue. According to Kennedy, the American consulate general was issuing visas more quickly than the British could obtain passage on ships for them.[16] Hull, however, did not find Kennedy's analysis of the situation satisfactory. Despite Hull's public statement that the State Department was already doing all it could to speed up the process, he insisted that Kennedy do more to remedy the problem. ER's speech and the outcry from the press and public about State Department obstruction had lit a fire under the secretary. The uproar may also have persuaded the president that something had to be done. After receiving information that the processing of visas was being held up because of a shortage of medical facilities for examining the children,[17] Hull demanded in a cable on July 11 that the American Embassy streamline the visa process and make it possible for a large number of children to reach the United States by August. He told Kennedy that he trusted "that all necessary steps have been taken to expedite the issuance of visas to qualified refugee children under the minimum requirements" and that medical examinations of the simplest kind would be conducted to avoid delays:

> Interested persons [meaning, no doubt, both ER and FDR] have been assured that every step has been taken to facilitate the issuance of visas to qualified applicants, that no delay whatever exists in acting in these cases, and that under the present arrangements 13,000 children can leave Great Britain for the United States by August first.[18]

During the entire refugee crisis, from 1933 to 1945, this was the only time the State Department issued such a clear, forceful directive regarding the speeding up of the visa process.

But the results of ER's initiative and the pressure from the public and the press it helped generate did not end there. On July 13, as a result of the groundwork laid by Joseph Alsop's memo and negotiations with the leadership of the USCCEC, the Departments of Justice and State unveiled a new immigration plan for the children. The announcement came as a surprise after the earlier assertions by Hull and FDR that the delays were not the fault of American visa policy. Under the new plan, the State Department would issue visitor visas to about 13,000 British children under the age of sixteen by August 1, as long as they expressed a commitment to return home at the end of the war. Since foreign governments were now permitted to pay transportation costs, a greater number of children without the means to cover their own passage would be able to come. In addition, the State Department would accept corporate affidavits from organizations approved by the attorney general, such as the USCCEC, rather than affidavits from individuals only. The corporate affidavits would be backed by a trust fund valued at $50 per child to cover any contingencies that might arise. Finally, American consuls could issue visas to children selected by USCCEC representatives abroad "from the war zones" without requiring approval of their names by the State Department. The department expected that "during the period of emergency" 10,000 more children would hold visas and possess the required travel documents than available ships could accommodate, making it possible to move them quickly once transportation was available.[19] The agreement appeared to apply to children from other European war zones as well as Great Britain, but this would not turn out to be the case.

By encouraging Alsop's effort to find a legal basis for a change in the State Department's regulations regarding the British children and by calling on her listeners in her radio broadcast to "insist" that the department cut the red tape holding back the issuance of visas, ER publicly challenged the president and State Department to change the government's visa policy. Despite the State Department's initial denial that a problem existed and FDR's support for the department's position, the State Department, in the end, reached a surprisingly liberal agreement with the USCCEC that would have permitted a large number of children to find refuge in the United States for the duration of the war. It was a remarkable accomplishment. ER worked hard before and after American entry into the war to obtain visas for individuals and for groups of refugees, but aside from her understated endorsement of the Wagner-Rogers Bill, her radio address about the British children was her one public effort to alter American refugee policy.

Unfortunately, the newly opened door quickly closed again. On the problem of transportation, Kennedy was essentially correct. Even if the process of issuing visas were expedited, the shortage of ships to transport the children would still prevent many of them from leaving. Furthermore, the British were becoming increasingly reluctant to expose the children to the danger from German submarines. On July 18, the British government temporarily suspended its plan to send children to the United States because it could not spare the war vessels to guard the ships that would carry them.

Although the British government withdrew from the program, it permitted British parents to send children overseas at their own risk. The London-based American Committee for the Evacuation of British Children took over responsibility for evacuating the children at the end of July.[20] In the hope that it would still be feasible to send children to the United States, the USCCEC published "The Bombers Are Coming," an illustrated fundraising flyer that reminded Americans: "Right now children are being killed and maimed. Bombs do not discriminate." The USCCEC appealed for funds to transport the children, whose "anguished parents" had registered them for evacuation, and to resettle them in homes in the United States. The flyer assured its readers that American refugee policy now made it easy for the children to enter the United States: "Our doors are now wide open to save as many children as possible."[21]

The danger posed by German submarines operating in the North Atlantic ended that hope, however. Although FDR signed a bill at the end of August that modified the Neutrality Act to allow American vessels to enter war zones to rescue children—a bill that ER worked to get passed—the German government would not guarantee safe passage for these ships as the bill required.[22] On September 17, sixty-nine children perished when the Germans torpedoed the British ship *City of Benares*, and on October 2, the British government permanently terminated the program to send children to the United States and the British dominions. Soon after that, the USCCEC abandoned its plans to facilitate the admission of the children, ended its campaign to raise $5 million, and laid off over half its staff. The USCCEC had succeeded in bringing approximately 1,000 British children to the United States and assisted private sponsors to bring 1,500 other children. The dream of bringing many more was now unattainable.[23]

AFTER THE BRITISH ABANDONED THE PLAN of sending children abroad, the USCCEC continued to oversee the placement and long-term care of children who had already reached the United States. The USCCEC also began planning the evacuation of refugee children from unoccupied France.[24] Unlike the British children, most of the children the USCCEC sought to rescue from France were Jews or non-Aryan Christians. Some of them were orphans, and some had been separated from their parents by the war or had been smuggled out of Germany or countries occupied by Germany. Some had parents who had been placed in internment camps by the Vichy government of France led by Prime Minister Pierre Laval. Since Vichy authorities were not permitting refugees to depart by ship from Marseille or other French ports, the route for getting the children out was through Lisbon, the only European port from which passengers could still embark for the United States.

On November 1, 1940, Pickett met in New York City with Marshall Field, Eric Biddle, Louis Weiss, Marion Kenworthy, Viola Bernard, Justine Polier, and Adele Levy of the USCCEC to discuss bringing 350 Jewish children from France to the United States. Pickett told them that the AFSC relief staff in France could gather information on the children and provide someone to escort them to Lisbon.[25] The next day Pickett met with Ernst Papanek, an Austrian Jew who had helped smuggle 2,000 children out of Poland, Czechoslovakia, and Germany and helped care for them in France. Papanek had immigrated to the United States in 1940. He worked for the Children's Aid Society and would later become closely associated with the circle of people around ER, including Justine Polier. In 1949 he became head of the Wiltwyck School, a school for delinquent boys on whose board ER, Polier, and Levy served and to which Bernard was a consultant. Many of the children rescued by Papanek, including the 350 he discussed with the USCCEC, were under the care of the Oeuvre de Secours aux Enfants (OSE), the French Jewish humanitarian organization for which he had worked.[26] Since the Vichy government could not guarantee reentry of refugee children who were not French citizens into France after the war, the children would not normally be eligible for visitor visas and the children would have to be admitted with immigrant visas under the quota.[27]

When Clarence Pickett met with ER in New York on November 9, 1940, he reported in his journal that they had a "good discussion" about various topics, including the problem of obtaining visas for refugees.[28] Pickett no doubt conveyed to her the USCCEC's concern that the State Department was obstructing the visa process and told her that Marshall Field, Louis Weiss, and Eric Biddle of the USCCEC would be meeting with the president to discuss the problem—plans she no doubt encouraged and, probably, helped arrange.

Two days later, before meeting with the president, Pickett, Field, Weiss, and Biddle met in New York with Edward F. Pritchard Jr., a young lawyer in the Justice Department's Immigration Division who was interested in helping refugees; George Warren, executive secretary of the President's Advisory Committee on Political Refugees (PACPR); and leaders of three of the principal refugee organizations. These leaders were Joseph Hyman of the American Jewish Joint Distribution Committee (JDC), the main Jewish relief organization operating in Europe, which worked closely with the AFSC throughout the Nazi period and helped fund some of its work; William Rosenwald of the National Refugee Service, the largest refugee agency in the United States; and Patrick Malin of the International Migration Service, each of whom furnished examples of problems they had encountered in obtaining visas for refugees. The group concluded that "the basic difficulty is an attitude on the part of most of the State Dept [*sic*] which is determined to reduce immigration to a minimum." As Pickett noted in his journal after the meeting:

It seems evident that there is a definite determination to obstruction on the part of a number in the State Department, but that there are some who are on the other side, especially Sumner Welles, the secretary. There was fear expressed that the constant flow of information to the President about the dangers of immigration was affecting his attitude, and this meeting will attempt to overcome them.[29]

The meeting with the president on November 12 yielded no concrete results, but Pickett reported that Field, Weiss, and Biddle believed their testimony on the visa problem "had made some considerable impression upon the mind of the President."[30] Although the president may have been sympathetic to the USCCEC, he left it up to the Justice and State Departments to work out their differences over American refugee policy with each other. Representatives from the Justice and State Departments reached an agreement in late November, but the difficulties of obtaining visas continued.

The effort to bring small groups of refugee children to the United States from unoccupied France sometimes succeeded, but only in a handful of cases. One small success that gave the USCCEC hope was the evacuation of twenty-six children from France in December 1940 by Martha Sharp and the Unitarian Service Committee in cooperation with the USCCEC. In this case, the State Department accepted a combination of individual consular affidavits and guarantees by the USCCEC to the Justice Department that the children without individual affidavits would not become public charges.[31]

In February, however, the State Department ruled that the agreement worked out with the USCCEC in the summer of 1940, after ER's intervention, that permitted children from Great Britain to enter the United States on visitor visas and with corporate, rather than individual, affidavits, did not apply to unoccupied France. Nevertheless, the USCCEC achieved a modest success after the State Department granted another exception to a group of 119 children who arrived in New York from Lisbon on June 21, 1941. It was the first large group of children to reach the United States under the sponsorship of the USCCEC since the children rescued by the Unitarian Service Committee.[32] Many of the children had been living before the German invasion in homes run by the OSE; many were being rescued from French internment camps. The AFSC chose and assembled the group in southern France and the JDC arranged the transportation of the children to Lisbon. In Lisbon they were given visitor visas and affidavits in lieu of passports after a representative of the AFSC or the JDC verified that each child was covered under the USCCEC corporate affidavit.[33] From Lisbon, under the care of the USCCEC, the children sailed for New York on the SS *Mouzinho*, a Portuguese ship chartered by the JDC. Once the children arrived in New York, the USCCEC took responsibility for their reception, and since all but one of the children were Jewish, German Jewish Children's Aid handled the placement of the children in families.[34]

On June 7, 1941, after the children had spent four days and five nights traveling from Marseille to Portugal, Morris Troper, the JDC's representative in Lisbon, wrote to ER to tell her about the successful rescue of the children. As the children were about to leave France, the train stopped at the station at Oloron, where the French authorities gave the children three minutes to say goodbye to fathers and mothers interned at the Gurs camp who arrived at the station under police escort. "Knowing they were to see their parents," Troper wrote, the children "refused to eat their breakfasts on the train that morning but wrapped up bread and rolls and bits of sugar and handed them to their parents when they met."

When the children reached Lisbon, he told ER, "they looked like tired, wan, broken, little old men and women. None dared to laugh aloud and few smiled." While the children waited for a ship to carry them to New York, the AFSC supplied them with new shoes and clothing and a physician from Vienna, a refugee himself, attended to their medical needs. The children enjoyed an unfamiliar opportunity to rest and play in accommodations near the beach. "One of the most pathetic sights I have ever seen," Troper told ER, "was that of these children, freed of restraints, trying to learn to play again.... After a few days here they smiled and laughed a little—but apprehensively, as though they might be punished for it. The results of experiences which no child should ever have to go through cannot be shaken off easily."

Troper, who recalled discussing the refugee situation at the White House with ER and Adele Levy in April, thanked ER for her "continued activity on behalf of Europe's child victims which has been so largely instrumental in the achievement of the results we have had."[35]

In the summer of 1941 the USCCEC published "Our Job Goes On: Rescue *and* Refuge," a fundraising brochure that sought to build on the publicity generated by the arrival of the children from Lisbon on June 21. Nearly 1,000 refugee children had arrived in the United States under the auspices of the USCCEC over the past year, Marshall Field reported. But the number of other children the USCCEC would succeed in saving depended "entirely on the funds made available to us *now*."[36] A substantial portion of Morris Troper's letter to ER of June 7, 1941, appeared in the brochure, including his moving description of the children's farewell to their parents at the Gurs camp and their strained efforts to play again on a beach near Lisbon.

The USCCEC experienced ongoing difficulties in raising sufficient funds to carry on its work. In January 1941, at Marshall Field's request, ER had written to Norman Davis, head of the American Red Cross, in support of the USCCEC's request for $150,000 to help support local child welfare agencies in supervising and caring for the 1,000 child refugees already in the United States.[37] On June 21, 1941, Marshall Field again turned to ER for help, reminding her of the discussion at the last USCCEC board meeting about the need to raise more funds by the end of September if it were to carry on its mission. They would begin the campaign with a dinner in New York City. He said it would be an "enormous help" if ER would come to it and "help acquaint the public with our needs." ER agreed to do so but was unable to attend because of the death of her mother-in-law, Sara Roosevelt.[38]

The dinner launched a campaign to raise $145,000 to care for children already in the United States and $358,800 for the rescue of 600 more children who had escaped from Nazi-controlled countries to unoccupied France.[39] On October 10, Marshall Field reported to ER and the other members of the USCCEC that two groups of children sponsored by the USCCEC had arrived in September: forty-five of them on the *Mouzinho*, fifty-six on the *Serpa Pinta*, another Portuguese ship.[40] By the beginning of November, the USCCEC had raised only $200,000 of its $503,800 goal. It decided to bring fifty more children to the United States.[41]

Limited funds; the difficulty of obtaining visas from the United States, exit permits from France, and transit visas from Spain and Portugal; and transportation problems all slowed the ability of the USCCEC to accomplish its mission. The entry of the United States into the war against both Japan and Germany after the attack on Pearl Harbor on December 7, 1941, made the task even harder. The USCCEC continued its efforts to bring small groups of children to the United States, but with limited success. In 1942, as a later chapter of this book will recount, the USCCEC, with ER's assistance, would nearly succeed in rescuing 5,000 mostly Jewish children from southern France, but the developing military campaign against German forces would thwart that initiative.

7

THE EMERGENCY RESCUE COMMITTEE, SUMNER WELLES, AND THE OBSTACLES TO RESCUE

"These poor people may die at any time"

THE FALL OF FRANCE in June 1940 and the extreme danger into which that placed antifascist refugees from Germany, Austria, Spain, Italy, and other countries who had taken refuge in France shook Eleanor Roosevelt deeply. As a result, she became intensely involved not only in the efforts of the United States Committee for the Care of European Children (USCCEC) to rescue children endangered by the war, but also in the work of the Emergency Rescue Committee (ERC), an organization formed for the purpose of rescuing political figures, writers, artists, and intellectuals who were trapped in southern France. Some of them were Jews, which made them doubly vulnerable since all Jews were in danger, but the ERC's purpose was to rescue them because of their political activities. These political refugees were at risk of arrest by the Gestapo or the collaborating French authorities, deportation to concentration camps, or execution by a firing squad because of their antifascist activities or writings. Many of them had played prominent roles in the political and cultural life of Germany and Austria or other countries now occupied by the Germans.

The active role ER played in the ERC's efforts would pit her against Breckinridge Long, whom FDR had appointed special assistant secretary of state in charge of emergency war matters in 1939 after the outbreak of the war. As the man overseeing the State Department's visa division, Long's antisemitic, anti-immigrant bias and excessive fear of subversives entering the country led him to thwart the work of both the USCCEC and the ERC. ER's work with the ERC also brought her into conflict with her husband, whom she prodded to order the State Department to pursue a more liberal refugee policy, and sometimes with Undersecretary of State Sumner Welles, whom she frequently contacted about refugee matters.

Welles himself is a puzzling figure. He was an old friend of Eleanor Roosevelt and of the president. He had roomed with ER's brother, Hall, at Groton, and held her wedding train when she married Franklin. He was one of the few people who addressed her as "Dear Eleanor" in his correspondence. Until his resignation from the State Department in 1943, he diligently investigated delays in the issuing of visas to individuals ER brought to his attention. Nevertheless, ER's pressure on Welles to speed up the process of issuing visas yielded frustratingly limited results.

ER'S INVOLVEMENT WITH THE FOUNDERS of the ERC began on June 15, 1940, when Karl B. Frank, an Austrian-born Jewish socialist who headed the American Friends of German Freedom, asked to speak to her about the plight of anti-Nazi refugees. She agreed, and on June 25 she met in New York with Frank, Clarence Pickett, and Varian Fry, a journalist and editor working at the time for the Foreign Policy Association. They presented ER with a list of anti-Nazis who were in particular danger. Joseph Lash, who also attended the meeting, reported later in a memoir that ER immediately called the president. FDR wondered why it wasn't "taken for granted that everything possible was being done" to help get the people on the list out of France. He "kept bringing up the difficulties" while ER "tenaciously kept pointing out the possibilities."[1] After the meeting, ER sent the list on to Assistant Secretary of State A. A. Berle Jr.: "You will see," she noted "that it is compiled and submitted by a responsible committee." She hoped that

> if it is safe and possible to do so, it can be put into the hands of our people in Europe with the request that they do everything they can to protect these refugees. I do not know what Congress will be willing to do, but they might be allowed to come here and [be] sent to a camp while we are waiting for legislation.

Noting that the list includes "a number of names already on lists upon which we have been working," Berle, who was sometimes more receptive to refugee concerns than most of his colleagues, responded sympathetically, but not optimistically:

> I need hardly tell you that the difficulties are extreme. There is now almost no communication with the occupied parts of Europe. I have been asking the groups with which I was in touch to advise these people to get to Africa, or, if possible, to Portugal (this last is extremely difficult) in the hope that we might, in time, be able to take some of them off from African ports....

If they are clear of the German lines, we have at least a sporting chance to do something to permit their entry.[2]

After her meeting with Frank, Pickett, and Fry, ER expressed her own sorrow about the situation in her My Day column. "My heart is heavy when I think of the tragedies which haunt the lives of many grown people," she wrote. The United States had welcomed some of the refugees "who have been marked people in their own countries because of their active opposition to Fascist or Nazi regimes," but many others remained in danger. There were reasons beyond the humanitarian one for rescuing these people, she noted, for they could be of great value to the United States, just as earlier political refugees had been:

> They know how Communists, Nazis and Fascists work. They know how propaganda is spread, how young people are influenced. They are as good material as the political refugees who came with Carl Schurz, the German, or Kosciusko, the Pole, whose statues we have taught our young people to honor because of their love of liberty.

On July 2, she prodded Sumner Welles to assist the German refugees in France: "Their situation and the situation of the Spanish refugees seems to me particularly pitiful and if there is anything that can be done to help them I hope we are going to be able to do it." Welles assured her "that we are doing everything that we can.... The practical way in which we can be of help, however, is not easy to find under present conditions. I know you understand the situation."[3] She did and she didn't. She recognized the difficulties but would grow increasingly disgusted with State Department policies that created additional obstacles.

Aware that they could not rely on the American government to take an active role in rescuing political refugees, Frank, Fry, and their associates concluded that only a determined private initiative could do the job. Someone had to contact the refugees who were in hiding, help them secure the necessary papers, and assist them in finding their way out of France. At the meeting with ER on June 25, Pickett offered the assistance of the American Friends Service Committee's (AFSC) staff members already in France, but Fry later reported to ER that he and Frank had told Pickett that the AFSC staff could accomplish very little. The circumstances required a different sort of person, one willing to work under cover and take risks:

> Since the French government has seen fit to agree to turn over to the German government all German nationals in their territory requested by the German government, what is urgently needed now is a new Scarlet Pimpernel[4] who will go to France and

risk his life, perhaps many times over, in an attempt to find the intended victims of Hitler's chopping block, and either provide them with means to keep alive in hiding or, if that is possible, to get them out of France before the French authorities reach them.

Fry asked ER if she or the president could recommend a person capable of doing the job. Fry himself had offered to go if no one else could be found, he told her, but in many respects, he did not think he was the most suitable person for the assignment:

> My French and German are both halting, I have published things which have aroused the ire of the German government, and I have had no experience whatever in detective work. The ideal candidate for the job would, it seems to me, be an adventurous daredevil who speaks French and German fluently, can play the innocent American convincingly, understands the political implications of the work he is doing, and is entirely willing to risk his life to see that it is done to the best of his or any man's ability. If you or Mr. Roosevelt can find such a man for us, you will remove the one barrier that still prevents us from bringing effective aid to the German anti-Nazis now trapped in France.

Asking the First Lady and, through her, the president of the United States, to recommend such an agent, was an extraordinary request. It expressed faith in her and trust that the president would do nothing to block the plan—a faith and trust that ER must have encouraged by the depth of her support for the goals of the proposed mission.

Fry assured her that he and his colleagues knew the names of the men in need of rescue, had the money to assist them, and could raise more money, if necessary. The nature of the mission, however, required a degree of subterfuge:

> [I]t is obvious that no one who went to France for the avowed purpose of doing what we want to do would have any success at all. He would either be arrested or requested to leave the country within twenty-four hours. In the circumstances, we may have to set up another committee whose ostensible purpose would be something quite different—such as locating missing Americans.[5]

Could the president of the still neutral United States actually condone such an undercover operation by a private organization? When ER sent Fry's letter to FDR on July 2 with the question, "What about this?" FDR told her that Fry's "suggestion may have all the merit in the world but it most certainly cannot be authorized or abetted by the Government of the United States." When ER replied to Fry, she didn't mention this exchange with her husband. She merely said, "the President has seen your letter."[6]

On July 17 Karl Frank wrote to ER asking once more for her help. He informed her of the formal establishment of the Emergency Rescue Committee, which had selected Frank Kingdon, a clergyman and the president of the University of Newark, as chairman. Ingrid Warburg, a member of the German Jewish banking family who had immigrated to the United States in 1936 and dedicated her life to assisting German refugees, took on the position of Kingdon's executive assistant. The committee also included the theologian Reinhold Niebuhr; Freda Kirchwey, editor of *The Nation*; and Robert Hutchins, president of the University of Chicago, among others. Since the ERC needed to send someone to France in whom everyone had confidence, as soon as possible, Frank told her in his letter, Fry had agreed to assume this role. He described Fry as "one of those silent, sincere and modest persons who would be best fitted to do the necessary work," and, contrary to Fry's own assessment of his qualifications, told her that "we are all sure he will be the right person for the next steps." The problem faced by the ERC was to obtain a passport for Fry as soon as possible. Frank asked ER to help secure it. When Frank wrote again in mid-August, he thanked ER for helping Fry "get his papers so quickly."[7] While the American government could not abet the ERC's plan, ER could and did.

During the period when the ERC was getting organized, other individuals and groups were also pressing the State Department to act. Initially the department seemed willing to cooperate. Assistant Secretary of State Breckinridge Long agreed to authorize consuls to issue emergency visitor visas to a list of European intellectuals and labor leaders compiled by the Jewish Labor Committee (JLC) once they had been vetted to make sure they would not engage in activities hostile to the United States. The JLC sent Dr. Frank Bohn to Marseille to make arrangements for the people on its list. Other groups also submitted lists, sometimes quarreling among themselves about whose list should take priority.

To create an orderly process, Justice and State Department officials reached an agreement on July 26 with James McDonald, in his role as chairman of the President's Advisory Committee on Political Refugees (PACPR), and its executive secretary, George Warren, authorizing the PACPR to serve as a preliminary screening committee.[8] Under this arrangement, the ERC would screen candidates proposed to it for rescue, write summaries of their background indicating why they were in danger, and send the names and biographical information to the PACPR. The PACPR would then review the lists and information compiled by the ERC and other groups, identify the refugees it judged had a good reason to come to the United States and would make good citizens, then submit their names to the Justice Department. After the Justice Department checked its files for information on the individuals on the lists, it would send an approved list on to the State Department. Finally, the State Department would search its own files, and if it found that the individual had a legitimate reason to immigrate to the United States and posed no threat to the United States, it would send a cable to the appropriate consulate authorizing it to issue an emergency visa. By law, the consuls retained the power to make the final decision, but Long said he would send out instructions to all the consuls indicating that the department expected the consuls to issue visas to those recommended in the manner just described.[9]

The State Department agreed to admit the political refugees on special visitor visas outside the quota and not to require that the refugee have an exit permit from France before the consul issued a visa. Normally, as was the case with the British children, someone applying for a visitor visa had to demonstrate that they would be able to return to a home outside the United States after the visa expired. Since that was clearly not going to be possible for political refugees, the State Department waived the usual six-month limit on visitor visas on the condition that the refugee begin efforts as soon as they arrived in the United States to move on to another country.[10]

A few days after the PACPR and the State Department reached their agreement, Mildred Adams, the ERC's executive secretary, asked Tommy, ER's secretary, to tell ER how pleased the ERC was with the new arrangement: "We realize that the quick action which has come in this matter is in large part due to her understanding and efforts." When Tommy forwarded information on the visa case of Dr. Willi Wolf to the ERC in early August, Adams promised to process it as quickly as possible and added, optimistically: "It sounds like a simple case and the newly established visa routine should make it easy." Adams was pleased to learn that the ERC could use ER's name in advocating in such cases: "Her backing helps a great deal."[11] When Varian Fry left for France in August, the ERC believed that with ER's assistance the emergency visa process was now on track. Despite his cooperation in establishing the procedure, however, Long had other intentions, which would soon become apparent.

VARIAN FRY ARRIVED IN FRANCE in mid-August 1940 to carry out the ERC's mission and set up headquarters in Marseille. He disguised his agency as a relief operation called the Centre Américain de Secours (American Assistance Center). Although he lacked some of the qualifications he had identified in his letter to ER as necessary for the job, Fry did possess a passionate opposition to Nazism that sprang, in part, from a visit to Berlin in 1935, where he witnessed a mob pulling Jews from cars along the Kurfuerstendamm and beating them. The mixture of viciousness and gaiety the crowd displayed made an indelible impression on him.[12]

Fry also possessed the ability to conduct interviews, track down leads, and gather information that he had acquired as a journalist. And, although he completely lacked any experience in managing a clandestine operation, it turned out that he had a talent for finding illegal ways to accomplish his ends. When refugees failed to obtain documents legally, he employed Bill Freier (the political cartoonist later known as Bill Spira) to create false French exit permits.[13]

Fry faced formidable obstacles. Not only did the armistice agreement between Germany and the French government at Vichy require the French to turn over to Nazi authorities, "on demand," any German refugee within its territory, but the Gestapo itself was searching for German anti-Nazis in unoccupied France.[14] To get refugees to Lisbon, where they could depart for North or South America, Fry arranged for a network of guides to usher them to the Spanish border and over the Pyrenees into Spain. Refugees then had to cross through Spain and into Portugal, both of which remained neutral, though under the rule of right-wing authoritarian governments. Initially, Spain allowed the refugees to travel on to Portugal if they had a Portuguese transit visa, and Portugal accepted large numbers of refugees on a temporary basis. But by late September 1940, as a shortage of vessels stranded thousands of refugees in Portugal, the Portuguese consuls in France stopped issuing transit visas unless the applicants could show they had a valid visa for another country and had already booked passage on a ship departing Lisbon. The situation improved in January when the Vichy government began to issue exit permits, but by then the Spanish government required that transit visas be screened in Madrid by the Gestapo before being issued.[15] Therefore, even if a refugee received an American visa, the difficulty of getting exit permits and transit visas to cross through Spain to Portugal as well as the difficulty of obtaining passage on a ship leaving Lisbon caused further delays or blocked the refugee from leaving France altogether. ER would become painfully aware of all of these obstacles as she sought to support the efforts of the ERC and to assist other refugees trying to flee Hitler's Europe.

Although these other problems often stymied refugees seeking to escape from France, obtaining American visas in a timely manner or obtaining them at all remained a major obstacle. The cumbersome system set up in July, which provided for a careful two-layered review of political refugee cases by the ERC and the PACPR even before the PACPR made recommendations to the Departments of Justice, followed by reviews by the departments of Justice and State and finally by the consuls, would have been a time-consuming process, even if it had been faithfully carried out.

When Fry first arrived in France he received support for his work from Hiram Bingham IV, the American vice consul in Marseille in 1940–41, who was sympathetic to political refugees.[16] Despite the bureaucratic hurdles imposed by the State Department, Bingham cooperated with Fry by issuing visas whenever possible to the refugees on the ERC's list. But the Vichy authorities, under pressure because of the terms of the German armistice agreement, objected to Fry's activities. The *prefecture* complained about Fry to Hugh Fullerton, the American consul general in Marseille. Fullerton, in turn, reported the complaint to the State Department. He then called Fry to the consulate to show him the State Department's cabled response, which stated:

> This government cannot countenance the activities as reported of Dr. Bohn [the Jewish Labor Committee representative in Marseille] and Mr. Fry and other persons in their efforts in evading the laws of countries with which the United States maintains friendly relations.[17]

On September 23 Fullerton told Fry to close the Centre Américain de Secours immediately and get out of France before the Vichy government arrested or expelled him. In addition, after the State Department complained to the ERC about Fry's activities, the ERC itself asked him to return to the United States. The ERC worried that the antagonism between Fry and the American consulate and embassy would make it harder to obtain urgently needed visas for the political refugees on its list. Fry refused to leave. Fry's task became still more difficult when Bingham was transferred to Lisbon and later on to Buenos Aires. Fry later reported that Bingham's successor, William L. Peck, "seemed to delight in making autocratic decisions and refusing as many visas as he possibly could."[18] As Fry's difficulties with the consulate in Marseille and the State Department, as well as with his sponsoring organization, increased, it became harder for ER to support his activities.

DURING THE EARLY FALL OF 1940, while ER continued to help facilitate the work of the ERC and USCCEC, she intervened to assist another group of refugees seeking to escape from Hitler's Europe. On September 10, a Portuguese ship, the SS *Quanza*, arrived at Norfolk, Virginia, with approximately eighty-one refugees aboard, most of whom were Jewish. The passengers had obtained what they thought were valid Mexican visas, but when the ship docked in Vera Cruz, Mexico, because their visas were fake, the Mexican government refused to admit them. The situation resembled that of the *St. Louis*, whose predominantly Jewish passengers thought they had valid Cuban visas but were denied permission to land when they arrived in Havana in May 1939. As the *St. Louis* slowly made its way up the East Coast of the United States on its way back to Europe, the passengers and the refugee organizations advocating for them appealed to the American government and FDR personally to permit them to enter the United States. The government refused. Granting them visas without the usual review would have violated American immigration regulations and taken up quota numbers for which other refugees had been waiting for months. When the *St. Louis* returned to Europe, Great Britain, France, Belgium, and the Netherlands agreed to take them in, rather than force them to return to Germany. Some later died in concentration camps after the Nazis occupied most of Western Europe, but about two-thirds of them survived, and half of the 937 refugees who had been on the ship immigrated to the United States later on.[19]

No record of ER responding to the plight of the refugees on the *St. Louis* has been found,[20] but the passengers on the *Quanza* experienced a different fate, partly due to ER's intervention on their behalf. When the *Quanza* stopped in Norfolk to load coal as it began its journey back to Europe, members of the USCCEC and the PACPR lobbied the State Department to allow the passengers to enter the United States. ER herself appealed to FDR and called Breckinridge Long to ask him to talk to FDR about the case. The Justice Department favored admitting the refugees aboard the ship, and when James McDonald communicated this to Long, it seemed to sway him.[21] Nevertheless, Long argued for admitting only half the refugees, at most. After lengthy negotiation, however, the Immigration Service of the Justice Department arranged for the admission of all of the refugees aboard the *Quanza*. The incident was among the small, infrequent victories for those seeking to open America's doors wider.[22] Rabbi Stephen Wise attributed the success of the PACPR in this case partly to ER: "One of the things that could be done could only be done because Eleanor Roosevelt and Marshall Field appealed to the Skipper [FDR] for the liberation of the refugees on the *Quanza*. All of them were released."[23]

THROUGHOUT THE FALL OF 1940, ER received news of delays and obstruction in the issuing of American visas to political refugees screened by the ERC and PACPR. As Fry ran into obstacles at the American consulate in Marseille and at the embassy in Vichy, he sent cables back to the ERC reporting on the difficulties he was having. The ERC, in turn, asked ER to assist in trying to speed up the process.

On September 6, 1940, ER forwarded a letter to Sumner Welles that she had received from Karl Frank about the difficulty of securing visas for refugees in France: "I am enclosing this letter," she wrote, "because it explains the situation better than I can do. Is there no way of getting our Consul in Marseille to help in getting a few more of these poor people out?" In response, Welles tried to allay her concerns about the slowness of the visa process, but when she shared Welles's reply with Karl Frank, he told her that he was grateful for Welles's "careful words" and "reassuring tone," but that "information reaching us daily indicates that matters in Marseille and Lisbon, while improved, are not yet as satisfactory as they should be."[24]

While the ERC was urging ER to intervene to speed up the issuing of visas to political refugees, the State Department was proceeding, instead, to tighten its policy. On September 10, Herbert C. Pell, the American minister in Lisbon, sent a memo to the

State Department warning that the special emergency visa system was not functioning as intended. Those on the approved lists of political refugees were often among "the least desirable element" of those applying for visas, and in some cases there was reason to believe they were German spies. Pell especially resented the fact that "some of the most active organizations pushing immigration cases" were "racial" (meaning, presumably, Jewish). Other applicants whom Pell considered more "desirable" failed to meet emergency visa requirements because they had no one in the United States advocating for them. Pell suggested reinstituting the system in place before the July agreement that directed consuls to reject visa applications if there existed "any doubt whatsoever concerning the alien."[25]

Adopting Pell's line of reasoning, Breckinridge Long sent FDR a letter on September 18 stressing the State Department's security concerns and proposing that the State Department "modify slightly" the emergency visa process. He charged that the PACPR had stretched the definition of "political refugee" and had not investigated the backgrounds of the refugees thoroughly enough. Instructing the consuls to conduct "a more careful examination" of visa applications "would contribute largely to closing the loopholes against the penetration of German agents." Therefore, he proposed limiting the special emergency visa program to a few special cases of individuals in imminent danger—hardly a slight modification. The president agreed with Long's recommendation and on September 19 the State Department informed the PACPR of the change in policy. The State Department circulated new instructions to its diplomatic posts in Europe directing consuls to examine visa applications more thoroughly and reject any applicant who had engaged in suspicious political activity in the past or could possibly pose a danger once in the United States.[26]

The effect of the change of policy on the number of visas issued to political refugees was devastating. On September 23, Karl Frank informed ER that the ERC had received a report from Fry that the Department of State had ordered the consul in Marseille not to issue any more visitor visas after October first.[27] ER forwarded Frank's telegram to Sumner Welles for an explanation and Welles turned to Breckinridge Long for advice: "What reply do you think I should make to Mrs. Roosevelt . . . ?" His question suggests that he himself may not have been fully informed about the details of how the system operated and, like FDR, depended on Long's judgment without challenging it. In his reply, drafted by Long, Welles told ER, "The news from Mr. Frank is not quite accurate. The authority to issue visitor visas for the refugees was limited to October 1 by original order. However, before the expiration of that date it was extended to November 1. Of course it can be extended again depending upon developments there." Welles did not inform ER of the change of policy that resulted from Pell's memo, but claimed, instead, "We have been giving every attention to the plight of the refugees." He blamed the problems that were occurring on "the extracurricular activities" of Fry and Frank

Bohn, to which the French government had objected. He also informed her of the State Department's request to the ERC that it ask Fry and Bohn "to cease and desist" their illegal actions and suggest that they come back to the United States.[28]

As the virtual strangulation of the emergency visa program became evident to the PACPR, James McDonald and George Warren met with Welles and Long to express their anger that the State Department was not living up to its agreement. The September 24 meeting was lengthy and contentious. Long recorded in his journal that McDonald saw him as an "obstructionist and was very bitter and somewhat denunciatory." Sure, however, that he could persuade FDR that he was doing what was necessary to protect the United States against radicals and subversives, Long did not worry when McDonald threatened to take the matter up with the president. After the meeting, however, Sumner Welles sent a cable to the consulates abroad reaffirming the procedures for issuing emergency visas established by agreement in July. Welles's intervention, which indicated that he had not adopted Long's obstructionist approach, improved the situation temporarily. George Warren reported to the PACPR on October 30 that after Welles sent his cable "a remarkable improvement in the issuance of visas" occurred.[29]

A few days after the meeting with Long and Welles, George Warren met with ER to inform her at length about the problems created for the PACPR by Breckinridge Long. He then followed up with a letter to which he attached documents refuting the claims Long had made in his September 18 letter to the president. Once again, as in the case of the British children, ER became deeply involved in the debate over refugee policy. On September 28 she sent Warren's letter and accompanying material on to FDR with a cover note: "Mr. Welles promised to explain to you that Mr. Long's letter to you was entirely erroneous regarding the situation." The consuls had approved visas for only a small number of the names submitted by PACPR to the State Department. The situation might be resolved if the consuls were instructed to carry out the terms of the agreement between the State Department and the PACPR. She explained that McDonald felt that the committee's "good faith" had been "impugned" and was "so wrought up about it" that he wished to speak with the president. "These poor people," she told FDR, "may die at any time" and "are asking only to come here on transit visas." She requested that he meet with McDonald and get the matter resolved as soon as possible.[30]

The president agreed. "Please tell me about this," he wrote in a memo to Welles. "There does seem to be a mix-up. I think I must see McDonald." But he met first with Long, who came armed with some exceptionally effective ammunition. FDR was already convinced of the danger of German espionage and sabotage. He believed that the background of every visa applicant needed to be thoroughly checked to weed out individuals who could threaten American security. Long reinforced that conviction. To bolster his argument, he supplied FDR with cables he had just received from Laurence

Steinhardt, the American ambassador to the Soviet Union, who expressed his belief that many of the labor leaders and intellectuals whom the PACPR had recommended for visas were not what the PACPR claimed them to be and that the PACPR was deliberately misrepresenting them to the State Department. Steinhardt, whose charges possessed greater authority because he was a Jew, complained that contrary to the provisions of the Immigration Act of 1924, the arrangement with the PACPR now placed the burden of proving that a refugee should not be admitted to the United States on State Department officials, rather than placing the responsibility on the refugee to demonstrate that they were worthy of admission. Entry into the United States was a "privilege, not a right," he insisted. After meeting with FDR, Long recorded in his journal that the president completely supported the State Department's handling of visa applications.[31] FDR often left visitors with the impression that he agreed with them even when he was just listening, so Long's assertion may not have been entirely true. But the fall of France in June and the massive air campaign against Great Britain that followed shocked the United States and intensified FDR's concern for national security. Under these conditions the arguments Steinhardt and Long were making carried great weight.

When McDonald and Warren laid out their case on behalf of the political refugees in a memo to the president on October 8, they were unaware of Long's preemptive lobbying of FDR in support of the State Department's position. In the memo, McDonald and Warren objected to the very limited number of visas issued to date and told FDR that they could find no basis for fearing that the refugees whom the PACPR had carefully screened would be a threat to American security. At the meeting with FDR on October 9, in which Francis Biddle and Henry Hart of the Justice Department, who were more sympathetic to the refugees than Long, also participated, FDR cited the concerns raised by Long about national security and read passages from Steinhardt's cable. When McDonald began to criticize Long, the president reportedly stopped him. Nevertheless, FDR recognized the peril the political refugees were in and expressed sympathy for them. According to George Warren's report on the meeting, the president wanted "properly qualified intellectual, political, and other refugees" to be rescued but "expressed concern that extreme care be taken to prevent the admission of those whose activities might be inimical to the interests of the United States." He wanted the Justice and State departments to speed up the process so that those qualified could be "rescued from the trap" in which the invasion of France had put them.[32]

Reporting to ER on the October 9 meeting with FDR, McDonald thanked her for "having made possible the conference with the President." He expressed optimism "that the new arrangements to be worked out by Mr. Biddle and the State Department will offer a basis for the rescue of those in imminent peril."[33] McDonald was impressed with the president's knowledge of the issues and told Justice Frankfurter that he thought the meeting had served "to sharpen his perception of those points on which attempts had been made to mislead him. At the end, he must have known who are responsible for thwarting his will."³⁴ If FDR did, indeed, recognize that he was being misled or understand who was blocking the issuance of visas to political refugees, it did not motivate him to insist on a change in the State Department's handling of the process or in who was managing it. The results of the meeting with McDonald and Warren were the same as those of the later meeting, on November 12, between the president and representatives of the United States Committee for the Care of European Children (USCCEC), at which Marshall Field, Louis Weiss, and Eric Biddle tried to counteract "the constant flow of information to the President about the dangers of immigration" and unlock the gates barring the admittance of refugee children to the United States. Both meetings raised hope but in the end led to no real change. In both cases, relying apparently on the Justice Department's more liberal approach to the refugee problem to moderate State Department policy, FDR asked the two departments to work out their differences and agree on an efficient system for screening refugees and issuing visas.³⁵

At the meeting between the Justice and State Departments on October 18, Welles, Long, Biddle, and Hart agreed that the PACPR would continue to screen political refugees and forward their recommendations to the Justice Department. Although the questions of who should be considered a "political refugee" and in immediate danger and how to speed up the issuing of visas to those who qualified remained unresolved, McDonald wrote optimistically to ER: "You will, I know, be glad to hear that the meeting last Friday of the representatives of the Departments of State and Justice made real progress. Mr. Welles and Mr. Biddle, according to my information, drove straight through to an agreement which clears the way for effective action." He was grateful to ER for her "indispensable helpfulness."³⁶

ER had no reason to doubt the good intentions of Welles and Biddle, but the result of the negotiations between Justice and State reflected increased anxiety about national security, not a desire to speed up the process of admitting to the United States the political refugees who were in danger. Contrary to McDonald's optimistic report on the meeting, the Justice and State Departments continued to wrangle over the emergency visa program and the role of PACPR before reaching an agreement in late November. Under this new agreement, the PACPR would continue to carefully examine the background of political refugees seeking visas. It would also check the ability of their sponsors to support them. But a new committee was created, which included the State Department, Immigration and Naturalization Service, Army Intelligence, Naval Intelligence, and, later, the FBI. By the spring of 1941, the Interdepartmental Committee, as it was called, was reviewing all visa applications from the point of view of national security before making recommendations to the consuls for expedited consideration. The consuls would still make the final decisions and might be asked by the committee to look further into the cases or verify facts presented by the

PACPR. If a consul planned to exclude the applicant, he had to wire his reasons for doing so to Washington, so that the Interdepartmental Committee could try to resolve the issue. The new system added another layer of bureaucracy, creating additional opportunities to question whether a visa applicant might be a threat. Pickett would report in his diary eighteen months later that George Warren described the effect of the Interdepartmental Committee on the visa application process as "one of incredible obstruction to any possible securing of a visa." Pickett regarded it as "a profligate waste of time and energy because it takes time of personnel from the army, the navy, the FBI, Justice and State Department and results in almost no visas being granted."[37] McDonald, Pickett, Warren, and ER had tried to speed up the State Department's management of the emergency visa process but were met instead with further obstruction.

WHILE ER SOUGHT TO HELP the ERC and the USCCEC secure visas for political refugees and for children in danger in unoccupied France, she also received appeals for assistance in the cases of refugees from other parts of Europe who were experiencing difficulty obtaining visas. She usually followed her practice of sending these appeals on to Sumner Welles, but she occasionally used these cases to press the president hard to intervene with the State Department. Her note to FDR about the cases of Rosa Vogl and Erna (Vogl) Fischer of October 1, 1940 indicates that she was engaged in an ongoing argument with the president about State Department obstruction. The Vogls, she wrote, were "A good case in point. They have been able to come for a long time, but the Consul won't grant visas." FDR, obviously irritated by ER's insistence, replied: "I do not think this is a good case in point at all."[38] He pointed out that Eliot Coulter, chief of the Visa Division, had written to Edith Vogl on September 21 telling her that the documents supporting her mother and sister's visa applications were being sent to Prague by diplomatic pouch and would take about ten days to arrive. Coulter, FDR continued, told Vogl that "visas are not issued only on the recommendation of the Department of State," but Vogl "prefers not to believe it." Coulter's letter seemed to FDR "entirely correct" and went "as far as any human being can go." He suggested that Vogl wait for a response from the consul in Prague, which "may take two months." That much delay seemed reasonable to FDR, but not to ER, who believed that part of the delay was deliberate.[39] ER continued to challenge the State Department's handling of the process; FDR, trusting that the State Department procedures were necessary for national security, did not question either the procedures or how they were being implemented.

Another case in which ER became involved documents the deliberate obstruction to which ER objected. In early October, Frank Kingdon at the ERC sent ER a copy of a letter written by Hans (Bohumil) Lustig to an American contact (identified as "C") recounting his difficulties in obtaining visas for his wife and himself from the

American consulate in Lisbon. Kingdon did not know what could be done about the case, but "as a human document and a detail of one family's experience," he told ER, "it will stir you."[40]

Lustig, who was born Czech, was a screenwriter who had worked for the prominent Ufa film studio in Berlin, then taken refuge in Paris in 1933 along with several other Jews associated with Ufa (including Billy Wilder and Peter Lorre), fled to the south of France after the German invasion, and finally reached Lisbon where he waited for visas for himself and his wife.[41] The State Department had sent a "preferential cable" to the American consulate in Lisbon giving its approval for issuing visas to him and his wife, and Lustig had received a telegram from the source identified as "C" confirming the department's approval. When he went to the American consulate, however, Consul Taylor Gannett told him, at first, that the consulate had no dossier on their case. After Lustig showed him the cable from "C," Gannett "flushed," according to Lustig, "and said excitedly, 'Only the Consul may decide whether you will receive the visa. Washington can only suggest it, that is all.'" Since the Germans occupied Czechoslovakia, Lustig had no homeland to return to. "If we want to get rid of you after six months," Gannett told him, "we will not know where to send you." The fact that Lustig had a contract with MGM film studios was "of no interest to him," even when Lustig told him the arrangement had State Department approval. Later Lustig learned that Gannett had recently been informed of his "disciplinary transfer" from Lisbon because so many people complained about him. That may explain why Lustig found him so "unusually unobliging and extraordinarily unnerved."

The next day, when Lustig and his wife met with Douglas MacArthur II, another consul, their dossier miraculously reappeared. MacArthur read it thoroughly, including Gannett's notes made on the previous day. Lustig managed to satisfy Gannett's concern that there was no country to which he and his wife could return, by telling MacArthur that they had obtained visas for Costa Rica, where the United States could send them if it wished to expel them after six months. MacArthur "seemed to be willing to make things easier for us," but after speaking with Gannett, asked Lustig to provide "a thorough account of my journalistic and film career." Lustig emphasized that he was "particularly endangered" because he had composed anti-Nazi pieces for Radio Mondial and wrote the screenplay for an anti-Nazi film. There was no danger of his becoming a public charge, he pointed out, because of his contract with MGM. "All this seemed to have a favorable reaction," he reported, yet a committee composed of all four consuls in Lisbon would again review his case, and the cases of the six or seven other intellectuals named in the cable from the State Department for preferential treatment. The consuls' report would then have to be sent to Washington so that the State Department could check its own files for information on the applicants.

Meanwhile, the Portuguese government had granted a final extension of the Lustigs' transit visas for only one more month.⁴²

Lustig was precisely the kind of person whom ER believed the United States should welcome because he had been a leader in the fight against Nazism and Fascism in Europe, but also because he would make a valuable contribution to American culture. Lustig's description of the convoluted procedure and deliberate delaying tactics to which he and others were subjected—which he generously characterized as "certainly not in keeping with the intentions of Washington"—gave ER ammunition in her ongoing argument with FDR about the way American consuls and the State Department were carrying out the emergency visa program. It was the kind of "case in point" that she hoped would prompt him to intervene and order the department to speed up the process. She sent Lustig's letter to FDR with a penciled note: "FDR Can't they be helped?"⁴³

The president referred the matter to the State Department as he normally did. He asked Breckinridge Long to draft a memo in response and then sent Long's memo to ER without comment. It is impossible to know how carefully FDR read Lustig's letter and, if he did, whether it made any impression on him. In any event, he did not use the letter as a basis for questioning State Department behavior. Perhaps he felt that since Gannett was being transferred because of the complaints about him, the State Department had matters in hand, but the repeated scrutiny of Lustig's case, unwillingness to accept his anti-Nazi record and MGM contract as sufficient reasons to admit him, and the whole length of the process should have alerted FDR to the fact that the preferential visa program was failing to respond effectively to the desperate situation in which many political refugees found themselves.

As Long's memo to ER indicated, the State Department did not regard responding to the emergency refugee situation as an urgent responsibility of the department. Addressing a woman whom he probably regarded as overly emotional, he acknowledged that cases such as Lustig's were "distressing" and that reading about them produced a "definite sentimental reaction." But, he asserted, Washington could not "superimpose judgment upon that of the consul" in whom the law vested authority. He claimed, disingenuously, that the department had instructed the consuls to "regard generously" the preference lists submitted to the department by PACPR, while making sure that the intentions of the applicants were not "subversive" and their records were "clean."⁴⁴

Long's explanation may have seemed reasonable on the surface and probably reassured FDR, whose first obligation as president was to protect the nation from danger and not to engage in humanitarian acts if he believed they might undermine American security. But while Long acknowledged that individual cases were "distressing" to read about, his memo makes no allusion to the emergency situation that existed, with which the preferential visa system was supposedly designed to deal. Moreover, the consuls had not actually been instructed to treat applicants on the preference list "generously." On the contrary, the directive sent to them on September 19 had instructed them to screen candidates for emergency visas with great care and reject the applications of anyone they suspected might not serve the interests of the United States. In fact, Long had written a memo to two of his State Department colleagues back in June in which he outlined his strategy. It was probably not a strategy he would have shared with FDR. With the president, he focused on national security concerns. The June memo reflects, instead, Long's cynical determination to obstruct the visa process in every way possible. The State Department, he said, could

> delay and effectively stop for a temporary period of indefinite length the number of immigrants into the United States. We could do this by simply advising our consuls to put every obstacle in the way and to require additional evidence and to resort to various administrative advices which would postpone and postpone and postpone the granting of the visas.[45]

It was not difficult for consuls to slow the visa process in this fashion, and the Lustig case was a good example of how it was done. In his October memo to ER about the Lustigs, having made it clear that the Department of State could not order the consulate to issue them visas, Long concluded by telling ER that the Department of State had cabled the American consulate in Lisbon about Lustig and asked it to cable back a report on "the circumstances of the applicant's case." ER sent a copy of Long's memo to Frank Kingdon, regretting that it was "not more encouraging" and telling him that she knew "of nothing else which might be done," but her intervention, in the end, had an effect. In November 1940, Lustig and his wife sailed for New York. Although Lustig finally reached the United States and resumed his career as a screenwriter in Hollywood, his case provided ER with further evidence that the State Department was obstructing efforts to rescue even those who most deserved rescue.[46]

Other people close to ER also recognized that State Department policy was contributing to the tragic situation that trapped the political refugees. In a letter to ER on November 8, 1940, Martha Gellhorn expressed outrage at the State Department's obstructionism:

> How is it that practically any royalty can get into this country, and that visas for anti-Fascist refugees, who have proved their good faith in the prison camps of two or three countries, cannot be obtained? What is happening, when such things go on? Who decides it? Who runs such a show? Doesn't it look pretty grim and godawful to you? It scares me.[47]

Breckinridge Long's role in preventing the rescue of many of the refugees also received public criticism even at the time. Joseph Alsop, who had helped ER in July to loosen regulations strangling the program to bring British children to the United States, said of Long in his syndicated column for November 25:

> Those who worked for easier admission of the English children to this country saw him use every resource of his position to obstruct their effort and know that he would have succeeded if the President had not rapped him smartly over the official knuckles. Those who tried to help the European political refugees heard him argue that visas could not be issued to these unfortunates except in the discretion of the "independent" consuls, despite several indications that the "independent" consuls had received informal instructions from Washington. Mr. Long seems to have a knack for these imbroglios.[48]

In the person of Breckinridge Long, ER faced a skillful and determined bureaucratic infighter who used his long relationship and direct access to FDR and the warning of possible subversion from Ambassador Steinhardt to persuade FDR that the State Department's complicated, drawn-out screening process for visa applicants was justified. The fact that Sumner Welles believed that the operations of fifth columns in France and Norway had played a role in the rapid capitulation of those countries, and that the United States had to guard against subversion as a result, reinforced Long's case.[49] Neither FDR nor Welles appear to have recognized that Long's plan was not simply to screen visa applicants carefully, but to deliberately delay the process of issuing visas. Taking Long's explanations of the lengthy process of issuing a visa at face value, FDR did not question whether or not State Department procedures were adequately responding to the emergency situation that existed. ER, on the other hand, detected Long's intentions and repeatedly told her husband that something was very wrong. When she challenged him again a few days after Long drafted his memo on the Lustig case, FDR responded impatiently (or perhaps just unknowingly), "What does seem wrong?"[50]

ON DECEMBER 4, 1940, ER RECEIVED a letter from Ingrid Warburg, Kingdon's executive assistant at the ERC, indicating that the November agreement between Justice and State had not solved the problem of long delays in the issuing of visas. The lists of refugees recommended for special consideration were now being sent to the Justice Department and the Justice Department was sending the names "very quickly" to the State Department, but there the process slowed to a crawl. Warburg asked ER to seek a solution.[51]

When ER passed this information on to Welles, asking him once again if there was anything he could do to speed up the procedure for issuing visas, he sent her a long, detailed letter, prepared for him by Breckinridge Long, defending Department of State procedures: "I have made careful inquiry about the possible delay," Welles said, "and I can assure you that there is no unnecessary delay." Although the processing of visas involved "an enormous volume of work," he told her, and it had been necessary to expand the department's staff to handle it, he claimed that "every visa application received up to this date will be transmitted and out of the Department by tomorrow night." The department had to follow certain procedures: checking the department's files to see if they contained any negative information on the applicant, composing a summary of the facts of the case, and giving this memorandum to a department official for review. If the review uncovered no problems, the department sent a telegram to the consulate to which the applicant had applied authorizing the issuing of a visa. "I have gone into this at some length," Welles said, "because I thought you would like to understand exactly what happens and to realize that while some time elapses between the receipt of the case and the dispatch of the telegram, there is no delay, though the process does take several days."[52]

The problem with the explanation provided by Welles and Long was that the entire process was taking far more than "a few days." While ER appreciated his "writing her in detail," his assertion that there was "no unnecessary delay" contradicted what she learned through the ERC about the plight of refugees. It left her frustrated.[53] She knew from lengthy reports received by the ERC from Varian Fry and Jay Allen, a correspondent for the North American Newspaper Alliance, and forwarded to her by Ingrid Warburg, that the problems went much deeper than the bland assurances, composed by Long and provided to her by Welles, suggested. If the bottleneck wasn't in Washington, then it was at the consulates abroad.

Fry's reports focused on the difficulty of obtaining French exit visas and Spanish and Portuguese transit visas, as well as emergency visas from the American consulate, and on the need for more funds to support the refugees while they waited to secure the papers required to reach Lisbon. Allen's report, written in mid-November, painted a dismal picture of the American consulate in Lisbon. It indicated that the difficulties experienced by Hans Lustig in obtaining a visa from the American consulate there were endemic and not limited to Gannett, the consul with whom Lustig had initially dealt and who had already left by the time of Allen's report. Allen frequently heard "stories of crudeness and prejudice," especially on the part of one of the vice-consuls. He himself had witnessed "anti-Semitic outbursts, etc." Allen believed that "the delays and difficulties here seem to me due almost entirely to the conviction of the men in the visa office that the powers-that-be in the State Department have their thumbs down i.e. are exclusionist." The consuls believed, after Avra Warren, the chief of the

Visa Division, had paid them a visit, that Hiram Bingham was losing his post in Marseille because he had interpreted his instructions too liberally and issued too many visas.

After receiving Warburg's letter and the enclosed reports, ER learned that Fry had been arrested. On December 12, 1940, acting once again as a conduit for firsthand, unvarnished reporting on the effects of Nazi policies and the inadequate American response to the refugee crisis, ER sent Warburg's letter and the reports from Allen and Fry on to FDR. She wrote at the top of the letter: "Varian Fry, an American citizen, has been arrested in Marseille and is now on a prison ship."[54]

ER also contacted Sumner Welles about Fry's situation. Welles told her that Fry, along with several other people associated with Fry's organization, had indeed been jailed by the French police on December 2 but had experienced "no physical hardship" and was released on December 5.[55] Welles suggested that there were good reasons for Fry's arrest:

> The fact is that Mr. Fry had been directed by his principals in this country to leave France. This order was sent to him some weeks ago but he continued in his activities there. His activities brought him into contact with various persons whom the French police had on the suspect list and he was in company with some of those persons when arrested.[56]

On December 18, in response to Warburg's December 4 letter and the reports ER had sent him, FDR simply replied: "I suggest you take up with the State Department."[57] He did not comment on the issue of State Department delays in forwarding recommendations for emergency visas to the consulates, or on Allen's or Fry's reports on the desperate plight of political refugees and the behavior of American consular officials, or on Fry's imprisonment. Once again, he preferred to leave these matters to the State Department without, apparently, giving them specific instructions for what he would like to see done. At the same time, however, he invited ER to press her case with the department.

ONE OF FRY'S CHIEF COMPLAINTS in the report he sent to the ERC at the end of October 1940 was the lack of funds to carry out his work.[58] In December, the ERC launched a fundraising campaign to remedy the problem.[59] ER supported the ERC's efforts financially by sending $25 (equivalent to approximately $450 in 2020) and contributed regularly thereafter,[60] but, following her usual practice of not participating in fundraising events for causes that had political implications, she declined invitations to participate in the ERC's fundraising drive. She even turned down an invitation to speak at a Hollywood fundraiser for the ERC despite the offer of film director and producer Ernst Lubitsch to contribute $25,000 if she came to speak.[61]

She supported the ERC's cause publicly, however. In a My Day column on December 21 she argued vigorously that many of the refugees the ERC sought to rescue would strengthen the nation:

> We have today a very great opportunity. People who have been known and recognized in the world as great scientists, educators, writers and sociologists are all seeking new homes. It will be short-sighted indeed on our part, if we do not continue the policy which has worked so well in the past—to enrich our own land by inviting into our midst these people who have a contribution to make to civilization.[62]

Eleanor Roosevelt played a key role in the work performed by the Emergency Rescue Committee by responding immediately to its appeals for help, facilitating the issuing of a visa to Varian Fry, prodding her husband to act, helping to arrange meetings for the leaders of the ERC and PACPR with the president or State Department officials, repeatedly asking Sumner Welles to intervene in cases where someone was having difficulty obtaining a visa, and publicly drawing attention to the importance of the ERC's work. She continued her efforts throughout December 1940 and into the following year as the political refugees still trapped in unoccupied France remained in grave danger.

8

CONTINUING THE FIGHT ON BEHALF OF VISA APPLICANTS

The "little officials" in the State Department "still hold their places"

IN EARLY DECEMBER 1940 Dr. Anna Stein, a leader of the Buffalo, New York, chapter of the Emergency Rescue Committee (ERC), wrote to Eleanor Roosevelt asking for her help with the cases of twelve refugees whose names had been submitted to the President's Advisory Committee on Political Refugees (PACPR) but who had not yet received visas. The twelve people, mostly Gentiles but some Jews, were associated with an organization of non-Marxist socialists known as the Internationaler Sozialistischer Kampfbund or ISK (International Socialist Fighting Alliance). Some members of this anti-Nazi group continued to work underground in Germany for five years after Hitler came to power; others reestablished themselves in Paris and continued to carry on their anti-Nazi activities, including publishing and distributing anti-Nazi literature and lending support to the underground movement in Germany. When Germany invaded France, the French government interned some members of the group, along with other nonnatives of German origin, in the Gurs camp in southern France; others fled to the south in advance of the German army. Because "their names are well known to the Gestapo," they are in "great danger," Stein wrote in her appeal on the group's behalf. "Their devotion to the ideals of justice and liberty recommends them as desirable citizens in America."[1] Like Hans Lustig, they were exactly the sort of people ER believed it was essential to rescue.

Dorothy Hill and Eva Lewinski delivered Dr. Stein's letter to ER at her apartment in New York and discussed the refugee cases with her. Hill was one of the founders of the Buffalo chapter of the ERC and well known to ER as an active member of the network of women reformers to which ER belonged; Eva Lewinski was a Jewish member of the ISK group who had managed to get an American visa because she was on the endangered refugee list sent to the State Department by the Jewish Labor Committee.[2] Dr. Stein, herself a refugee from Germany, had arrived in the United States in September 1938. She had been a teacher at Country College in Walkemühle, Germany, the educational center of the ISK movement before 1933. Lewinski, who had been one of Stein's pupils at Walkemühle, joined Stein in exile in the United States in October 1940. Both of them began to work closely with the ERC and the Jewish Labor Committee to bring out other members of their group.[3] At ER's direction, Tommy forwarded the letter from Stein to Sumner Welles, who promised to check on the status of the twelve cases.

On December 27, ER met again with Eva Lewinski, this time at the White House. Paul C. Benjamin, a prominent social worker and champion of the unemployed during the Depression, who was also a member of the Buffalo chapter of the ERC, accompanied Lewinski. They had come to Washington to press the cases of those on the list that Lewinski had helped deliver to ER in New York on December 2, together with those of fifteen additional refugees.[4] Before ER had a chance to send the expanded list to Sumner Welles, Welles finally reported on the initial group of visa cases. He told ER that six of the cases had already been approved by the State Department and sent on to the consulates "for special consideration," two were under consideration by the State Department and would be "expedited," and four had not yet been sent to the department by the PACPR.[5]

On the same day Welles was writing to her, ER sent him the revised and expanded list that Lewinski and Benjamin had left with her and asked him for "a report as to why many of these people who actually have visas are finding so much difficulty." As he had done in the past, Welles sent ER's letter and the new list of refugees to Breckinridge Long and asked him to draft a reply.[6]

In the letter Long drafted, Welles told ER that the difficulty that people who already had visas were having lay with barriers that the Department of State had no power to remove: "traveling through hostile territory in which the Gestapo is active," "getting permits to cross frontiers," and "getting over borders and through lines which are controlled by the military authorities." He was referring to the same obstacles that Fry had detailed in his reports: getting exit permits from France and transit visas for passage through Spain and Portugal. In the case of Spain, where an agent of the German government ("presumably a Gestapo officer") screened the names of anyone wishing to travel through the country, Welles said that the State Department had appealed in "exceptional cases" to the Spanish Government, but not always successfully. Providing the names and addresses of particular individuals to the Spanish government might put them in danger, since it could make it easier for the German agent to locate and arrest them.

ER passed the information Welles had provided on to Lewinski and Benjamin in Buffalo. She also asked Tommy to send copies of Welles's letter and report to James McDonald at the PACPR and Frank Kingdon at the ERC.[7]

As her correspondence makes clear, ER played a significant role in pushing for a resolution to the cases on the ERC lists. When the ERC learned of inexplicable delays in the processing of visas for the individuals it sought to rescue and brought the problem to ER's attention, she sent the names directly to Sumner Welles and demanded an explanation. When she found that some of the names had never reached the State Department, she submitted the list to the PACPR and asked them for the reason. Thus she put pressure on both the State Department and the PACPR to act on the cases and to speed the processing of the visa applications whenever possible. Despite Welles's assurance that the cases were being "expedited" and that the consulates had been instructed to give them "special consideration," some of them dragged on for another six months. With the assistance of his colleagues, Welles sought information on each case and tried to explain the delays. In the case of Otto Pfister, Lewinski's fiancé, who was on one of the lists delivered to ER, the Interdepartmental Committee wondered how Pfister had managed to secure his release from a German internment camp by posing as a French soldier (he had actually posed as a French civilian). French soldiers ordinarily carried identification papers and Pfister was a native German. Wouldn't the Nazis have been able to recognize that? The Interdepartmental Committee apparently feared that the Nazis had coerced or persuaded him to become a German spy, despite his past engagement in anti-Nazi activities. Pfister had lived in France for twelve years, however, and his French was good enough to fool the Germans, as apparently the consul in Marseille eventually concluded. Pfister got his visa, but it took months and required the tenacity of Lewinski and her friends, who submitted testimony to Pfister's good character, plus ER's persistent application of her influence, to overcome the resistance of the State Department and the consul in Marseille.[8] Welles's intervention, while it focused special attention on a case, had a limited effect on speeding up the process.

THE DEPTH OF ER'S DISTRESS about State Department obstruction and her views on what needed to be done about it were recorded by Eva Lewinski in a memorandum of conversation she wrote after she and Paul Benjamin met with ER on December 27, 1940. The document provides the fullest available window into ER's private views on the refugee issue. Lewinski said in the memorandum that ER "knew all the details we came to explain to her of the difficulties which the refugees seeking to come to this country are meeting" and agreed that the pace at which emergency visas were being issued was "by far insufficient."[9]

One week earlier the State Department had issued a statement in response to criticism of its policies that claimed that the department had approved most visa applications for political refugees.[10] A *New York Times* (*NYT*) editorial took the State Department's assertions at face value and declared, "It is something of a triumph over red tape that out of about 2,000 individuals for whom various refugee committees have asked admission to this country half have already received visas, nearly all the others will receive them as soon as they can make use of them, and only about a dozen have been rejected."[11] But ER did not buy it. Lewinski reported that ER

> did not think that the articles in the New York papers give a real picture of the situation, nor did she agree with Mr. George Warren who, after a conversation with the officials of different administrations, and also with Mr. Cordell Hull himself, seemed to be reassured and to think that things would go on better now. In her opinion things are going on too slowly even after the examination of each case. Those who are obstructing a more liberal refugee policy still hold their places in the State Department. She herself makes many interventions, but not always with success.... She felt very sorry for all these facts.[12]

ER clearly believed that those officials who obstructed a more liberal immigration policy and continued to "hold their places in the State Department" should be removed. Given her ongoing argument with FDR about delays in the issuing of visas during the fall of 1940, she no doubt had urged FDR to do so. She expressed her low opinion of Breckinridge Long to FDR more than once. Justine Polier later remembered ER saying to the president in regard to Long,

> "Franklin, you know he's a fascist." And really cross, he said, "I've told you, Eleanor, you must not say that." She said, "Well, maybe I shouldn't say it, but he is."[13]

Since Long and the other obstructionists had not been removed, the only way to change the State Department's attitude, ER advised Lewinski and Benjamin, was to arouse public support for admitting more refugees and to put pressure on Congress:

> You have to push the public opinion all over the country, to make them understand that we do not object to investigation of these people who seek entrance to the United States, but that we have to go on quickly. And that these people for whom applications for visas are made are for the most part not Communists or fifth columnists, they are known for their fight for the democratic ideals of this country.

Lewinski, Benjamin, and their colleagues needed to make their congressmen understand that if they conducted "a reactionary campaign inside the Congress concerning the refugee problem," they could lose their seats. If Congress could be persuaded to support a liberal refugee policy, ER told them, that would influence the "little officials" in the State Department in Washington and in the consulates abroad, who "do not want to take any risk," to change their behavior.[14] She urged Lewinski and Benjamin to approach their local newspapers and hold mass meetings (as they had already done in

Buffalo). ER understood that the "little officials" in the State Department would continue to act, out of fear, with excessive caution unless the American public demanded the admission of more refugees.

ER's personal concern, her warmth and candor, made a deep impression on Lewinski. When Lewinski reflected on this meeting with ER in a memoir she wrote for her children years later, she said: "That I, an unknown refugee, should be able to enter the White House; that the wife of the President would receive me, shake my hand with great warmth, listen to what I had to say, ask questions, and then promise to try to help—was perhaps one of the most profound experiences that I had ever had."[15]

Back in Buffalo, Benjamin and Lewinski followed ER's advice about reaching out to the public, the press, and their congressmen. Benjamin wrote ER that he would ask the members of the Buffalo branch of the ERC "to write and to see their congressmen, urging consideration for these refugees now marooned in southern France."[16] He informed the press that as a result of their discussion of the refugee problem with ER, the Buffalo chapter of the ERC planned to invite local congressmen to a luncheon or dinner in order "to enlist their interest in speeding issuance of visas for political refugees in Lisbon, Portugal, and southern France." Benjamin said that after speaking with ER he felt "that there needs to be a tremendous upsurge of concern in this country for the democratic way of life and a swinging back to the old doctrine that the United States is and should remain a haven for the oppressed. Mrs. Roosevelt expressed the greatest concern for these people, who are in such danger," he said, "and I feel that it is up to us to arouse public opinion against racial and religious prejudices that might arise out of the attempt to give refugees a place in the United States."[17]

DURING HER MEETING WITH LEWINSKI and Benjamin at the White House on December 27, 1940, ER expressed a special interest in the case of Rainer Litten, the son of Irmgard Litten, a German refugee now living in England. ER had reviewed Irmgard Litten's book, *Beyond Tears*, in her My Day column in September 1940 after its publication in the United States. The book recounts the arrest, detention in several concentration camps, and torture of Hans Litten, another of Irmgard's sons, and her efforts to rescue him from the time of his arrest in 1933 until his death in Dachau in 1938. Irmgard was a Gentile, but Hans and Rainer's father was a Jew who had converted to Christianity to advance himself professionally. Hans, however, went to synagogue, studied Hebrew, and became active in a Jewish youth group while a teenager, reaffirming his Jewish heritage in defiance of the wishes of his father, who had become a prominent Königsberg jurist.[18] After Hans became a lawyer, he often defended leftist workers and Communists, although he was not a Communist himself. In 1931 he tried to bring criminal charges against several members of the Sturmabteilung (SA), the Nazi paramilitary group, who had murdered three people in an attack on a dance hall where

Communists often gathered. He called Hitler to the witness stand in hopes of showing that such violence was a deliberate policy of the Nazi party aimed at destroying democracy. When, to prove his point, he quoted from a pamphlet written by party propagandist Joseph Goebbels proclaiming that the Nazis would "make revolution" and "chase parliament to the devil" with the help of "German fists and German brains," Hitler became enraged and could not respond. From then on Litten was on Hitler's enemies list and was among the first people rounded up after Hitler came to power.[19]

Beyond Tears had originally been published by Editions Nouvelles Internationales, a publishing house established in Paris by ISK, the German anti-Nazi group to which Eva Lewinski and Otto Pfister belonged. This "deeply moving" book, ER wrote in My Day, was "painful to read" but made her feel "proud for the whole human race that such people as Hans Litten and his mother have lived in the world and kept faith to the end." She hoped the book would sound the alarm to the "many people who are not yet awake to the menace of power which knows no restraints except the measure of its own physical force."[20]

In September 1940, ER was also helping promote *Pastor Hall,* a British film based on a play by the German Jewish playwright Ernst Toller. The film dramatized the resistance of a German pastor to the Nazi suppression of Christian and democratic values in a German village and his eventual murder. In a prologue to the film, ER told viewers that she found the film "deeply encouraging," for it told the story of a man of "undying faith" who was willing to perish for his beliefs. Men like Pastor Hall, she said, represented the hope of future generations who must enter a world "dominated not by the destructive force of hatred, but by the creative power of love."[21] Like the story of Hans Litten, the film gave her a way to speak out much more directly against the persecution of innocent people by the Nazis than she had in the past. One of ER's correspondents told her that she "was deeply impressed by the fact that the wife of the President of the United States had the courage to prove that humanity and loyalty to democratic principles rank higher than diplomacy."[22]

Rainer Litten's case was on ER's mind when she met with Lewinski and Benjamin because she had recently received a letter from Gunther Jacobson, a New York immigration lawyer, telling her that Rainer had fled from Germany to Switzerland but was in danger of being sent back to Germany if he could not obtain an American visa. Jacobson appealed to ER for help and ER forwarded Jacobson's letter to Sumner Welles, asking him what he could do. Although Welles quickly cabled the consul general in Zurich, he received back a discouraging report. Rainer was an actor, did not speak English, and was without financial resources. He had obtained an affidavit from "a Mrs. Master" through a friend, but "Mrs. Master is understood to be in only moderate circumstances and is unknown to Mr. Litten." Therefore, the consulate did not consider it an adequate guarantee of support.[23]

Litten's case is an example of the overzealousness of consuls in excluding would-be immigrants on the grounds that they were "likely to become a public charge." Like the cases of Rosa Vogl and Erna Fischer, which ER had employed in her ongoing argument with FDR about the length of time it was taking to process visa applications, and the case of Hans Lustig, who suffered a long delay in obtaining a visa, this was "a good case in point." On January 23, after asking the ERC for assistance with Litten's case, ER sent Welles a note telling him that Ingrid Warburg thought that the American consul in Zurich was "unduly cautious" in questioning whether Mrs. Master, who, it turned out, was the sister of Edith Lehman, the wife of New York governor Herbert Lehman, had sufficient means to sponsor Litten.[24] She noted that Litten's mother had also pledged to turn over the American royalties from *Beyond Tears* to her son for his support. Later that day, Welles telephoned to say that he had sent a telegram to Zurich requesting that the consulate issue a visa for Litten.[25] A month later, on February 27, 1941, the consulate in Zurich finally did so. In this case, the weight of ER's influence, plus, no doubt, the risk of annoying the wealthy and politically prominent Lehman family, tipped the scales.

Despite ER's success in helping Litten obtain his visa, Litten remained stranded in Switzerland for many months while ER became increasingly irritated. When ER wrote Welles for a report on the case toward the end of March, Welles replied that he had requested a telegraphic report from Zurich on "Litten's alleged difficulty in making the necessary travel arrangements for his journey to the US." Over two weeks later, ER wrote: "I hope I will soon get the report on Rainer Litten. It seems to take a long time to get anything through!" When Welles replied two days later, he reported that Litten had not visited the consulate since receiving his visa on February 27. In the middle of May, ER received word from Morris Troper, the agent of the Jewish Joint Distribution Committee in Lisbon, that the JDC had hoped to send Litten to the United States in June, but their office in Zurich advised "case still unready." ER sent the message on to Welles and again exploded: "This message seems incredible. Is it true that the Litten boy's case is not yet in order?"

Welles responded that the delay Litten had experienced since receiving his visa apparently arose from his failure in trying to obtain the transit visas from Spain and Portugal that would enable him to reach Lisbon. Although the United States could not officially ask foreign governments to issue transit visas, the State Department had telegraphed the consul general in Zurich to find out what the obstacles were and promised that after receiving a report "if I feel there is anything we can do to be of help, I will have it done." In response to ER's incredulousness and in defense of the State Department's handling of the case, Welles said, "I do, however, want to make it clear that the Litten boy was given an American visa on Feb 27, and that he has not subsequently appealed to any of our officials for assistance."[26]

In August, Irmgard Litten sent a cable to the ERC reporting that her son had become very ill with an inflamed middle ear, required an operation, and could not travel before September 26 when his visa expired. Now he faced losing his American visa because of illness at a time when she understood there are "enormous difficulties in obtaining American visas or prolongations of previous ones," because "the authorities wish to protect the country from being infiltrated with doubtful individuals." At Ingrid Warburg's request, ER again contacted Sumner Welles to see what he could do. In Welles's absence, Breckinridge Long responded on September 3 reporting that the State Department had cabled "its advisory approval" to the consulate in Zurich of a new visa for Litten. ER's intervention had again been effective, but two weeks later Long reported that Litten told the consulate that he could not depart for the United States until after his operation and had not yet secured transit visas or steamship passage.[27] Litten never made it to the United States, but fortunately Switzerland did not deport him back to Germany and he survived the war. He resumed his acting career in Switzerland and died in Zurich in 1972.[28]

Litten's case illustrates some of the reasons for the long delays that characterized the manner in which the State Department and American consulates processed visa applications. These delays, which Breckinridge Long encouraged, angered ER. But Litten's case also highlights the other daunting obstacles, which ER recognized were not under the control of the State Department, that also blocked the rescue of even a small number of refugees seeking to escape from southern France and other parts of Europe: the difficulty of obtaining exit and transit visas from France, Spain, and Portugal, the shortage of transportation, and the slowness of communication, as well as unavoidable complications such as illness.

IN A LETTER TO ER IN JANUARY 1941, in response to further complaints ER had received from Varian Fry, Sumner Welles once again expressed confidence in the procedures established by the State Department:

> I believe that, despite some critics who are not aware of the facts, the machinery which we have set up to deal with the emergency refugee problem is functioning effectively and well.

He went on to assert that the State Department "acts promptly" on the names of refugees recommended by the PACPR and sends the recommendations to the consuls who grant these applicants "an immediate hearing." Refugees are arriving in the United States "in large numbers" and in other American countries as well.[29]

There is no reason to believe that Welles was insincere in what he told ER. He may have been misled by Long and others in the State Department into thinking that the review process was working more effectively than it actually was. The reports ER received from the ERC, relatives and friends of refugees, Jay Allen, and Varian Fry about the refugee situation continued to contradict Welles's complacent interpretation of the situation, however. As a result, she persisted in challenging the wall of reassurance that Welles threw up with the help of Long and Avra Warren. She had some success in moving forward the visa cases of individual refugees, but ER's pressure failed to motivate Welles to advocate changes in the system or in the way it was administered.

DURING THE FIRST FEW MONTHS OF 1941, up against the same obstacles encountered by ER, James McDonald became discouraged by the ineffectiveness of the President's Advisory Committee on Political Refugees (PACPR). In early February 1941, he turned to ER, who had continued to provide him with advice and moral support, in addition to serving as his liaison with the president. McDonald asked to see her about "a personal matter on which I covet your counsel."[30] He felt defeated by the State Department's rejection of emergency visas for some of the political refugees recommended by the PACPR and the slow processing of the applications it did approve. He had gotten the impression from the State Department that it believed the president did not want refugees to come to the United States and wished to see the work of the PACPR terminated. McDonald's reference to a "personal matter" in asking to meet with ER suggests that he was considering resigning his position as head of the PACPR. On March 2, after meeting twice with McDonald, ER wrote to him:

> I spoke to the Pres [sic] and he says he certainly does not believe that the people in the State Department thought that he wanted the committee's work to come to an end, or that he does not want to get proper refugees over here.
>
> The Pres thinks you are doing a very remarkable piece of work and he wants you to continue, and he wants the skeleton committee held together, because of the future.
>
> He feels that if a few of the people are turned down you should not become discouraged, because sometimes things are discovered in an investigation which make it necessary to refuse, and these investigations have to be made.

FDR continued to believe that the time-consuming review of visa applications conducted by the State Department was necessary for the nation's security. When he told ER that he wanted "the skeleton committee held together, because of the future," FDR apparently meant that he didn't expect much to be accomplished while the war went on but expected there would be opportunities once the war was over to resettle a greater number of refugees. When McDonald thanked ER for speaking with FDR, he asked her "to tell the President that we are appreciative of his expression of confidence and that as long as he feels we can be of use, we shall consider it a privilege to continue to serve."[31]

WHILE ER PRESSED THE CASES the ERC brought to her attention and helped reassure McDonald about the usefulness of the PACPR, the issue of Varian Fry's status remained unresolved. He continued to defy both the ERC's attempt to recall him and the State Department's demand that he cease operations and return to the United States. After Fry's passport expired on January 22, 1941, ER responded to an appeal for help from Fry's wife, Eileen, by trying to arrange for her to meet with Sumner Welles. When Eileen Fry called ER again to report that Welles could not see her and, instead, had made an appointment for her to see Breckinridge Long, ER expressed her irritation that Welles had shunted her off to his less sympathetic colleague: "Will you please look into this situation yourself and let me know?" Welles replied on February 22 that he was sorry he had been too busy to see Eileen Fry and enclosed the memo of conversation Long had written after he spoke with her.

"I reviewed with Mrs. Fry some of the activities of her husband which I said had been, from the point of view of the Department, of doubtful wisdom," Long wrote. "She said that those particular extralegal activities were no longer being prosecuted" and that her husband, as an agent of the ERC, was now "giving relief in the form of small sums of money to persons of Jewish or foreign nationality or who had lost their nationality."[32] This was, in fact, what Fry had told his wife in letters meant to mislead the Vichy censors and provide her with cover to plead his case.

Long then asked Eileen Fry if the ERC would be willing to request that the State Department issue Fry a passport for him to continue to carry out the relief mission she had described. When she said she was confident that they would, he asked her to obtain such a letter. By this time, however, relations between Fry and the ERC had become antagonistic and Kingdon would not endorse the renewal of Fry's passport or even meet with Eileen Fry. Fry, however, feeling that he could not "abandon my people," continued stubbornly on without the security of a passport.[33]

In March 1941 Warburg sent ER a copy of a letter Fry had written to the ERC back on January 24, which had been brought out of France by hand and thereby escaped censorship. "[It] is really a document," she told ER and suggested that the president might wish to read it, and Sumner Welles too, "if you think it wise."[34] In his thirteen-page letter, Fry expressed his "disgust" at the embassy's lackadaisical attitude toward the refugees he was trying to help. With "a few honorable exceptions," he charged, the members of the foreign service

> have no more interest in the refugees than they have in the Chinese coolies. Furthermore, many of them are violently anti-Semitic. Nearly all of them are snobs, and some of them are constitutionally dishonest.

Fry pleaded with the ERC to "get someone with the connection of Hamilton Fish Armstrong [editor of *Foreign Affairs*] and his upper-class background, to take the State

Department by the scruff of its neck and the seat of its pants and shake it until all visas fall out of its pockets."³⁵

We don't know what ER thought of Fry's letter (or FDR, if he read it), but it must have added fuel to her anger at the State Department that she had expressed to Lewinski and Benjamin. Nevertheless, on May 13, when Eileen Fry appealed to ER once again for her help in renewing Fry's passport, ER replied, "Miss Thompson gave me your message and I am sorry to say that there is nothing I can do for your husband." Despite her deep sympathy with Fry's aims, she understood that the State Department could not approve the use of illegal methods by a private American citizen in a nation with which the United States had diplomatic relations. "I think [your husband] will have to come home," she told Mrs. Fry, "because he has done things which the government does not feel it can stand behind. I am sure they will issue him a passport to come on even though it means that someone else will have to be sent to take over the work which he is doing."³⁶

Even after his failure to get permission to stay in France, Fry stuck tenaciously to his task, but events made his work nearly impossible. In June 1941, because of its concern about Nazi subversion, the American government demanded the withdrawal of German consulates in the United States by July 10. Germany responded by ordering the closing of American consulates in both Germany and German-occupied territory. This brought the emergency visa program to an end, although the cases of political refugees for whom visas had already been authorized but not yet issued remained active.³⁷

In addition, driven by fears that undesirable persons would enter the United States if the State Department did not exert even stricter control over the process, the State Department once again tightened immigration restrictions. Beginning July 1, the sponsors of visa applicants would submit affidavits to the State Department in Washington rather than to the consulates and, after investigating the affiants, the State Department would cable its recommendations to the consulates. The consulates would continue to retain the power to reject the application if they deemed it advisable. The new procedure "will highly centralize the granting of visas and slow up the process," Clarence Pickett complained in his journal.

The State Department also erected another new barrier to immigration: it would no longer issue visas to people who had relatives still living in countries under Nazi control. The reason for this new policy, Long explained to Pickett, was that the Polish, Russian, and German governments required anyone coming to America to send money to their relatives back home or distribute propaganda for their country in the United States. If they did not comply, their relatives would receive punishment. The State Department seemed to have "a plausible case," Pickett noted in his journal, "but also it is another item in the suppression of individuals." The new policy meant "almost a complete elimination of immigration."³⁸

News of the stricter State Department regulations provoked anguish among those who cared deeply about the survival of refugees. Albert Einstein, knowing "no one else to whom to turn for help" and believing that ER always stood "for the right and humaneness, even when it is hard," wrote to her on July 26:

> A policy is now being pursued in the State Department which makes it all but impossible to give refuge in America to many worthy persons who are the victims of Fascist cruelty in Europe. Of course, this is not openly avowed by those responsible for it. The method which is being used, however, is to make immigration impossible by erecting a wall of bureaucratic measures alleged to be necessary to protect America against subversive, dangerous elements.

Einstein urged ER "to bring the matter to the attention of your heavily burdened husband in order that it may be remedied."[39] ER sent Einstein's letter on to the president and reinforced Sumner Welles's recommendation that the president meet with his Advisory Committee on Political Refugees to discuss the issue.

At the meeting, McDonald read a memo prepared by the PACPR that called the new policy "unnecessary, illogical, ill-adapted to the purposes claimed for it, and cruelly burdensome on the refugees affected by it." The members of the committee asked that it be "cancelled or substantially modified."[40] In addition, they asked that the State Department simplify procedures, establish a board to review cases on appeal from the Interdepartmental Committee, and allow the sponsors of visa applicants to testify before the review board. FDR, in characteristic fashion, "did not commit himself definitely," McDonald told ER, but the members of the committee "received the impression" that the changes they had recommended would be adopted. At the PACPR's meeting in December, George Warren reported that "experience seemed to indicate that the so-called relative clause had been less rigidly applied in recent weeks." A review board had also been established. But in regard "to the simplification of procedures Mr. Warren said he could report no progress whatsoever."[41]

For Pickett and ER the unique circumstances of individual people took priority over blanket bureaucratic regulations, which by their very nature suppress individual freedom and ignore individual merit, and over the magnified fear that officials like Long employed in order to justify those regulations. Their interventions on behalf of individual visa applicants sometimes succeeded, usually with the help of Sumner Welles, but their protests had little impact on the "plausible" arguments and policies of government bureaucracy, which Welles himself endorsed.

ER FOUGHT WITH SUMNER WELLES over the new State Department rules when Joseph Lash, executive secretary of the International Student Service (ISS), and Trude Pratt, vice-chair of the ISS's executive committee, brought to her attention the plight of twenty-three Czech students whom they were trying to assist. The primary aim of the ISS, which had taken over the administration of the program begun by the Intercollegiate Committee to Aid Student Refugees, was to enable students to remain safely in the United States for the duration of the war.[42] ER played an important role in the organization by helping to secure the participation of prominent people in ISS programs, speaking at ISS events herself, and contributing to the ISS scholarship fund.[43]

On October 6, 1941, Lash sent ER a list of the Czech students, most of whom had been studying in French universities at the outbreak of war and had refused to return to Czechoslovakia after the Germans occupied it. When the Germans invaded France, the students had found temporary refuge in Marseille or Switzerland. The Czechoslovak Consulate General had filed requests for emergency visas for the students through the PACPR and the visas had been authorized by the State Department in the spring. But when the new regulations went into effect in July, the students had to get their visas reapproved and, since all of them had relatives still living in Bohemia and Slovakia, they had not yet succeeded in getting their visas reapproved. Lash asked ER, "Is there any possibility of waiving the requirements with respect to relatives in occupied territories? I do not believe that Czechoslovaks are the kind of people whom the Germans can use for espionage purposes in this country."[44]

When Tommy asked Sumner Welles for information that ER could use to frame her reply to Lash, Welles asked Avra Warren to draft a response. In the reply drafted by Warren, Welles told ER that after reexamining the cases of the students in question "in the light of information relating to the presence of close relatives in German-occupied territory," the State Department concluded that "the issuance of visas to the aliens in question would not be in the interest of the United States at this time," with the exception of a few students who planned to continue their theological studies in the United States. The Czechoslovakian Legation was now seeking admission of the students to England, Canada, or another British territory where they might enlist for military service in the Czech Legion. The United States had agreed to issue them transit visas for that purpose.[45]

Welles's explanation angered ER. She objected to a policy that made no distinctions among visa applicants from German-occupied territories: "I do not think the relations clause should apply to Czechs. I think it lays us open to accusation of not wanting to help any refugees." Welles replied, with an even greater than usual degree of rhetorical tiptoe, that the existence of close relatives in German-occupied territory was "a factor which must necessarily be taken into consideration along with all other factors in the case and which may or may not, in the aggregate, result in an unfavorable conclusion. I can assure you that there is no rule which interferes with our policy of granting asylum to worthy refugees." Unsatisfied with Welles's explanation, ER, in one of her sharpest responses to Welles's explanations, demanded action in the particular cases of the students for whom Lash had sought help: "If it isn't a hard and fast rule, please look into it again. Everyone feels they would not be influenced."⁴⁶

WHILE ER WRANGLED WITH WELLES over the Czech students, Varian Fry was returning to the United States. After his arrival in New York via Lisbon on November 2, 1941, the *New York Herald Tribune* (*NYHT*) reported that he "bitterly reproached the State Department for following a 'stupid policy' in controlling visas." Because many refugees were "entangled by red tape," they were "falling victims to a systematic round-up of anti-Nazis by Gestapo agents in unoccupied France."⁴⁷

In October 1941, Frank Kingdon asked ER if she would speak at a luncheon on November 4 welcoming Fry home. The ERC planned to invite 2,500 of its donors to attend. Tommy replied that ER's busy schedule and the work she was now doing as assistant director of the Office of Civilian Defense prevented her from accepting any more speaking invitations at that time. A week later Kingdon sent a second invitation, this time reminding her that despite being "constantly under the surveillance of Gestapo agents," Fry had carried out "one of the most important works of these times." Once again, ER regretted that she could not attend.⁴⁸ ER was indeed busy at this time, but she may also have felt that she had done all she could do for Fry behind the scenes and did not want to be publicly identified with a man whose surreptitious activities had angered the State Department.

Fry assisted in the rescue of about 2,000 people during his nearly fifteen months in France. Many of them, including Marc Chagall, Jacques Lipchitz, Heinrich Mann, Marcel Duchamp, and Hannah Arendt, were prominent in their fields and some would go on to make significant artistic or intellectual contributions to cultural life in America, as ER and others had predicted. Although modest compared to the scale of the problem, Fry's achievement stands out as one of the few significant rescue efforts made during the war. ER supported Fry's work by encouraging him at the outset, helping him get a visa, passing his reports and requests on to FDR and to Sumner Welles, and pressing Welles to expedite visas for individuals recommended by the ERC. When Welles told her that Fry was engaged in illegal activities that the American government could not tolerate, however, she recognized that she could do no more to help him.

Elinor Morgenthau and ER with Jane Addams, 1929. (COURTESY OF THE FDR LIBRARY.)

Clarence Pickett, executive director of the American Friends Service Committee and his wife, Lilly, 1942. (REPRODUCED BY PERMISSION FROM ARCHIVES/AMERICAN FRIENDS SERVICE COMMITTEE.)

Members of the President's Advisory Committee on Political Refugees posing with Undersecretary of State Sumner Welles, November 16, 1938. *L to R:* Hamilton Armstrong, Welles, George L. Warren, and James McDonald. (COURTESY OF HARRIS & EWING/LIBRARY OF CONGRESS.)

Columnist Dorothy Thompson (*rt.*) with Rep. Edith Nourse Rogers (R-MA), co-sponsor of the Wagner-Rogers bill, April 1939. (Courtesy of Harris & Ewing/Library of Congress.)

REFUGEE FACTS

AMERICAN
FRIENDS SERVICE COMMITTEE
20 SOUTH TWELFTH STREET
PHILADELPHIA, PA.

Cover of AFSC pamphlet *Refugee Facts*, 1939. (REPRODUCED BY PERMISSION FROM ARCHIVES/AMERICAN FRIENDS SERVICE COMMITTEE.)

Introduction to *Refugee Facts*. (REPRODUCED BY PERMISSION FROM ARCHIVES/AMERICAN FRIENDS SERVICE COMMITTEE.)

REFUGEE FACTS

MUCH of the recent news from the newly framed German Empire and from Italy has dealt with the harsh treatment accorded to various classes of citizens who are deemed undesirable by their governments. These stories have been paralleled by others describing the efforts being made to find lands in which those unfortunates may find refuge, and by discussions as to how far the United States should go in providing asylum for refugees. It is the purpose of this pamphlet to supplement these discussions with a number of little known but nevertheless important facts which have direct bearing upon the refugee problem and which in some degree run counter to rather widely held impressions. First, facts are presented, derived from U. S. Government records, having to do with the amount of recent immigration. This is followed by a discussion of the salient characteristics of immigrants who are now being received in the United States from Central Europe, which line of thought leads quite naturally into a brief appraisal of what we will be called upon to do for them and what they may do for us if given the chance.

Refugee children rescued by the U.S. Committee for the Care of European Children arriving in New York. From pamphlet *Our Job Goes On: Rescue* and *Refuge*, 1941. (Reproduced by permission from Archives/American Friends Service Committee.)

Varian Fry, agent of the Emergency Rescue Committee in Marseilles, 1940 or 1941. (Reproduced by permission from the United States Holocaust Memorial Museum.)

Telegram to Eleanor Roosevelt from passengers on the refugee ship *Quanza*, September 1940.
(REPRODUCED BY PERMISSION FROM NATIONAL ARCHIVES AND RECORDS ADMINISTRATION.)

Martha Gellhorn, war correspondent and close friend of ER. (Courtesy of the FDR Library.)

Assistant Secretary of State Breckinridge Long, who thwarted efforts to liberalize and speed up the visa process. (REPRODUCED BY PERMISSION FROM THE UNITED STATES HOLOCAUST MEMORIAL MUSEUM.)

Eva Lewinski, refugee and advocate for other anti-Nazi refugees. (COURTESY OF THE PFISTER FAMILY.)

Cartoon in a National Conference of Christians and Jews (NCCJ) bulletin, 1939. (FROM THE NATIONAL CONFERENCE OF CHRISTIANS AND JEWS RECORDS, SOCIAL WELFARE HISTORY ARCHIVES, UNIVERSITY OF MINNESOTA.)

ER and Rose Schneiderman with labor leader David Dubinsky, 1938. (FROM THE ARCHIVES OF THE YIVO INSTITUTE FOR JEWISH RESEARCH, NEW YORK.)

ER accepting petitions from residents of the Emergency Refugee Shelter, Oswego, NY, September 1944. (COURTESY OF THE FDR LIBRARY.)

9

COMBATING ANTI-IMMIGRANT SENTIMENT AND ANTISEMITISM ON THE HOME FRONT

"I'm not afraid and I don't want you to be afraid"

HANS LUSTIG WAS FORTUNATE in having a job at MGM waiting for him when he arrived in the United States in the fall of 1940, but the problems of most refugees did not end with admission into the United States. The Great Depression and the increasing turmoil in Europe reinforced the anti-immigration sentiment in the United States that had led to the passage of the 1917, 1921, and 1924 immigration laws. The unemployment rate in the United States, which had reached nearly 25 percent in 1933, dropped to 14 percent (7.5 million people) by early 1937, but FDR's decision to cut spending that year precipitated a recession that pushed the unemployment rate back to 19 percent (8–10 million people) in 1938 and well into 1939.[1] Many American workers feared that an influx of European refugees would displace them, and those still unemployed worried that they would have to compete with the new immigrants for the scarce jobs available.[2] Antisemitism and fears that Communists would be among the immigrants further stoked anxiety.

These anxieties created opposition to a liberalization of immigration restrictions. They also made it hard for refugees who did make it to the United States to find work and achieve acceptance in their new country. Refugees needed assistance adjusting to their new condition. To meet that need, refugee organizations created facilities for welcoming the newcomers, provided temporary quarters for housing them, and sought to place them with families or find them homes of their own. They assisted them with finding work and provided health and other human services. The American Friends

Service Committee (AFSC), which was at the forefront of refugee efforts domestically as well as in Europe, worked with the National Coordinating Committee for Aid to Refugees, whose members included both Christians and Jews, on placing newly arrived refugees in American communities.[3] The AFSC and other organizations also sought to educate Americans about the contributions immigrants made to the United States and win acceptance for people who came from different cultural and religious backgrounds.

Eleanor Roosevelt warmly embraced these efforts, praising them in her My Day column and encouraging those individuals and organizations that were addressing the problems immigrants faced. Her interest in programs that helped immigrants become oriented to American society went back to her earliest experience in social service when she worked with Jewish and Italian immigrants at the Rivington Street Settlement on the Lower East Side of New York. ER also addressed the issue of discrimination against immigrants in her speeches and took a special interest in initiatives aimed at overcoming the misinformation that created prejudice against them.

Although this work had begun before 1938, the events of that year, culminating in Kristallnacht, and the large increase in the number of refugees admitted to the United States as a result of the Roosevelt administration's somewhat more liberal policy during this period, made the task of absorbing new immigrants into the United States urgent.[4] In December 1938, when Dr. John Elliott, senior leader of the Ethical Cultural Society, came to tell her about plans to create "friendship houses" in many cities around the country to assist refugees, ER wrote Clarence Pickett that she thought it "a very wonderful idea." Elliott assured her that he could raise the money but said he needed guidance from Pickett and the AFSC, which had become expert at managing programs in which "people train by working together." Pickett replied that he thought the chairmanship would demand too much of his time but that one of his colleagues was helping Elliott flesh out the plan. Elliott went on to help found the Good Neighbor League Committee on the Émigré and the Community, an organization for fostering greater acceptance of immigrants by American society, and ER agreed to serve as its honorary president.[5]

One of the earliest organizations to establish hostels or friendship houses for refugees was the Women's Division of the American Jewish Congress (AJC). According to a fundraising pamphlet sent to ER in 1940, the refugee hostels operated by the Women's Division of the AJC had provided shelter to 3,000 men, women, and children since they opened in 1934.[6] When Carrie Chapman Catt wrote to ER in May 1940 urging her to visit Congress House, a refugee hostel in New York City founded by Louise Wise, the wife of Rabbi Stephen Wise, and write about it in her My Day column, ER readily agreed to do so. She wrote in her column that Congress House "must indeed seem a cheerful haven to strangers landing on our shores. I wish we could receive everyone who comes to this country with the same spirit which Mrs. Wise and her colleagues have been able to create in these houses."

In a later column, ER noted that she had failed to mention "one rather important fact" about Congress House: the Women's Division of the AJC "accepted refugees on an entirely non-sectarian basis. Not only Jewish, but Catholic and liberal Protestant refugees from Germany, have found a haven here."[7]

But while some individuals and organizations welcomed the new immigrants, hostility toward them remained strong. In January 1939, when the eminent Jewish American violinist Mischa Elman, himself an immigrant, launched a tour of twenty-five cities to raise funds for German refugees of all religious backgrounds, he received a threatening letter and had to have two plainclothes policemen escort him to Carnegie Hall and sit backstage during the concert. "What has happened to us in this country?" ER asked in My Day the next day. "If we study our own history we find that we have always been ready to receive the unfortunates from other countries, and though this may seem a generous gesture on our part, we have profited a thousand-fold by what they have brought us."[8]

Many organizations opposed to immigration spread false information about refugees to stir up prejudice against them. The American Coalition, for example, an organization of self-proclaimed patriotic groups formed in 1937 by Senator Robert Reynolds of North Carolina, campaigned not only to restrict immigration but to deport aliens, who, Reynolds claimed, populated American prisons, asylums, and relief rolls, in addition to taking jobs from Americans.[9]

To counter misinformation about immigrants, the AFSC distributed a pamphlet in the spring of 1939 entitled *Refugee Facts*. The manuscript "came into our hands," Pickett explained to ER, and "it seemed so pertinent" that the AFSC decided to publish it. The pamphlet had actually been produced by the American Jewish Committee, which had asked the AFSC to publish it but had covered the cost of printing. The American Jewish Committee no doubt felt that the pamphlet would carry greater weight with the public if it were published by a Christian organization. In addition to carefully checking the statistics, the AFSC added an introduction.

Pickett asked ER to write about *Refugee Facts* in My Day, but he worded his request carefully because of his sensitivity to the constraints that limited ER's freedom: "If you feel strongly impelled to say something about it in your column, we hope you will not feel restrained."[10] Probably because the issue mainly concerned refugees once they were in the United States, ER did not feel restrained. Although she rarely devoted a whole column to one topic, in this case she did. One of the most surprising statistics cited in the pamphlet, she noted, was that the nation had actually experienced a net loss of immigrants over the past six years:

> From 1932 through June 1938, a total of 241,962 immigrants were admitted into the United States for permanent residence. During this same period 246,449 immigrants

previously admitted to this country for permanent residence moved away, so that roughly, during the six years of the Nazi regime in Germany, 4,487 more aliens departed than were admitted to the United States.

ER called special attention to the refugees described in the pamphlet who had created jobs by bringing their technical knowledge with them and restarting their businesses in the United States. Three refugees whose wool hosiery firm previously exported goods to the United States from Germany had reestablished their business in Massachusetts and employed thirty-eight American workers. A refugee who arrived with a patented process for making gloves now sold $100,000 worth of goods in the United States each year. These facts, she wrote, "seem to indicate that these immigrants will contribute to our well-being as have similar groups in our past history."[11]

To ER, integrating immigrants into American society was part of making democracy successful. In the fall of 1939, when she gave one of her "sermons on citizenship" at the New York Herald Tribune Forum on Current Problems, she noted that the other speakers had focused on the threat from Communist and Nazi groups. She agreed that it was necessary to protect the nation against the influence of such groups but argued that it was more important to address human needs, including those of immigrants. She told her listeners that they need not fear the threat of Communism and Fascism if they made democracy serve everyone:

> I believe in democracy and in my inward power to work for democracy and to make it seem worthwhile to other people. And for that reason I'm not afraid and I don't want you to be afraid. I want you to make this country a land where we do not live under fear, but where we work to make life worth living.[12]

ER'S ATTITUDE TOWARD THE REFUGEE problem, both in its overseas and domestic manifestations, was bound up in her evolving conception of national defense. After the fall of France she came to the firm conclusion that the United States could reach no accommodation with Hitler. She hoped that someday military force would no longer be needed to settle disputes, but as the menace of Nazi military aggression grew, she became more and more committed to FDR's program of building strong military defenses and supplying the French and British with weapons to defend themselves. At the same time, she continued to believe that an essential element of national defense was for citizens to make a deeper commitment to improving the lives of everyone. Modern weapons and men trained to use them constituted the first line of defense, she said in a speech to the Herald Tribune Forum in 1940, but a well-armed, well-prepared military force also needed "something which will create in these trained men an unbeatable spirit." Citizens in totalitarian states felt that they were participating in a revolution; citizens in the United States must feel that they, too, were participating in an inspiring process of transformative change.[13]

ER was adapting her "sermons on citizenship" to the new circumstances in which America found itself. The nation was now preparing for war. Building a society that met everyone's needs would create national unity and lift morale; it would give Americans something worth fighting and dying for. The reception of refugees to the United States continued to be one of the areas needing improvement.

The passage of the Alien Registration Act (Smith Act) at the end of June 1940 required anyone residing within the borders of the United States who was not a citizen or national to register as an "alien." Each alien was finger-printed and filled out a questionnaire about his or her background, memberships in organizations, occupation, and employment. He or she was then assigned a registration number and issued an identification card by the Immigration and Naturalization Service (INS). Although the INS attempted to soothe the fears of immigrants about this process in a series of public service announcements over the radio, the law did nothing to dissipate the widespread suspicion of recent immigrants and it officially stigmatized them as outsiders. Over five million immigrants eventually submitted alien registration forms.

To dispel prejudice against refugees, ER, Clarence Pickett, and their colleagues sought to strengthen the argument made in the 1939 pamphlet *Refugee Facts* that far from becoming a drain on American resources, immigrants had made substantial contributions to the American economy. At the end of 1940, at ER's instigation, Agnes Inglis, in her role as executive secretary of the Committee for Selected Social Studies, began a study of refugees and employment that ER hoped would illuminate the situation of refugees nationwide. In May, as the study proceeded, ER wrote a My Day column deploring the prejudice against immigrants that arose, in part, from the fear of spies infiltrating America's growing defense industry. She thought it "perfectly natural" that Americans "should be extremely anxious now to keep foreign agents from retarding our defense industries, or from creating dissension among us through their activities." She recognized that identifying aliens who had entered the country illegally required the authorities to "question many people who are entirely innocent of any subversive activity." But because that was necessary, only government officials of "the highest caliber" should "have anything to do with these activities." Ordinary citizens should report suspicious activity to these authorities. But most people who had entered the country recently were either citizens or becoming citizens and were "probably more devoted to the democratic form of government than many of our citizens who have taken their allegiance to democracy for granted." These new citizens "must be given the same opportunity that the rest of us have to earn a living and to lead their own lives protected by the laws of our land."[14]

In her weekly radio broadcast on November 3, 1941, in order to refute the view of "very simple people" that the government cared more about assisting refugees than in helping "what they call 'Americans,'" ER asked Agnes Inglis to report on some of the results of her study. According to the *New York Herald Tribune*, Inglis said that "since 1933 150,000 refugees from Hitler-dominated countries had settled in the United States, approximately half of them in New York and only 3 percent were wholly dependent on relatives or relief agencies. The remainder, she said, earn an average of $18 a week, while 2,700 of them in New York alone manage or have set up enterprises that employ 9,000 persons."[15]

Broadcasting these facts may have moderated the attitude of some people toward refugees, but not enough to alter the resistance in Congress and among the majority of American citizens to liberalizing the nation's immigration policy.

ANTISEMITISM ALSO REMAINED AN OBSTACLE to national unity and intensified as the threat of American involvement in another European war increased. It also became a propaganda tool for anti-interventionists, such as the America First Committee and its spokesman, Charles Lindbergh. On September 11, 1941, Lindbergh gave a speech in Des Moines, Iowa, in which he charged that since September 1939 three groups had, by devious means, pushed the United States toward involvement in the European conflict: the British, the Jews, and the Roosevelt administration. To Lindbergh the Jews were not a part of "us." Like the British, they had "reasons which are not American" for pushing the United States into the war. They were understandably "looking out" for their own interests as a people, but Americans "cannot allow the natural passions and prejudices of other peoples to lead our country to destruction." The "greatest danger" of the Jews "to this country," Lindbergh charged, "lies in their large ownership and influence in our motion pictures, our press, our radio and our government." They used the media they controlled to celebrate the glory of war in plays and movies, provide biased coverage of events in newsreels, withdraw advertising from newspapers and magazines that published antiwar articles, and label people advocating nonintervention "traitor," "Nazi," and "anti-Semitic."[16]

ER did not respond directly to Lindbergh's speech in My Day but continued to fight prejudice in her column, speeches, and in correspondence with supporters of Lindbergh's position who wrote to her. When one correspondent complained to her about "the Jews who are madly trying to bring pressure on the administration to start the shooting" and about Henry Morgenthau, who "naturally wants us to save several million Jews at the sacrifice of several American Gentile boys' lives," ER replied: "If we sit back and accept whatever may be done to us, and allow Hitler to dominate the world, you will be far worse off than you or anyone can imagine. . . . You are extremely unwise to be prejudiced against any group, because one prejudice leads to another, and who knows when one's own particular group may be attacked."[17]

WITH THE JAPANESE ATTACK ON Pearl Harbor on December 7, 1941, the American declaration of war on Japan the next day, and the declaration of war by Germany on the United States four days later, the debate ended over whether the United States should and could isolate itself from a conflict that raged all over the world. Antisemitism remained a corrosive and undermining force in America during the war, however, and ER remained determined to resist it together with intolerance directed against African Americans. Not wanting Americans to lose sight of what they were fighting for, she continued to campaign for greater equality both within the military and on the domestic front.

The United States Congress itself was rife with antisemitism. In 1944, the columnist and radio commentator Walter Winchell criticized Congressman John Elliott Rankin of Mississippi for the manner in which he spoke the Jewish names of voters who urged him to support a bill that would create a federal ballot for soldiers voting in presidential and congressional elections. He called him "Rankin of the House of Reprehensibles." Rankin responded on the floor of the House by saying that Winchell's true name was "Walter Lipshitz" and spelled it out to make it appear obscene. Many of his fellow congressmen laughed at this, and when he said he had told a friend that Winchell was a "kike—a Jew so loathsome that other Jews despised him," they laughed again. When Rankin finished his speech, according to the newspaper *PM*, "virtually all the Republicans and about half of the Democrats rose to their feet applauding Rankin."

When Morton Greenwald, one of ER's correspondents, read an account of Rankin's speech and the reception it received, he sent the clipping on to ER and asked her:

"Is this the America of the 4 Freedoms? . . . .

"Is this what thousands of soldiers, sailors, marines, many of whom are Jews, are fighting to preserve and come home to?

"Is this the America I, a Jew, am supposed to live and fight, and die for?

"*Is it?*"

ER replied, "Unfortunately, there are always small minded and mean men in this world. That, however, should not make you feel our freedom is not worth fighting for because, fortunately, there are a great many who are shocked by such statements and whose determination to eliminate prejudice is strengthened by them."[18]

One way ER expressed her commitment to fighting antisemitism was by continuing to support the work of the National Conference of Christians and Jews (NCCJ).

In 1943, while promoting a reading list published by the Chicago Round Table of the NCCJ entitled "Reading for Democracy," she reported that she kept receiving letters "which point up the prejudices in which so many of us indulge, even in wartime." Prejudice against race or religion seemed "out of place," she wrote, "in a country with so many racial origins and so many religions." Now, as America fought in Europe and Asia, its "soldiers fight and die, side by side, and are comforted by priests, ministers or rabbis, as the case may be, quite regardless of whether the dying boys belong to the particular church represented near them at the moment."[19]

At the end of July 1942, James Waterman Wise, research consultant to the Council Against Intolerance in America, asked ER to contribute the lead article to *American Unity*, a monthly manual for teachers and other educators, which the council planned to launch in September and distribute free of charge to 10,000 teachers, principals, and superintendents throughout the United States. *American Unity* would provide educators with "factual material keyed to current events, lesson plans, assembly programs, and discussions of vital problems." By highlighting "the contribution of men and women of every race, faith and color to the upbuilding of our nation," it would "expose the hate-mongers as traitors to our country."

In her article ER wrote that democracy could not achieve victory unless it succeeded in promoting attitudes that went beyond mere tolerance:

> Tolerance is not a word which I like, when it means mere apathetic acquiescence in the rights of other people. If democracy is to win out, we must do more than acquiesce. We must fight for the basic rights of individuals and of nations. No child must leave school without the realization that these rights are dear to him and can not be retained by him unless he makes sure that they apply to all other people as well.

She went on to vigorously articulate a set of human rights that reflected FDR's vision of the Four Freedoms and foreshadowed the Universal Declaration of Human Rights. As she and her colleagues would do in 1948 in drafting the declaration, she included economic and social rights, as well as civil and political rights in her list:

> More people must feel that their right to worship God as they see fit does not hamper their political, economic or social rights. All people have a right to free worship and free self-expression. All people have a right to be governed in a way which they themselves choose. All people have a right to demand an economic system which will free the world from starvation and give everyone an opportunity, throughout the world, to work for the standard of living which they desire. All people have a right to freedom and respect as individuals regardless of race or creed.

In a passage that anticipated the famous statement she made in 1953 that human rights "begin in small places, close to home," she added: "We must learn to accept the democratic processes in the school room and in the home, and we will then live our lives so that each generation will move forward with a real understanding of democracy. Only thus can we achieve a real victory over insecurity and fear, for which all of us strive."[20]

Although ER had not relinquished the idea, expressed in her 1938 article on the future of the Jews, that there was a "Jewish problem" that needed some kind of remedy, such as a wider dispersion of the Jews geographically and professionally, her commitment to racial and religious equality ran deep. The stereotypes of Jews that she still sometimes repeated echoed the culture of her time, but for her they did not express a desire to deny Jews their civil, political, economic, or social rights. She spoke out against prejudice, advocated equal rights to housing and jobs for all people, and refused to speak to groups that she knew rejected Jews as members. There is no evidence that her occasional references to the negative stereotypes of Jews that she had absorbed as a child and whose expression remained socially acceptable among many people at the time made her less active in combating antisemitism, less sympathetic to the plight of Jewish refugees, or, later on, less horrified by news of the Holocaust.

10

A FAILED ATTEMPT AT RESCUE

"Only prompt emigration can save the children from deportation and early death"

WITH AMERICA'S ENTRY into the war in December 1941, the efforts to rescue European refugees had entered a new phase. As long as the southern part of France remained unoccupied by the Germans, some opportunities to get refugees out of that region remained, but the difficulty increased. In August 1942, Varian Fry, now living in New York City, wrote to Eleanor Roosevelt warning that "the refugees in France now face the greatest danger which has come their way since the armistice of June 1940." Information sent to the Joint Distribution Committee (JDC) and the Emergency Rescue Committee (ERC) by underground contacts in France indicated that the Vichy government had agreed to deport 16,000 foreigners and French Jews from the occupied zone and 10,000 Jews and Gentiles from the unoccupied zone of France "to an unknown destination in eastern Europe." Three thousand six hundred internees from the Gurs, Vernet, and Les Milles detention camps had already been deported. Children over five years old in the unoccupied zone and over two years old in the occupied zone were being deported with their parents. Children under those ages were being left behind, virtually as orphans. The Vichy government had ceased issuing exit permits altogether "without distinction of race or nationality" and Spanish and Swiss authorities were barring entry into their countries of those attempting to escape.

"My own feeling," Fry wrote in his letter accompanying the report,

> is that we ought not to seem, by official silence, to condone such brutal and barbaric treatment of defenseless men, women and children. I hope that you will agree with this and that you will use your influence to get the State Department to

make a vigorous public statement. I also hope that you will mention these events in your column.

ER sent a copy of the report to Sumner Welles: "Could we protest and may I mention in my column?"[1] Welles replied that the State Department had

> protested not once but several times to the head of the French Government against this inhuman program. Heads of our relief organizations in unoccupied France have protested to Marshal Petain. Representatives of other civilized states have followed suit. All this, however, has made no impression on Laval.

Although Welles saw no reason why ER could not use the information in the report in her column, she chose not to because of Welles's assurances that both the American government and relief organizations had strongly protested. These protests had also been publicized in the press.[2]

ER did write in My Day at this time about another atrocity: the treatment of Polish women at the Ravensbrück Women's Preventive Detention Camp in Germany. In July 1942, she received a letter from Flora McPherson, a British woman in London whose husband still lived in Warsaw. McPherson enclosed a detailed report on the Ravensbrück camp, where many women had already "died from maltreatment, torture, massacre, murder and hunger." McPherson asked ER to publicize the Nazis' brutal treatment of the women in the camp in hopes of raising such "a storm of protest from women all over the free parts of the world" that they would save at least some of their lives.

The Ravensbrück concentration camp, which opened in 1939, was unusual in that it housed only women, although a small camp for men was later established next to it. The largest group of prisoners in the camp were Polish women, but it also included Roma, Germans, and other women from all over occupied Europe. About 15 percent of the women were Jewish, many of whom, if they survived their treatment in Ravensbrück, were shipped to Auschwitz in 1942–43 and murdered. Toward the end of the war the installation of gas chambers would accelerate the death rate at the camp. Of the approximately 130,000 women who were housed at Ravensbrück at one time or another, only 15,000 to 32,000 survived.

In August, ER sent McPherson's letter, together with the enclosed report, to Archibald MacLeish, then head of the Office of War Information, asking him if it would be wise for her to write anything about it. MacLeish answered that he did not ordinarily think it was constructive to publicize atrocities unless doing so was related to "a possibility of action." But the "heartbreaking and yet subdued" style of the report on Ravensbrück and his trust in ER led him to encourage her to use the material. In ER's hands, he felt sure, the story could be made into "an affirmative, moving instrument." It was clear to MacLeish that "the German purpose is not merely to visit horrors upon defenseless people for the sake of horror but rather to maim and cripple and eventually to exterminate races of which the Nazi government disapproves." For that reason, he believed that the story had great value in the ideological struggle between Nazism and democracy for it presented "the most precise opposite to our purpose to provide a greater freedom and a richer life for all men everywhere."[3]

After receiving MacLeish's blessing, ER participated, along with Dorothy Thompson, Clare Booth Luce, and Pearl Buck, in a broadcast on September 23, 1942, to the women of Poland. ER told them that if young people, like the young Polish soldier who had recently visited the White House, committed themselves to the fight to win the war and then make an equal effort to create a better world for everyone after the war, then "I think there is no question but what the reward for your sufferings, the reward of your courage, will surely come."[4]

In her My Day column, ER quoted from a passage in the report on the Ravensbrück camp that described how the women prisoners were forced to go barefoot on streets strewn with hard gravel until their heels developed festering sores. They were not considered ill until they collapsed. If one of the women talked to a Jew, she was shut in a dark cell for 42 days.[5] ER expressed outrage at the treatment of the women prisoners simply by presenting these facts, then responding to those facts in her seemingly innocent fashion: "How can the Nazis hope to create loyal and friendly citizens in a country which they have conquered by cruel treatment? Certainly, if they want goodwill, they go about it in a strange fashion."

Like ER's statement after Kristallnacht that the Nazis had exhibited "a woeful lack of imagination" in seeking "to achieve legitimate objectives of orderly government" through violence, ER's criticism of the treatment of the women prisoners at Ravensbrück seems woefully inadequate to the situation she is describing. But it also possesses a certain canniness. The fact that the Nazis obviously had no intention of generating "goodwill" or creating "loyal and friendly citizens" transforms the naïve surface of her question and statement into irony. Was ER responding in this indirect way because of instructions from FDR and the State Department or because she herself believed that in her role as wife of the president she should not too bluntly condemn Nazi atrocities? Or was this style an intentional strategy for exposing evil? Judging from the way she sometimes used this indirect method to express disapproval even after FDR's death when she was freer to speak out (and did so), it is apparent that her style expressed an instinctive, perhaps deliberate intention. Jacob Blaustein, who worked closely with ER when she chaired the UN Human Rights Commission during the postwar years, noted that behind an "attentive, innocent expression," ER possessed "a thoroughly practical mind, capable of unsuspected toughness. Much like Socrates," he recalled after her death, "she would ask questions in a tentative manner, hesitating, often professing ignorance. And by this gentle strategy she often extracted a 'yes' or 'maybe' where a frontal attack would have produced a 'no.'" Blaustein quoted a State Department diplomat who, after watching her exercising this talent, remarked: "Never has anyone seen naiveté and skill so gracefully blended."[6]

Perhaps ER developed her naïve yet pointed style partly because of her position as wife of the president and pressure from her husband's administration not to take confrontational stands on foreign policy, but its roots lay deep in her spiritual nature. While she reluctantly came to the conclusion that only armed conflict would stop the Nazis, her focus throughout the war was on relieving human suffering: advocating for and assisting refugees, promoting equal rights for African Americans, mitigating the effects of internment on Japanese Americans, providing services to women workers in the armaments industry and their children, and bringing comfort to American soldiers. Like the Quakers, whom she continued to admire, support financially, and rely on in doing some of her good works, she concentrated on helping the victims of oppression, not on condemning the oppressors. She says nothing to sugarcoat or excuse the Nazis' treatment of the women prisoners at Ravensbrück, but instead of simply condemning it, sets up a contrast between Nazi cruelty and the behavior of a good government, which would indeed solicit the "goodwill" of the people and seek to create "loyal and friendly citizens" through its policies. Such a government, supported by an active citizenry, was, of course, the goal that ER and Clarence Pickett ardently promoted through their words and actions. ER admired Dorothy Thompson's eloquent expressions of outrage, but she herself often preferred to expose evil gently and indirectly.

AFTER AMERICAN ENTRY INTO THE war, ER continued to take a special interest in the rescue and care of refugee children. Because of the increased obstacles to rescue caused by the conflict and the limited funding the United States Committee for the Care of European Children (USCCEC) succeeded in raising, most of the efforts she participated in had modest goals and results. In May 1942, after the USCCEC had been unsuccessful in bringing children to the United States for several months, ER reported that fifty children, many of whom had been interned in concentration camps in France, would be arriving shortly in the United States under her organization's sponsorship.[7] Another group of thirty-nine children, whose parents had died or disappeared into concentration camps, were rescued from internment camps in unoccupied France by the American Friends Service Committee (AFSC) and arrived in the United States under the sponsorship of the USCCEC on July 30.[8] The numbers were pitifully small, but under the circumstances the USCCEC faced, the rescue of each child represented a small victory.

A month later, on August 31, a few days after receiving the report from Varian Fry about the deportation of Jews from France, ER received a telegram from an emergency committee made up of leading relief organizations in Geneva that proposed a much larger rescue operation. The committee urgently sought her assistance in gaining the admission to the United States of 5,000 Jewish children under the age of sixteen who remained in France after the deportation of their parents. The committee called upon the USSCEC to act immediately.[9] After ER sent the telegram on to Marshall Field, the USCCEC met in emergency session and committed itself to evacuating 1,000 of the children. The American Jewish Joint Distribution Committee agreed to contribute $400,000 to $450,000 to the effort. It planned to use some of that money to charter a Portuguese ship to transport the children to the United States. The USCCEC planned to raise approximately $500,000 to meet the remaining expenses.[10]

At its meeting on September 9, the President's Advisory Committee on Political Refugees (PACPR) voted to endorse the plan to rescue the children. At the suggestion of James McDonald, ER helped arrange a series of meetings with Justice and State Department officials for the PACPR's executive secretary, George Warren.[11] Afterward, McDonald reported to ER that Warren felt that "the prospects of rescuing at least some hundred of the children are now excellent."[12] Given her lack of trust in the State Department, ER no doubt spoke with the president about the plight of the children as well and urged him to act.

On September 17, the State Department sent messages to the consuls in Marseille, Nice, and Lyon authorizing them to issue quota visas for 1,000 of the children. In this case, to make it possible to act quickly, the State Department agreed to accept guarantees of support from the USCCEC for all the children rather than requiring individual affidavits for each child.

ER, meanwhile, met with members of the USCCEC board to discuss how the organization would implement the initiative. By this time, the AFSC, Joint Distribution Committee, the International YMCA and YWCA, and French child welfare agencies were already preparing to select the children who faced the most danger, provide adults to escort them, and secure transportation for them from Lisbon to the United States. Assurances had already been received that private homes would be available for the children once they arrived in the United States.[13]

After receiving cables from France indicating that children facing deportation were in more urgent need of rescue than previously thought, the USCCEC decided at its meeting on September 21 to try to rescue all of the 5,000 children who needed to escape. McDonald and Warren presented the request to Sumner Welles, who promised he would recommend to the president that he endorse the proposal.[14] When Welles got back to them, he informed McDonald and Warren that the president had approved the request. The president did not think it "desirable, however, that any public statement be made concerning this decision on the part of this Government."[15]

Even with the United States now engaged in the war against Germany and even in a situation crying out for a humanitarian response, FDR felt he would risk arousing antisemitism, perhaps anger the Vichy government headed by Laval, and derail the project if his administration announced a plan to rescue Jewish children before an agreement and arrangements were firmly in place. In keeping with the president's wishes, the USCCEC withheld an announcement of the rescue plan. When the press asked Welles on October 8 to comment on a report that 1,000 refugee children would be coming to the United States from France, he downplayed the decision. Without mentioning the children's Jewish identity, he confirmed that the United States planned to admit refugee children whose parents had been deported from France but declined to disclose how many were coming.[16]

The following day, Marshall Field announced the USCCEC's plans for the refugee children, although he, too, did not say how many would be coming or identify them as Jewish. "Urgent cables from overseas relief organizations," he said, "warn us that only prompt emigration can save the children from deportation and early death."[17] Finally, on October 15, the extent of the rescue effort and the fact that the children were Jewish were made public when the *New York Times* reported from Vichy, France, that the French government had agreed to accept American visas for 5,000 Jewish children under the age of 18 and permit them to leave for the United States. The State Department had authorized American consuls in France to issue emergency visas that would enable the children to enter the United States for the duration of the war. Under the agreement with the French government, which had been negotiated by S. Pinckney Tuck, the American charge d'affaires in Vichy, the children would return to Europe after the war if their parents could be found.[18]

For once, it appeared that the State Department and the president fully backed the USCCEC effort. As in the case of her success in getting the State Department to revise the terms on which British children could come to the United States in the summer of 1940, ER had used her influence to alter American policy. By facilitating the USSCEC's negotiations with the department, she appeared to have helped rescue a large number of Jewish children from unoccupied France.

Unfortunately, it was not to be. Notwithstanding the *Times* report that the French had agreed to the plan, obstacles remained. Laval would have been happy to have unburdened France of the children, but German officials opposed sending them to the United States for fear that their story would generate anti-Nazi propaganda. Laval, whose freedom of action was circumscribed by his need to appease the Germans, was also angry that the plan had been made public. When his government issued instructions for exit permits for the children, only "bona fide orphans" were included. Since the parents who had been deported to Eastern Europe were considered to be still alive, this ruling excluded all but about one hundred of the children. Tuck managed to get the number increased to five hundred and arrangements for their departure were underway when, as in the case of the British children in the summer of 1940, the progress of the war intervened.[19]

On November 8, 1942, United States forces landed in North Africa and the Vichy government broke diplomatic relations with the United States. Two days later, Germany broke its armistice agreement with the Vichy government and invaded unoccupied France. Although Vichy continued to function under Laval with limited powers in most of metropolitan France until August 1944, it did so under German domination. On November 30, 1942, Marshall Field reported to ER that the refugee children would be unable to emigrate, but that negotiations were continuing with the French and Swiss Red Cross on providing transportation for the children to the Swiss border. He requested that the USCCEC urge the State Department to ask the Swiss government to instruct the Swiss legation in France to resume the negotiations with the Vichy government for the children's release that Tuck had begun. While the negotiations for the children still in France continued, the USCCEC hoped that as many as 500 children who reached Spain and Portugal might be rescued.[20] These hopes, too, were dashed. Although some of these children were later rescued, the hope of rescuing a substantial number of children from southern France soon faded. The relief groups had run out of time. Although political and bureaucratic resistance in the United States had finally been overcome, the circumstances of the war thwarted what would have been one of the largest rescue operations in the history of the European refugee crisis.

SOME CHILDREN FROM SOUTHERN FRANCE continued to slip across the border into Spain, and during the winter of 1943, the USCCEC succeeded in bringing several small groups of children who had managed to reach Portugal to the United States.[21] In the spring of 1943, however, the State Department dealt yet another blow to efforts to rescue children by ruling that anyone who departed from Germany before March 15, 1938 (the date of the Anschluss) could not be classified as a refugee. The reason for this ruling was unclear, but it meant that many children in Spain and Portugal became ineligible for evacuation to the United States under the arrangement that the USCCEC had worked out with the State Department. "Many of these children were refugees in the same sense that they had been on the road ahead of Nazi pogroms prior to the 1938 Anschluss date," Robert Lang, now the executive director of the USCCEC, wrote to Louis Weiss. The Spanish would not allow these children to stay in Spain permanently and they now faced the same risks as the children who had been trapped in unoccupied France.[22]

On May 20, 1943, as ER and her colleagues became increasingly discouraged by the resistance of American consuls to issuing visas for refugee children, Tommy relayed a telephone message from ER to Sumner Welles:

> We are finding a great deal of trouble, not only in the United States Committee for the Care of European Children, but in other committees working to bring children out of Europe. It seems almost impossible to get visas. These people want to know whether they should keep on trying.[23]

Welles replied that the State Department had instructed consuls in Spain and Portugal to issue visas to children recommended by the USCCEC who were under sixteen years of age and had arrived there before March 1938. Some of the eligible refugee children had already arrived in the United States; others would be sailing soon. The State Department's willingness to make an exception for these children was welcome. The fact was, however, that very few children who were unaccompanied by parents fit into this category.[24]

The USCCEC did keep trying, but from January 1943 until the end of the war only 111 more refugee children arrived in the United States under the care of the USCCEC. After the war, when it was again possible to rescue European children, the USCCEC continued its work before finally disbanding in 1953. By that time, it had brought a total of 4,177 refugee children to the United States, a tragically small number considering how many were lost in the Holocaust, but a significant achievement considering the obstacles the USCCEC faced.[25]

The USCCEC's achievement was significant in another way as well. The way in which the USCCEC carried out its rescue effort reflected the democratic values, especially a person's right to be treated as an individual, not as a stereotyped member of some group, that ER and her colleagues fought for throughout the refugee crisis. As Kathryn Close put it in her final report on the USCCEC program:

> From the moment of selection in Europe each child began to have the experience—perhaps his first in many years or even in his entire life—of being regarded as a person in his own right, with his own reactions, fears, wishes, hopes and potentialities adding up to his own personal needs. In America he participated in plans being made for him not as a representative of a group of unfortunates but as one particular person. What firmer support could be offered for a deprived child's future than such a consistent regard of his own individuality? Here was foundation stone

quarried by the experience and basic theories of all American social work, from the bedrock of American democracy.[26]

FROM 1939 ONWARD, ER'S RELATIONSHIP with Sumner Welles provided a bridge between her and those who had the power to issue visas. When he resigned as Undersecretary of State in August 1943, she lost the personal channel to the State Department that had sometimes made her efforts effective.[27] Cordell Hull and William Bullitt, Welles's rivals at the State Department, had used information they had obtained about Welles's homosexual activities to pressure FDR to get rid of him.[28] ER's correspondence with the State Department had fallen off as it became more difficult to get refugees out of occupied Europe and as she received fewer appeals for help in individual cases. After Welles's departure, it fell off still further.

As old friends, ER and Welles mutually respected and trusted each other. She could be frank with him and she could rely on him to respond to her complaints. Although Welles vigorously defended American refugee policy and its implementation by the State Department, he occasionally pushed his colleagues to act more flexibly. In the case of individual refugee cases referred to him by ER, Welles sought detailed information from American embassies or consulates in Europe about what was causing delays. When regulations permitted, he requested State Department staff and consuls to expedite the processing of visa applications. At times, he too became impatient with his department's rigidity. In a memorandum to Avra Warren about a query from ER about the case of Mr. and Mrs. Oscar Von Halle and their son Gerd, Welles told Warren that he was "getting increasingly concerned about cases of this kind":

> It is, of course, obvious that as a matter of proper procedure visas cannot be issued in regions where there are no American consuls to issue them. On the other hand, in order to take care of thoroughly deserving, bonafide cases where we can obtain all of the evidence that is absolutely necessary to assure us that the applicants are desirable, is it not possible to conceive of some exception to the general rule so as to make it possible for these people to get exit permits?[29]

Nonetheless, while ER's colleagues in the rescue campaign expressed their conviction that the Department of State and the consuls abroad deliberately obstructed the issuing of visas as a matter of policy, Welles continued to insist that in most cases the time it took to issue a visa was perfectly normal. His insistence that the visa process was functioning well made it more difficult for ER and her allies to persuade FDR that something was wrong with the way the State Department was managing the visa process and to do something to correct it.

Often Welles gave her a specific reason why someone's visa was delayed or denied. Sometimes the problem was that the applicant was so far down on the quota list that Welles estimated it would take as long as several years before the consulate would even consider the case. At other times, the consulate reported that it had not received the person's application or the necessary affidavit of support or that the affidavit they had received did not offer sufficient proof of the sponsor's financial ability to support the refugee in the United States. Sometimes the applicant was found to have been a member of the Communist Party or some other political organization believed hostile to the American government or was suspected of being a Nazi or Soviet agent. In other cases, Welles told her that the problem lay in an area over which the State Department had little or no power—such as obtaining an exit visa from the Vichy government, transit visas from Spain and Portugal, or transportation to America and the funds to pay for it—not in the visa process itself.

ER recognized that there were legitimate reasons why the State Department would refuse to issue visas to certain individuals, but she did not accept the long delays in processing applications and grew exasperated with the bureaucratic explanations, often written by Breckinridge Long, that she received from Welles for why such a lengthy process was necessary. Her efforts ensured that the cases she wrote to Welles about got careful attention, however. In some of those cases her intervention did in fact shorten what would have been an even longer process or would not have happened at all.

Although she achieved some modest success, it is impossible to conclude that ER's bombardment of Welles for information on individual visa cases and her expressions of impatience and, at times, incredulity and outrage, at the glacial pace of the process had more than a small impact on accelerating the issuance of visas. Only a fundamental change in policy, procedure, and the attitude of those implementing the regulations would have significantly increased the flow of refugees to the United States.

The degree to which Welles himself was captive to the system is striking. Welles was in charge of the overall supervision of American visa policy, but Assistant Secretary of State Breckinridge Long and the chief of the visa division (Avra Warren and, later on, Howard Travers), who were far less sympathetic than Welles to the refugees, were responsible for carrying out policy and directing the activities of the consulates abroad.[30] While Welles asked the State Department's visa division or the consuls abroad to look into why the processing of individual cases dragged on for so long, he failed, nearly always, to challenge the explanations drafted by Long, Warren, or another colleague or insist that they interpret the standards for admission to the United States more liberally. During their struggle with the State Department in October 1940, the members of the President's Advisory Committee on Political Refugees concluded that Welles was "fair and objective when actually confronted with a situation" but would "not make an initial move."[31] His troubled relationships with Cordell Hull and William Bullitt at the

State Department, who disliked and distrusted him, might have limited his power to make changes, but, in fact, there is no evidence that he felt change was necessary. The historians Richard Breitman and Allan Lichtman point out that one of the reasons for the rigidity of America's restrictionist refugee policy had to do with bureaucracy: "Even those who championed the cause of European Jews found themselves confined to the channels and bound by the procedures of the bureaucratic system."[32] Welles appears to have been a captive both of the system and his own personality. The historian Irwin Gellman describes Welles as "rigid, dogmatic, and opinionated" throughout his career and too focused on "technical details." By maintaining a "narrow focus," he "often missed the larger picture." Welles's devotion to bureaucratic procedure may have blinded him to the failure of the system to do the work of rescue effectively.[33]

Despite his consistent defense of State Department procedures, Welles was sympathetic to the plight of refugees and the suffering of European Jews.[34] Refugee advocates, such as Stephen Wise, felt they could trust him, while they did not trust Breckinridge Long.[35] But Welles shared the fears of FDR and his State Department colleagues that subversives would infiltrate the United States among the refugees and threaten the nation.[36] He was also keenly aware that the majority of Americans opposed allowing more refugees into the country and worried that if the State Department loosened its regulations, it would expose the department to more criticism from Congress and the public. Despite its restrictionist policies, the department already had received criticism from some Americans for admitting too many Jews.

One indication of Welles's ongoing sympathy for refugees—especially Jewish refugees—is that after leaving office, he expressed dismay that the Allies had no specific plans for the care of refugees once they won the war. In August 1944, a year after his resignation, he called for the Intergovernmental Committee on Refugees to do what it had failed to do in the past. "It is regrettably true," he wrote, "that the plans which should long since have been completed to deal with the refugee crisis which will become acute as soon as the war in Europe is over have not yet been formulated, much less adopted." He noted: "Pitifully few Jewish refugees have been enabled to make their way to Palestine" and urged that the British lift the bars to immigration. He envisioned Palestine becoming "an autonomous state, under an international trusteeship, constituted after agreement with the Arab states of the Near East."[37] As early as the fall of 1942, he had privately expressed the conviction that only the establishment of a Jewish state would provide a solution to the Jewish refugee crisis.[38] ER would only come to that conclusion much later.

11

RESPONDING TO NEWS OF THE EXTERMINATION CAMPS, 1942–45

"This hour of extremity"

IN LATE AUGUST 1942, at about the same time Varian Fry sent his report to Eleanor Roosevelt about the deportation of thousands of foreign Jews and Gentiles from France "to an unknown destination in eastern Europe," Gerhart Riegner, the World Jewish Congress representative in Geneva, received information from a German industrialist that the Nazis had begun to implement plans to deport all Jews in German-occupied territory to camps in Eastern Europe. There the Nazis would exterminate them with poison gas. Riegner asked the American consulate in Geneva to pass this report on to the American government, seek its verification, and inform Rabbi Stephen Wise of the news. He also asked the British consulate to convey the information to Sidney Silverman, Great Britain's representative to the World Jewish Congress. After Wise received a copy from Silverman, he questioned Sumner Welles about it. Welles asked him to keep the report private until the department could assess its veracity. On November 24, three months after receiving the alarming news, Welles finally got back to Wise to tell him that further convincing evidence confirmed Riegner's report.[1]

In response to this revelation, the leaders of the major American Jewish organizations called upon the Jews of all free lands to observe a day of mourning, fasting, and prayer for the Jews of Europe on December 2. Editorials condemning the murder of the Jews appeared in some of the nation's leading newspapers, and Christian leaders urged Christians to join their Jewish brethren in this day of prayer and mourning.

Although the *New York Times* and other papers reported on the Nazis' mass murder program on November 26, ER did not express her shock at the terrible news in her My Day column until December 3, following the day of mourning.[2] Responding cautiously, she wrote as if she had just learned of the killings:

> There was a small item in the paper this morning which filled me with horror. I noticed yesterday that in many parts of the country work had stopped for a few minutes while people prayed for the Jewish victims of Hitler's cruelty. This morning I saw that, in Poland, it was reported that more than two-thirds of the Jewish population had been massacred.
>
> There seems to be little use in voicing a protest, but somehow one cannot keep still when such horrors are going on. One can only pray that it will dawn upon Hitler that the Lord is not patient forever and that he who puts other people to death by the sword, is often meted out the same fate.[3]

Although oddly muted by the way she places the events she is describing at a distance from herself ("There was a small item in the paper," "I noticed yesterday," "This morning I saw that"), and by her statement that "There seems to be little use in voicing a protest," her column is more explicit in identifying Hitler's crimes than any statement she had made previously. She "cannot keep still" and must express her anguish. "Hitler's cruelty" fills her "with horror." More importantly, she names the group that is suffering ("the Jewish victims") and conveys the scope of the massacre ("more than two-thirds of the Jewish population"). FDR had condemned Nazi crimes in more forceful language in recent months, but until December he had chosen to focus on "all the victims of Nazi crime" rather than calling particular attention to Hitler's program to exterminate the Jews as ER was doing in her column.

The previous summer, at Rabbi Wise's request, FDR sent a message to the Madison Square Garden protest rally held on July 21 in which he said, "The Nazis will not succeed in exterminating their victims any more than they will succeed in enslaving mankind. The American people not only sympathize with all victims of Nazi crime but will hold the perpetrators of these crimes to strict accountability in a day of reckoning which will surely come." In August, he again pledged that the perpetrators of the crimes would be punished, but he did not mention the Jews specifically. In October he called for the establishment of a United Nations Commission for the Investigation of War Crimes.[4] Now, in December, with the knowledge of the scale and systematic character of Hitler's extermination plans verified and made public, leaders of the major Jewish organizations in the United States met with FDR to urge the president "to act now in behalf of the Jews of Europe." One of the memoranda they presented to him described in horrifying detail the methods of "outright slaughter and slow death" employed by Hitler. Two million Jews had already perished and the five million Jews remaining in Nazi-occupied Europe now faced total annihilation. The members of the delegation said that the expectation that the victory of the democracies would bring an end to the Nazi menace gave the Jewish people hope, but asked: would the Jews of Europe "live to see the dawn of this day of freedom? Unless action is taken immediately, the Jews of Europe are doomed."[5]

FDR responded by assuring the Jewish leaders that the United States would do everything possible to save the European Jews who were still alive.[6] On December 17, the United States joined Great Britain and nine exiled Allied governments in issuing a statement condemning Germany "for carrying into effect Hitler's oft-repeated intention to exterminate the Jewish people of Europe" by transporting Jews from all of the occupied nations to camps in Eastern Europe under "conditions of appalling horror and brutality" to be "massacred," worked to death, or left to die of exposure. The declaration promised "that those responsible for these crimes shall not escape retribution."[7] The statement did not, however, specify what the Allies would or could do to rescue the Jews still alive.

ON DECEMBER 10, 1942, RABBI WISE sent ER the latest issue of the *Congress Weekly*, which contained the texts of the two memoranda the Jewish leaders had given to the president. Wise asked ER to convey the facts about "this titanic horror" to the readers of her My Day column and suggest some ways in which "the civilized world should act to save Hitler's victims." ER, who apparently felt that her December 5 My Day column was a sufficient response on her part, replied: "I am, of course, horrified as is every one, but I have written and spoken on the subject and do not know what more I can say."[8] She had spoken out, but not with forcefulness or in the kind of detail Wise believed the crisis demanded.

Two months later, as Rabbi Wise became more and more deeply disturbed by the failure of the Roosevelt administration to attempt the rescue of Jews who still survived, Wise again appealed to ER, who had "led the country on so many occasions in demanding compassion and justice for oppressed peoples." Although Wise continued to support the administration's position that the successful prosecution of the war must take first priority, he also knew that time was running out for the Jews. In "this hour of extremity," he told ER, before the Allies can achieve victory, the Jewish people of Europe "are threatened with total extermination." Would she address a protest rally being planned for March 1 at Madison Square Garden and "utter that word of compassion which may give courage to the imperiled and even to those who have the power to save them?" ER once again rebuffed Wise, citing "a previous engagement," but added, "I join with you in hoping that something can be done."[9] The participants in the event, attended by 21,000 people, passed a resolution demanding that the Allies take practical steps to rescue as many Jews as possible.

One of the reasons ER stayed away may have been that she anticipated the criticism of the administration's lack of action in attempting to rescue Jews that Jewish leaders expressed at the rally. Herman Shulman, chairman of the special committee of the American Jewish Congress on the European situation, said at the rally that "months have passed since the United Nations issued their declaration denouncing the unspeakable atrocities of the Nazis against the Jews and threatening retribution." The nations promised that "immediate practical steps would be taken to implement it" but had taken no action.[10] ER would not have wanted to be in the position of defending the administration and was not herself in a position to offer a possible course of action. Whatever the reason for her silence, Rabbi Wise must have been disappointed that ER, known more than anyone in America for her humanitarian concern, was unwilling to "utter that word of compassion" or mention the rally afterward in her column.

AS JEWISH LEADERS, LIKE WISE and Shulman, grew frustrated that the Roosevelt administration was failing to act swiftly to rescue European Jews before it was too late, a different kind of pressure began coming from a new organization not associated with the mainline Jewish groups. Its leader was a Palestinian Jew named Hillel Kook, who had changed his name to Peter Bergson when he came to the United States. In December 1941 he and others had formed the Committee for a Jewish Army of Stateless and Palestinian Jews, which sought the establishment of an army of 200,000 soldiers based in Palestine that would fight alongside British forces in the region. But Bergson and his colleagues soon turned their primary energies to demanding that the Roosevelt administration act to save as many of the Jews still trapped in Europe as possible.

Bergson successfully recruited some members of Congress, including freshman congressman Will Rogers Jr., Democrat of California, and a few prominent figures from the theater and film world to join his organization and press for action. With the help of the Hollywood scriptwriter Ben Hecht, he employed bold public relations tools, such as full-page newspaper ads sounding the alarm, demanding vigorous rescue efforts, and soliciting funds. The aggressive tactics of Bergson and his colleagues disturbed the established Jewish organizations in the United States, whose leaders worried that the wrong kind of pressure would alienate the president and undermine their efforts to persuade him to act.

After Hitler's extermination plans became public in late 1942, Hecht created a pageant to convey the scope of the tragedy to American audiences. "We Shall Never Die," staged by Moss Hart with music by Kurt Weill, was first performed before 40,000 people at Madison Square Garden on March 9, 1943, and then traveled to other cities. ER saw the pageant in Constitution Hall in April as part of an audience that included seven Supreme Court justices, two cabinet members, thirty-eight senators, and hundreds of congressmen. ER praised the memorial to "the two million Jewish dead of Europe" in her My Day column for its heartrending portrayal of Nazi cruelty:

> The music, singing, narration, and actors all served to make it one of the most impressive and moving pageants I have ever seen. No one who heard each group come

forward and give the story of what had happened to it at the hands of a ruthless German military, will ever forget those haunting words: "Remember us."

The pageant brought home to ER the agony of Hitler's victims. Later on, after attending a ceremony at which "The Black Book of Polish Jewry," an account of the annihilation of the Warsaw ghetto, was presented to some members of Congress, she would again express the pain she felt: "I hope that many people will see this book," she wrote. "It is a horrible book, a book which explains the terrible statistics of martyrdom of the Jews in Warsaw, and makes one ashamed that a civilized race anywhere in the world could treat other human beings in such a manner."[11]

Despite her anguish, however, ER did not make the "We Shall Never Die" pageant the basis of a call to action to rescue the Jews who still remained alive. She used it, instead, to reinforce her warning to Americans that they must refrain from the cruel treatment of minorities in their own country and overcome prejudice toward refugees from abroad:

> All the way through, I thought how important it is in this country that we do not for a moment allow intolerance and cruelty to creep into our dealings with any of our own people, or with any people who have taken refuge among us.[12]

In June ER received a letter from a correspondent warning that Hitler was slaughtering Jews "systematically at the rate of Eight Thousand each day." If something was not done immediately, "there will be no Jews left in Europe at the end of the war." ER replied, "I am just as concerned over this situation as you are," but insisted that "until the war is won, there is very little anyone can do."[13] That was, in essence, the Roosevelt administration's position at the time.

A month later, the journalist and educator Max Lerner sent a telegram to ER asking her to send a message "of hope and encouragement" to the Emergency Conference to Save the Jewish People of Europe planned for July 20–25 in New York. The conference, Lerner told her, would propose plans to the Allied governments "for immediate action" to rescue those who could still be saved.

In response, ER sent a carefully worded message, which expressed deep sympathy for the goals of the conference, but, in a series of qualified statements ("any help that can be extended," "it is hard to say what can be done," "if it is possible to evacuate them"), communicated skepticism about whether much could actually be done to save the European Jews:

> No one in this country will withhold any help that can be extended and I send every good wish to your committee which is trying to save the Jewish people of Europe.

> It is hard to say what can be done at the present time but if you are able to formulate a program of action I am quite sure that the people of this country who have been shocked and horrified by the attitude of the Axis powers toward the Jewish people will be more than glad to do all that they can to alleviate the sufferings of these people in Europe and to help them reestablish themselves in other parts of the world if it is possible to evacuate them.[14]

Although she said it was difficult to know what could be done, she certainly knew about the proposal to create temporary havens for refugees in the United States, Africa, or elsewhere. She may not have known how to rescue Hitler's victims and get them to those camps but, if a way were found, she believed—with greater optimism than the record of the American response to Nazi persecution warranted—Americans would support doing it.

The Emergency Conference to Save the Jewish People resulted in the establishment of the Emergency Committee to Save the Jews of Europe. A fortnight after the conference ER met with Bergson to discuss the goals of the new organization. After the visit, Bergson sent her the report of the Emergency Conference, whose principal recommendation was the establishment of a government rescue agency. ER sent Bergson's letter on to the president who responded: "I do not think this needs an answer at this time."[15]

ER did not reply directly to Bergson's letter, but on August 13, before hearing back from FDR, she wrote a My Day column in which she again expressed her distress at the plight of the Jews, who had "suffered in Europe as has no other group." She emphasized the horrifying scope of the slaughter: "The percentage killed among them in the past few years far exceeds the losses among any of the United Nations in the battles which have been fought throughout the war." She also made a deeper commitment to the need for rescue than she had before, ending her column with a warning about the consequences of not acting:

> I do not know what we can do to save the Jews in Europe and to find them homes, but I know that we will be the sufferers if we let great wrongs occur without exerting ourselves to correct them.

This was not the urgent call for rescue that the Emergency Committee to Save the Jewish People of Europe no doubt hoped for, but it was a stronger statement than Rabbi Wise had persuaded her to make. Apparently moved by the impact of "We Shall Never Die," the appeal from Max Lerner, and her meeting with Bergson, ER now went beyond her version of the administration's mantra—"until the war is won, there is very little anyone can do"—to a moral commitment to the need for rescue.

She said she did not know how it could be done, but it was morally imperative that America make the effort.¹⁶

Most of her August 13 column, however, was not about the suffering of the European Jews and the need for rescue. It was about the shortsightedness of antisemitism. She held a mirror up to her audience. She knew that many of her readers were antisemitic, and she knew that antisemitism was one of the principal obstacles to generating sufficient pressure within and without the administration to persuade it to take effective action to save the Jews. Her goal was to warn her readers about the danger of prejudice, but the way she addresses the issue also reveals the way negative stereotypes of Jews remained part of her consciousness. She began by stating, more strongly than in her 1938 article on the future of the Jews, that the Jews are like every other people in the world:

> There are able people among them, there are courageous people among them, there are people of extraordinary intellectual ability along many lines. There are people of extraordinary integrity and people of great beauty and great charm.
>
> On the other hand, largely because of environment and economic condition, there are people among them who cringe, who are dishonest, who try to take advantage of their neighbors, who are aggressive and unattractive.¹⁷ In other words, they are a cross section of the human race, just as is every other nationality and every other religious group.

Despite her assertion that people with such personal qualities may be found in any group of human beings, in listing the negative characteristics often attributed to Jews in particular, ER reinforced the stereotype. But she also laid the foundation for her argument that whatever her readers might think of Jews, they would be wise to support efforts to rescue those being persecuted in Europe. Many Jews, she pointed out, had lived in Germany, Poland, Romania, or France for generations and regarded themselves as natives of those countries. Any group in any country, including the group to which her readers belonged, could suffer the same fate as the Jews. It was therefore a matter of self-protection for people everywhere to protest "against wholesale persecution, because none of us by ourselves would be strong enough to stand against a big enough group which decided to treat us in the same way."

From the beginning, the struggle in the United States to aid the Jews of Europe had been carried out in the face of widespread antisemitism. While ER directed her efforts both toward rescuing Jews and other refugees from Europe and toward fighting prejudice against Jews and other immigrants in the United States, she functioned within the antisemitic ethos of her time. She had not entirely shed her consciousness of the old Jewish stereotypes, but she also appears at times, as she does in this column, to be deliberately making concessions to her prejudiced readers in order to persuade them of a larger point: yes, you may keep your negative attitudes, but you must, at the same time, respect the human rights of all people. She employed the same strategy when she argued for equal rights for African Americans without publicly advocating an end to social segregation. ER grants her readers a basis for their prejudices (some Jews do have unpleasant characteristics) but urges them to recognize that the crisis of European Jews requires them to look beyond their "individual likes and dislikes." Mass persecution is a problem that "far transcends prejudices or inclinations." All human beings, whether we are fond of them or not, have a right to survive and grow.[18] Americans, like the schoolchildren she had written about in *American Unity*, needed to recognize that the individual rights they held dear could only be preserved if they applied "to all other people as well."[19]

IN NOVEMBER 1943, THE EMERGENCY COMMITTEE's allies in Congress increased the pressure on FDR to take practical steps to rescue the Jews. Will Rogers Jr. and Representative Joseph C. Baldwin, a New York Republican, introduced a resolution calling on the president to establish a rescue commission whose purpose would be to set up refugee camps in Spain, Portugal, Morocco, Switzerland, Turkey, and Sweden as temporary havens where Jews would remain safe until the end of the war. Although the House Foreign Relations Committee failed to act on the resolution, it passed the Senate in a unanimous vote on December 20 and it appeared likely that the House would take up the matter again after the Christmas recess.[20]

Another development, however, obviated the need for the resolution. During the fall of 1943, pressure for vigorous action to rescue European Jews grew within the Roosevelt administration itself. Under Henry Morgenthau's direction, a group of Treasury Department officials, including Josiah E. DuBois Jr., John Pehle, and Randolph Paul (all of them non-Jews), documented the State Department's deliberate subversion of proposed rescue efforts. At the end of December, DuBois prepared a "Report to the Secretary on the Acquiescence of this Government in the Murder of the Jews." In it, DuBois accused Breckinridge Long of systematically blocking the issuing of visas. He also blamed the State Department for obstructing the transfer of funds the World Jewish Congress proposed to use to finance the rescue of Jews from Romania and France. Before submitting the report to the president, Morgenthau softened the title to "Personal Report to the President," but he included the charge that some members of the State Department were antisemitic and the warning that public knowledge of State Department behavior could cause the administration considerable political harm.

The thorough work performed by the Treasury Department officials, together with the growing public and congressional pressure, persuaded FDR to act. At a meeting on

January 16, 1944, at which Morgenthau, Pehle, and Paul presented the report, FDR quickly agreed to the establishment of an independent rescue agency outside the State Department.[21] FDR did not recognize or did not wish to recognize, however, that Breckinridge Long acted deliberately to obstruct rescue efforts. In a memorandum written after the meeting at which Morgenthau and Pehle presented FDR with their report, Pehle wrote, "The President seemed disinclined to believe that Long wanted to stop effective action from being taken." That was the only part of the report the president questioned.[22] His loyalty to Long blinded him. Neither ER nor McDonald had been able to overcome that obstacle.

The War Refugee Board, as it was called, began work with John Pehle as its director. Since its backers considered it unrealistic to ask Congress for funds to support its mandate, the agency's work was hampered by a tiny budget of $250,000 that came from the president's wartime contingency fund and its reliance on private contributions, largely from Jewish groups. Having no powers of its own, the War Refugee Board depended on frequently uncooperative diplomats and military authorities, who were worried that rescue efforts would interfere with combat operations, to carry out its work. Although Edward Stettinius, Welles's successor as undersecretary of state, removed Breckinridge Long from his position, the State Department continued its foot-dragging tactics.

In March 1944, in response to a request from the World Jewish Congress, DuBois and a colleague, Joseph Friedman, drafted a statement for FDR condemning the Nazi program of extermination. Although it was redrafted at FDR's request to make it less heavily focused on the Jews, the final version went much further than any statement FDR or the Allies had made in the past. It identified "the wholesale systematic murder of the Jews of Europe" as "one of the blackest crimes of all history" and promised aggressive efforts at rescue:

> In so far as the necessity of military operations permit this Government will use all means at its command to aid the escape of all intended victims of the Nazi and Jap executioner—regardless of race or religion or color. We call upon the free people of Europe and Asia temporarily to open their frontiers to all victims of oppression. We shall find havens of refuge for them, and we shall find the means for their maintenance and support until the tyrant is driven from their homelands and they may return.[23]

These promises were kept only to a limited degree. Nevertheless, despite the many ways in which its work was hampered, the War Refugee Board managed to rescue an estimated 200,000 Jews during the remaining months of the war.[24] The accomplishments of the War Refugee Board proved that something could be done to save Jews who remained alive. Had it been established earlier and been adequately funded and empowered, many more would have been brought to safety.

THE COMMITMENT TO CREATING TEMPORARY havens to protect victims of Nazi and Japanese persecution for the duration of the war went largely unfulfilled, with one exception. In the summer of 1944, the War Refugee Board established the Emergency Refugee Shelter at Fort Ontario in Oswego, New York. It was the kind of haven that many advocates of rescue, including the Emergency Committee to Save the Jewish People of Europe, had been calling for. Refugees could be speedily sent to such a camp—in Africa, the British colonies, the United States, or elsewhere—free from the delays imposed by visas, affidavits, background checks, and other obstacles. There, they could live out the rest of the war in safety, then return to their homes or be screened and issued the necessary documents for immigration to another country. In her letter to Assistant Secretary of State A. A. Berle Jr., back in June 1940, ER herself had suggested that the anti-Nazi refugees in unoccupied France might be brought to a such a camp in the United States until Congress passed legislation, presumably to permit their temporary or permanent entry into the country, but the proposal fell on deaf ears.

The shelter at Oswego housed approximately 1,000 refugees, most of them Jewish, brought to the United States from southern Italy. It provided ER with a chance to observe one result of the War Refugee Board's work and another opportunity to engage personally with refugees. In September she and Elinor Morgenthau visited the camp. ER was an experienced inspector of public institutions and had learned to burrow behind window dressing temporarily arranged for the visit of an influential person. Her My Day column about her visit to the Fort Ontario camp reflected her keen observation of the details of life in the camp and her desire to understand how it was organized and how it related to the local community of Oswego. Perhaps because she knew that the establishment of the camp might provoke controversy and hoped to encourage the establishment of additional havens for refugees by showing that its cost was minimal, ER emphasized that "only the absolute necessities of life are being provided." Food cost forty-five cents per day for each person and furniture consisted of iron cots with cotton mattresses, army blankets, and "an occasional bare table and a few stiff chairs." She admired the efforts of one woman to make her austere surroundings beautiful. The woman had covered her clothes, which hung from hooks on the wall, with unbleached muslin cloth, then "painted and cut out figures of animals, stars and angels, which were placed all over the plain surface." Other people had cut colorful illustrations out of magazines and newspapers to decorate their walls. "The effort put into it speaks volumes for what these people have undergone," ER wrote, "and for the character which has brought them through. Somehow you feel that if there is any compensation for suffering, it must someday bring them something beautiful in return for all the horrors they have lived through."

She approved of the way the residents of the camp were participating democratically in the building of community, having elected a committee that made decisions about the structure and policies of the camp in close cooperation with Joseph Smart, the camp director. The town of Oswego had also formed a committee to work with the camp committee in managing relations between the two communities in the areas of education, recreation, and business.[25]

ER quickly learned that the camp residents, who had hoped in coming to America to leave the onerous restrictions of life under military occupation or in refugee camps behind them, were frustrated by their confinement. When she asked the head of the camp committee, Dr. Juda Levi, what the greatest problem for the residents was, he replied, "The fence." When she spoke in the camp auditorium she said, "I know the fence troubles you. I know the restrictions are plentiful. But at least the menace of death is no longer everpresent."[26] She made it her job to open up greater opportunities for the education and development of the many talented individuals among the refugees, such as helping to make it possible for some of them to attend Oswego State Teachers College.

During and after her visit to Oswego, ER received many requests from residents of the camp asking for her help with various problems. Characteristically, she took careful note of each person's needs, passed the information she gathered on to Joseph Smart, and asked him what could be done in each case. Smart replied that "practically all of the communications which you received from residents of Fort Ontario during your visit requested services which we were equipped to provide. I have written each person a letter telling them that you were greatly interested in his problem, and that it can be handled by their seeing the appropriate person on our staff."[27]

When Dr. Arthur Ernst, one of the refugees living in the shelter in Oswego, appealed to ER about their being allowed to stay in the United States, she reminded him that they had been told before they came that they were being allowed refuge with the understanding that they would return to their countries of origin after the war. The president had announced this condition when he explained the plan for the shelter in a memorandum to Congress in June 1944. For that reason, only Congress could alter the terms of the agreement, but she assured him, "Some of us hope that Congress may be induced to do so." ER told Dr. Ernst that "the President can not ask Congress to [alter the original agreement] because it might prevent his being able to induce Congress to let other people in on a similar agreement."[28] Oswego would turn out to be the only such haven provided in the United States, but ER still hoped that would not be the case.

Several months after FDR's death on April 12, 1945, and the German surrender on May 6, Joseph Smart resigned as director of the Oswego shelter and formed "Friends of Fort Ontario—Guest Refugees" to take up the cause of the camp residents. ER, Reinhold Niebuhr, United Nations Relief and Rehabilitation Administration (UNRRA) director Herbert H. Lehman, the labor leaders John L. Lewis and David Dubinsky, Albert Einstein, Thomas E. Dewey, and others appeared on the letterhead of the organization. ER and others lobbied Congress and the State and Justice Departments to permit the refugees in the shelter who wished to stay to do so. Ruth Gruber, a journalist who had been sent by Harold Ickes to accompany the refugees on their voyage from Italy to America and who became the chronicler of their experience, became a passionate advocate. Restrictionists in Congress and the Truman administration resisted, however, and it appeared that most of the residents of the shelter would be forced to return to Europe. An appeal initiated by the National Refugee Service and the United Jewish Service in Kansas City that reached Truman through three of his close friends, including his Jewish friend Eddie Jacobson, apparently helped change Truman's attitude. But the crucial factors were the growing awareness of the enormity of the refugee crisis in Europe, the British decision to allow more refugees to enter Great Britain, and Truman's effort to persuade the British to allow a large number of refugees to enter Palestine. How could the United States fail to allow the small number of refugees in Fort Ontario to remain in the United States and still ask other countries to do their part to relieve the refugee crisis? In December 1945 Truman issued a directive ordering government officials to employ "every possible measure" to enable the immigration of refugees to the United States and to make the admittance of the residents of Fort Ontario and refugees in the American-occupied zones of Europe a priority. Truman's directive permitted the acceptance of affidavits from approved nongovernmental organizations for groups of refugees in place of the affidavits from individual sponsors. In late January and early February, the refugees in Fort Ontario who had chosen to stay in the United States were bused to Niagara Falls, Canada, so that they could reenter the United States as immigrants. With the support of friends and relatives and the assistance of religious and refugee organizations, they were resettled in the United States.[29]

Oswego satisfied ER's strong desire to support communal efforts to assist people who were down and out, help them get back on their feet, and open up opportunities through which they could fulfill their aspirations. In that regard, her relationship to the Oswego camp was like her relationship to Arthurdale, the community that she and Clarence Pickett helped establish for unemployed coal miners in the early nineteen thirties. It also foreshadowed her keen interest in the children's villages and kibbutzim she visited during the trips she made to Israel beginning in 1952. In all of these cases, she took a personal interest in the fate of individual people in the community while supporting governmental and nongovernmental programs to help all the members of the community build better lives for themselves.

AFTER THE WAR ER FELT that more could and should have been done to rescue Jews from the Nazis. Moshe Kol, the director of Youth Aliyah, reported after her death that the only time he saw ER falter in responding to a question from the press was when she was asked if in her opinion, everything possible had been done during the presidency of her husband, Franklin D. Roosevelt, to save Jews during the period of the holocaust? She refused to discuss the subject. She evaded the question. I saw it gave her pain. She just could not answer it with the forthrightness she generally afforded the questions of the press.[30]

The fact that she was not very successful in her efforts to pressure her husband and the State Department to admit more Jewish and non-Jewish refugees to the United States does not diminish the significance of the work she did to open America's doors wider. Her reticence about the persecution of the Jews by the Nazis during much of the 1930s and her understated comments on Kristallnacht, on the Ravensbrück camp, and on the news of the Nazi death camps can be only partially explained by the constraints of her position. Her tendency to express herself in response to horrific events in a style of naïve indirectness, whether or not it carried an ironic intention, did not adequately address those crises. There is no doubt, however, about ER's commitment to rescuing Jews, as well as other victims of Nazi persecution. Few people tried harder than ER to save those who suffered persecution, particularly children. But her persistence met with stubborn resistance, and the fact that she was not in a position of power limited her range of action. Looking back after the war, she felt she should have made still greater efforts. In 1952, after visiting a village of immigrants in Israel, she told Ruth Gruber, "I wish I had done more for the Jews. . . . I should have done more."[31] Israel's success in rehabilitating survivors of the Holocaust would give her great joy and a deep sense of relief at seeing the Jewish people renewed.

12

A MARCH TO A BETTER LIFE

"From the land of persecution to the Land of Promise"

THE ONLY PLACES JEWISH refugees from Hitler's Europe were unreservedly welcome were the Jewish communities in Palestine, which urgently needed more settlers to help develop the land and achieve the goal of building a Jewish homeland. Responding to information she received from her Jewish friends, Eleanor Roosevelt began taking an interest in these settlements in the mid-1930s. Most of her Jewish friends and colleagues, with the exception of Justine Polier, did not consider themselves Zionists,[1] but they recognized that with immigration to the United States and other countries severely limited, Palestine offered a refuge. As a result, they often contributed funds to support Jewish settlements there. Like her friends, ER did not advocate a separate Jewish state, but she too regarded the settlements in Palestine as a haven for Jewish refugees fleeing from Nazi persecution.

ER believed that the Balfour Declaration of 1917 had established a legitimate basis for Jewish settlement in Palestine, and as her views on the future of Palestine evolved, the declaration remained the fundamental guide to her thinking. The declaration had been in the form of a letter from Arthur Balfour, the British foreign secretary, to Lord Rothschild, a leader of Britain's Jews, declaring that the British government supported the creation in Palestine of "a national home for the Jewish people." The declaration was incorporated into the British Mandate for Palestine adopted by the League of Nations in 1922.

Many Americans endorsed the Balfour Declaration in the period leading up to the founding of Israel. The United States Congress unanimously passed a joint resolution in 1922 endorsing the establishment of a Jewish national home in Palestine and legislatures in thirty-three states followed suit. Every president from Woodrow Wilson to

Franklin Roosevelt expressed their support. It was, of course, easier for Americans to be enthusiastic about immigration to Palestine than to favor the easing of visa regulations or the liberalization of American immigration quotas.

Although the meaning of the phrase "a national home for the Jewish people" was open to interpretation, the Balfour Declaration stimulated Jewish immigration to Palestine and nurtured the Zionist dream of eventually establishing a Jewish state. The number of Jews in Palestine more than doubled between 1922 and 1931 (from 83,790 to 174,606), many of them fleeing virulent antisemitism in Poland and Romania. After Hitler came to power, large numbers of Jewish immigrants to Israel began coming from central Europe. By 1935 the Jewish population in Palestine had again more than doubled to 375,000.[2] American Jewish groups became a major source of funding for immigration and settlement-building.

FDR favored Jewish immigration to Palestine and pressured the British government several times not to place limits on it. In July 1936, after the influx of Jews seeking to escape persecution in Europe provoked an Arab revolt in Palestine and the British considered restricting Jewish immigration in order to ease tensions, FDR directed the State Department to send a message to the British government saying the United States "would regard suspension of immigration [to Palestine] as a breach of the Mandate." On August 5 he proclaimed, "Men and women of Jewish faith have a right to resettle the land where their faith was born and from which much of modern civilization has emanated." His actions helped persuade the British not to impose new restrictions at that time.[3] In the fall of 1938, in response to an appeal from Rabbi Stephen Wise, FDR once again put pressure on Great Britain to admit more Jews to Palestine.[4] This time his efforts failed; in May 1939 the British issued a White Paper restricting Jewish immigration to 75,000 a year until 1944, when it would end entirely unless the Palestinian Arabs approved of allowing more Jews to enter the country.

ER ALSO OPPOSED BRITISH EFFORTS to restrict immigration to Palestine, but her interest in Palestine as a refuge for Jews had another dimension as well. The Jewish immigrants to Palestine were engaged in cooperative efforts to create new communities. Her attraction to these pioneer settlements reflected the commitment to community-building that led her to collaborate with Clarence Pickett and the American Friends Service Committee (AFSC) on resettling out-of-work coal miners. That interest also prepared her to support the work of several Jewish organizations that provided practical training to European Jews. ER's close friend, the labor leader Rose Schneiderman, solicited ER's interest in ORT,[5] an organization "For Constructive Relief for the Jews of Eastern and Central Europe." ORT was established in 1880 to train European Jews to support themselves as skilled laborers or farmers. Its rehabilitation programs perfectly expressed

ER's belief in preparing impoverished or displaced persons to help themselves. In March 1937 several leaders of Women's American ORT, including Schneiderman, wrote to ER thanking her for speaking at an ORT dinner several years before and describing the progress ORT had made since that time. ORT, they wrote, "now maintains over 300 training centers, teaching Jews trades and agriculture in the countries of Europe, where their position is so precarious. Through this training they become productive citizens of their country; or, if they emigrate, they go with a skill in hand." Noting the "interesting resemblance" between some of ORT's work and the New Deal subsistence homestead program, they invited ER to the group's tenth anniversary luncheon in New York and asked her to speak briefly about the Resettlement Administration, the government agency that oversaw the establishment of subsistence homesteads such as Arthurdale. After ER regretted that she would not be able to attend, ORT's president, Emily Rosenstein, asked her to send a message like the "beautiful paragraph" from ER's previous speech:

> [It] is more worthwhile to help people to help themselves than to give simple charity. After all, if we help a condition which exists, like starvation, there is really not so much merit; but if we have the vision to prevent it and to help people beforehand, we have shown three great qualities, imagination, sympathy, and vision. And those three qualities, all of you who have worked in this work before have already shown.[6]

This approach to assisting people in need by helping them acquire the skills to help themselves was identical to the AFSC approach to human problems that ER so strongly endorsed.

Having failed to get ORT on ER's calendar for 1937, Rosenstein tried to induce her to speak the following year, even offering to change the date of ORT's annual luncheon to make ER's attendance possible. ER again sent her regrets, saying that she would be away.[7]

Her response to another invitation suggests she may have had other reasons for turning down the invitations to speak at the ORT luncheons. In April 1938, Schneiderman wrote ER that she had accepted the chairmanship of the National Women's Committee of the Jewish National Fund, which sought to raise $100,000 to establish a Leon Blum Colony in Palestine. Shocked by the crisis faced by European Jewry, a crisis intensified by the effect of the Anschluss on March 12 on Austrian Jews, Schneiderman decided she must act. She felt the need to explain to ER that she was doing so not as a Zionist but because something had to be done:

> It is the first time I have undertaken any work in connection with the Jewish cause..., first because I never believed in Zionism. I am not a Zionist today. I love my adopted land and don't want to live in any other country of the world. But whatever one's

philosophy may be, one has to face the stark realities affecting the Jewish people of Europe. Refuge must be given them wherever possible. Palestine of course affords the kind of haven, although it doesn't offer complete security, nevertheless, it is a place where the young men and women of Jewish faith can reestablish themselves and in cooperation with one another, work out their destinies.

Schneiderman's statement sums up the viewpoint of most of ER's Jewish friends prior to 1945. Schneiderman went on to ask if ER would come as the guest of honor to an afternoon tea planned by the Women's Committee for the end of May or early June 1938.[8] ER was interested but asked Tommy to clear Schneiderman's invitation with the State Department. George Summerlin, chief of protocol, replied that, while ER was free to use her own judgment, he did not think that "any particular purpose would be served" by her attending such a tea:

The President and Secretary of State are constantly bombarded with requests for their support in behalf of organizations interested in the colonization of Palestine. They have consistently taken the stand, however, that in view of the troubled situation in Palestine, and since American Jewry itself appears to be divided regarding the advisability of further colonization there, it would be unwise for them to appear to "take sides."

He also thought it would be unwise, given "the urgent needs of many of our fellow citizens," for ER to publicly approve a campaign "to raise funds for a particular group of citizens in certain foreign countries."[9]

Once again ER bowed to the constraints of her position and took Summerlin's advice, but to Schneiderman, she simply made the excuse that May and June were too "crowded with engagements." Undiscouraged, Schneiderman wrote again on May 18, 1938, asking if ER could speak at a fundraising dinner for the Leon Blum Colony in November or December on a day scheduled to fit her calendar. "The campaign, if successful, will make it possible for at least 10,000 young people to find a refuge," she told her.

ER again put Schneiderman off but this time was much more encouraging, telling Schneiderman that if the committee set a date, she would "try very hard to come." In September Tommy wrote to Schneiderman that ER could attend the Leon Blum dinner if it were held on December 6, 1938. The committee changed the date they had previously set, and ER attended the dinner. Schneiderman wrote to ER afterward that the dinner was a great success, clearing approximately $23,000.[10]

It is not clear why ER decided to ignore the earlier advice she had received from the State Department and accept the invitation to the fundraising dinner for the Blum Colony. Perhaps the worsening situation of Jews in Germany and Austria, as well as the prospect of creating a refuge for 10,000 young people, persuaded her to use "her own judgment," as Summerlin had said she was free to do. Writing in My Day after the event, however, she was careful not to directly endorse the project. As she often had on other occasions when responding to potentially controversial foreign policy matters, she turned the spotlight on American problems in need of remedy. Rather than talk about aiding the resettlement of Jews in Palestine, she called her readers' attention to the problem of minority rights in the United States. The speakers at the dinner upset her deeply, she said, for they all celebrated how fortunate Americans were to live in a free country, when in fact not all Americans were free:

> Are you free if you cannot vote, if you cannot be sure that the same justice will be meted out to you as to your neighbor, if you are expected to live on a lower level than your neighbor and to work for lower wages, if you are barred from certain places and from certain opportunities?[11]

It became easier for ER to support causes such as the Blum Colony and ORT after the outbreak of war in Europe as FDR steered the nation gradually toward active opposition to Hitler. In November 1940, she spoke to 1,500 at a benefit dinner in Chicago marking ORT's sixtieth anniversary. She spoke fervently, praising ORT for helping people acquire skills that enabled them to "start again in new ways of endeavor." She herself compared ORT's work explicitly to the programs of the AFSC.[12] ER continued to support ORT's fundraising efforts throughout the war after it moved its activities to allied and South American nations and trained workers to produce weapons and other materials for the military.[13]

ER also appeared and spoke regularly at events sponsored by the United Jewish Appeal (UJA) beginning at least as early as November 1941 and mentioned some of them in My Day. Since January 1939, the UJA had served as the fundraising organization for the Jewish Joint Distribution Committee (JDC), which worked closely with the AFSC in conducting relief and rescue programs in Europe; the United Palestine Appeal (UPA), which aided immigration to Palestine; and the National Coordinating Committee for Aid to Refugees and Emigrants Coming from Germany (later the National Refugee Service, NRS), which helped refugees settle in the United States. Between 1939 and 1945, the UJA helped rescue over 160,000 Jews from extermination by the Nazis and brought relief to thousands of displaced Jews.[14] During this period, the UJA reached out to Gentiles as well as Jews by expressing its goals in nonsectarian terms and emphasizing the contribution the JDC, the UPA, and the NRS were making to defending democratic values and winning the war. Prominent Gentiles, like New York governor and presidential candidate Thomas E. Dewey, as well as FDR, endorsed the UJA campaigns. The UJA "sustains the spirit of freedom and democracy," FDR proclaimed in 1943. ER joined in this chorus of praise, and her participation in UJA meetings and her statements of support both during and after the war helped draw large audiences to UJA events and encourage both Jews and Gentiles to contribute.¹⁵

ER's close friend Adele Levy, who had worked with ER on the Wagner-Rogers bill and the United States Committee for the Care of European Children (USCCEC), was the first national chair of the Women's Division of the UJA and helped ensure that ER played an active role. "Of all the things in which I am interested, this organization, which helps care for the persecuted Jews in Europe, is closest to my heart," Levy told ER.¹⁶ It became a tradition for ER to serve as the guest of honor at the opening meeting of the Women's Division of the UJA each year. After the 1945 meeting, ER praised the contributors to the UJA who tightened their belts in order to donate more to the cause: "There are not many of us who give so generously that we make an actual sacrifice and perhaps even have to ask the family as a whole to share in that sacrifice."¹⁷

ER'S DEVOTION TO ORT AND the UJA expressed her desire to do what she could personally for the persecuted Jews of Europe. But the Jewish organization that would eventually come to mean the most to her was Youth Aliyah. The work of Youth Aliyah was closely aligned with several of ER's deepest concerns: the welfare of children, providing people with the tools to live independent productive lives, and the creation of democratic communities. Beginning in the early 1930s, Youth Aliyah rescued Jewish children from Nazi persecution in Germany and later from other countries. The organization brought the children to Palestine, where they received training in agriculture and various trades and became the builders of new communities and eventually a new nation. In Modern Hebrew *aliyah* is the word for "elevation" or "going up," and is used both for ascending to the *bimah*, the platform in the synagogue where the Torah scroll is read, and for moving to Israel. As the British journal *Palestine* put it, "This movement of the youth from the land of persecution to the Land of Promise bears something of the character of the old pilgrimage. It is a march to a better life."¹⁸

Youth Aliyah was led by the dynamic Henrietta Szold, the daughter of a Baltimore rabbi. Szold's response to the conditions of America's urban immigrant population mirrored the efforts of Jane Addams, Lillian Wald, and the other leaders of the Progressive reform movement in the United States. When Szold began working as a teacher, she recognized that the Russian immigrants arriving in Baltimore did not understand English and lacked the skills necessary to earn a living. To meet their needs, she founded a night school where she taught English, civics, and vocational skills like dressmaking and bookkeeping. Szold's school was similar in many ways to the settlement houses founded by Addams and Wald.

From her students, Szold learned about Zionism. She began to read Zionist literature and contribute to Zionist publications. In 1909 she visited Palestine, where she encountered some of the same conditions that she and other social reformers were addressing in America's immigrant population. She was shocked by the poverty, poor sanitation, and disease among both Jewish and Arab residents of Palestine and became a passionate advocate for aiding the Jewish settlements in that land.

In 1912 Szold founded Hadassah, the Women's Zionist Organization of America, whose motto was "The Healing of My People." Building on the experience of the social reform movement in the United States, Hadassah did pioneering work in Palestine in the field of public health. It sent the first American nurses there just ten months after the organization's founding. Szold asked the nurses to visit Lillian Wald's Henry Street Settlement in New York before they left for Palestine to study its methods and, following the Henry Street model, they settled in a poor neighborhood of Jerusalem and offered health services to its inhabitants.[19] Over the years, Hadassah established modern medical facilities in Palestine modeled on American practices. These facilities served both Jews and Arabs. In 1920, Szold moved permanently to Palestine to oversee Hadassah projects; and in the 1930s, when Hadassah became the American sponsor of Youth Aliyah, Szold took over the direction of its operations in Palestine.[20] By the 1930s Hadassah had become the largest Zionist organization in the United States and an important player in shaping the development of Jewish settlement in Palestine.[21] It also shaped the lives of many Jewish women in the United States, offering them a mission that was both idealistic and practical.[22]

Hadassah's work naturally appealed to ER, whose earliest experience assisting impoverished people had been at New York City's Rivington Street settlement house. Like Wald, who was one of the leaders who inspired her to work for progressive causes in the 1920s, ER became a strong advocate of public health programs in the United States. It was probably her close friend Elinor Morgenthau, who shared ER's interest in public health, who first encouraged her to speak at Hadassah events. When she and Morgenthau spoke to 4,000 women at Hadassah's annual convention in 1934, ER praised Hadassah's efforts to raise the level of health care in Palestine.[23]

ER's association with Youth Aliyah began at a time when the need to find places of refuge for Jews had become acute. Efforts to permit more refugee children to enter the United States would fail. Youth Aliyah offered another way to rescue them. ER first mentioned Youth Aliyah in a My Day column in June 1938 when she praised the organization for training young people in a two-year course that covered "every department of rural work and the running of a home," thereby offering "real hope for future security to children many of whom have come from areas where life has been extremely precarious." Youth Aliyah, like ORT, was doing the kind of work she admired the Quakers for doing in the United States: the children were being "helped to independence," not given charity.[24] Capitalizing immediately on ER's My Day column, Hadassah issued a press release the following day under the headline, "Mrs. Roosevelt Lauds Project for Removing Refugee Children to Palestine."[25]

In the fall of 1938, in an effort to further stimulate ER's interest, Junior Hadassah sent her a pamphlet about Meier Shfeyah, one of the youth villages established by Youth Aliyah in Palestine. ER responded by describing the village in My Day:

> In a little pamphlet which was sent me by Junior Hadassah, there are some pictures of a home where underprivileged children and the children of refugees are being brought up.... The children, with the guidance of a director and instructors, carry on the entire life of the village. They have to have their ups and downs, for we know that even in well regulated villages the unexpected will happen. They have to deal with the vagaries of the other children and the elders in the community; with the creatures of the animal world and with dame nature.
>
> These children are certainly receiving a training and preparation for real life which is superior to that given by most schools.[26]

Later, in recognition of the interest ER had expressed in their community, the children of Meier Shfeyah created a book with a cover of inlaid Palestinian olive wood and dedicated it to "The First Lady of the Land of Liberty." The book, handwritten in English, contained pictures and stories about the lives of the 165 refugee children at Meier Shfeyah. It also incorporated products of the work the children did in their farm school and domestic science classes, including a sheaf of wheat with a bit of the soil in which it was grown and pieces of embroidered material used in making the girls' dresses. It is hard to imagine a more tactile representation of the lives of these children. In presenting the gift to ER in February 1940, Nell Ziff, national president of Junior Hadassah, noted that communities such as Meier Shfeyah not only assisted refugee children to become self-reliant adults, but also contributed to the task of "re-establishing the Jewish Homeland."[27] In accepting the book, ER recognized its significance in illustrating how such children could acquire skills and become self-supporting. She planned to show the book to the president and "also to a great many children in this country in underprivileged places where they are helping to rebuild their lives, because I think it will give them courage."[28] ER loaned the book to the Palestine Pavilion at the New York World's Fair where it was displayed in a case at the center of the Hall of Culture and seen by thousands of people during the 1940 season.[29] Given the situation of Jews in Europe, it is hard to overestimate the importance to American Jews of having the blessing of the First Lady for the work they were doing to nurture the settlements in Palestine.

In 1938, a month after ER had written about Meier Shfeyah in her column, the outbreak of violence in Germany on Kristallnacht made Youth Aliyah's mission still more urgent. Marian Greenberg, National Youth Aliyah Committee chairman, made that mission more vivid to ER when she asked ER to send a message to be read as part of a national broadcast marking Szold's seventy-eighth birthday. With her request,

Greenberg enclosed a Hadassah pamphlet that called attention to the reasons Jewish parents in Central Europe were willing to send their children to Palestine in the care of Youth Aliyah: "Suppose your child were deprived of the right to go to school, learn a trade or profession, or earn a livelihood?" The pamphlet reported that by 1938 Youth Aliyah had brought more than 2,200 Jewish boys and girls between the ages of fifteen and seventeen out of Germany, Austria, and Poland and trained them in agricultural settlements and at trade schools in Palestine. It now sought 1,000 American sponsors to rescue 1,000 additional children over the next three months. In response to Greenberg's letter, ER sent a message for use in the broadcast in which she praised the "intelligence and self-sacrifice" with which Szold carried on her work and wished her continued success.[30]

In early January 1940, Elinor Morgenthau helped arrange a meeting between Gisela Warburg, national chairman for Youth Aliyah, and ER at the White House. Warburg and two of her colleagues were seeking to establish an ongoing relationship between ER and Youth Aliyah by inviting her to head the National Youth Aliyah Advisory Committee then in process of formation. ER said that if she accepted the position, she would not have time to attend meetings or do any work. Tamar de Sola Pool, Hadassah's national president, assured her that this would not be necessary. What they asked of her was to lend her name and to mention the work of Hadassah whenever she could. Under those conditions, ER was "very glad indeed to accept." Elinor Morgenthau also accepted a position on the advisory committee, as did Clarence Pickett.[31]

Having secured ER's agreement, Hadassah set about forming the rest of the committee, using ER's name to encourage others to join. With ER on board, Greenberg wrote to Szold, "the rest was plain sailing." The primary reason for creating the advisory committee, Greenberg said, was to "dress up the stationary" that Hadassah used when appealing to the British Colonial Secretary to issue more certificates for the young refugees sponsored by Youth Aliyah to enter Palestine. The certificates were essential to Youth Aliyah's continued operation.[32] The dressed-up letterhead may have helped. Greenberg was able to tell ER in early May 1940 that the British government had granted Youth Aliyah 1,600 new certificates. "In these dark days," she said, "one may derive some comfort from the realization that the work of rescue and reconstruction is still going on even if it is impossible to keep pace with the grinding forces of destruction."[33]

Although ER agreed to head its advisory committee, mentioned its work favorably in My Day, and responded enthusiastically to reports of its progress, Youth Aliyah would not become deeply important to her until her first visit to Israel in 1952.

IN 1940, WHEN THE HADASSAH leaders appealed to ER to join the Youth Aliyah advisory committee, ER asked one question: "Is there room in Palestine?" The question reflected the views of Isaiah Bowman, the Johns Hopkins geographer whom FDR had commissioned in 1938 to appraise possible sites for refugee settlements around the world. Bowman had told her that Palestine could not even sustain the population it already had, much less absorb a large number of new immigrants. The leaders of Hadassah, however, assured her that the answer to her question was "yes."

Bowman's opinion of Palestine's limited capacity did not discourage ER from joining the advisory committee, but Bowman's views continued to shape her attitude toward immigration to Palestine for some time to come.[34] His influence is evident in ER's answer to a letter she received in June 1943 in which the correspondent proposed that the United States pressure Great Britain to allow Jewish refugees from Nazi-occupied Europe to enter Palestine. ER categorically rejected the idea that large-scale immigration to Palestine was practical: "they would soon starve if Palestine were their destination, as Palestine can not support any more people."[35]

Jewish leaders, however, continued their effort to dissuade ER of that view. After Rose Halprin, chairman of the Post-War Planning Committee of the American Zionist Emergency Council, and several of her colleagues met with ER in late November 1943 to discuss the issue of immigration to Palestine, Halprin wrote to tell her that "several experts, renowned in their respective fields, have of recent years reported on the absorptive capacity of Palestine and have indicated that the country could, through scientific development, absorb a population several times the present number." Halprin enclosed a six-page report drawing on the work of these experts.

The report noted that the ruins of towns, aqueducts, and terraced hillsides suggested that Palestine had once sustained a population of three to four million people, many more than the 1,500,000 it did at the end of 1943. The absorptive capacity of a country, the report argued, depended not just on natural resources but also on "the energy and the creative ability of its inhabitants." Given "modern technical advantages" and "a hard working and intelligent population," Palestine could reasonably be expected to sustain a population well above the number it supported in ancient times. Currently only 1.5 percent of the land in Palestine was irrigated. American experts estimated that ten times that amount could be irrigated by drawing on existing water sources. Much more could be irrigated by tapping into newly discovered below-ground sources and by bringing water from the Jordan River to the large unsettled areas around Beersheba. The credibility of the report was no doubt strengthened in ER's mind by citing the large-scale irrigation project similar to the Tennessee Valley Authority (TVA) proposed for Palestine by Dr. Walter S. Lowdermilk, assistant chief of the U.S. Soil Conservation Bureau. TVA was a program dear to the hearts of both FDR and ER, and the idea of applying New Deal strategies to the economic development of Palestine would have been very appealing to ER. The irrigation project proposed by Lowdermilk, the report estimated, could expand the farming population of Palestine from approximately 800,000 to 2 million or more.

The report also cited the rapid expansion of industry in Palestine (production having increased fourfold between 1933 and 1942), the abundance of oil reaching

Haifa through a pipeline running from Iraq, and the hydroelectric projects of the Jordan Valley.

Although the country imported more than it exported at that time, the fact that most of the capital invested in the country came with the immigrants themselves or was contributed by Jews abroad meant that the Jewish settlements in Palestine, unlike other development projects, were unencumbered by a large debt burden. Based on the settlers' recent achievements, the report concluded that "a large increase in the Jewish population is possible without displacing the native population." In fact, the report said, the increase in the Jewish population of Palestine had resulted in an increase in the Arab population because the Jews had introduced improvements in health care and in other areas that had lengthened the life expectancy of the Arabs.

ER wrote on the letter: "A very convincing statement" and sent the report on to FDR, who replied: "I wish you would have a talk with Dr. Isaiah Bowman about this."[36] After ER spoke with Bowman, Bowman sent her a follow-up letter in which he told her that after "a careful reading" of the report Halprin had sent her, he had concluded that it "provides no facts, arguments, or points of view not already well known and carefully weighed." In a three-page memorandum enclosed with his letter, rather than repeating his argument about Palestine's absorptive capacity, he chose instead to focus on the political problems that mass immigration to Palestine would greatly intensify and the larger issue of how to rescue Jews under threat of annihilation.

Bowman's analysis of the political situation drove to the heart of the problem. A large expansion of the Jewish population of Palestine would require an "increasing use of force" to defend it, and, like other observers at the time, he did not anticipate that the Palestinian Jews would be capable of managing the task themselves: "Palestine, as a Jewish State (which is more than a Jewish Home) would not have the power to defend itself against wider regional opposition." If Great Britain were to agree to the establishment of a Jewish state, it would be unlikely to do so unless the United States joined it in guaranteeing its security. And, if the United States became a joint guarantor, it would become responsible "for the consequences of the political acts" of that state: "Are we prepared as a nation to do that? Who can guarantee the willingness of the American people to continue to back up guarantees to Palestine, a small and chronically troubled country 6,000 miles away?" The answer to this question would eventually be "yes," but in 1944, in the midst of a global war, it seemed unlikely that most Americans would favor assuming such a burden.

Another issue concerned the role to be played by the new world organization being planned by the Allies to keep the peace after the war. If that organization were going to succeed, Bowman wrote, it could only do so by applying force justly: "The Arab world would feel deeply wronged by the mingling of constantly expanding Jewish claims and rights on the one hand, and the wider commercial and military interests of the guaranteeing powers on the other."

Bowman professed deep sympathy for the Jews ("Only a heart of stone would deny the Jews full and sympathetic consideration") but argued that their future depended on multiple solutions, not just on immigration to Palestine. "Is it in their long-term interest," he asked, "to create a growing problem of security in the Near East that may require for its solution the more or less immediate use of American bayonets?" Perhaps because of Bowman's failure, after a long search, to find a practical and politically acceptable area of the world for the large-scale settlement of Jewish refugees, he did admit that "The answer may prove to be *yes*, if there is no other way," but "in all the wide world" did there have to be "a solution by force in just this particular area of 10,000 square miles?" The answer to that, he added, was inevitably, "It is not just 10,000 square miles, but the Holy Land!" And "From that point on, emotion controls the argument, emotion supported by 'wrongs too deep for tears.'" Bowman cautioned that statesmen had to consider other factors in addition to emotion and not forget that "emotion also affects the Arabs and the Americans as well as the Jews."

Halprin's memorandum and Bowman's response to it educated ER to the difficulty of finding a solution for the future of Palestine. Eventually she would conclude, as Bowman put it, that "there is no other way," except for the creation of a Jewish state, but she had not yet reached that point. She directed her secretary to "Keep statements for reference."[37]

ALTHOUGH SHE WOULD REMAIN SKEPTICAL of Palestine's capacity to absorb large numbers of additional settlers, ER was appalled at the measures the British took to prevent Jewish refugees from reaching Palestine. In December 1941 the *Struma*, an unseaworthy and overcrowded ship commissioned by the New Zionist Organization and the Zionist underground military group, the Irgun, and carrying hundreds of Jewish refugees, arrived in Istanbul from Constanza, Romania. The ship remained in port for seventy days, while the passengers appealed to the British authorities to issue certificates for entry into Palestine. The British, fearing there might be spies and subversives among the refugees who lacked visas and seeking to limit immigration to Palestine as much as possible, refused to issue the certificates. The Turkish authorities refused to allow the passengers to land or permit the repair of the ship's engine, which had died. On February 23, 1942, after the Turks towed the ship out of the harbor into the Black Sea, a Russian submarine apparently torpedoed it by mistake and it sank, carrying 768 Jews to their deaths, including over 100 children. Only one passenger survived.[38]

On March 8, Justine Polier wrote a letter to ER appealing for help and enclosing a memorandum citing the sinking of the *Struma* as the most tragic consequence of Britain's refusal to permit Jews to enter Palestine. British "policy not only violates all considerations of justice and humanity by virtually condemning to death these anti-fascist Jewish refugees," the memorandum stated, "but is in defiance of military necessity. For, many of these refugees who have gone to their deaths or are languishing in internment are able-bodied men with military training or skilled technicians and laborers whose contributions to the war effort could be an extremely vital one." Not even "the logic of official policy" demanded the exclusion of these refugees, because the war was preventing "even the limited immigration quota permitted by the British White Paper policy" from being filled.[39]

ER immediately sent the memorandum on to Sumner Welles, then undersecretary of state, telling him it seemed "perfectly shocking" to her: "Why, because of a technicality of not having visas when these people come from countries where they can not get visas anyway, they should be turned back I cannot see. It just seems to me cruel beyond words."

Welles sent her a statement by the British undersecretary of state for the colonies placing blame on the Jews on board the *Struma* who had sailed to Turkey with the "intention of effecting their entry illegally into Palestine" and on the Turks and the submarine that sank the ship. Welles added: "This is one of the most shocking tragedies which have taken place in a tragic year. Naturally I am doing everything I can to prevent a recurrence, but the British are adamant in their refusal to prevent any increased immigration into Palestine for fear of Arab unrest." Welles's response did not satisfy ER. "Why not try to give asylum and guarantee that such refugees will continue to Africa and South America?" she replied. "This policy is so cruel that if it were generally known in this country, it would increase the dislike of Great Britain which is already too prevalent."[40] As Justine Polier said in an oral history interview many years later after reading from these letters, this was among ER's sharpest remarks on the plight of Jewish refugees, expressed in an irate tone that ER rarely adopted.[41]

In response, Welles said he wished "your suggestion could in fact be carried out," but a lack of ships "to transport these unfortunate people either to Africa or to South America" and the "well-founded fear" of the nations in South America that there "would undoubtedly be some subversive agents planted by the German authorities" among the refugees, made this impossible.[42] The State Department, he said, echoing Ambassador Steinhardt's influential 1940 warning, had "reason to know by experience that when the Gestapo permits a quantity of refugees, such as that on board the *Struma*, to leave Nazi-controlled territory, it does so only with some ulterior purpose in mind." If "safe shipping communications were available," Africa would make a more practical destination, he said, but that solution also posed problems because no facilities existed for caring for the refugees in British-controlled east Africa, the most likely destination. Furthermore, the refugees themselves possessed no resources or means of making a living in countries where they did not speak the native language. Months of preparation would be needed to create conditions adapted to the refugees' needs. Nevertheless, Welles said he would ask the Intergovernmental Committee on Refugees to seek a solution.⁴³ Welles did so, but it did not lead to any alternative plan for the refugees trying to reach Palestine.⁴⁴

Welles also wrote to the British Foreign Office about the *Struma* tragedy and forwarded to ER the reply defending British policy that he received. The Foreign Office, which described the refugees on board the *Struma* as "of enemy nationality," said that a change in British policy on the immigration of Jews to Palestine "at a critical moment of the war would involve a risk of dangerous repercussions on the non-Jewish populations of the Middle East by which the whole conduct of the war might be affected." The message ended with a pointed recognition that the United States was in no position to criticize others on the issue of refugees: "The Government of the United States is, of course, aware that Her Majesty's Government is not alone in finding it necessary to restrict emigration from enemy countries under the stress of war."⁴⁵

The British responded more generously to appeals from Hadassah to assist a large group of Jewish child refugees stranded in Teheran. The British issued certificates for their immigration to Palestine, but Iraq would not permit the children to be transported through its territory. In early December 1942, Hadassah president Tamar de Sola Pool asked Elinor Morgenthau to deliver an urgent appeal to ER asking her to intervene on behalf of this group and to urge the president to do so. Although ER did not play a major role in Hadassah's effort, her attention to the problem no doubt increased pressure on the State Department to find a way to transport the children to Palestine. Hadassah remained in touch with her during the rescue effort through Morgenthau. Ultimately, Paul Alling, who handled the matter for the State Department's Near Eastern Division, put Hadassah in touch with the War Shipping Administration, which in turn referred the organization to John McClay at the British Ministry of War Transport. McClay succeeded in finding British ships to take the children first from Basra to Karachi, then through the Suez Canal to Haifa. On February 19, 1943, de Sola Pool and Gisela Warburg wrote to ER with the news that "the 835 Polish refugee children who had been stranded in Teheran, and in whose fate you took such a deep interest, are about to arrive in Haifa."⁴⁶

BRITISH COOPERATION IN THE RESCUE of the Teheran children was an exception. As a result of the severe restrictions Great Britain placed upon the immigration of Jews to Palestine, pressure continued to grow in the United States to persuade Great Britain to change its policy. In April 1944, Will Rogers Jr. invited ER to join the Sponsoring Committee of the American League for a Free Palestine, an organization formed by Peter Bergson to support the creation of a Jewish state in Palestine. Aware of ER's "deep appreciation of the inhuman disaster which confronts the Hebrew people of Europe," he felt sure she would want to back "this new freedom movement." The purpose of the organization, he told her, was to open Palestine to the immigration of European Jews, promote the organization of a Hebrew Palestine Army that would participate in the invasion of Europe and the occupation of Germany, and "secure recognition of the Hebrew people of Europe and Palestine as a nation with rights of representation in the councils of the United Nations and at the peace table." Both for political reasons and because ER continued to believe Isaiah Bowman's negative assessment of the absorptive capacity of Palestine, she did not feel she could accept Rogers's invitation: "There are diplomatic angles in which I should not be involved," she told him. She advised that the first of the organization's three purposes "should be qualified since there seems to be a limit to the number of people the land at present will support without aid."[47]

THE UNSETTLED QUESTION OF THE future of Palestine made some supporters of FDR worry that Jewish voters would turn away from him in the presidential election of 1944. In early October, Freda Kirchwey, editor of *The Nation*, wrote a note to ER expressing her alarm. She reported that many of her Jewish friends were telling her that unless "prompt measures are taken," many Jewish voters who voted for FDR in 1940 would vote for the Republican candidate, Thomas E. Dewey. They reported that Dewey's Jewish advisers were planning an attack on Roosevelt "for failure to do anything effective about Palestine (whether he could or not is beside the point!)." In addition, Dewey would come out in support of a Jewish Commonwealth bridging both sides of the Jordan River, thus "outbidding all Democratic promises."

ER responded to Kirchwey's letter on October 4, telling her that she had shown her letter to FDR and he had told her, "He does not know what can be done."[48] FDR was reluctant to take a position on the future of Palestine that contradicted the policy of America's British ally in the midst of the war, but the political pressure on him made it necessary for him to act. On October 11, at a meeting with Stephen Wise at the White House, FDR agreed to send a letter to be read at the Zionist Organization of America convention that stated: "I know how long and ardently the Jewish people have worked and prayed for the establishment of Palestine as a free and Democratic Jewish commonwealth. I am convinced that the American people give their support to this aim, and if reelected, I shall help to bring about its realization."[49] After the publication of the statement, Kirchwey wrote to ER again, telling her how pleased she was that the president had sent "such a forthright, vigorous statement" to the convention. Kirchwey's Jewish friends who previously expressed concern about weakening support for FDR "now say that they have direct evidence of a shift in feeling among the Jewish organizations they run or are in touch with." In the end, FDR received support from 90 percent of Jewish voters in 1944, just as he had in 1940.[50]

In March 1945, ER received a letter from a woman in Los Angeles who complained that FDR's promise during the campaign of a homeland for the Jews in Palestine remained unfulfilled. ER's reply again shows that she had absorbed Isaiah Bowman's views on the problems a Jewish homeland in Palestine would face: "You seem in no way to understand the difficulties about Palestine. Palestine is not a land cut off from the rest of the world. It is a land surrounded on all sides by lands owned by the Arabs." While the president sympathized with the wish of the Jews for a homeland, ER told the woman, he also recognized the significance of Palestine to the Arabs, not only for those who lived there but for the Arabs as a people. For the Jews, "Palestine is their homeland and because of its history, it has a religious meaning to them, but unfortunately it also has a religious meaning to the Arabs." If the Arabs were "not at least friendly to an increase in the Jewish population in Palestine," then other nations would have to guarantee the security of Palestine with military force. Although the Jews had said they could defend themselves, the Arab superiority in numbers "might mean a massacre of everyone now in Palestine if anything is done which is contrary to the Arabs' desire." It was a problem that the UN needed to address, ER concluded, not just Great Britain and the United States.[51]

After the war, when President Harry S. Truman appointed ER to the first American delegation to the newly established United Nations organization, she would find herself in the midst of the debate about how to handle this complex and troubling problem.

13

THE POSTWAR REFUGEE CRISIS AND THE FUTURE OF PALESTINE

"A duty to lead"

THE DEATH OF FRANKLIN ROOSEVELT on April 12, 1945, liberated Eleanor Roosevelt both from the responsibilities of being the First Lady and from the restraints on her freedom to speak her own mind that the position had imposed upon her. Initially, it also reduced her influence, although her decision to continue to write her My Day and If You Ask Me columns provided her with a medium for reaching a wide audience. Continuing invitations to speak to a wide range of groups also gave her many opportunities to express her views. The fact that she had established herself in fields of political action well beyond the traditional role of First Lady meant that she could carry on those activities into the post–White House years. But a new field of action opened up for her as well. In December 1945 President Harry Truman appointed ER to the American delegation to the United Nations. Established shortly after FDR's death at an international conference in San Francisco, the UN was holding its first session in London in January 1946. Its founding had opened a path toward the establishment of an international legal system and mechanisms for keeping the peace that ER and her colleagues in the international women's peace movement had promoted in the 1920s and 1930s. The refusal of the United States to join the League of Nations in 1919 had contributed to its failure, but this time the United States took a leading role in the founding of the new international organization. FDR had been its chief architect during its planning phase.

At first, ER was unsure that she possessed the skills necessary to perform effectively in her new position, but she soon proved herself wrong. She studied every briefing paper given to her by the State Department and brought the moral commitment, passion, patience, tact, and guile that she had developed over her long years of political activism to her task. The rest of the American delegation consisted of a bipartisan group of prominent men: Secretary of State James Byrnes, former secretary of state Edward Stettinius, Senate Foreign Relations Committee chair Tom Connally (D-TX), and ranking Republican member of the Senate Foreign Relations Committee senator Arthur Vandenberg (R-MI), plus several alternates, including the future secretary of state John Foster Dulles. They regarded ER's appointment as a public relations ploy by Truman in order to draw political capital from her late husband's popularity and from her own. They assigned her to represent the United States on the Third Committee, which dealt with Social, Humanitarian, and Cultural Affairs and where, as she put it, they didn't think she could "do much harm."[1]

But she would not accept obscurity. Even after she began to assume the responsibilities of her new position, ER knew that she possessed a power she had not had before: "For the first time in my life I can say just what I want," she told reporters on the ship taking the delegation to London. "For your information it is wonderful to feel free."[2] The journalist S. J. Woolf, writing about ER after she had served on the delegation for a year, reported that she listened attentively to the speeches of the other delegates on the Third Committee, and when she disagreed with what was being said, she "could barely disguise her feelings." Even before the speech had ended, she would pick up the triangular "United States" sign in front of her and wave it to indicate her desire to respond.[3]

It turned out that the first explosive issue to come before the UN at its inaugural meeting in London was where the thousands of people uprooted by the war should go. After the liberation of the death camps and slave-labor camps, thousands of people, including many Jews, wandered through the devastated cities and countryside looking for something to eat. Some tried to return home; some feared to return home and fled westward. The Allies gathered up many of them and placed them in displaced person (DP) camps where they waited for the occupying forces to determine their future. The problem of where they would all go would take another three years to solve. ER played a prominent role in seeking a solution to this crisis.

The question before the UN at its first meeting was whether hundreds of thousands of refugees, both Jewish and non-Jewish, living in DP camps in Europe should be forced to return to their countries of origin, as the Soviet Union and its Communist allies insisted, or should be free to seek asylum elsewhere. Since the issue fell under the purview of the Third Committee, ER debated the question with the Communist representatives serving on that committee. She won "hands down," as she put it, then fought it out all over again in the General Assembly with Andrei Vishinsky, the Soviet delegate to the UN. Vishinsky was an aggressive debater who had presided over the Great Purge trials of 1934–38 in the Soviet Union. The men on the American delegation worried that ER would not be a match for him, but no one else on the delegation was prepared to speak on the issue. Vishinsky charged that the refugees who did not want to return to their countries of origin were collaborators, war criminals, or traitors; ER argued that many of the refugees feared persecution by the governments now in power if they returned home. She did not think the Soviet Union would approve of forcibly repatriating Republican refugees to fascist Spain and insisted that refugees decide for themselves under what sort of government they wanted to live. ER again prevailed. Knowledgeable and articulate about the issue of refugees, she emerged from these encounters as a stateswoman of international stature and champion of refugees and human rights. She reported to Joseph Lash that after her performance Dulles said to her: "I feel I must tell you that when you were appointed I thought it terrible and now I think your work here has been fine! So—against odds, the women inch forward, but I'm rather old to be carrying on the fight."[4]

AFTER THE FIRST MEETING of the General Assembly adjourned in mid-February 1946, ER traveled to Germany to see firsthand the conditions faced by the refugees in the DP camps. In her two-and-a-half-day visit, she visited four camps, including one for Jews. The problem of how to resettle these refugees seemed daunting to her. She did not envy the UN committee charged with examining the problem and coming up with recommendations.

At the Zeilsheim Jewish DP camp, survivors of the Holocaust spoke to her about their hopes for the future. Many of them wanted to go to Palestine. She answered with an "aching heart," wondering, "When will our consciences grow so tender that we will act to prevent human misery rather than avenge it?" Both the children and adults in the camp looked much older than their years and their "feeling of desperation and sorrow" overwhelmed her: "An old woman knelt on the ground, grasping my knees," she reported. "I lifted her up, but could not speak. What could one say at the end of a life which had brought her such complete despair?"[5]

The day after she returned to New York, she spoke to a crowd of 2,000 people at a rally inaugurating a fundraising drive for the Women's Division of the United Jewish Appeal of Greater New York. Reminding her listeners that they were surrounded by the comforts of a city physically untouched by war, she tried to give them a sense of the pervasive destruction in Germany: the bombed-out homes and apartment houses everywhere; the lack of food, shelter, and heat that "beat upon one every minute." She described in great detail the meager rations of the inmates of the Jewish DP camp and the efforts of families to create some semblance of home, despite the lack of privacy. But she was especially struck by something she felt could only be conveyed in a question: "What would happen to us if suddenly we had no real right to appeal to a government of our own?" This powerlessness—"a kind of spiritual uprooting" or sense of "being lost"—haunted her whenever she was in one of the camps. She recalled that when she visited the coal mining region of the United States during the darkest days of the Depression, the people she met at least felt they had the right to tell their government their troubles. In the DP camps, "There just is nothing to hold onto." The remedy for this spiritual malady was not handouts: "Charity is a wonderful thing," ER said, but it does not retrieve a lost sense of security, "the feeling that we have roots." As in the coal fields of West Virginia, ER recognized that what the people in the DP camps needed was not relief but rehabilitation: the opportunity to become citizens of a country again and to rebuild independent lives.

The final point ER wanted to convey to her listeners in New York was her feeling that Americans had been spared "untold misery" for a reason: America was "expected to give leadership" in the broken postwar world.[6]

ONE CONCRETE WAY IN WHICH the United States could provide leadership was to provide funding for the United Nations Relief and Rehabilitation Administration (UNRRA), which had been established by the Allies in November 1943 to aid European refugees, and for its successor, the International Refugee Organization (IRO). Another was to persuade Great Britain to allow more refugees to enter Palestine. The third, of course, was for the United States to admit many more refugees than it had before and during the war, thereby setting an example for the rest of the world. President Truman and ER supported all three ways of solving the refugee crisis in Europe, but Congress and the American people resisted spending money on overseas aid to refugees and remained strongly opposed to admitting more refugees to the United States.

In November and again in December 1945, ER urged Congress to pass legislation appropriating funds for UNRRA, which depended in large part on the financial support of the United States to do its work: "It would seem impossible for the members of Congress to go home and enjoy their Christmas vacations with the weight of the suffering of the world constantly before them, and no action yet taken to alleviate it."[7] She was relieved when Congress finally passed the bill.

When a decision was made to replace UNRRA, which was running out of funds, ER participated vigorously in the UN debates on the constitution of the IRO, which was established in April 1946 and took over the task of finding homes for displaced persons in 1947. She helped make sure that under the IRO refugees could choose resettlement if they had valid reasons for preferring it to repatriation. She then led the campaign to convince Congress to authorize American participation in the new organization and appropriate funds to cover the American share of its budget (45.75 percent). ER also led the effort to secure American funding for the newly established

United Nations International Children's Emergency Fund (UNICEF). She turned once again to Clarence Pickett to help pressure the new Congress, which had come under the control of the Republicans in the November 1946 elections, to commit the United States to the new organizations. Although the American Friends Service Committee (AFSC), as a tax-exempt organization, could not lobby Congress, Pickett said it would do its best to educate the public about the importance of the two agencies. He told her he would also ask the Friends Committee on National Legislation, which did have the right to directly advocate for legislation, to work on the issue: "You can be sure we will do everything we can to muster support for both agencies."[8] With the help of strong support from the State Department, Congress finally appropriated funds for UNICEF in May 1947 and for the IRO in late June.

ORGANIZING AND FUNDING AN EFFECTIVE international refugee agency was only the first step in solving the Jewish refugee situation. While UNRRA and then the IRO tried to do their work, the crucial question was where the refugees would go. President Truman thought a substantial number of them should go to Palestine. On August 31, 1945, in reaction to a report by his emissary Earl Harrison on the appalling conditions in the European DP camps run by the United States, Truman appealed to Great Britain's new Labour government to admit immediately 100,000 of the surviving Jews in Europe to Palestine. Great Britain continued to resist liberalizing its immigration policy in Palestine, however, for fear of stirring up further Arab unrest. In a My Day column on November 7, ER deplored British intransigence and urged opening Palestine as soon as possible to the "miserable, tortured, terrorized Jews who have seen members of their families murdered and their homes ruined." These refugees were now stateless, she noted, since they did not wish to return to "the countries where they have been despoiled of all that makes life worth living." It was natural for them to want to immigrate to Palestine, "where they will feel again that sense of belonging to a community which gives most of us security." Although she felt that it was vital that large numbers of Jews be admitted quickly to Palestine, she also said that Americans had to "face the fact" that they too "may be asked to assume some responsibility." Americans could not "sit comfortably" by and allow fifty of "these emaciated, miserable people" to die every day, which she had been told was now the case.[9]

In mid-November, two and a half months after Truman first asked Great Britain to admit 100,000 Jews to Palestine, British prime minister Clement Attlee and Foreign Secretary Ernest Bevin rejected the request, in effect, by proposing instead the creation of the joint Anglo-American Committee of Inquiry to study the issue of Palestine and recommend a plan of action. Britain hoped that by drawing the United States into the development of a policy on Palestine, the United States would assume some responsibility for carrying it out. When the committee issued its report in April 1946, it recommended that 100,000 Jews be admitted immediately to Palestine, just as Truman had requested, but it also called for other countries to admit some of the Jewish displaced persons. As for the future of Palestine, the committee advocated delaying the establishment of a Palestinian state or states until hostilities ceased. In the meantime, the British would continue to administer Palestine under its mandate until a UN trusteeship could be created.[10] Although the deliberations of the Anglo-American Committee were exceedingly contentious, its members unanimously endorsed the report.[11]

ER was pleased with the committee's recommendation to immediately admit 100,000 refugees to Palestine. She told James McDonald, who had served as a member of the committee, that she also favored defending the Palestinian Jews with military force. She recognized, however, that the United States was unlikely to make such a commitment:

> I think we should have the courage to tell the Arabs that we intend to protect Palestine, but I suppose that is asking too much of us at the present time, though it would only take a small air-force it would seem to me to keep them in order.[12]

Protecting the Jews would probably have been more difficult than she thought, but her advocacy of military force was one measure of her firm conviction that there was no other way to rapidly alleviate the misery of the Jews still in the European DP camps than by allowing large-scale immigration to Palestine. The almost seven-month delay caused by the establishment of the Anglo-American Committee frustrated her. "There was really no need for a committee of inquiry," she wrote in My Day, but the United States had agreed to it, for "the obvious reason" that it "believed Great Britain would accept the report of such a group and try to implement it."[13] Truman appointed a task force to work on doing just that and called for the British government to accept the Joint Committee's recommendations. Britain, however, continued to resist. In rejecting Truman's appeal, Bevin remarked that "the agitation in the United States, and particularly in New York, for 100,000 Jews to be put in Palestine . . . was because they do not want too many of them in New York."[14]

WHILE ER STRONGLY SUPPORTED the recommendation of the Anglo-American Committee of Inquiry, as did most Americans, she also recognized that Bevin had a point. The United States had "a duty to lead" in accepting its share of Jewish refugees. She reiterated the point she had made over six months before: "It is not fair to ask of others what you are not willing to do yourself." Bevin's remarks had given "a great many of us pause. We should not so conduct ourselves that such things can be said about us by responsible statesmen."[15]

In a My Day column written a week later, ER urged Americans to be more generous:

> It might be unwise to bring into New York, which already is larger than any city should be, a great number of any particular group. But certainly throughout this country we could scatter our share of displaced persons without upsetting our economy. We are not yet at the point where an increase in population is a menace. In fact, it would be quite possible to absorb far more than our share of the displaced people in Europe who are seeking homes.[16]

Anti-immigrant and antisemitic sentiment remained strong after the war, however, and Congress continued to resist the admission of refugees. Truman sympathized with the displaced persons, but the steps he had taken to allow more of them into the country were proving ineffectual. In December 1945 he had ordered that displaced persons be given preference under the current American immigration laws. His directive also permitted the State Department to accept corporate affidavits rather than requiring affidavits from individual sponsors.[17] ER supported the president's policy, but his directive had made little difference in the number of refugees admitted, partly because many displaced persons were from Eastern Europe and the American immigration quotas for those nations were very low: Poland, 6,524; Latvia, 236; Estonia, 116; Lithuania, 386. Despite these limits, Congress opposed even the small increase made possible by Truman's directive. A Gallup poll taken at the time showed that the American public also overwhelmingly opposed an increase in immigration. Nevertheless, Truman kept trying.

In August 1946 Truman said he would propose legislation to allow a substantial number of displaced persons to enter the United States.[18] In November, ER noted in My Day that Mrs. Julius V. Talmadge, president general of the Daughters of the American Revolution, opposed Truman's plan. Given the fact that Truman was not proposing to increase America's immigration quotas, but merely to carry unfulfilled quotas from month to month, ER could not understand why some people were "so fearful of holding out even so mild a helping hand." Because the American economy in the postwar period, unlike the Depression years, was growing, she could now compare the nation's needs to the late nineteenth and early twentieth centuries: "The years of high immigration in the past were usually prosperous, because at that time we were expanding. At present, we are again in need of labor. And the types of immigrants we could obtain would, in many cases, be of a very high order."[19]

There was a division at this time among American Jewish organizations about American immigration policy and the future of Palestine. ER had friends in both camps. After news of the Nazi program for the extermination of the Jews reached the United States in 1942, nearly all Jewish organizations in the United States, which had remained disunited up to that point, joined in demanding a Jewish homeland in Palestine. The two exceptions were the non-Zionist American Jewish Committee and the anti-Zionist American Council for Judaism, formed in 1942 to actively oppose the Zionist goal. A minority of American Jews supported the American Council for Judaism's position, but the organization appeared more significant to non-Jews than it was because its leadership included Lessing Rosenwald, former chairman of the board of Sears, Roebuck, and Arthur Hays Sulzberger, the publisher of the *New York Times*.[20] ER knew Rosenwald well because she had served with him on the board of the Julius Rosenwald Fund since 1940, together with her good friend Adele Levy, Rosenwald's sister. The Rosenwald Fund financed the construction of schools for black children in the rural American South, fellowships for talented blacks, medical services, and other efforts to promote the welfare of black Americans. Along with Justine Polier, Rosenwald and Levy were among ER's most important partners in the fields of both black civil rights and Jewish refugees.[21]

Truman's plan for opening America's doors to a large number of refugees pushed the Zionist and non-Zionist American Jewish groups farther apart. The Zionists, led by Abba Hillel Silver and Stephen Wise, continued to press for the creation of a Jewish homeland, while the non-Zionists and anti-Zionists began campaigning to allow at least 100,000 Jewish displaced persons to come to the United States. Many Zionists supported the effort to bring Jewish displaced persons to the United States, but an influential minority did not, fearing that relieving the pressure created by large numbers of Jews in the European DP camps would undermine the drive for a Jewish state.

ER allied herself with the non-Zionist and anti-Zionist groups by serving as a vice chairman and adviser to the Citizens Committee on Displaced Persons (CCDP). The CCDP was a nondenominational organization founded by the American Jewish Committee and the American Council for Judaism to persuade Congress and the public to alter American immigration policy. Adele Levy also lent her support to the organization and Lessing Rosenwald furnished much of the funding. The founders of the CCDP were careful to recruit a group of prominent non-Jews to participate in the group's organizational meeting and serve on its board. ER backed the group not only because she was not a Zionist but because of her personal ties to some of its leaders and, most importantly, because she believed that whatever the outcome of the debate over Palestine, the United States needed to admit far more Jewish refugees than it was doing. Even before the CCDP started its campaign, support came from other quarters.

The Protestant Federal Council of Churches of Christ in America and the Catholic weekly *Commonweal* both called for the United States to admit more refugees. An editorial in *Life* magazine declared it a disgrace that the nation had failed to do so. Even the State Department supported the admission of displaced persons to the United States—largely because it opposed the creation of a Jewish state in Palestine and because many displaced persons were fleeing Communism in Eastern Europe—a far cry from the days when Breckinridge Long did everything he could to keep refugees out.[22]

In his State of the Union address in January 1947, President Truman said the United States could take pride in the economic and food aid it had supplied to other nations since the end of the war, but it had failed to accept its share of displaced persons. Only about 5,000 of them had entered the country since May 1946. The agencies in charge of immigration were doing all they could within the limits of existing laws, he said, but he urged Congress to pass "suitable legislation as speedily as possible" to allow a "substantial number" of displaced persons to enter the United States.[23]

While Truman's appeal to Congress was vague, and he failed to follow it up, the CCDP launched a campaign at the end of January 1947 to secure legislation that would allow 400,000 displaced persons from Europe to enter the United States over the following four years. The leaders of the CCDP knew that in order to win broad public support, the campaign needed to be aimed at bringing European displaced persons of every background, not just Jews, to the United States. Since only a minority of the refugees in the European DP camps were Jewish, it was necessary to set a high goal in order to include as many of the Jews as possible.[24] Just as they did during the debates over the Wagner-Rogers bill in the 1930s, the sponsors of the legislation had to overcome what Earl Harrison, who had become the committee's chairman, called "inspired falsifications" intended "to create the impression that a regular swarm of persons from Europe has been and is now coming to this country."[25] According to Harrison fewer than 300,000 immigrants had arrived in the United States over the previous decade, although 1,500,000 visas could have been issued within the quota restrictions. By making use of the quotas that remained unfilled during the war years, the legislation advocated by the committee would allow 100,000 immigrants to enter the United States each year for four years above the normal annual quota of 154,000. America would be doing its part.

ER strongly endorsed the proposed legislation, which was introduced in the House by Representative William G. Stratton (R-IL), and she and Levy worked to get the bill passed. In many respects, the battle over the Stratton bill resembled the struggle for passage of the Wagner-Rogers bill, despite the greatly altered circumstances of the postwar period. As the supporters of the Wagner-Rogers bill had done in 1939, the CCDP drew up a plan to care for the refugees after they arrived. In advocating for the Stratton bill, the committee emphasized that it would not weaken the standards for admission to the United States. As Lessing Rosenwald explained in a letter to ER, the additional immigrants would be admitted without distinction as to race, religion, or national origin. The restrictions in force under the current immigration laws would "be in no way modified." People with communicable diseases, anarchists, applicants likely to become public charges, and others deemed undesirable under current law would still be excluded. Rosenwald told ER that the committee had raised approximately $250,000 to support its effort, and he hoped ER would do whatever she could during her upcoming speaking tour to publicize the committee's goals. ER did so and also promoted passage of the bill in her My Day column.[26] Responding to the people who often asked her if all the displaced persons wishing to immigrate to the United States were Jewish, she wrote in her March 5 column that "only about 20 to 25 percent" were, but they were "the ones most cruelly attacked under the Hitler regime" and were dying at a higher rate in the camps, probably because their ill treatment had worn down their resistance to disease. The majority of the displaced persons were Poles, Balts, Ukrainians, and Yugoslavs of Catholic or Protestant background.[27]

In June 1947, ER reported in My Day that the General Federation of Women's Clubs, which had at first opposed the Stratton bill, now supported it. In debating the bill, one member of the organization had said that displaced persons should stay in their own countries rather than come to United States. "Perhaps," ER said, "the member did not realize that these displaced persons have no country." Some Americans think the displaced persons are likely to become a burden, she noted: "Actually, just the reverse is true." As she had done in the late 1930s, when she drew on the findings published in the American Friends Service Committee's pamphlet *Refugee Facts*, ER told her readers that "Statistics show that most of the refugees who were fortunate enough to come to this country during the war years are now not only self-supporting, but employers of other people. Not a little of our success in the past has come because we have had new people coming to our country with fresh ideas and fresh determination to succeed."[28]

As in 1939, such arguments coming from ER and other supporters of the bill failed to move Congress, whose members received seven letters opposing the admission of displaced persons to every letter supporting it. Despite the CCDP's repeated statement that 80 percent of the displaced persons were non-Jews, many Americans still assumed that most of the displaced persons were Jews, whom they often equated with Communists. Although the CCDP managed to rally strong support from newspapers, plus a broad spectrum of religious, union, and other organizations, as well as the public at large, it was not enough to sway Congress to pass the Stratton bill or a similar bill introduced in the Senate by Republican senator Homer Ferguson (R-MI).[29] When ER learned that Congress would not pass the Stratton bill before it adjourned at the end of July but would instead appoint a committee to examine the American immigration system and the situation of displaced persons, she expressed her disgust in My Day:

"We hardly need any more investigation, since all the facts are already known. This is simply the kind of delaying tactics we blame the Russians for using."

Unfettered by the constraints that tempered her public statements about the Wagner-Rogers bill during her husband's presidency, ER sharply criticized congressional inaction in her column. Doing nothing about the refugee problem in 1947 meant leaving "desperate people with no hope." She had heard rumors of a possible death march by Jews in the European DP camps and believed that American "inaction is the type of thing that would drive refugees to that kind of desperate action." Should such a thing occur, "members of our Congress can have it on their consciences if thousands more of the Jewish people die."

In advocating on behalf of the European refugees, ER returned to one of the great themes of the "sermons on citizenship" she delivered in the 1930s: the power of fear to sap the will to act morally. She knew there were "obvious reasons" why some people feared bringing people from the DP camps into the country, but she thought "this fear is far more dangerous than the people whom we might bring in." Americans had grown "pusillanimous" when, in fact, "Good new blood will do us no harm." She attributed a toughness to the refugees, which Americans, because they had been spared the devastation endured by Europeans, lacked. Americans were "suffering from fear of the unknown. But these people have seen so much that was unknown that they have learned how to accept it and stand up to it."[30]

Undeterred by congressional foot-dragging, ER kept pushing. In August, she wrote to her friend Charl Williams, head of the National Education Association, telling her that she had heard from a friend at the CCDP that the Parent Teachers Associations (PTAs) were not actively working to obtain passage of the Stratton bill. She asked Williams to urge the PTAs to do so. The National Executive Committee of the PTA had approved a resolution on June 5 backing the bill, but state chapters of the organization had done very little to follow up. Williams replied that she was writing to PTA leaders asking them to take action.[31]

When Congress adjourned at the end of 1947, however, it still had not passed the Stratton bill or any other bill admitting additional refugees to the United States.

IN JANUARY 1948 A SENATE subcommittee began preparing a new immigration bill that became known as the Wiley-Revercomb DP bill after its sponsors. The new bill initially called for the admission of only 100,000 displaced persons over a two-year period, but by the time it reached a vote that figure had been raised to 200,000. The bill was highly discriminatory, however. It stipulated that only refugees who had arrived in the DP camps by December 22, 1945, would be admitted. It also set aside 50 percent of the visas for agricultural laborers and 50 percent for refugees who had fled the Baltic

States and Eastern Poland after their annexation by Russia. These provisions gave preference to the refugees who had been in the camps the longest, to agricultural workers who were needed in the Midwest, and to those who could not return to their home countries for political reasons, but they excluded more than 100,000 Jews permitted to leave Russia and others fleeing pogroms in Poland in the spring and summer of 1946. "The date of December 22, 1945 was deliberately written into this bill because the date prohibited Jews from taking part in this program," charged Senator J. Howard McGrath (D-RI). He expressed his sorrow that the Senate was incorporating "the principles of narrowness, intolerance, and bigotry" into the law.[32] The Senate made its prejudices still clearer by passing an amendment that set aside half the German and Austrian quotas for so-called *Volksdeutsche*, who in this case were ethnic Germans expelled from the parts of Germany absorbed by Poland and the Soviet Union after the war.

In June, after the Senate passed the bill, Earl Harrison, chairman of the CCDP, lamented that the *Volksdeutsche* were being "handed special privileges over the victims of Nazi oppression."[33] ER, however, glossed over the bill's discriminatory provisions. She thought it was "fair that there should be some distribution on a percentage basis, with consideration for the numbers remaining in the different nationality groups in the displaced person camps," but she hoped that the United States would not "be too exacting in our standards." Perhaps not wishing to criticize a bill that represented a step forward, considering how resistant Congress had been to any increase at all in the number of displaced persons entering the country, she tried to look at the sunny side of the matter: Although "200,000 is not many," she told her My Day readers, "it is something" and, once the bill passed the House, "may start the ball rolling in other countries." Although Senator McGrath remarked that "the mountain has labored but brought forth a mouse," ER thought the bill "a welcome mouse!"[34] As ER often told her friends, "If you have to compromise — be sure to compromise up."[35]

When the House debated its own version of the DP bill, some of the same arguments that had been made against refugees in the 1930s resurfaced and ER again tried to counteract them. In her June 12 My Day she quoted Representative E. E. Cox (D-GA) who called the displaced persons "the scum of all Europe — an aggregation of loafers." The DP camps, he charged were "hotbeds of revolutionists" and if these refugees came to the United States they would "join those who are gnawing away at the foundation of our constitutional government." Appealing again to the kind of information summarized in *Refugee Facts* in the late 1930s, ER pointed out that, in truth, most of the displaced persons had skills and wanted to work. Some had professions and had been prominent in their fields before being driven out of their homes. Immigrants with similar backgrounds had done very well in America. She was relieved when the House passed a more liberal version of the bill. The House version moved the cutoff date by which refugees had to have arrived in the DP camps to April 21, 1947, which would have allowed the Jews coming from Russia and Poland in 1946 and after to qualify for admission.[36] The conservatives on the House-Senate Conference Committee prevailed, however, and most of the restrictive provisions of the Wiley-Revercomb Senate bill survived. President Truman signed the compromise bill, known as the Displaced Persons Act, which admitted 205,000 refugees over two years, but he was deeply disappointed with it, calling it "flagrantly discriminatory."[37] William Haber, Jewish adviser to the American army in Europe, called it "the most anti-Semitic Bill in U.S. history."[38] Nevertheless, despite the way the bill was worded, in practice many Jews were admitted. The Displaced Persons Commission (DPC), appointed by the president and charged with administering the bill, interpreted its provisions much more liberally than either supporters or opponents of the bill expected. After a tough fight in 1950, Congress amended the bill, making it less restrictive and expanding the number of displaced persons admitted to the United States. In reaction to criticism of its procedures, however, the DPC for a time administered the amended bill more strictly, excluding some Jews who wished to immigrate to the United States. Nevertheless, Truman's 1945 directive and the 1948 and 1950 DP bills enabled close to 100,000 Jews to resettle in the United States, about 16 percent of the total number of displaced persons admitted between July 1, 1948, and June 30, 1952.

ER had been in the forefront of efforts to pry open America's doors to greater immigration, but it had not been easy, even as the nation was making a strong economic recovery after the war. As the historian Leonard Dinnerstein sums it up, "strong national prejudices, procrastination in Congress, and some less than dynamic leadership from the White House combined to prolong the miseries of those Jews who survived the Holocaust."[39]

BETWEEN THE END OF WORLD WAR II in 1945 and 1948, the resistance of the United States and other nations to immigration, along with the conditions in Europe that made refugees unwilling to return to their countries of origin, increased the importance of Palestine as a possible haven for Jewish refugees. ER's long-term ally on refugee matters, James McDonald, had concluded even before the end of the war that Palestine was the only practical destination for large numbers of Jewish refugees. In November 1944, he sent Justice Felix Frankfurter the text of a talk that reflected his long, frustrating experience with the refugee issue. Its title summed up its message: "The Record of a Quarter of a Century of Intergovernmental Efforts on Behalf of Refugees Points Imperatively to Palestine as the Primary Solution of the Vast and Tragic Problem of Jewish Refugees." The record clearly shows, he told Frankfurter, that "the governments and the intergovernmental organizations have almost never faced the realities of the tragedy of the refugees but that instead they have been guilty of face-saving maneuvers while millions of innocent men and women have been needlessly sacrificed." Only Palestine offered hope for those who had survived.[40]

ER's old friend Sumner Welles came to the same conclusion. In a speech on April 1946, he said that Palestine had become "more and more indispensable" as a refuge for the Jewish people. Welles also expressed his belief "that Palestine must become not only the promised National Jewish Homeland, but also an independent Commonwealth into which the entrance of the Jewish people who wish to make that holy land their permanent home must never be restricted, save insofar as economic limitations may require." It would be a democratic commonwealth in which the rights of all the people of Palestine, whatever their race or faith, would be protected. Welles was not yet prepared to publicly support the establishment of a separate Jewish state, but predicted that if unlimited immigration were permitted, Palestine "in all probability" would "in the future possess a majority of citizens of the Jewish faith," and that, he said, "is its rightful destiny." In May 1947, after the British asked the UN to take responsibility for Palestine's future, Welles went further. He came to the conclusion that the only possible solution to the problem was some form of partition, a solution the UN would soon approve.[41]

Like McDonald and Welles, whose opinions helped shape her attitude toward Palestine, ER's views about the future of Palestine evolved as violence and intransigence on both sides of the Jewish-Arab conflict made a unified Palestine a less and less viable option. In January 1946 Aline Goldstone, one of the leaders of the American League for a Free Palestine, the group founded by Peter Bergson to support the establishment of a Jewish state, wrote to ER criticizing her for characterizing the surviving Jews of Europe as merely "miserable, wretched human beings about whom something must be done." ER, she complained, was looking at them as "objects of pity and charity" rather than as human beings with "the right of nationhood" and the right to determine their own future in "what they consider, and rightly, I believe, their national territory, Palestine."[42] ER replied that while the Jews of Europe should be regarded as the equals of any other human beings, they urgently needed food, clothing, and shelter first of all. As to their future destination, ER remained undecided.

ER looked at the problem not as a Zionist like Goldstone, but as a pragmatist who was sympathetic to the Jews but recognized that the question of Jewish settlement in Palestine raised complex issues. "Nobody questions [the Jews'] right to self-determination," ER said, but she enumerated the obstacles to their creating a state of their own in Palestine. As before, the difficulties with large-scale immigration of Jews to Palestine explained to her by Isaiah Bowman remained persuasive in her mind. First of all, she said, the Arabs believed the land was theirs. ER thought they were willing to let the Jews who already lived in Palestine remain, but they were opposed to the immigration of a large number of Jewish refugees and to the establishment of a Jewish state.

In addition, ER believed that the Jews were not strong enough to defend themselves. As a result, it "would seem like suicide" to permit the Jews to immigrate to Palestine unless Britain and the United States were prepared to defend them. The other obstacle to permitting European Jews to immigrate to Palestine was the uncertain capacity of Palestine to support a much larger population. Probably remembering the contradictory reports she had received in 1943 from Bowman and Rose Halprin, ER noted that "Some reports are agreed that it can, others disagree."[43] The second option, therefore, was to resettle Jewish refugees in other countries of the world, "and apportion them according to population." It was "not a simple question."[44]

After the British rejected the recommendation of the Anglo-American Committee of Inquiry to permit 100,000 Jews to immigrate to Palestine, ER continued to express an ambivalent view of the Palestine problem. In a My Day column on August 19, 1946, she deplored the British policy of intercepting refugee ships bound for Palestine and interning the passengers on Cyprus. She also deplored the use of force by the Jews in Palestine but felt their actions were understandable given how much the Jews wanted to create a home for themselves and how harshly the British treated them. She understood why the Arabs did not welcome the Jews and, at this point, did not believe that partitioning Palestine into Jewish and Arab states was a viable solution. She also downplayed the desperate character of the struggle. The Jews, she claimed, were "not asking for a vast increase in land." They only wanted "to keep what they have, with slight additions for economic needs" and "be allowed to take in refugees." In addition, she thought many Jewish refugees preferred to settle in other countries.[45]

ER's hedging of the issue provoked a scathing critique of her column from Sarah Siegel, one of her Jewish readers, who challenged ER's column point by point. In response to ER's statement that many of the Jewish refugees in Europe did not wish to go to Palestine because they saw brighter futures elsewhere, she cited James McDonald's statement on the radio that 99 percent of the Jewish refugees in Europe wanted to go to Palestine and not to any other country. In regard to ER's assertion that Jews were not seeking "a vast increase in land" in Palestine, but "only to keep what they have, with slight additions," Siegel said that, on the contrary, the Jews were claiming "their internationally acknowledged rights under the Balfour Declaration," which permitted them to live, work, and purchase land anywhere in Palestine. Siegel challenged ER's continued questioning of Palestine's absorptive capacity and claimed that the Arabs were better off since the Jews had arrived.

Ignoring ER's opposition to British policy on Palestine and her admiration for the crusading spirit of young Jewish settlers, Siegel interpreted ER's column to mean that ER felt that "the Jewish problem" was "a question of kind hearts and philanthropy; if the good people of America or Britain or other counties will open their gates and let the beggars in, all will be well." That, Siegel felt, missed the point:

Don't you see, Mrs. Roosevelt, . . . [that] as long as the homeless people remain homeless and a minority in other people's lands, they will always be open to suspicion on the part of their neighbors and at the mercy of these neighbors, and will continue to be the convenient scapegoat whereby the Hitlers of the future can climb to power?

In reply, ER conceded that McDonald knew better than she how many refugees wanted to go to Palestine, but that she had been told that "a fair number" were willing to immigrate to the United States. She insisted that the question of Palestine's absorptive capacity had not been settled. Finally, while the lives of some Arabs had been improved because of the economic development brought to Palestine by Jewish settlers, she believed the lives of others had been made more difficult. For that and other reasons, Arab leaders objected to further Jewish immigration.

ER's ideal was the pluralistic and democratic society that she had been seeking for many years to build in the United States: a society in which everyone possessed equal rights and was free to practice their own religion without prejudice. That is what she wanted for the Jews. ER was not yet willing to embrace the Zionist argument being made by Siegel that the Jews would only be secure if they established their own state in which they were a majority and in charge of their own government. Not all Jews wanted a Jewish state or national home, she told Siegel, and most Jews in the past had been citizens of the countries where they lived and simply wanted to be free to practice their religion, as Protestants and Catholics did. She recognized that "change has come" and that Jews might decide "to establish and fight for the right to the land." But she hoped that was not true.[46] At this point, the issue for ER still came down to finding homes for thousands of refugees in Europe, not to creating a Jewish state.

The ambivalent nature of her August 19 column reflected ER's distress at the intensifying violence created by Britain's refusal to accept the recommendations of the Anglo-American Committee and at the harshness of British policy in Palestine. Britain's harshness had increased over that summer. On June 29, 1946, British soldiers raided the Jewish Agency and seized a large number of documents containing information about the agency's activities, including its participation in violence against the British. The incriminating documents were taken to British Mandatory headquarters in the King David Hotel in Jerusalem. Around the same date, the British arrested over 2,500 Jews from throughout Palestine who were suspected of anti-British activities. On July 22, in response to the arrests and to destroy the evidence collected by the British raid on the Jewish Agency, the Irgun, under the leadership of Menachem Begin, bombed the southern wing of the King David Hotel, which housed the Mandate's Secretariat and the offices of the British military command. Ninety-one people were killed, including many Arabs and Jews.

ER condemned the attack in My Day, finding it "difficult to understand" why, after so many innocent Jews had died in the world, Jews would "carry on this same kind of senseless performance, except that it seems to be a trait of human nature to want to retaliate in kind, no matter what the consequences may be." She knew "well what the Jews have suffered" and was "not proud of the way in which so-called Christians have acted during these past years," but ever-escalating violence would make a just solution to the Palestine situation even harder to achieve.[47]

In the aftermath of the attack, the British rounded up almost 800 Jews in Tel Aviv and sent them to a detention camp. British authorities also severely restricted civil liberties for all Jews in Palestine, carried out random searches of people and homes, imposed curfews, and set up roadblocks. These policies turned Palestinian Jews further against British rule, and the Irgun and Lehi, another terrorist organization (formerly called the Stern group), intensified their attacks on the British. On August 12 the British announced that they would no longer permit "unscheduled" immigration into Palestine. Anyone attempting to enter would be sent to Cyprus or some other place of detention.

The tough measures adopted by Great Britain failed to quell Jewish resistance, however, and by February 1947, Britain had had enough. Bevin asked the UN to take responsibility for resolving the question of the future of Palestine.

AS A SPECIAL SESSION OF THE UN General Assembly to discuss the issue was about to begin, ER's criticism of Great Britain's handling of the Palestine problem and of her own government's policy on the issue grew even sharper. When George Henry Hall, 1st Viscount Hall, said in the House of Lords that he could not "imagine that the [British] Government would carry out a policy of which it did not approve," ER wondered in My Day how the UN could be effective if its decisions were not respected. The British had previously rejected the recommendations of the Anglo-American Committee of Inquiry and now, after Britain had requested the special session of the UN to come up with a solution, Lord Hall was implying that Britain would veto any UN plan it did not like. While Great Britain temporized, the suffering of the refugees continued. The tragedy of Palestine she wrote, was that "those who are being kept out of Palestine are the waifs and strays of horror camps" who had already endured so much. "I deplore terrorist tactics," she said, "but I deplore even more the attitude of self-righteous governments." She included her own. In some of the harshest language she used during the debate about the future of Palestine, she charged that the position of the American government had "never gone beyond pious hopes and unctuous words," but a "day of reckoning" would arrive: "The preventable suffering of human beings brought on by other human beings cannot be overlooked from on high forever."[48]

In May the UN formed the Special Committee on Palestine (UNSCOP) to study the Palestine problem and recommend a solution. Violence in Palestine continued, however, and ER remained critical of the measures Great Britain took to suppress it. Writing to Secretary of State George Marshall in late May 1947, she charged that Great Britain had established "a police government" in Palestine, "with a forgetfulness of all we think of as British principles and justice." She felt that the American position on Palestine at the UN had been vacillating. Either the United States should insist that the principles of the Balfour Declaration be upheld, "in spite of the Arabs," or it would have to retreat from the commitment it had made to the declaration years before. In response, Marshall evaded the issues ER raised. Great Britain, as the mandatory power in Palestine, was charged with maintaining law and order, he told her, and the purpose of the recent special session of the UN had been to form the Special Committee on Palestine, not to consider substantive matters related to Palestine.[49]

In August, the British navy rammed and boarded the *Exodus*, a ship carrying 4,500 Jewish refugees and survivors of the Holocaust seeking to immigrate to Palestine. Two refugees and a crewman died in the fight for control of the ship. After the British towed the ship into the port of Haifa, they transferred most of the passengers to three prison ships, which they sent back to Europe and anchored off the coast of France. The French government expressed its willingness to take in the refugees, but most of them refused the offer, wishing instead to be sent to the British internment camps on Cyprus. After receiving a telegram from Helen Waren, a Broadway actress who had entertained American troops in Europe for the USO, describing the horrendous conditions aboard the ships, ER appealed to Truman: "Since they want to go to Cyprus," she wrote in her telegram, "some pressure might be brought to bear on Great Britain to allow them to do so. Their plight is pitiful and I hope you may feel that you can exert some influence on Great Britain."

In Truman's reply he pointed out that Americans had funded the *Exodus* and its organizers knew "that they were trying to do an illegal act." He worried that such tactics would backfire:

> The action of some of our United States Zionists will eventually prejudice everyone against what they are trying to get done. I fear very much that the Jews are like all under dogs—when they get on top they are just as intolerant and as cruel as the people were to them when they were underneath. I regret this situation very much because my sympathy has always been on their side.[50]

In the midst of her correspondence with Truman, ER received a letter from Eva Warburg Unger informing her of the conditions endured by Jewish orphans in the British internment camps on Cyprus. Unger was a resident of the Givat Brenner kibbutz in Palestine and the sister of Ingrid Warburg, the executive assistant to Frank Kingdon at the Emergency Rescue Committee in the early 1940s. The children, Unger told ER, were confined by barbed wire, surrounded by machine guns, and living on "very little water and bad food." They were survivors of Nazi concentration camps or had been hidden somewhere for many years during the war. Each day they remained in the camps would "make it more doubtful" that it would be possible "to reeducate them to 'normal' and happy boys and girls." ER sent Unger's letter on to Truman, together with the following sharp words:

> I have just received the enclosed letter of which I am sending you a copy. The British still seem to be on top and cruelty would seem to be on their side and not on the side of the Jews.[51]

In the end, although the American government urged them not to do so, the British shipped the refugees from the *Exodus* back to the British zone in occupied Germany and placed them in displaced persons camps.[52] These people, ER wrote in My Day,

> have gone through so much hardship and had thought themselves free forever from Germany, the country they associate with concentration camps and crematories. Now they are back there again. Somehow it is too horrible for any of us in this country even to understand.[53]

During the summer of 1947, members of the UN Special Committee on Palestine visited Palestine to interview the various parties to the conflict and try to find a compromise solution. The Arabs refused to cooperate with the committee because they believed that any solution other than a unitary state, which would have an Arab majority, violated their right to self-determination as guaranteed by the UN charter. The Jews, on the other hand, cooperated fully and vigorously lobbied the members of the committee for the creation of their own state. The committee's report, issued on September 3, recommended the partition of Palestine into Jewish and Arab states.

Nearly all members of the American delegation to the UN and State Department officials opposed partition and believed that the United States should reject UNSCOP's recommendations. ER, however, argued during the debates within the American delegation that the United States should firmly back the partition plan. She became adamant on the subject. After watching the conflict between the Jews and the Arabs intensify and believing that UNSCOP's recommendations were the result of a careful assessment of the alternatives, ER's reluctance to endorse the creation of separate Arab and Jewish states disappeared. When Loy Henderson, head of the Office of Near Eastern Affairs in the State Department, warned that partition would generate bitter opposition among the Arabs and an ongoing conflict in the Middle East, ER told him, according to Henderson, "I think you are exaggerating the dangers. You are too pessimistic.... I'm confident that when a Jewish state is once set up, the Arabs will see the light; they will quiet down; and Palestine will no longer be a problem."[54] The naïveté of her statement is consistent with her view expressed elsewhere that if the Arabs were dealt with decisively, they would accept the creation of a Jewish state. Henderson and the opponents of Jewish statehood were, of course, correct. The Arabs did not quiet down. But ER never wavered in her support for partition.

Truman, on the other hand, agonized over what position the United States should take and whether it should actively urge other nations to vote for partition in the General Assembly. The American Zionists lobbied for strong American backing of the UNSCOP report. In addition, the leaders of the Democratic Party warned the president that not supporting partition might hurt the party's chances in the 1948 elections, especially in states like New York with large Jewish populations. State Department officials, on the other hand, cautioned the president against angering the Arabs and weakening American influence in the Middle East. Truman also worried about the danger that the United States might have to commit American troops to defend the Jews, possibly provoking the Russians to intervene as well. After much hesitation, appeals from his close Jewish friends, Eddie Jacobson and Abraham Granoff, advice from his White House advisors, David Niles and Clark Clifford, both of whom supported partition, and a weighing of the arguments from all sides, Truman finally authorized the State Department to publicly support partition. The announcement was made at the UN on October 11. At first, however, Truman accepted the State Department's low-key approach to the General Assembly vote. Not wishing the United States to be identified as the leader in the establishment of a Jewish state and, in fact, hoping that the partition plan would fail to receive the two-thirds majority it needed for passage, the State Department refrained from pressuring smaller nations dependent on the United States (notably Haiti, Liberia, and the Philippines) to vote for partition. In the last two days before the final vote, however, when it appeared that the plan would fail, intense pressure directed at the White House persuaded Truman to intervene personally. Truman and his White House staff made it known to the wavering nations that the passage of the partition plan was vital to the United States. This last-minute effort was successful, and on November 29, 1947, the UN General Assembly voted in favor of partition. The Arabs rejected the plan and, following the vote, proceeded to attack the Palestinian Jews.[55] The Arab response deeply disturbed ER, who regarded it as an assault upon the fundamental mission of the United Nations. While she would sympathize with the Arab people who suffered because of the fighting that ensued, she could not forgive the Arab leaders for their defiance of the UN.

14

COMMITTING TO THE ESTABLISHMENT OF A JEWISH STATE

"A moral obligation"

A S THE PARTITION PLAN'S strongest champion within the Truman administration, Eleanor Roosevelt urged its vigorous implementation with the help of an international police force, if necessary. The president and Secretary of State George Marshall could not easily ignore her views. The UN Human Rights Commission (HRC), which was drafting an international bill of human rights, had elected her its chairman and the reputation she had earned in her debates at the UN with Andrei Vishinsky on the refugee issue gave her stature. She was also the widow of a popular president, a much sought-after speaker, and, not least, a widely read columnist, a role that gave her immediate access to the American public. She did not refrain from using the power of her pen in her debate with Truman and Marshall about American policy.

ER did not think the partition plan was an ideal solution to the conflict. She would tell one critic that she did not know whether the majority report of the UN Special Committee on Palestine (UNSCOP) that recommended partition "was wise or not." But after lengthy investigation, first by the joint Anglo-American Committee of Inquiry, then by UNSCOP, "nothing better was suggested."[1] She believed it was the best way to ensure that the Jewish refugees in Europe would find new homes—in a place where they were welcome and needed. Equally, if not more importantly, she regarded the implementation of the plan as the first crucial test of the UN's authority and ability to solve world crises. The Arab nations, she thought, were being shortsighted in not abiding by the UN's majority decision, for if the UN failed and the world were to "return to the condition of each individual nation looking out for itself," the small nations would suffer most and "live in continued uncertainty."[2]

Other factors governed the views of most of her colleagues on the American delegation to the UN and in the State Department, including Marshall, Loy Henderson, Undersecretary of State Robert Lovett, and Secretary of Defense James Forrestal. As states in Eastern Europe and the Balkans came under Soviet control or influence, the struggle to contain the Soviet Union came to dominate their thinking. If the United States sought to impose the UN partition plan on the unwilling Arabs, they believed it could lead to the Arabs canceling American and British oil concessions. Loss of access to Middle Eastern oil would undermine the Marshall Plan for the recovery of war-devastated Europe and put the United States at a disadvantage in a potential conflict with the Soviet Union. In addition, weakened American influence in the Middle East would invite inroads by the Soviet Union into the region.

ER, too, was keenly aware of the need to prevent Soviet expansionism, but she had little use for the argument about the Arabs and oil. The strategic importance of oil was much overrated, she believed. Since the Arabs had no other major customers for their oil besides the large nations, they were unlikely to cut off the supply. Even if they did, she thought, the United States would find a substitute for oil if necessity demanded it, just as it had developed sulfa drugs and penicillin during World War II.[3]

The opponents of partition in the State Department believed that partition violated the principle of self-determination, which America had championed since World War I. In 1947, the Arabs in Palestine numbered approximately 1.2 million, whereas the Jews numbered only 600,000. The creation of a Jewish state would deny the Arab majority the right to choose its own form of government.[4] Ordinarily, ER would have shared this view, but her sympathy for the Jews who had survived the Holocaust and her anger at the Arabs for defying the UN overrode other considerations.

ER believed the United States had assumed a responsibility for helping to implement the UN plan when it backed the UN Special Committee on Palestine majority report and led the effort to persuade other nations to vote for partition. She worried that the United States might renege on its obligation, however. In January 1948, after she read an article by *New York Times* correspondent James Reston in which he reported strong opposition to the UN plan among some officials in the State and Defense Departments, ER expressed her concern to Marshall and Truman.[5] She urged that the embargo on shipping arms to the Palestine area, which the United States had imposed in early December 1947, be quickly lifted and that a UN police force be supplied with modern equipment. Strong military force "is the only thing which will hold the Arabs in check," she told Marshall. Not enforcing the UN's decision would put the new organization in danger of becoming as ineffective as the League of Nations had been.[6] Knowing that officials in the State and Defense Departments opposed a police force in which the Soviet Union participated, for fear that the Russians would use Palestine as a base for subversive activities throughout the region, ER suggested that the police force be composed of troops from smaller nations.

In his reply to ER's letter, Marshall told her that the United States was waiting for the report of the UN Commission on Palestine before deciding how to proceed. The commission, which was composed of representatives from five small nations, had been charged by the UN General Assembly with managing the transition to Arab and Jewish states as the British Mandate ended. Truman assured ER that he and Marshall were working on a plan to enforce partition.[7]

Despite these assurances, ER kept pressing for action. At the end of February, as the UN Security Council was about to take up the security report of the Commission on Palestine amid continuing violence in Palestine, ER joined Herbert Lehman, former director general of the UN Relief and Rehabilitation Administration (UNRRA), Senator Elbert Thomas (D-UT), and Sumner Welles, now the honorary president of the American Association for the United Nations, in urging the formation of a UN international police force as soon as possible and its deployment in Palestine to enforce the partition plan. They also called for the lifting of the arms embargo on any party to the conflict that accepted the plan.[8] The State Department, however, proposed a different approach. On February 21, Marshall recommended to the president that the best way to stop the violence in Palestine was to put the country under a temporary UN trusteeship after the British Mandate ended on May 15 rather than seek immediate compliance with the partition plan.

On March 19, Warren Austin, United States permanent representative to the UN, gave a speech at the UN that signaled the change in the American position on partition that Marshall had recommended. The purpose of a temporary UN trusteeship, he said, would be "to maintain the peace and to afford the Jews and Arabs of Palestine further opportunity to reach an agreement regarding the future government of that country."

Austin's proposal shocked the supporters of partition. The National Council of Jewish Women called it a "political bombshell."[9] Benjamin Cohen, a Zionist who was ER's chief ally in debates on Palestine within the American delegation to the UN when he served as a counselor to the State Department, wrote an op-ed piece criticizing Austin's speech and arguing that only a small, well-equipped international force would be required to enforce the partition plan.[10] Sumner Welles, who saw "no shadow of justification" for the reversal of American policy, quoted a representative of one of the Latin American nations, who said that first the United States "convinced us that partition was the only answer. Now they are trying to convince us that partition is insane."[11]

ER was outraged. In a letter to Marshall, she said that the United States had assumed "a moral obligation" when it endorsed the Balfour Declaration and tacitly agreed to the establishment of a Jewish homeland by permitting Americans to invest capital in the formation of Jewish settlements in Palestine. As to the UN, she could "hardly see how it can recover and have the slightest influence, since we were the only ones who could give it any force and we now have been the ones to take it away." She would "have to state my feelings publicly," she told Marshall, and if, as a result, he wished her to resign from the Human Rights Commission, she would do so. She quite understood that "it is extremely difficult for you to have someone serve under you who openly criticizes the attitude of the Administration." ER also wrote Truman, enclosing a copy of her letter to Marshall and repeating her offer to resign.

Alarmed by the vehemence of ER's opposition to the new policy, Marshall hastily arranged for Charles "Chip" Bohlen, special assistant to the secretary of state, to explain the administration's thinking to ER. Marshall also told her he would be "most unwilling" to accept her resignation from the UN Human Rights Commission. "I think you can do a great deal of good there," he told her, "however much it may complicate matters to have you criticizing the attitude of the administration."[12] The resignation of a great champion of Jewish refugees would also have embarrassed the administration and increased criticism of its failure to back implementation of the partition plan.

Truman also responded to ER, reconfirming his commitment to the UN by telling her, "If the United Nation fails all is chaos in a world already beset with suspicion, divisions, enmities, and jealousies." He hoped that her conversation with Bohlen would "dispel at least some of [her] doubts and misgivings" about administration policy. As for her resignation from the American delegation, he told her it would be "calamitous": "There is no one who could, at this time, exercise the influence which you can exert on the side of peace." He tried to reassure her by telling her that the UN trusteeship proposed for Palestine would be temporary. It was not intended to replace the partition plan but merely to maintain the peace once the British Mandate came to an end.[13]

ER publicly voiced her objections to the Truman administration's trusteeship plan in two My Day columns, written after Marshall and Truman had responded to her letters. In the first column, on March 26, she began by summarizing her interpretation of the history of the Jews in Palestine. She agreed with the statement in a *New York World-Telegram* editorial that "The ideal Palestine solution is a free democratic country in which all enjoy equal rights and live in peace together." That was what she believed the Jews themselves originally envisioned after the Balfour Declaration. She thought they regarded the British Mandate as a means of providing stability during the "settlement and growth of a nation." At first, she believed, the Arabs "were not greatly distressed at the idea of not holding sway over Palestine at some future date," but after a small group of Arabs grew rich from selling oil to Great Britain and the United States, their attitude changed. This version of the history of Palestine under the British Mandate assumed that the Jews hoped eventually to outnumber the Arabs in Palestine and thus "hold sway" in a democratic nation in which they were the majority. Her belief that the Arabs were not very unhappy with this scenario until some of them got rich from selling oil ignored the rebellion of Palestinian Arabs against Jewish settlement, especially in the period 1936–39, and their deep attachment to the land in which they lived.

After the UN Special Committee on Palestine issued its majority report, ER noted, the United States had used its considerable influence to secure an affirmative vote for partition in the General Assembly. Once the Arabs violently rejected the plan, however, she thought the United States had encouraged the Arabs to believe they could succeed in preventing implementation of the plan:

> I feel that our evident reluctance to accept responsibility and carry out whatever requests the UN might make of us, whether of a military or an economic nature, led to increased resistance by the Arabs.

By not fully backing up the UN decision, with force if necessary, she believed the United States had undermined the ability of the UN to act as peacemaker.[14]

The meeting with Charles Bohlen, which took place on the day her first column appeared, did not change her mind. She told him that if the United States had adopted "a firm line" with the Arabs after the UN vote in favor of partition, the Arabs might have accepted the plan in principle. As she had said in an earlier My Day column, "No one expected either the Jews or the Arabs to be completely satisfied with the U.N. majority report," but hoped that the two parties would "attempt to work out a solution to the whole problem, beginning with the majority report as a basis and seeing how it could be improved upon."[15] The proposal for a UN trusteeship for Palestine, on the other hand, was "a step backward."[16] In a letter to the president after her conversation with Bohlen she said she could not see how it made "anything simpler or safer than it was before."[17]

In her second My Day column, filed on the day she met with Bohlen, ER charged that the administration's decision was motivated by fear. "I dislike actions . . . taken from fear," she said, reiterating one of her most strongly held convictions, "since they are very apt to be unwise and unjust." Given the record of violence by extremists in both camps, she wondered who would enforce an armistice during the UN trusteeship while the Arabs and Jews negotiated an agreement. The trusteeship government would face the same problem as before: if it permitted the immigration of Jews to Palestine, the Arabs would protest; if it did not allow immigration, the Jews would protest. Meanwhile, the "miserable, desperate" Jews held by the British on Cyprus and languishing in the displaced persons camps in Europe would continue to "become less able to be valuable citizens anywhere." Since "all the argument and effort" put into reaching an agreement acceptable to everyone had failed, "the one already adopted by the UN might as well be implemented." That was not a ringing endorsement of partition, but it recognized that further delay would not produce a "perfect solution."[18]

After rumors circulated that she was considering resigning from the Human Rights Commission, ER told readers of My Day that she had offered to resign because she felt the need to publicly disagree with the administration, but that the president had assured her that her disagreement "did not in any way embarrass him" and urged her to stay on. She appreciated this "extremely generous attitude" and planned to remain at her post as long the president and secretary of state wished.[19]

AS IT TURNED OUT, events on the ground made ER's argument with Marshall and Truman no longer relevant. As the British withdrew their forces and administrative personnel in preparation for ending the Mandate, fighting intensified between the Jewish and Arab forces, despite UN efforts to arrange a truce. By the end of March, the defensive strategy adopted by the Jews had failed and they risked losing Jerusalem and their settlements in the Galilee. Their only chance, they concluded, was to go on the offensive to try to seize the transportation network and the Arab towns controlling the crossroads in the center of the country, as well as the key high ground throughout Palestine. With the help of fresh shipments of arms from Czechoslovakia and dissension among leaders of the Arab forces, the new strategy succeeded. By May Jewish military successes had imposed a de facto partition of Palestine. The breakdown of the British Mandate's administrative structure—its police force, courts, and public services—and the fact that the Arabs did not create a governmental order of their own also gave the Jews an advantage as they went about setting up an administrative system in the areas under their control. Although the part of Jerusalem under Jewish control remained extremely vulnerable, the threat did not deter the Jews from moving ahead with the formation of their own state.[20]

When it became clear that David Ben-Gurion, now chairman of the newly formed Zionist Council of State (the provisional Jewish government in Palestine), would announce the establishment of the State of Israel when the Mandate ended on May 14, ER joined Jewish leaders and Truman's political advisors, led by Clark Clifford, in pushing the president and Marshall to recognize the Jewish state promptly. ER didn't know what the administration's plans were, she wrote to each of them, but she had been told by Jewish organizations that the Soviet Union would recognize the Jewish state as soon as it was declared. She thought "it would be a mistake to lag behind Russia" and "again follow instead of lead." She hoped that whatever policy the United States followed that "it be clear and consistent." On her letter to Truman she wrote a postscript by hand: "I failed to say that I personally believe in the Jewish State."[21] With the establishment of Israel now at hand, ER cast aside her doubts about what she knew to be an imperfect resolution of the Palestine problem.

When the United States recognized Israel, however, ER was disgusted by the way Truman handled the announcement. Ben-Gurion declared Israel a state at midnight on May 14, 1948, at the moment the British Mandate came to an end. Without explaining his decision in advance to the American delegation in New York or America's allies, Truman immediately announced that the United States was granting de facto recognition to the new state, making the United States the first country to do so. Although Dean Rusk, who was in charge of the State Department's UN desk, called Warren Austin to inform him of the president's decision, Austin was apparently so upset by it that he went home without sharing the information with his colleagues. The United States had beaten the Russians to it, but the members of the American delegation in New York, who had been working to arrange a ceasefire between the Arabs and the Jews, were stunned at not having any explanation of the American action to share with other diplomats at the UN. ER had gotten what she wanted—may even have felt a little responsible for Truman's decision—but was embarrassed at the unexpected way it had come about. "Much as I wanted the Palestine State recognized," ER wrote Marshall the following day, "I would not have wanted it done without the knowledge of our representatives in the United Nations who had been fighting for our changed position." She had "seldom seen a more bitter, puzzled, discouraged group of people" than some of those she saw at the UN after Truman's announcement. Once again, she felt, the United States had weakened the UN and lost the confidence of the nations it hoped to lead. After ER sent Truman a copy of her letter to Marshall, he wrote to say that he regretted that she was upset by the way in which the recognition of Israel had been handled. "There was not much else to be done," Truman told her, given that there was "a vacuum in Palestine" and the Russians were eager to be the first to recognize the new nation.[22]

Some of the opponents of partition in the American delegation and in the State Department were so deeply unhappy with Truman's decision to recognize Israel that they considered resigning, although in the end Marshall and Dean Rusk persuaded them to stay. Truman, they believed, was motivated purely by his desire to secure the support of Jewish voters in the presidential election in November and was therefore allowing domestic politics to undermine the defense of America's interests abroad.

ER was not unappreciative of the importance of Jewish voters to the Democratic Party, but her forceful advocacy of the partition plan and recognition of the Jewish state had to do with her concern for the plight of Jewish refugees and her desire to make the UN an effective agency for settling disputes, not with electoral politics. It is not clear to what extent her passionate stance influenced Truman's decision, but as one of the few people within the administration who wholeheartedly, publicly, and consistently supported the creation of a Jewish state once the General Assembly voted for partition, she kept presenting him with persuasive arguments that transcended domestic political considerations for recognizing a separate Jewish nation. Her advocacy, and that of experts on foreign policy such as Sumner Welles and Benjamin Cohen, provided cover for Truman as he made the decision to recognize Israel against the advice of his own State Department.

FROM 1946 THROUGH 1948, ER advocated forcefully for the admission of displaced persons to the United States, for large-scale Jewish immigration to Palestine, and, once the UN adopted the partition plan, for the plan's implementation. Her main role at the UN, however, was her leadership of the Human Rights Commission (HRC), the committee charged with drafting an international bill of human rights. After the formation of the commission in 1946, ER became its chair and directed its work until 1951. Serving in the role of chairman of the HRC provided her with an opportunity to guide the incorporation of principles for which she had fought during the New Deal into an international document.

ER approached the task of drafting an international bill of human rights with an urgency that arose in part from the horrors of the Holocaust; in part from her recognition that the nations of the world, including her own country, had failed to protect Jews and other victims of Nazi persecution. How could such violations of human rights be prevented in the future? "We who wrote this document," ER said after the adoption of the Universal Declaration of Human Rights (UDHR), "felt that World War II had perhaps had, as one of its causes, the wiping out of the rights of certain human beings by Hitler and that if we could make it impossible for human rights and freedoms ever again to be ignored, ever again to be wiped out, perhaps we would take away one more of the causes that underlie war."[23] The drafting of the UDHR and the subsequent covenants, which sought to establish human rights standards and international constraints on the violation of human rights, offered a promising way to achieve that goal.

As James Loeffler has documented in his book, *Rooted Cosmopolitans: Jews and Human Rights in the Twentieth Century*, Jews had played a prominent role in the development of the concept of human rights during the first half of the twentieth century and in the incorporation of human rights into the UN Charter. Hersch Zvi Lauterpacht, a Zionist from Galicia and leading expert on international law, coined the term "crimes against humanity" and wrote an early draft of an international bill of rights that became an important resource for the UDHR. Raphael Lemkin, another Jewish lawyer, coined the term "genocide" and got the word included in the indictment of Nazi leaders at the Nuremberg trials. ER worked with some of the Jews who helped advance the cause of human rights, including René Cassin, a key member of the HRC who wrote the second draft of the UDHR, and her friend Justine Polier, who was both a Zionist and a passionate defender of the rights of African Americans and children. She also developed a warm working relationship with Jacob Blaustein, a non-Zionist who lobbied successfully at the founding conference of the UN in San Francisco for the inclusion of human rights provisions in the UN Charter, including the establishment of the Commission on Human Rights. Blaustein, who headed the American Jewish Committee, regularly made proposals to ER and the HRC regarding the UDHR and the human rights covenants. Blaustein shared ER's optimism about the UN human rights program. Before the establishment of Israel, he believed that enshrining universal human rights in international law, rather than establishing a separate nation state, was the best way for the Jewish people to protect themselves against persecution.[24] Both Blaustein and ER were staunch anti-Communists who believed that advocacy for human rights was a powerful weapon that the United States could use effectively in its competition with the Soviet Union for influence throughout the world.

Jewish organizations naturally followed the deliberations of the HRC closely and lobbied the commission to include provisions in the UDHR and the human rights covenants that they considered important for the protection of Jews in the future. The World Jewish Congress and the consultative councils of Jewish organizations put a particular emphasis on how the UN planned to review complaints of human rights violations and implement the human rights enumerated in the declaration. They called for a provision requiring that the laws of every UN member state conform to the UN Charter. They advocated for the creation of a tribunal before which individuals or groups could bring complaints against their own governments. They worried that many provisions in the draft bill would permit discrimination as long as it was "legal," thus making it possible for governments to deny human rights by passing discriminatory legislation as the Nazis had done. The Jewish groups also believed that a declaration would not suffice; only the legally binding covenants that the HRC was also working on would protect people from human rights abuses.[25]

The most striking difference between the American Bill of Rights and the French Declaration of the Rights of Man on the one hand and the UDHR on the other is that the UDHR includes economic and social rights as well as civil and political rights. The representatives of the newly independent and undeveloped nations on the committee felt strongly about including these rights because they believed that unless issues like illiteracy, disease, and poverty in their nations were addressed, civil and political rights would mean little. The Soviet Union and other Communist nations supported the inclusion of economic and social rights because they felt that the Communist system was more effective than capitalism in realizing them. The State Department would have been happier with a declaration that included only civil and political rights because most of its officials believed that education, health care, and an adequate standard of living were not rights, but goals that governments might help facilitate, but not guarantee. Their view reflected the belief of many Americans. As the role of government expanded during the New Deal, however, ER, like her husband, embraced the idea that people had a right to education, a living wage, and the other needs of a viable life.

In a speech on "Humanistic Democracy and the American Ideal" in 1939, ER defined the American ideal as "opportunity for education for every child," the "chance to come into the world healthy and strong," and the "opportunity to earn a decent living under decent conditions."[26] And in the article she wrote in 1942 for *American Unity*, she spoke explicitly of people's "political, economic or social rights," including the "right to demand an economic system which will free the world from starvation."[27]

ER regarded the founding of Israel, which occurred in the same year as the adoption of the UDHR, as a realization of human rights (social and economic, as well as civil and political) for a people who had suffered the worst human rights disaster in history. She also believed that Israel, as a nation founded by a people who had repeatedly suffered human rights abuses throughout the centuries, would respect the rights of all its citizens, including Arabs, and even be a beacon of human rights in a region where governments often violated the rights of their own citizens. ER's relationships with some of the leading Jewish advocates of human rights, such as Blaustein and Polier, reinforced ER's identification of Jews with the promotion of human rights. So did the fact that Jews such as Lauterpacht and Cassin played prominent roles in the drafting of human rights documents. Lauterpacht himself hoped that Israel would become a model of human rights that other nations could emulate.[28] In a message to the National Conference of the Christian Committee of the United Jewish Appeal in 1950, ER said that Israel deserved their support because of its commitment to protecting the rights and freedoms of all its citizens.[29] She did not acknowledge that Israel's definition of itself as a Jewish state made this commitment problematic. Future events would undercut ER's idealistic vision. Attacked persistently by Arab terrorists, thrice waging war with its Arab neighbors who refused to accept its right to exist, and, after 1967, assuming the role of occupying power, Israel received increasing criticism for violating the rights of the Arabs under its jurisdiction.

ER RIGHTFULLY REGARDED HER ROLE in drafting the UDHR as her greatest achievement. The skill with which she chaired the HRC and guided the UDHR through the UN greatly enhanced her prestige as an advocate of human rights. After the declaration's adoption by the General Assembly, the delegates rose to give her a standing ovation. Her success endeared her to the Jews who felt a special stake in the declaration. The Arabs, on the other hand, regarded her strong support for the partition plan and for the state of Israel as a betrayal of the very rights enumerated in the UDHR.

Wadad Dabbagh, an Arab "wife and citizen of Palestine," who wrote to her in May 1948, just before Israel declared itself a state, questioned ER's commitment to human rights. Dabbagh viewed ER as a Zionist sympathizer whose position on Palestine was not justified by the facts. Dabbagh accused the Jews who complained of persecution in Europe of becoming "despotic" after arriving in Palestine and committing "all the unlawful acts of which they were the victims" in the countries from which they came: "They avenge themselves upon the innocent Arabs who used to live peacefully in their homes for immemorial times." She urged ER to suspend her support of the Zionist movement until she had had a chance to go to Palestine and see for herself how the Zionists were "driving us [out] of our homes, depriving us of our lands, robbing us of our means of living, and encroaching upon our resources and upon the wealth of our country."[30]

In her reply ER expressed sympathy for those who suffered on both sides. Once war broke out, she said, "there is nothing but misery for everyone concerned." But she blamed the Arabs for bringing their troubles upon themselves. The Arabs had "protested wrongly" against the UN report, she said, and argued, optimistically, that by proposing to make Palestine a single "economic unit," the proposed plan would enable "the two nations to live peacefully side by side even though there was partition and to gradually work out a mutually acceptable plan."

As she had done in the past when challenged to justify the creation of a Jewish state, she cited the Balfour Declaration as the origin of the current reality. The half million Jews who had immigrated to Palestine had come with the expectation that they would be permitted to create there a "national home." In addition, she referred to the provisional agreement signed by Emir Feisal, the Hashemite emir of the Arab kingdom of Hejaz, who led the Arab revolt against the Ottoman Turks, and Chaim Weizmann at the Paris Peace Conference in 1919. Under the terms of that agreement, Feisal pledged that the Arabs would permit large numbers of Jews to immigrate to Palestine, as long as the Jews respected the rights of Arab peasant and tenant farmers and assisted the Arabs with economic development. Feisal had made such an agreement, but ER was apparently unaware that Feisal added a codicil to the Arab version of the agreement, following the signatures, saying that the Arabs would only redeem their pledge if the Arabs were granted independence. Moreover, by the end of 1919 he had ceased to cooperate with the Zionist Jews.[31] Given the Balfour Declaration's endorsement of Jewish immigration to Palestine and what she thought was the Arab acceptance of the declaration's aims, she thought it "unrealistic and stupid" to "turn around now and behave as though no agreement had existed and that something unforeseen is occurring." Thousands of Jews had been encouraged to settle in Palestine and begin restoring their ancestral homeland. The clock could not be turned back. She did not blame the Jews for what had happened "because they are living up to what, for a long time now, they have considered were unquestioned agreements." She did not blame the Arab people either, but she did blame the Arab leaders and was "deeply sorry" for the suffering endured by both the Arab and Jewish people because of the refusal of the Arab leaders to abide by the vote of the UN General Assembly.[32]

Dabbagh found ER's answer unsatisfactory. She had read ER's recent statement on the UN draft declaration of human rights and wished to provide ER with "some more facts about the tragic story of the poor Arabs of Palestine" so that ER could "do them some justice in the name of those Human Rights."[33] The Arabs had fought on the side of the Allies against the Ottoman Turks during World War I in an effort to achieve their independence, she said, but were then "deeply frustrated by the Balfour Declaration." The Arab leaders had never agreed to its terms, she told ER. In fact, the anniversary of the declaration was a day of mourning throughout the Arab world: "It reminds us of the difference between theory and practice in the matter of human rights." The "injustice" of the declaration, she said, had resulted in repeated Arab rebellions against its consequences ever since. In 1918, she said, there were only 56,000 Jews in Palestine, now there were three-quarters of a million. These Jews are "strangers to Palestine," she said, but "are planning to take it, either by expelling the Arabs out of their homes or by exterminating them." She cited the massacre of Arab villagers at Deir Yassin and in other Arab villages and the expulsion of Arabs from villages and cities taken over by the Jews. "We are not a savage people who can be colonized or exterminated in such a barbarous way," she said, citing the Arab contributions to European civilization. "I am sure, dear Madame, that you can do something, and you are going to do it in the name of Justice and Human Rights, which you are admirably defending and advocating."

It is impossible to know whether Dabbagh's appeal created any doubt in ER about the justice of the partition plan or generated thoughts about the moral complexity of applying the principles of the UDHR to the situation in Palestine. Dabbagh's letters certainly did not change ER's fundamental attitude. She would go on making the same arguments about the conflict between the Arabs and the Jews even more emphatically in subsequent correspondence and public statements. Dabbagh was "astonished" when ER sent a curt one-sentence reply to her second letter: "I have your letter of June 30 and I regret there is nothing I can do to help in the situation about which you write."[34] Perhaps Dabbagh had touched a sensitive spot in appealing to ER on the basis of the human rights declaration that ER had played such a key role in creating. In any event, the issue would continue to haunt her as she fended off similar criticism for the rest of her life.

IMMEDIATELY AFTER BEN-GURION declared Israel a state, armies from five Arab countries attacked the new nation. As the conflict intensified, ER continued to hope that the UN, with strong backing from the United States, would intervene to settle the dispute in a way that would ensure Israel's survival and implement the partition plan. But the military success of the Israeli forces, rather than the UN, would eventually determine the outcome of the conflict.

Although outnumbered and initially outgunned, the Israeli forces were highly motivated, better disciplined and led, and possessed a greater knowledge of the terrain on which they were fighting than the invading forces. The Haganah, the Jewish army in Palestine, had developed as a force to protect Jewish settlers from Arab attacks and was, according to one British Cabinet member, "the most formidable fighting force in the Middle East because it was not a private army but simply the whole Jewish community organized" to ensure its survival.[35]

On May 20, the UN appointed Count Folke Bernadotte, a Swedish diplomat and member of the Swedish royal family who had helped rescue inmates of Nazi concentration camps near the end of World War II, to mediate a truce and assist the two sides in negotiating a solution to the conflict. Toward the end of May, when the Arabs rejected a ceasefire ordered by the UN Security Council, ER urged once again that the UN create a military force as soon as possible in order to ensure that groups such as the Arab League would obey its decisions.[36] She again chastised Great Britain and members of the American government for seeming to be more interested in Arab oil than in solving the problems of the Jews and the other residents of the Middle East, but she thought most Americans admired the courage of "a small group fighting for liberty and the creation of a Government of their own."[37] As the war continued into the summer, with a brief truce in June, many more people, the great majority of them Arabs, fled or were driven from their homes. In the end, over 80 percent of Palestinian Arabs became refugees. During a fragile ceasefire finally established by Bernadotte in July, Bernadotte appealed to Secretary Marshall and to the UN to provide assistance to these refugees. He believed that the work of mediating the conflict would not succeed unless the "most urgent aspects of [the] great human disaster affecting 330,000 destitute Arab refugees from Jewish-controlled areas and 7,000 Jewish refugees" were addressed.[38]

After seeing a copy of the appeal, which Marshall may have passed on to her in the hope that she would publicize the problem, ER devoted a My Day column to Bernadotte's description of the humanitarian crisis and urged her readers to help. Characteristically, she began by calling attention to the plight of women and children: "He says that thirty percent of these refugees are children under five years of age, and over ten percent are pregnant women and nursing mothers." The refugees lacked food and medical care. They lived on the side of roads under burlap screens or without any shelter at all. When the rains began in September they would be cold. Epidemics might break out and "thousands of children and women, who have no responsibility for the conditions existing in these areas, will die." The people living in the areas to which the refugees had fled could not meet the needs of the refugees who were overtaxing the local water supply. The United States government had promised aid but would probably be able to provide only about half of what was needed, ER told her readers: "Therefore it is asked that private organizations, church groups particularly, cooperate with the government by sending what they can through government channels immediately."[39]

ER sent a copy of her column to Marshall, expressing her hope that he would receive the assistance he needed. Marshall replied that her "support of Count Bernadotte's appeal will have a powerful effect." Truman had directed the State Department to ask for contributions from private sources, and Marshall reported to ER that American companies and relief organizations had contributed "generously," including one oil company that donated $200,000. By the end of August, according to the *New York Times*, the United States had sent relief supplies and money totaling over $800,000 to assist the refugees.[40]

On September 16, Bernadotte submitted his report and recommendations to the UN. The following day he was assassinated by members of the extremist group Lehi, who believed that Bernadotte was secretly assisting the British and their Arab allies. That idea made "no sense at all to me or to a lot of other people," ER wrote in My Day and noted that the act was a setback for the nascent peacekeeping efforts of the UN, for it would discourage diplomats from accepting the responsibility of mediating conflicts in the future. More immediately, the "ruthless stupidity" of the assassination was "a hard blow" to the Israeli government as it struggled for recognition as a new state. Internal division would not "strengthen the cause of this young nation before the world," but ER thought that the government "will prove itself strong enough to dominate what is, in essence an outlaw group."[41]

Bernadotte had intended the report he submitted to the UN before his death to serve as a basis for negotiations, not as the final plan for a settlement of the conflict, but since both the Jews and the Arabs rejected parts of Bernadotte's plan and the Arabs refused to negotiate, it did not provide an avenue to peace. Bernadotte's principal recommendations were that the UN quickly adopt clear, decisive resolutions aimed at ending the violence, establish a Palestine conciliation commission to carry out its directives, accept as fact the existence of the Jewish state of Israel, affirm the right of Arab refugees to return to their homes as early as possible or be adequately compensated for the loss of their homes if they chose not to return, and settle the political future of Arab Palestine.[42] He believed that the demilitarization of Jerusalem, which he thought should be under UN control, would require a well-armed UN military force, but such a force should only be deployed if both the Arabs and the Jews agreed to the demilitarization of Jerusalem in principle.[43]

ER agreed with Secretary of State Marshall that the UN should accept these proposals, but she disagreed with Bernadotte's assignment of the Negev to the Arabs. In October, she asked her old friend Bernard Baruch to try to persuade Secretary of State

Marshall that the American endorsement of the Bernadotte Plan "was not tantamount of complete acceptance of all the recommendations contained in it, but only as being a good basis for negotiations." She thought granting the whole of the Negev to the Arabs was "highly unfair." The Western Galilee, which Bernadotte proposed the Arabs trade to Israel in exchange for the much larger Negev, was not adequate compensation, she said, given that "in Jewish hands the Negeb would be developed and may turn out to be the only place where they can receive immigration." ER said she had made these arguments at meetings of the American delegation, but didn't think she had much influence, her only "real backer" being Benjamin Cohen.[44]

The original partition plan voted on by the UN in November 1947 had given the Negev to the Jews, and ER felt that the United States should continue to support that provision of the plan rather than Bernadotte's proposal. Although Marshall publicly supported Bernadotte's recommendation, in a speech on October 28 Truman once again overruled his state department by fully endorsing the original partition plan. "Israel," he said, "must be large enough, free enough and strong enough to make its people self-supporting and secure."[45] That was ER's view as well.

By the time of Truman's speech, however, the issue had already been settled on the ground. Fearing the loss of the Negev because of Bernadotte's plan, the Israelis broke the truce on October 14 and attacked the Egyptian army in the Negev, effectively destroying it as a serious threat. In response to the fighting, the UN Security Council drafted a resolution calling upon the two sides to withdraw their forces to the positions they had held prior to October 14, a move that would only affect the Israelis since their forces had driven back the Egyptians. The UN threatened sanctions if the two parties did not comply. At a meeting of the American delegation to the UN in Paris on November 3, attended by Secretary Marshall, Austin, John Foster Dulles, Philip Jessup, Bohlen, and ER to discuss the draft resolution, ER expressed her concern that voting for the resolution would make it appear that the United States no longer supported the UN partition plan. A resolution intended to enforce a truce would, in effect, dictate the terms of a final settlement. To address her reservation, Marshall proposed adding vague language stating that the resolution did not in any way alter the "rights, claims or position [of interested governments] with regard to a peaceful adjustment of the future situation of Palestine." ER continued to believe, however, that the resolution signaled a change in the U.S. position. The United States was vacillating again, she felt, as it had in March by advocating a temporary UN trusteeship, rather than unequivocally supporting partition. In a letter to Marshall, written after the meeting, she told him that she had left the meeting "rather bewildered." If the United States was not changing its position, what was it doing? ER understood that the United States was trying to allay British fears of angering the Arabs, but she continued to wonder if the problem could have been solved and much bloodshed averted if the United States had taken a firm position with the Arabs and Great Britain on partition from the beginning. Like Sumner Welles, ER believed, as she put it, that "Israel without the Negeb could not possibly be independent and self-supporting in that part of the world." For that reason, if Israel were not granted the Negev, it would fight for it (as, in fact, it had done). For the negotiations over partition to succeed, she insisted, the United States had to make it absolutely clear to Great Britain and the Arabs that it backed Israel: "It is one of those situations in which one can not remain neutral though one can be fair."[46] After Ralph Bunche negotiated a ceasefire agreement between Israel and Egypt in February 1949, the Negev remained in Israeli hands.

In a ceremony honoring ER in 1949, Abba Eban, who served simultaneously as Israel's ambassador to the United States and representative to the UN, praised ER for her steadfastness on the issue of the Negev. When his delegation had to "resist a movement for the mutilation of Israel at its very birth," he said, ER was "a source of mature counsel, a ready defense in adversity. The cruelty of depriving us of that desert [the Negev] which represents our main national opportunity was apparent to her, as it became apparent to the entire delegation of the United States and to the General Assembly itself which withheld its endorsement of any proposal restrictive of Israel's national rights."[47]

Israel gained 21 percent more land during the 1948 war with the Arabs than had been allocated in the partition plan and proved itself decisively on the battlefield, but its success intensified the Arab desire for revenge. A permanent peace agreement and recognition by the Arab states of Israel's right to exist remained out of reach. Bunche successfully negotiated separate armistice agreements with Jordan, Lebanon, and Syria, as well as Egypt, but Israel remained in a state of perpetual low-grade war along its vulnerable borders with its Arab neighbors. Frequent raids by the *fedayeen* (guerrilla groups armed and trained by Egyptian intelligence), as well as the Egyptian blockade of Israel's access to the Red Sea, would eventually lead to the 1956 Suez Crisis.[48]

THE 1948 ARAB-ISRAELI WAR deepened ER's commitment to Israel because it decisively confirmed Israel's ability to defend itself and opened the new state to thousands of Jews still living in the DP camps in Europe. She also developed a romantic vision of the Jewish soldiers who participated in the war. They appeared to her very much like the American colonists who fought for independence against the British in the American Revolution. ER's disdain for British colonialism and its policies in Palestine under the Mandate ran deep. The fact that the Jews had struggled against British rule in Palestine as well as against the Arabs reinforced her identification of the Israelis with the Americans who fought in the Revolution.[49]

In September 1948, after Israel's surprising success in repelling the attacking Arab armies, ER heard a group of young Israeli soldiers speak at a United Jewish Appeal event. They were there as part of Israel's public relations campaign to build support for the new nation in the United States. By commenting on the event in My Day to her large American readership, ER greatly amplified the story that Israel wished to convey of heroic fighters overcoming all odds. She also merged Israel's founding narrative with the story of America's founding. The Israeli soldiers spoke about how their small, ill-equipped forces frequently confronted situations that "would seem practically impossible for them to meet," ER wrote, yet repeatedly "accomplished what seemed the impossible." She "wondered if that had been the way some of the young men around General George Washington had felt as they faced the British Army without shoes, in the dead of winter, with scant food and very scant equipment." She imagined that many of those close to Washington must have "held much the same kind of conviction about freedom and the cause of their small nation as these youngsters hold." For the Jewish soldiers, Palestine was "a holy country . . . dedicated to save the Jewish people" from persecution.

When ER speculated about the motivations of the Arab soldiers in the conflict, on the other hand, her remarks expressed disdain about the possible motives of the Arab participants. The deep commitment expressed by the Jewish soldiers made her "almost want to talk to some of the young Arab soldiers . . . to find out whether a different dream was alive in their hearts and shone from their eyes or whether they more nearly approximated the young Hessians of our own Revolutionary War, who fought for the sake of fighting and the pecuniary returns." But she didn't talk to any Arab soldiers or obtain any other personal knowledge of what the Arabs felt was at stake.[50]

ER's depiction of the Israeli soldiers as tough, resourceful freedom fighters came at the beginning of a major shift in the image of the Jew in American popular culture, a change that would culminate ten years later in the publication of Leon Uris's bestselling *Exodus* and the making of the popular film starring Paul Newman based on the novel. In the years after World War II, as Michelle Mart has shown in her book *Eye on Israel*, images of the Jew as a despised dishonest outsider or a helpless victim of Nazi persecution began to give way to images of a "new Jew" who was strong, virtuous, and heroic.[51] Beginning in 1948, ER contributed to this change through her celebration of Israeli soldiers and pioneers in her written and spoken descriptions of Israel. The old cultural stereotypes of Jews that ER still echoed during the 1930s and early 1940s disappeared from her discourse.

The soldiers ER met in New York showed her their strength not only as warriors but in their commitment to building their new nation. Still concerned about the land's absorptive capacity, ER asked them how the desert area of the Negev could "possibly support hundreds of thousands of Jewish refugees." They answered immediately: "It is a desert now, but where there are settlements it blooms. It can bloom everywhere." The conviction that shone in the Israeli soldiers' eyes made her believe "that no kind of work would seem too arduous to them if the fulfillment of their dreams were in sight."[52] When ER went to Israel for the first time in 1952, the itinerary arranged by her hosts provided abundant confirmation that the confidence expressed by the Israeli soldiers enabled them to triumph over the many obstacles the young nation faced. Upon her return to the United States, ER drew on her impressions of what she saw to help burnish Israel's image for her American audiences.

15

VISITING ISRAEL AS WORLD PATRON OF YOUTH ALIYAH

"I saw what had been done"

T HE FOUNDING OF ISRAEL and the end of the barriers to immigration imposed by the British allowed thousands of Jews to immigrate to the new state. In June 1950, when the International Refugee Organization (IRO) was about to close up shop, there were still 539,579 refugees whom the IRO had been unable to resettle. But there were very few Jews among them because of Israel's open immigration policy. In the first three and a half years of Israel's existence, the new state welcomed an astounding 685,000 immigrants, a figure greater than the number of Jews already living in the country (655,000).[1] The ability of Israel to absorb so many new immigrants and to survive as a viable nation depended heavily on the financial support of Americans, both Jews and Gentiles. Eleanor Roosevelt played a prominent role in the ambitious fundraising effort that made the massive influx of immigrants into Israel possible and helped sustain the nation in its early economically troubled years.

After the end of World War II, the United Jewish Appeal (UJA) challenged American Jews to donate huge sums of money to care for the survivors of the Holocaust, find them homes in Palestine or elsewhere, and sustain the Jewish settlements in Palestine. With the help of prominent Christians, such as ER, the UJA also reached out for support to the Gentile community. Now completely free of the constraints she had felt about raising money for particular causes while she was in the White House, ER joined enthusiastically in this work. In 1946 she spoke at UJA events in support of what she described in My Day as the "exceptional drive" of the UJA to raise $100 million (over $1.8 billion in 2020 dollars) "for the rescue and rehabilitation of the Jews of Europe." ER told her My Day readers about the Community Committee of New York for the UJA, whose honorary chairmen were Governor Thomas E. Dewey, New York mayor

William O'Dwyer, Herbert H. Lehman, and Bishop William T. Manning. Its executive committee, she pointed out, was composed of "men of many races and many faiths." ER felt that if every community in the United States were to form such a committee, it "would help to increase the feeling of brotherhood throughout the world." Of the six million Jews murdered, she told her readers, two million were children. She had recently met a couple who had come to America from a concentration camp near Frankfort. They had seen their children burned to death and yet, because of the "extraordinary tenacity" with which people hold on to life if given any hope, were struggling to begin again. Americans—Catholics, Protestants, and Jews alike—who had "been spared such cruelty," ER said, had "a joint responsibility" to assist the Jews who remained in Europe "to return to some kind of normal living."[2]

In January 1947, ER's old friend Henry Morgenthau Jr., who had left his post as secretary of the Treasury after Truman became president, became general chairman of the UJA.[3] ER actively supported Morgenthau's efforts by speaking frequently at UJA fundraising events. Another well-known Christian who joined ER in supporting the UJA was Nelson Rockefeller. For UJA's 1947 campaign, which had set the ambitious goal of $170 million, he and ER organized a National Christian Committee, composed of eighty prominent Americans, to help the UJA achieve its objective. Thomas Watson, president of IBM, became its national chairman. The group pledged generous sums of money and agreed to partner with the UJA in 225 cities by setting up citizen committees, as ER had suggested in 1946, and encouraging churches to take up collections for the cause.[4]

After the founding of Israel in 1948, when many American Jews came to care deeply about the success of the new nation, ER became even more important to the Jewish community. As American Jews shared in their nation's growing prosperity after World War II, many moved to the suburbs, and, with antisemitism on the decline, they came to enjoy a more secure place in America's mainstream. Most of them did not desire to immigrate to Israel, but they took pride in Israel's existence and its accomplishments reinforced their own growing confidence. Both religious and secular Jews were eager to hear and read about Israel, evidenced in the nearly one hundred books published about Israel in the United States by the mid-1960s, including *Israel Without Tears* (1950) by the popular journalist and lecturer Ruth Gruber; *My Promised Land* (1953) by the *Hadassah Newsletter* columnist Molly Lyons Bar-David; and Leon Uris's *Exodus* (1958), to name just a few.[5] ER helped satisfy this appetite for inspiring stories about Israel and helped affirm the warm relationship that many American Jews formed with the new nation.

One indication of ER's affirmation of a special bond between American Jews and Israel appears in her response to a request in 1949 from Lessing Rosenwald asking her to send a message to the America Council for Judaism's annual conference. While ER strongly supported Rosenwald's efforts to pass a bill to admit displaced persons to the United States, she was equally strong in her disagreement with the ACJ's position on Israel. The anti-Zionist council, which advocated "complete secular integration of Americans of Jewish faith with their fellow citizens of other faiths," as Rosenwald put it, rejected the idea that American Jews possessed a unique responsibility for Israel. American Jews, Rosenwald told ER, owed "no obligations to the State of Israel not shared by other Americans" and should simply offer it "the measure of goodwill accorded to any other foreign state that lives with us in peace and friendship." ER did not agree, replying pointedly, "I hope that your Council will take a special interest in the State of Israel since while you are Americans, your religious affiliation must make you especially sympathetic to the efforts now being made by the small State of Israel to give a chance for life in the future to many of the refugees of Europe."[6]

Leaders of the UJA greatly valued ER's participation in its campaigns. They turned to her again and again as a speaker at UJA events and published her statements, as well as statements written by UJA fundraising staff that she had approved, in their newspaper ads and other appeals for contributions. In 1950, Lea Horne, chairman of the UJA of Greater New York, told ER that she was "one of our staunchest supporters" and "a vital part of this great cause." She thanked ER for speaking at two luncheons, which raised over a million dollars, "much of it due to your drawing power and the inspiration of your presence there."[7] It is impossible to calculate how much money ER helped raise for the UJA over the years, but it was probably well over one hundred million in today's dollars.

After the formation of the American Financial and Development Corporation for Israel in 1950 under the chairmanship of Henry Morgenthau Jr., ER participated in the campaigns organized by the corporation to sell State of Israel bonds. She also became a member of the organization's advisory council. Most of the money raised for Israel up to that point had gone to aiding the refugees in Europe and helping them get settled in Israel and elsewhere. The bonds provided capital for the industrial and agricultural projects needed to make Israel economically independent. Although the concept of a Jewish nationalist state was opposed to the secular, universalist principles of American liberalism, most American Jews, who were overwhelmingly liberal, ignored that underlying contradiction by insisting that Israel was extending the values of American liberal democracy into the Middle East and serving as a bulwark against Communist expansion. They took pride in the fact that Israel was a multiparty democracy with a free press and a government committed to providing health care and education for its citizens and promoting economic equality. When ER herself bought a bond in honor of Elinor Morgenthau, who had died in 1949, ER made a statement, probably prepared by the campaign's publicity department, in which she said that by buying bonds to strengthen Israel's economy, "we are also strengthening its capacity to serve humanity and to serve the highest interests of democracy and world peace."[8]

ER'S SPECIAL CONCERN FOR REFUGEES had always been for children. She had supported the efforts of her friends to pass the Wagner-Rogers bill that would have brought 20,000 Jewish and non-Aryan children to safety in the United States, publicly challenged the State Department and her husband on the issue of admitting British children to the United States for the duration of the war, and intervened with FDR and the State Department in the attempt to rescue 5,000 Jewish children from unoccupied France in 1942. The welfare of children, both Jewish and Gentile, remained one of her highest priorities after the war.

This concern expressed itself most strongly in her association with Youth Aliyah, the organization whose work had captured ER's imagination in the late 1930s and whose National Advisory Committee she had joined in 1940. Hadassah, Youth Aliyah's financial sponsor in the United States, drew ER closer to the work of the organization in 1949 when it presented her with the first Henrietta Szold Award for distinguished humanitarian service. ER donated the $1,000 she received with the award toward the creation of a music library at Ramat Hadassah Szold, Youth Aliyah's new reception center at Alonim. Although her contribution to Youth Aliyah had been largely through lending her name to Hadassah's fundraising efforts, speaking at Hadassah events, and praising Youth Aliyah in My Day, that support had been much appreciated. The citation read in part: "in recognition of her participation with Hadassah in the rescue and rehabilitation of 40,000 Jewish children through Youth Aliyah."[9] The award itself was as much a way of identifying ER publicly with Youth Aliyah and eliciting a deeper commitment from her as it was a way of thanking her for her previous support.

Material sent to ER before she received the award explained the importance of the new reception center at Ramat Hadassah Szold. The 40,000 children Youth Aliyah cared for between 1934 and 1949 came from 44 countries and spoke many different languages. The youngest children Youth Aliyah ordinarily accepted were ten years old, and Youth Aliyah served as their guardian until they reached the age of eighteen. Some of the children who arrived between 1934 and 1949 were orphans; others were placed in the care of Youth Aliyah by their parents, who were unable or unwilling to emigrate. Youth Aliyah provided the parents with a means of freeing their children from the intolerable circumstances they faced in their native lands. By 1949, 25,000 children had finished their training in agriculture, trades, the arts, and other vocations under the direction of Youth Aliyah. Fifteen thousand were still in training in 200 agricultural settlements and institutions. Many of these children had lived for long periods in concentration camps or in hiding, enduring privation and trauma. Youth Aliyah had developed an educational system, involving both study and work, designed to restore them to health and confidence, as well as to give them the practical and citizenship skills they needed to contribute to the building of the new nation. Now, after independence, 1,500 children were arriving in Israel each month and Youth Aliyah had to expand to meet their needs.[10]

In an article in the *New York Herald Tribune*, William L. Shirer estimated that a training program on the scale planned by Youth Aliyah for a nation with under one million people and a low birthrate would have a considerable impact: "75,000 children who assimilate the social and cultural ideals of their new homeland through daily living and instruction can become a very potent factor in its development."[11] Youth Aliyah's programs and the vital role the children participating in them were playing in the growth of Israel had enormous appeal to ER, who had spent much of her life advocating for adequate education, medical care, nutrition, and housing for children and for educating people of all ages in active citizenship.

YOUTH ALIYAH BECAME A MAJOR PART of ER's humanitarian work in 1952 after she met with Moshe Kol, Youth Aliyah's director, at a session of the UN in Paris. Kol proposed that she become the World Patron of Youth Aliyah and invited her to Israel to see his organization in action. ER readily accepted Kol's proposal.[12]

Before leaving for the Middle East, ER decided to visit several of the Arab countries on Israel's borders. This plan appears to have originated with Charles Malik, who succeeded ER as chairman of the UN Human Rights Commission. He wanted her to learn more about the culture of the region, its need for economic assistance, and the Arab perspective on Israel. As a result, she added Lebanon, Syria, and Jordan to her itinerary. Malik was a Lebanese Christian and Western-educated philosopher, a champion of liberal Western ideas who had served as rapporteur during the drafting of the Universal Declaration of Human Rights (UDHR). He and ER were on the same side in the debate within the commission on the rights of the individual person as opposed to the sovereign power of the state. ER came into contact with other Arabs at the UN, but Malik was the only one with whom she worked closely. Although not entirely trusted by his Muslim Arab colleagues, Malik strongly supported the cause of the Palestinian Arabs.

Malik no doubt hoped that a visit to several Arab countries would modify ER's attitude toward Israel, but her anger at the Arabs for defying the authority of the UN and her relief that many survivors of the Holocaust had found refuge in Israel made her unreceptive to the Arab point of view. In addition, her many relationships with American Jews with whom she had worked since the 1920s in many of the fields that most engaged her nurtured her sympathy for Israel. In 1947, she had also formed a warm friendship with David Gurewitsch, her personal physician, who had been a member of the German Zionist Youth Organization as a boy and went to Palestine in 1934 after graduating from medical school in Switzerland to serve as a physician at the Hadassah Hospital in Jerusalem. Gurewitsch accompanied ER to Israel during her 1952 tour. Malik, on the other hand, was one of the few Arabs she knew. Without Arab friends and few Arab colleagues, she had very little opportunity to hear the Arab side of the argument, feel she had a personal stake in the welfare of Arabs, or respond to Arab needs.

ER's lack of sympathy for the Arab point of view also stemmed from her full embrace of the Israeli version of events before, during, and after the 1948 war. In response to a letter she received in the summer of 1951, ER said that most of the Arab refugees had fled out of fear or at the advice of their leaders, who told them they would soon be able to return with the victorious Arab armies. She later noted that about 170,000 Arabs had stayed put and continued to live safely in Israel.[13] Because of the research Benny Morris, Ilan Pappé, Avi Shlaim, and other "New Historians" have done in Israeli archives, we now know that many refugees were deliberately driven from their homes and villages by the Haganah or frightened into leaving by the Haganah or the acts of the Irgun and Lehi. But ER believed the story her Israeli hosts told her and discounted the Arab version of events.[14] Now, she told her correspondent, it was "unrealistic" to expect that those who left could return to Israel since an enormous number of Jewish refugees had streamed into Israel since 1948 and moved into areas once occupied by the Arabs.[15] In many cases, ER wrote in a My Day column later that year, the Arabs would have no homes to return to because "their houses are rubble, having been destroyed after they fled." She does not say why they were destroyed or mention the appropriation of the lands of "absentee" Arabs and the redistribution of Arab property to Jewish settlers.[16] In addition, ER argued in her column, if the Arab refugees were to return, they would bring with them their deep dissatisfaction: "Why should the new state of Israel take people, who would be dangerous citizens, antagonistic to them and their ideas, back into the country?" The Jewish immigrants who had been "flooding into Israel from all over the world," on the other hand, were "imbued with a love of Israel and a belief in the experiment being tried out there." She believed the Arabs would find it much more difficult to make a living in Israel than if they resettled in neighboring Arab countries where "there is land lying idle and where they would not be up against so much competition." ER knew little or nothing about conditions within Arab societies, such as tensions between Sunni and Shiite Muslims or shortages of jobs, that would have made the acceptance of Palestinian refugees by other Arab countries far more difficult than she imagined. In any event, she urged the correspondent whom she felt was being unrealistic about the possibility of the Arab refugees returning to their land to adopt a purely pragmatic view of the situation: "We must look at things as they are and not as we wish they were."[17]

ER was not alone in this view. Elfan Rees, a member of the English clergy who visited the Arab refugee camps many times beginning in 1949 and became the expert on the refugee problem for the Commission of the Churches on International Affairs and the World Council of Churches, came to a similar conclusion. He described the Arab leaders as "positively uncharitable and unhelpful" toward the refugees and criticized pro-Arab American Protestant leaders who, he felt, were "playing the political game of the Arab states by preferring to have the refugees remain a bartering factor" rather than advocating their integration into Arab societies. There was land available for the refugees in Iraq and Syria, Rees asserted, where "by faith, by language, by race and by social organization," the refugees would be "indistinguishable from their fellows." Furthermore, these nations needed manpower for their development.[18]

On the eve of her departure for Lebanon, Malik wrote ER a note expressing his hope that she would meet people who could help her understand the "basic problems" of the Middle East, which were "much deeper" than the issue of Arab refugees, although that was "certainly a great problem." Malik hoped she would be inspired with a sense of the region's long history as the seedbed of civilization and recognize the region's potential for entering "another one of its brilliant periods," if "the rising generation can be seized with a mighty task of construction and hope, grounded in freedom and in a worthy spiritual content."[19] ER would make an effort to assess how the Arab nations she visited were approaching their need for economic development and to learn something about American and UN economic aid programs in the region, but she would not perceive signs pointing toward a realization of Malik's vision.

Malik arranged for ER to be the guest of the Lebanese government while she was in his country from February 10 to 13, 1952. While there, she visited three refugee camps, dined with business leaders and government officials at the home of a wealthy businessman, and spent an evening with Bechara el Khoury, then the president of Lebanon, and his wife. She also visited the homes of a typical farmer and a typical worker, as she had requested.

Stephen Penrose, a friend of Malik's who was president of American University, organized a tea at which ER engaged in a long conversation with a group of professors about the Arab point of view on Palestine. They told her that the UN had made a huge mistake in voting to partition Palestine into separate Jewish and Arab states. In the unified state favored by the Arabs, they said, the Jews would have had the status of a protected minority. The group claimed that the Arabs and Jews had lived in peace in Palestine until the Jews began to create their own government, an assertion that ER said she knew was inaccurate. The group worried that Israel would seek to acquire more territory because of the need to resettle the 700,000 immigrants from Europe and nearby Arab states. ER told them that supporting a strong UN as a bulwark against aggression was the best way to prevent this from happening, but she felt her effort to reassure them failed.

While in Lebanon, ER reported, she also met with a group of educated refugees who told her "how cruelly they had been driven from their homes in Palestine and forced to abandon their possessions at a moment's notice." The members of this group had been able to reestablish themselves in their professions, but "their eviction still rankled and they declared they would never be satisfied until they could return to their homes in Palestine." ER felt "desperately sorry for them," recognizing, she said in a patronizing way, that they were "simply the helpless victims of the history of their times, and have been caught in a struggle that is beyond their understanding." But she sympathized a great deal more with the much larger number of refugees who lived in the refugee camps without an opportunity to move on with their lives.[20]

Penrose was himself a strong advocate for the Arab position. He was one of several Americans who had lived and worked in the Arab world and sympathized deeply with the Arab people.[21] They were actively opposed to the establishment of a Jewish state and made their opinion known to the State Department, which largely shared their point of view. The university that Penrose headed was a highly respected institution that had been founded by American missionaries in 1862 but from the beginning was devoted to promoting American civic values rather than to evangelism.[22] It attracted Arab students from throughout the Middle East and its graduates were influential in the region. ER possessed none of Penrose's experience and, as a result, lacked his social and emotional foothold in the Arab world.

Penrose had vigorously articulated his views on the rights of the Palestinian Arabs in a speech at the World Council of Churches conference that met in Beirut in 1951. That speech reveals how much his narrative of events surrounding the establishment of Israel diverged from the one ER frequently repeated when challenged to justify her views. Penrose did not think that the Balfour Declaration promised the Jewish people a state of their own. The declaration was a "masterpiece of ambiguity," he said, designed to satisfy the Zionists without disturbing the Arabs. But its key passage, Penrose argued, clearly limited its intention:

> His Majesty's Government views with favor the establishment in Palestine of a national home for the Jewish people and will use their best endeavors to facilitate the achievement of this object, *it being clearly understood that nothing shall be done which may prejudice the civil and religious rights of existing non-Jewish communities in Palestine*, or the rights and political status enjoyed by Jews in any other country. [italicized by Penrose]

To Penrose that passage meant "quite obviously" that "the national home for the Jewish people in Palestine could not mean the establishment of a Jewish state inasmuch as the latter would certainly 'prejudice the civil and religious rights of existing non-Jewish communities in Palestine.'"[23]

It is difficult to dispute Penrose's argument. It is also difficult to know what the term "national home" could mean if it did not mean a Jewish state. The declaration was, as Penrose, says, ambiguous. In her own statements on the Balfour Declaration

ER did not directly address the point Penrose was making about the rights of the Arabs and other non-Jewish communities in Palestine. She interpreted the declaration quite differently. At one of the press conferences she held during her Middle East tour, she went further than she had in the past in finding a basis for a Jewish state in the declaration by telling the Arab journalists that she "had always assumed that when Lord Balfour pledged British support for a Jewish national home in Palestine, he had meant that the Jews should have their own country under their own government." When an Arab questioner asserted that Lord Balfour had told Chaim Weizmann that this was not what it meant, ER recalled a conversation she had with Weizmann in which he had told her just the opposite. Given how "completely at variance" the two interpretations were from each other, ER concluded, "this was simply one of those emotional questions about which feelings run so high that neither side can concede even the possibility of another point of view."[24] Recognizing that this was true did not appear to create any doubt in ER's mind about her own commitment to a Jewish state.

In regard to the UN partition plan, Penrose called the role of the United States in securing its adoption by the UN "one of the blacker pages in the history of American international politics." The plan, he argued, had created an "unworkable" patchwork of Jewish and Arab zones of control in order to create areas where the Jews would have a majority and placed more than half of the country, including its most fertile land, under the governance of less than one-third of the population. Like Loy Henderson and other State Department officials who had opposed the plan, Penrose argued that it violated "the principle of self-determination" first set forth by the American president Woodrow Wilson. It was therefore natural that the Arabs came to question the sincerity of the UN and the United States in espousing that principle. Penrose admitted that both sides had committed "dreadful deeds" when warfare broke out after the adoption of the partition plan, but he argued that the Zionists "made better use of the terrorist tactics" by frightening many Arabs into fleeing. He did not believe that "this wholesale displacement and resultant destitution" of the Arabs could in any way "be justified as essential to the solution of the Jewish problem in Europe."

While ER sympathized with the Arab refugees, she regarded the Arab refusal to cooperate with a UN plan to provide employment for the refugees and permanently resettle them in other Arab lands as unrealistic and cynical. Penrose, on the other hand, believed that the Arabs had rejected the resettlement plan because of their deep sense of injustice and "their conviction that cooperation under present circumstances would imply acceptance of the status quo." Since they regarded the status quo as "intolerable," they would not cooperate until it changed and saw no point in direct negotiations with Israel until it did. Penrose believed that a change in the status quo would only come about through determined efforts by the UN and the United States to change the attitudes of both sides.[25] Over the years that followed, however, the status quo only became more intolerable from the Arab point of view.

While in Lebanon ER no doubt heard many of the arguments Penrose made in his 1951 speech either from him, the group of Arabs he gathered together to present to her the Arab perspective, or from other Arabs she met. Although what she heard sharpened her awareness of Arab grievances, it did not change her views on partition or on the best way forward. On the Arab side, it is clear from the response in the Arab press to ER's visit that she was perceived as an embodiment of an American policy that heavily favored Israel over the rights of the Arabs. ER's visit did nothing to alter Arab perceptions. According to the American legation's report, those who listened to her speak to the YWCA and women's organizations in Beirut were impressed in the beginning by "her humility and desire to inform herself on Arab problems," but several of them said afterwards that ER's speech had given them "no new hope of a fair settlement of the refugee problem."[26]

The Arab press in Lebanon attacked her for her role in the creation of the Jewish state and for what it regarded as her indifference to the fate of the Arabs displaced at its founding. It appeared hypocritical to them, as it had to Wadad Dabbagh, that a woman who enjoyed a reputation as a great champion of human rights would not condemn what they saw as violations of their rights.[27]

IN DESCRIBING THE REFUGEE CAMPS in the three Arab countries she visited after she returned home, ER reported that the refugees lived in tents "on steep hillsides" or "on hot, barren plains," lacked adequate nutrition, and suffered from respiratory diseases in the winter and dysentery and fever in the summer. Because of the unwillingness of the Arab states to create employment and permanently resettle the more than 700,000 refugees displaced by the 1948 war, they depended largely on the United Nations Relief and Works Agency for Palestine Refugees for food, shelter, medical care, education, and other needs. Although Jordan had made some effort to draw some of the refugees into the economic life of the country, unemployment among the Jordanians and Lebanese themselves made such efforts difficult. The refugees, ER said, were an "economic burden" to the countries where the camps were located, vulnerable to Communist organizers, and a continuing threat to peace in the Middle East. But what most troubled her was "the loss of skills, the death of pride, the breakdown of morale" that resulted from lack of employment and hope for the future. She told her Arab hosts that whether the refugees were resettled or returned to their homes in Israel, they "would be of no future use unless their skills and work habits were preserved." Her point always won "at least passive agreement" but she felt their assent arose out of "perfect politeness—and complete inertia." What the refugees needed, ER felt, was not handouts but the opportunity to become independent, productive citizens of a country once again.[28] As she had said in 1946 after visiting the DP camps in Germany, "Charity is a wonderful thing," but it does not retrieve "the feeling that we have roots."[29]

At the press conference ER held at the end of her visit to Israel, she was less restrained than she had been while traveling in the Arab countries. The refugees had been trained by Arab leaders and Communist organizers, she charged, and the children drilled to shout in English, "We want to go home." These outbursts "made no impression" on her "since it was obvious that with different training they would change their minds."[30] These remarks drew a strong reaction in the Arab press, which said that they showed her callousness about the refugees and her prejudice in favor of the Jews.[31] Later, after returning home, she repeated these comments in a speech to the Nation Associates.[32]

S. Roger Tyler, the American consul in Jerusalem, reported that the reaction of the Arab press in Jerusalem to ER's visit "ranged from violent imprecations to mere factual reporting of her movements. There was no instance of a genuine expression of pleasure or welcome."[33] An editorial in the Palestinian Arab newspaper *Falastin* greatly exaggerated ER's influence upon Truman, claiming that when she threatened to "flare up" after Warren Austin announced in March 1948 that the United States would now support a UN trusteeship for Palestine rather than the immediate implementation of the partition plan, "Truman submitted, America submitted and States tied to America's apron strings submitted to Mrs. Roosevelt's will." To the editors of *Falastin*, ER was "partly responsible for the establishment of the National Home, the creation of Israel and the dispersion of the Arabs." They asked her to shed her "Americanism" and her "Judaism" and "with a clean Christian conscience meditate on the Palestine crime committed by the U.S. against a peaceful and peace-loving nation in their own homeland."[34]

In her speech to the Nation Associates after she returned to the United States, ER said she had come away convinced of two things: that the Arabs and Israelis would make progress toward peace only if the UN succeeded in resettling the Arab refugees in countries outside of Israel and that there was "nothing to be done *but* to resettle them" since there was "no home for them to go to in most cases." But Arab resistance to resettlement blocked the way.[35] Ali Ash Sheikh Said Al Qaderi, a resident of the Bared River refugee camp in Lebanon, made the depth of that resistance clear in a letter he wrote to ER after her return. He pledged that the Arabs would "refuse every plan or decision which forbids us from going back to our own country or which aims to settle us outside Palestine" and told her that they nurtured in their children a love of Palestine and a desire to take "revenge of the oppressor."[36]

BESIDES SEEKING GREATER UNDERSTANDING of the Arab point of view on Israel and visiting the Arab refugee camps, ER's other motive for visiting the Arab countries was to assess the possibilities of their economic development. Her views on Israel and the Middle East were heavily influenced by the politics of the Cold War. In 1949, as part of its effort to contain the Soviet Union and counteract its influence, the Truman administration initiated the Point 4 program, which provided technical assistance to developing nations in many parts of the world. Its aim was to stimulate economic development and create opportunities for investment in these countries. ER strongly supported this and later nonmilitary foreign aid programs, which promised to assist the nations of the Third World to raise the standard of living of their citizens, and she wanted to observe the conditions they were designed to address. She believed these economic programs rather than military aid were the most important means of reducing the appeal of Communism in the Middle East. In each of the three Arab countries to which she traveled, she visited factories, farms, and shops and spoke with workers in their homes or places of employment, as well as with businessmen, educators, and government officials. ER observed that she was "fully conscious of a certain amount of hostility" behind the outward politeness of the government officials who were her hosts, but she found that when she talked to people individually or in groups in their homes or shops, "the atmosphere was friendly and hospitable."

During her travels through the Arab countries, ER observed what she described as "appalling poverty" of a kind unfamiliar to most Americans, and she questioned the people she met about plans for economic development.[37] Her brief visits to the Arab states did not provide much opportunity to get to understand the cultures of these countries. She measured what she observed by Western standards and, particularly, by the entrepreneurial standard of America's "can do" culture. From that perspective, what she found was not encouraging. While some economic development plans were being carried out, she mainly observed that much more needed to be done. In Syria, the schedule she had asked the American legation to arrange with the Syrian government included visits to a textile factory, a typical worker's home, two Palestine refugee camps, and an agricultural school.[38] At a textile mill in Damascus the owners of the mill showed her the living quarters being constructed for their foremen and said they planned to build a housing project for their workers. When she wrote about this experience later on, after having visited both the Arab countries and Israel and having spoken with officials of UN and American development programs, she said that she had found in both Lebanon and Syria that such projects were "being done on a charitable or benevolent basis, a kind of paternalism, rather than for sound economic reasons." She felt that the leaders of these countries had "accepted the thought of change" but had "no idea of the number and extent of the changes that will be necessary" and were not "making the long-range plans that must precede any real and effective economic development." In addition, "as far as I could see," people did not enter government service "to work unselfishly, with the idea of serving the country and their people," but for "private profit" and they felt that to do so was "entirely legitimate." Although she came to these conclusions partly as a result of conversations she had with the Arabs she spoke with, her views were no doubt strongly influenced by the analyses of the

American diplomats who helped arrange her itinerary in each of the countries she visited and by the American and UN economic development officials who briefed her along the way. To bring about the kind of changes she thought the region needed would require a great deal of outside help from the UN and the United States, she believed, but because of long experience with imperialism, the leaders of these nations were distrustful of American motives and reluctant to accept help for fear of becoming dominated once again by an outside power. For this reason, she noted, Syria had rejected assistance from the American Point 4 economic development program and Jordan had only recently accepted its help.[39]

WHEN ER PASSED THROUGH THE MANDELBAUM GATE, crossing from Jordan into Israel in the middle of a divided Jerusalem, she felt she was entering a very different atmosphere. In the Arab world, she felt discouraged by the Arabs' lack of experience, training, and planning, and, above all, by her perception that the Arabs lacked the motivating spirit she believed was required for the sort of economic development needed to raise their standard of living. In Israel, on the other hand, she was inspired by the energy, excitement, and sense of purpose she felt its people expressed as they went about the task of building their new nation. Her response was strongly influenced by the welcome she received from representatives of Youth Aliyah, Hadassah, and the Israeli government who wanted to show off what they were accomplishing and enlist her in championing their cause back in the United States. She entered Israel not as an ordinary visitor, but in her role as the prospective World Patron of Youth Aliyah and valuable Hadassah supporter.

Unlike other American Zionist organizations, whose primary goal had been achieved by the founding of Israel, Hadassah's opportunities to fulfill its purpose greatly expanded with the opening of the new state to immigration. As the work of building a nation for the Jewish people captured the imagination of many American Jews, particularly the Jewish women in America's burgeoning suburbs, Hadassah's membership grew to over 300,000, making it the biggest voluntary organization of women in the world. The increased financial support that followed this expansion in membership enabled Youth Aliyah to build more training centers and youth villages and permitted Hadassah to greatly expand the construction of medical facilities.[40] Hadassah hoped to engage ER more fully in making its accomplishments known and raising funds to carry its work forward.

In her 1952 visit, ER focused most of her attention on visiting Youth Aliyah and Hadassah facilities. Her many years of experience in promoting child welfare, public health, adequate housing, vocational education, and community building in the United

States during and after the Depression and New Deal prepared her for a deep appreciation of Israeli efforts to rehabilitate children, establish cooperative communities, and create a health system. The way Hadassah and Youth Aliyah approached solving social problems by collecting and analyzing data and bringing in experts (often American) to evaluate programs and make recommendations, a method Henrietta Szold had brought with her from America, was also familiar to ER.

There was an important difference, however, between what American social reformers had achieved and what Israel was doing. The reform movement in which ER participated in the 1920s and 1930s in the United States helped bring about permanent improvements in the fields of child welfare, public health, and social security and helped shape the emerging American welfare state. But Arthurdale and the other cooperative settlements sponsored by the New Deal's Subsistence Homestead program that ER championed in the 1930s did not become important models for the way Americans lived. In the early days of Israel, on the other hand, the kibbutzim functioned as building blocks of the new nation. The devotion ER once lavished on the Subsistence Homestead of Arthurdale and the commitment she shared with the Quakers to providing displaced people with the practical skills, resources, and hope necessary for building self-sustaining lives, she now directed toward Israel. The promise of a more community-based, cooperative society, which the New Deal in the end failed to fulfill, now seemed, in Israel, a realizable goal.

ER's first visit to Israel made an enormous impression on her. In addition, it strengthened the confidence of Israelis that they would receive the outside backing they needed to survive. After she visited a tuberculosis hospital in Jerusalem, a frontier hospital in Beersheba, and the Eddie Cantor village in Maale Hahamisha, Julia Dushkin, a member of the Hadassah Council in Israel Executive Committee, wrote to ER that she had "left an indelible impression" upon the people she met: "Your coming to Israel at this time has enhanced the feeling of security of the many here to whom your very presence is a symbol of their greater personal safety for in you they see the personification of the world's interest in their better destiny."[41]

ER toured the country with her usual tireless energy, attentiveness to the individual people she met, and appetite for detailed information about the operation of the programs and projects she inspected. The *Jerusalem Post* reported that on one fourteen-hour day, she visited the Yuval Gad pipe works at Migdal Ascalon and a Mekorot pumping station, traveled to a Bedouin encampment where she drank coffee with Suleiman Ali-Buzeil, Sheikh of the Negev and head of the Bedouin tribe in the region, stopped at the Hadassah hospital in Beersheba where Dr. K. J. Mann, director of the Hadassah Medical Organization, took her on a tour, saw the newly built part of the town, and spoke with a Romanian family in a nearby immigrant absorption camp. Her "searing pace . . . exhausted her escort," the *Post* reported, but at the end of the day she told Vera Weizmann, wife of Israel's president, Chaim Weizmann, "I never feel tired when I'm absorbed."[42]

ISRAEL STRONGLY APPEALED TO ER in many ways, partly because of the way she associated its experience as a new nation with America's history and the American spirit. In 1948, she had identified the young Israeli soldiers she met in New York with Washington's troops in the American Revolution. Now, she compared the building of Israel with the early settlement of her own country, telling reporters in Jerusalem that in Israel she "almost felt at home because the early American pioneers must have had a similar faith in themselves and in the future of their country." Israel, she said, was an "invigorating country to be in" not only because of its "vitality," but because of the perception that "all the pressing problems are somehow being solved."[43] It was this self-confident spirit, more than anything else, that separated Israel, in ER's mind, from the Arab countries she visited. She associated it with the character traits she believed had enabled Americans to build their own country under adverse conditions. Many American Jews, and Christians as well, shared this perception of Israel as a pioneering country, in which farmer warriors had fought against the British and against the native inhabitants of the land on which they settled, just as American frontiersmen had fought for their independence in the early days of American history. ER's communication of this simplified, romantic version of events to her American audiences reinforced an image of Israelis as heroic actors in an exciting drama.[44]

ER found these frontier qualities especially alive in kibbutz Degania near the lake of Galilee and in the person of its leader, Joseph Baratz. Baratz had helped found the settlement as a young man in 1909. He had struggled with his wife, Miriam, and other early settlers under harsh conditions to harness water for irrigation and make the land productive. They had also fought to protect the settlement, helping to repel an attack from Syrian forces during the 1948 war. ER's visits to Israel bound her emotionally to its cooperative agricultural settlements, its youth training centers, and its children, and no one bound her more closely to the land of Israel than Joseph Baratz. During her first visit, ER began a warm friendship with Baratz, who embodied for her an indomitable creative spirit, both idealistic and realistic, that she found immensely appealing.[45] One may wonder if part of the appeal of Baratz and other pioneers she encountered in Israel was how completely they dispelled the old stereotypes of the Jew that ER had once harbored.

Drawn by Baratz and the thriving community that he led, ER visited Degania each time she traveled to Israel, and Baratz visited her in Hyde Park and New York City. In the correspondence the two friends carried on until ER's death, Baratz shared news about his family and his pleasure in the agricultural cycle at Degania. He also expressed concern about his nation's ongoing vulnerability in the hostile neighborhood in which it existed and his regret that ongoing raids by Arab guerillas along Israel's borders hampered the work of its agricultural settlements. In this "beautiful season, not so hot during the day and delightful in the cool of the evening," Baratz wrote her in October 1955, "we are concluding the date harvest, which this year our flourishing date palms made more abundant than ever. . . . If only we may be permitted to work, we [could] create so much—in the fields, in the gardens, and in the creation of new beauty and happiness."[46]

In 1956, when he and the other members of the community of Degania were about to celebrate the settlement's fiftieth anniversary, Baratz expressed to ER his wonder at the miraculous fact of Israel's existence. He and the other pioneer settlers had been called "dreamers," he told her, but never imagined what eventually took place: "We certainly did not believe that we would see a Jewish State—and in seeing it, we feel ourselves the most blessed people in the world."[47]

Baratz also ran Gordon House at Degania, home to the A. D. Gordon Agriculture and Nature Study Institute, which housed zoological, botanical, and geological specimens, books, and equipment for the study of agriculture and the flora and fauna of the Jordan Valley. The institute played an important role in the education of Degania's young people. ER visited Gordon House and over the years that followed sent contributions for its support. Gordon (1856–1922), who spent the last few years of his life at Degania, was a prominent Zionist thinker. He believed that physical labor, and especially agricultural labor, from which Jews had been cut off for many centuries, would rejuvenate the Jewish people and create a spiritual bond between them and Eretz Yisrael—referring, like the term "Promised Land," to the geographical area, not the later state. Gordon's philosophy, whose essence Baratz no doubt conveyed to ER and which had guided the community of Degania and other kibbutzim, would have appealed to ER, whose involvement in the experiments at Val-Kill and Arthurdale during the 1930s expressed her interest in reviving rural communities in the United States. When Speaker Yosef Sprinzak welcomed ER to the Knesset he recognized her special grasp of Israel's quest for spiritual as well as material renewal:

> In the difficult task which lies before us we have need of friends, who are great in spirit and who will understand our position here—friends who are capable of conveying to the wide world the real meaning of our approach to the Renaissance of the Jewish State.
>
> We know that in your dynamic life your interests lie not only in social welfare, but no less in spiritual welfare.
>
> From my good friend, Yosef Baratz, of Degania, I learned that you were interested in "Beit Gordon," which is in Degania.

The moral content of Gordon's ideals, inspired by the teachings of the Prophets, is essentially the same force which brought forth our pioneers, our youth, and the creators and defenders of the fundamentals of our life.[48]

In 1956, ER wrote a foreword to *A Village by the Jordan*, Baratz's story of the founding and growth of Degania. It was "the story of the striving of people for a better existence," she wrote, and more specifically, "of a desire to live in common and share in common with others." She found inspiration in the "unselfishness of action" that characterized the lives of Joseph and Miriam Baratz, their family, and fellow villagers. "The story," she said, "gives us much to think about because it deals with high aspirations, and it gives a lift to one's daily life."[49]

THE DISPARITY THAT ER PERCEIVED between the dynamic spirit of Israel, embodied by Joseph Baratz and the pioneers of Degania, and what she felt was the absence of such a motivating drive in the Arab countries she visited was noted by other observers as well and posed a challenge for American policy in the Middle East. After hearing ER speak at the State Department upon her return from Israel, Richard Funkhouser, officer-in-charge of Syria-Iraq-Lebanon Affairs, wrote to her asking advice about the problem created by the sharp contrast between what he called the "remarkable youth, energy, dynamism and confidence of the State of Israel" and "the incompetence, backwardness and confusion of the surrounding Arab States." The Arabs themselves recognized this difference, Funkhouser said, and it made them fear that "it will be impossible to hold the dynamic Israel state within its present limits." Funkhouser wanted to know whether ER could assess how realistic this fear was and what could be done to allay "this real or imaginary fear in the minds of the Arab States."

ER replied that the Arabs should seek a guarantee through the UN that neither side would acquire land from the other except by mutual agreement. But beyond that she hoped, unrealistically, that if the two sides would act pragmatically, the disparity between the Arabs and the Israelis offered an opportunity. The Arabs needed to reach a settlement with Israel that would enable them to develop their own countries.[50] The economic development of these countries was essential, she believed, to winning the competition between Western democracy and Soviet Communism. In *India and the Awakening East* (1953), her account of her travels in the Arab countries, Israel, Pakistan, and India, her main purpose was to assess how well these countries were equipped to resist Communism, adopt democratic governance, and develop themselves economically. Communism promised one of the most important freedoms, the freedom to eat. She worried that the Arabs, Pakistanis, and Indians did not recognize that this was a false promise because freedom and prosperity were connected. She regarded Israel, on the other hand, as a bridgehead of democracy in the developing world, a country that could serve as a model for other newly independent nations to emulate rather than succumb to the seductions of Communism. Israel, ER said later, was "the one country that really understood democracy" in a region where most nations had "no understanding of it."[51]

Israel was also a model of economic innovation. If the Arabs would only enter into a peace agreement with Israel, she wrote in *India and the Awakening East*, the Arabs could acquire technical assistance from Israel's experienced administrators and trained technicians who had brought skills from the developed countries of Europe and America. In exchange, the Israelis would gain access to the Arab oil, food, and raw materials they needed for their own development. Such an arrangement would raise the standard of living in Arab countries and open markets for Israeli goods. Instead, ER said, the Arabs hoped to obliterate Israel, which, even if possible would be an enormous loss to them as well as the Israelis. In a stunningly negative assessment of Arab capabilities, she claimed that they "would not put into the country the hard and intelligent work that the Jews have. And unless they did, all development would stop; the land would deteriorate, barren plains and dry deserts would appear where tree-planted fields and productive farms now flourish."[52]

ER applauded the end of colonial rule that began after the end of World War II. But she had not completely shed a colonialist mentality. She regarded the Arabs the way the Puritan colonists of New England regarded Native Americans: the native people did not make use of the land, whereas the new settlers would make it productive through the virtue of hard work. The implication of ER's harsh judgment was that the Israelis deserved the land because they had the energy, the skill, and the will to develop it. Their resourcefulness would benefit not only themselves but the land and its native inhabitants. Her vision of a benevolent colonialism resembled that of some of the pioneering Jewish settlers of Palestine themselves. Moshe Smilansky, a leader of the orange growers of Rehovot, wrote in the 1930s: "We are returning to our homeland that has waited for us as wasteland," bringing with us "the great values of a new civilization" as "a gift to our ancient land, and to the people who have settled it while we were away, and to the other peoples of the surrounding Orient. . . . Never did a colonial project bring so much blessing as the blessing brought upon the country and its inhabitants by our project. Every piece of land upon which our feet have stepped turned good. We did good to us and we did good to all that are with us."[53]

ER had an optimistic view of history, which seems at times naïve but also inspiring. It is partly why she appealed, and still appeals, to so many people. She believed that nations could learn, with the help of the United Nations and the International

Court of Justice, to settle their differences through compromise and a willingness to abide by international law and the decisions of the UN. She believed that people could change, could become more loving and respectful of each other, and begin to cooperate when they realized that it served their mutual interests. She applied this optimism to the situation in the Middle East. In a speech she gave after her return to the United States, ER said that if the emotional core of the Arab-Israeli conflict (the Palestinian Arabs' loss of their homes) could be removed or dissipated by resettling the refugees, then "the logic of the situation" would lead over time to the Arabs and Israelis actually working together to solve problems. There was a nationalistic "stirring" among the Arab people, a desire for an improved standard of living, she said, but the leaders of the Arab states did not know how to use their newly gained freedom to meet the needs of their citizens. "I think if one could just transfer a little of the ability to administer and organize," possessed by the Israelis, "into the Arab governments, their business circles, their agriculture, one would find the problems of the Arab countries solving themselves very rapidly."[54] She thought it was largely the stubbornness of the Arabs and their unwillingness to recognize their own self-interest that prevented them from accepting the existence of the Jewish state and allowing Israel to apply its skills to the economic development of the region. ER's view was encouraged over the years by the Israeli leaders with whom she discussed Israel's future. After meeting with Israeli president Yitzhak Ben-Zvi at a reception in Jerusalem in 1962, ER told her My Day readers that Ben-Zvi felt "strongly about the contribution Israel could make to the well-being of the whole Near East area if only Egypt could be induced to give up its dream of driving the Israelis off the map."[55] Ben-Gurion still held onto this dream in 1973 on his deathbed when he told Ruth Gruber that he thought peace would come from Egypt because its youth "know what we can contribute to them, and what they can contribute to us. They have diseases like trachoma and bilharzia that we cured over fifty years ago. We have so much we can help them with, and they have natural resources that can help us."[56]

In an ideal world and from a purely pragmatic point of view, such an arrangement made good sense. In fact, beginning in the 1950s Israel pursued a foreign aid policy that brought development assistance to some of the emerging nations in Africa, including Ghana.[57] If the Arabs had accepted partition, they too might have benefited from such programs. But ER's vision of Israeli-Arab cooperation reflected a naïveté about the intense nationalist sentiments that motivated the Arabs after the end of Ottoman and European colonial rule, about the effect of colonization and then dispossession on the Palestinian Arabs, and about the power of historical narratives to constrain political choice. She also failed to recognize that the great cultural, economic, and political differences between Israel and the Arab states, far from offering an opportunity for cooperation, represented an enormous impediment.

Once again, as she had done in 1938 in *This Troubled World*, ER held up an ideal as a kind of challenge to the reality created by political passions. At the same time, her belief that cooperation between Arabs and Israelis was possible provided her with another rationale for supporting Israel. If Israel had the potential and the willingness (which ER believed it did) to function as a catalyst for economic and social change in the Middle East, should the Arabs agree to make peace, that, from ER's perspective, further justified Israel's existence.

16

IMMIGRANT CHILDREN AND THE TASK OF CULTURAL INTEGRATION

"The successful integration of the youth from many lands into a united people"

After her 1952 trip, Eleanor Roosevelt visited Israel three more times: in 1955, 1959, and 1962, the year of her death. On each trip, Moshe Kol, the director of Youth Aliyah, later recalled, she asked to return to the places she had been before so that she could "evaluate the development which had taken place"[1] since her last visit. She also visited new training centers, youth villages, kibbutzim, irrigation works, medical facilities, and other projects she had not seen previously. Although she took an interest in many aspects of Israeli life, her special focus remained on children. When ER wrote or spoke about Israel, she recognized the enormous challenges Israel faced in education, vocational training, health care, housing, job creation, and military preparedness while absorbing a flood of immigrants from sharply different cultural backgrounds, but she painted an idealistic picture of the efforts the Israelis were making to address them. She was a good observer who asked probing questions, but her perspective was necessarily shaped by her Youth Aliyah, Hadassah, and Israeli government hosts. She saw what they wanted her to see and heard their positive presentation of the work they were doing. The depth of her knowledge was also limited by the shortness of her visits to Israel and the crowded itineraries she followed.

ER took her second trip to Israel in March 1955 with her close friend Trude Lash (formerly Trude Pratt), who had been her colleague in refugee work in the late 1930s and 1940s and in the field of child welfare, in which Lash was expert. Lash, ER told a Hadassah official, was her "eyes and ears for child work."[2] At the time of their trip to Israel, Lash was executive director of the Citizens Committee for Children of New York, a group that advocated for programs to meet the needs of New York City children, particularly those from low-income families.³ Lash's goal on the trip was to study Youth Aliyah's programs and the possible application of their methods to child welfare programs in the United States. She agreed to write an article for the *Hadassah Newsletter* about the trip and to give ten talks to Hadassah groups about what she and ER experienced in order to stimulate interest in the work of Youth Aliyah.

ER's second trip to Israel introduced her to one of the most difficult problems Youth Aliyah faced: how to integrate children from Morocco and other countries in North Africa and the Middle East into the modern nation Israel was building. Beginning in 1951 more than 70 percent of immigrants to Israel were coming from these countries.⁴ The children posed a different challenge from the children who had been traumatized by the Holocaust and the war in Europe. The North African and Middle Eastern children came from families that lived under conditions and practiced customs very unlike those of their European counterparts. Some of the children, like those from Europe, came to Israel unaccompanied by their parents. In some cases the parents were dead, but some of the North African and Middle Eastern children came because their parents felt their children had no future in the countries in which they lived. The parents, who often hoped to join their children in Israel later on, entrusted their children to Youth Aliyah, which took responsibility for their care, education, and integration into Israeli society. Even more than on her first visit, ER was fascinated by the scale and speed with which Youth Aliyah carried out its task.

ER and Lash began their trip in France with stops at two camps for Moroccan immigrants near Marseille. One of the camps housed Moroccan families while they waited for a boat to take them to Israel; the other, operated by Youth Aliyah at Cambous, served Moroccan children, ages seven to fifteen, who were going to Israel alone. Moshe Kol probably suggested this prelude to ER's second visit to Israel since it allowed her to see the children at the very beginning of their journey toward citizenship in their new country. The children spent two months at the camp, where they studied Hebrew, Israeli history and geography, and agricultural work and began a process of orientation to the unfamiliar circumstances they would encounter in Israel. ER felt the beds the children slept on in order to see how comfortable they were, made "a minute inspection" of the rest of the camp, and inquired about the children's background. She asked for details about the medical, hygienic, educational, and administrative arrangements at the camp, examined documentation on the psychological state of the children, and discussed the emotional state of the children with the camp's psychiatrist. She had lunch with 180 children, who entertained her with songs and recitals, and she conversed with some of the children in French.⁵

The Moroccan Jews were among the poorest in the world. The children at Cambous were being asked to make a rapid transition from a Third World culture to the fundamentally European culture of Israel. Some of the children were illiterate. Most of the children were accustomed to sleeping in their clothes and had never slept in a bed. They had never seen a toothbrush, eaten at a table, or used forks and knives. ER regarded their customs as primitive and their education at Cambous as a step toward civilization. "Most of the things babies learn in more advanced communities," she wrote, "have to be learned by these children at whatever age they leave Morocco."[6] Lash was impressed by the skill of the educators at Cambous. "Only an absolutely devoted staff could take these youngsters from a strange civilization, from so many varied backgrounds, scared youngsters, many of whom understand none of the languages staff members understand and—without force, without relying on strict rules—get them to accept and to learn willingly so much in such a short time."[7]

Despite what their teachers were able to accomplish, however, Lash and ER recognized that the challenges for these children would be great. Many of them had histories that were "almost unbelievable," ER said in a speech to the Hadassah convention after her return. She wondered if they would "ever be able to overcome the past." ER recounted a conversation with one little boy whose father had given him a wristwatch before he departed and hoped his parents would join him in Israel before too long: "His big eyes opened wide and he said: 'We were ten children and seven of us died. My mother felt the evil eye was on her so our parents decided to send me and my brother to Israel to live. My little brother, seven years old, stayed with my mother to die.'"[8] Yet ER saw the children of Cambous playing, dancing, and singing Israeli songs and "realized that when they said the word 'Israel' it was said with an intonation which meant that to them it had become the symbol of life. Many of them were not at all sure that they would ever again see the families they had left behind. But Israel meant life to them."[9]

ER'S VISIT TO CAMBOUS EXPANDED her awareness of the task Israel faced: the absorption of a large number of immigrants from diverse cultural and economic backgrounds into a unified nation. Already an assimilationist based on her experience of immigration to the United States and living well before the time when the ideals of "multiculturalism" and "diversity" became current, it was a small step for ER to go further and accept the need for the thorough melding of immigrants into one Jewish nation that Israel was trying to achieve. The fact that the Arabs still living in Israel would remain unassimilated in a Jewish state did not appear to trouble her, although she did believe they should enjoy the same rights as other citizens.

Beginning in the 1970s Israeli educators would begin taking a more pluralistic approach to educating children from diverse backgrounds, but in the 1950s their policies were decidedly assimilationist.[10] Aryeh Deri, a Moroccan immigrant who emerged as a leader of Sephardic Jewry in Israel in the 1980s and founded the ultra-Orthodox Shas Party, believed the effect of assimilation on the culture the Sephardic immigrants brought with them had been devastating. He told the Israeli journalist Ari Shavit that the leaders of the Ashkenazi Labor Party that dominated the Israeli government until the late 1970s

> thought that most of the people who emigrated from the Arab world were primitive and therefore had to be put through a process of secular European indoctrination. The melting pot was a Western melting pot that was supposed to totally transform us. Those Labor Ashkenazim didn't honor our civilization. They did not see the beauty of our tradition. That's why they severed us from our roots and our heritage.[11]

The "Zionist imperative," writes the historian Erica Simmons, "called for all immigrants to shed their Diasporic pasts and subsume themselves, whatever their backgrounds, in a new identity." Youth Aliyah, which "wanted youngsters to shed the social habits acquired in other countries and contexts," played a significant role in the effort to achieve this goal.[12] ER shared Youth Aliyah's belief in the benefits of this process and did not recognize its negative side.[13]

The fact that most of the children immigrating to Israel arrived unaccompanied by their parents and not speaking Hebrew made it necessary to meet all their needs—emotional and social as well as educational—but it also provided an extraordinary opportunity. By living together with teachers and mentors in training schools and youth villages, the children would be motivated to adapt more quickly to the new life they would be leading. The pull exerted upon them by the natural tendency of immigrant parents to cling to old ways and their native language would be absent.

Visiting Israel four times during its critical early history, ER observed the evolution of institutions and methods for turning a wave of young immigrants into productive citizens who were committed to the survival of the new nation. Israel was, indeed, an exciting experiment to watch. As the authors of a report on Youth Aliyah's innovative methods for educating "high-risk adolescents" wrote in 1974: The need to integrate "a diversity of languages, cognitive styles, cultural and religious traditions, levels of technological development, and social aspirations into a cohesive national and cultural unit" transformed Israel "into a vast laboratory for both naturalistic observations and scientific experimentation in areas of cultural redevelopment through education."[14] Much of the money raised by private organizations, primarily by Hadassah, and substantial sums allocated by the Israeli government went into supporting this ambitious educational program. "The results," ER felt, "justify both the money spent and the effort which has gone into the building of these future citizens." ER admired the comprehensive services Israel provided to children from infancy to maturity and the programs designed for children from various backgrounds and degrees of preparedness. She and Lash were eager to see the entire range of institutions and programs run by Youth Aliyah and other organizations. She visited children's villages where the children lived together under the supervision of teachers and mentors. "The directors practically take the place of parents," she wrote afterward, "and, while encouraging great independence and self-reliance in the children, still give them a sense of love and protection which creates a fine group of young citizens for this new country." She visited trade schools where "the child studied four hours a day and did five hours of manual work under a master mason, carpenter, or tinsmith." She saw camps where children lived temporarily while they mastered a particular skill, such as driving and maintaining a tractor. She visited another camp that evaluated children with psychological problems, then sent them to schools or camps that seemed "best fitted to correct their particular troubles."[15]

At Pardesiya, ER and Lash visited a Youth Aliyah training facility that trained teenagers who had arrived with their families, including some who had not attended school before coming to Israel. The students were from the *ma'abarah* (a camp for absorbing refugees) in Pardesiya and came mainly from the Middle East and North Africa. Many immigrant families believed their teenage children should work to assist in their family's support but would allow them to attend a school like the one at Pardesiya because the students got paid while there and learned a trade. The students at the Pardesiya training facility could also live at home since Youth Aliyah had located it right at the camp.[16]

When ER revisited the places in Israel she saw in 1952, Lash reported in her article in the *Hadassah Newsletter*, ER was startled by the changes that had taken place. Where there had been "only scraggly seedlings," there were now "long rows of stately eucalyptus trees." Where there had been sand, there were "orange groves, avocado plantings and banana plantations." ER and Lash saw "new villages everywhere, rows of gleaming white apartment houses in Tel Aviv, new factories, new industries."

As ER and Lash toured the country, they often talked about what Israel needed the most. In the beginning, ER concluded it was achieving economic independence, for in 1955, Israel still remained heavily dependent on outside financial aid and investment. Finance minister Levi Eshkol told them that Israel "must narrow the gap between what we spend and what we produce, and slowly, slowly, we are doing it." But as ER and Lash met with more children and teachers, ER came to believe that the foundation of Israel's well-being would be "the successful integration of the youth from many lands into a united people." They found that Israelis were nearly unanimous in their conviction that the future of Israel would depend on whether it would be possible to "imbue" its immigrant children, "from many racial and cultural backgrounds, from countries as far apart as Poland, India, Holland and Iraq—with the certainty that they belong together, that they must help their country with untiring and selfless willingness to serve it."[17]

The challenge was immense. The school population had quadrupled in the past four years and ER called the shortage of teachers "appalling." The fact that children who arrived with their families were often expected by their parents to go to work at the age of fourteen when compulsory education ended made it difficult to keep them in school after that age. Partly for that reason, the army, in which all Israeli boys and girls, with some exceptions, were required to serve, played a significant role in the process of integrating the new immigrants. In 1949, Ben-Gurion had written that the function of the army was not only to defend the state, but to "serve as an educational and pioneering center for Israeli youth—for both those born here and newcomers."[18] The children from North African and Middle Eastern countries were the special targets of this educational effort. When describing the part played by the Israeli defense forces, ER wrote in My Day that the army was "looked upon as a continuation of the educational system," and was "expected to do part of the job of teaching all citizens the rudiments of democracy." For those children who arrived in Israel with little education, the army helped fill the gap, ER said, and even played a role in teaching them agriculture.[19]

Lash and ER were amazed by the evident transformation of the immigrant children in a short time. At Cambous the children "were just beginning to smile," but in Israel, they found, the children laughed "easily and quickly" and welcomed ER with "beautiful radiant faces." At the Youth Aliyah training centers in Israel, Lash found that it was "impossible to tell national origin" because the children already appeared "changed."[20] But Lash and ER also learned that "the obvious success in the tremendous task of cultural integration does not mean that there are not failures or serious difficulties." Dr. Louis Miller, a Hadassah psychiatrist, explained to them that "'acculturation' was sometimes too fast; that the newcomers followed rules easily and quickly, but tests showed they did not always understand the reason for these rules and soon forgot their newly acquired knowledge."[21] Despite such setbacks, ER and Lash were correct in concluding that Youth Aliyah's programs were attaining the goals its leaders set for them. The results of an examination that tested the intelligence, achievement, personality, and knowledge of Hebrew of Israeli students upon their entrance into the army indicated in 1974 that graduates of Youth Aliyah "attained the average of the total Israeli population and even surpassed it in certain areas. They came very close to Kibbutz-born children, who obtained the highest scores in these tests."[22]

IN ADDITION TO THE EDUCATIONAL PROGRAMS conducted by Youth Aliyah, ER also took a keen interest in Hadassah's medical programs. When the leaders of Hadassah heard that ER was returning to Israel, they decided "they must show her something new and different and exciting, the like of which she could not have seen anywhere else in the world." They chose Hadassah's Community Health Center at Bet Mazmil (later named Kiryat Hayovel), a facility designed to serve a primarily immigrant community, which was developing a new way of integrating health education, preventive medicine, and the diagnosis and cure of disease with recreational programs and other community activities. It was a good choice for a woman who had long advocated comprehensive approaches to health care.

ER's hunger for details about every aspect of the programs conducted at Bet Mazmil is evident in Hadassah's report on her visit. The facility sought to assist immigrant families to adapt physically and emotionally to the society in which they were now living. The professional staff included specialists in anthropology, biostatistics, and psychiatry who were developing methods that they would apply in Arab villages as well as in immigrant settlements. ER, who knew about the nature of health administration from experience with health policy in the United States, wanted to know how the goal of an integrated health service could be achieved when several medical agencies were involved. She was told that Hadassah had been successful in persuading the health insurance companies, the municipality, and the government to cooperate so that all medical services were delivered through the health center. That alone, ER said, was a remarkable step forward in creating a new model for community health centers.

ER wanted to know about some of the difficulties faced by a typical immigrant family. After telling ER in detail about the origins of one family, the employment and health problems of the father and mother, and the behavior problems of one of the children, the Hadassah official who accompanied ER became uneasy about getting off schedule, but ER, "patently fascinated by all she heard," wanted to hear more about the problems immigrants had in adapting to a new culture, such as changes in their traditional diet. The approach to such issues was usually indirect, they told her. Rather than dictate that they drink milk, one nurse combined milk into a dish with potatoes and peanuts, foods they were used to eating.

While the Israeli Foreign Service officer escorting ER's party kept "desperately pointing to the time," ER's attention remained focused on the "brightly colored charts showing the age structure of each family in the community."[23] ER wanted to know about it all.

ER'S DEVOTION TO ISRAEL, INSPIRED by its success in fighting for its existence, then by her first trip to the country in 1952, then by her return visit in 1955, flowed from two emotional sources. First of all, she saw how programs run by Youth Aliyah and other Israeli agencies had already revitalized the desperate men and women she had visited in the displaced persons (DP) camps of Europe. What Israel had done for its immigrants was, like the programs of the American Friends Service Committee for impoverished Appalachian coal miners, a transformation of their lives so that they could begin again. Youth Aliyah did it so rapidly, on such a tremendous scale, and in such a thorough way, that it astounded her. Second, ER recognized how important it was to the

Jews that Israel provided them with a national home. After enduring for generations as a persecuted minority in other countries and suffering unbelievable horrors during the Holocaust, they were now in charge of their own destiny.

In a speech to the Hadassah Convention after her return from her 1955 visit, ER told of an incident in Haifa the previous spring when "a very charming, good looking young woman" came to see her with her husband and two children. The woman told her that she had spoken to ER at a DP camp shortly after the war. ER remembered the encounter very well. The woman had lost all her family, except one little girl of about ten months old, "who looked as though she were going to die." ER had not expected either of them to survive. But after leaving the camp, the woman managed to reach Haifa, start life over again, marry an Israeli, and have a son. The woman's daughter had grown into "a lovely child," ER said. "You would never have dreamed what she had been through as a baby." For the small family that now stood before her, "life had really become a promise fulfilled." More than anything she saw in Israel, this family represented the meaning of Israel for ER.

The accomplishments of Hadassah and Youth Aliyah impressed ER so much that she regarded them not only as the fulfillment of the promise of Israel for the Jewish people, but "as the guide for changes that must come eventually to the whole Middle East" and, in fact, to the world. The success of the democratic nations' effort "to build a better world in which all people can live with greater hope and greater happiness," ER said, will "depend on the determination of our people to do on a world-wide scale just what Hadassah and Youth Aliyah are doing in Israel."[24] It was a wonderful vision. Israel's achievement was in many ways a special case, however, brought about by the unique historical circumstances in which the Jews found themselves. After centuries of dispersal and persecution, culminating in the Holocaust, the Jews seized the opportunity to become a nation once again. Many of the European Jews brought skills with them and Americans, both Jewish and Gentile, provided know-how and generous financial support. Both the suffering that lay behind the Jews and the future they felt was now within their grasp inspired an extraordinary energy, resourcefulness, and determination as they pursued their pioneering tasks.

ER'S ADMIRATION FOR THE WAY Youth Aliyah had adapted its methods to meet the needs of North African and Middle Eastern children intensified her interest in the organization's work after her 1955 trip. One of the ways that her deepened commitment expressed itself was in the fundraising trips she made on Youth Aliyah's behalf to Canada, Great Britain, and various parts of the United States. She even took her campaign on behalf of Youth Aliyah to Mexico, where she was welcomed by the Jewish community of Mexico City and spoke to the local Youth Aliyah council.[25] Her personal experience of Israel provided rich material for the fundraising speeches she delivered in these various countries.

ER's trip to Great Britain in 1957 was especially significant for Youth Aliyah. She was a beloved figure in Great Britain, partly because her husband's crucial contribution to Great Britain's defense during World War II was still fresh in people's minds, but also because she herself had made a much-appreciated visit to Great Britain in 1942 in the middle of wartime to help lift morale. Youth Aliyah, on the other hand, was not well known outside of the Jewish community. But the attention ER attracted from the British media because of who she was gave her multiple opportunities to promote the work of Youth Aliyah to a broad audience in press conferences and interviews on television and radio, as well as at fundraising events for the organization.

The high point of ER's trip was a dinner at Grosvenor House in London in her honor attended by 700 people, including many prominent individuals. Among them were Eliahu Elath, the Israeli ambassador to Great Britain; Israel Brodie, the chief rabbi of Great Britain; Solomon Gaon, the Haham (chief rabbi) of the Sephardic congregations of the British Commonwealth; Robert Balfour, the third Earl of Balfour and the nephew of Arthur Balfour; and ER's old friend Lady Stella Reading, who had directed the Women's Voluntary Service in Great Britain during the war. A report on ER's trip in the *Youth Aliyah Review* called the dinner "probably the most memorable in the history of Youth Aliyah."[26]

Her fame helped make her fundraising efforts in Great Britain an enormous success. Moshe Kol, who helped host her visit, reported afterward that Youth Aliyah had raised 25,000 pounds during her visit. Equally important, Kol wrote, was that "Youth Aliyah became very famous through the whole of the British Press, Television, Radio." That opened up opportunities to appeal to Jews and others "who were outside our work," but would now consider supporting Youth Aliyah.[27]

At a dinner given by the Manchester Friends of Youth Aliyah in her honor, ER said that even though the people of Israel were trained to defend themselves, she felt that the people wanted peace. "They have been through experiences which it is better that they should forget but it is the kind of experience which makes them value a peaceful life, which makes them long to develop security."[28] She knew the depth of that longing from her friend Joseph Baratz of Degania, who loved the earth's fruitfulness and wished that his community could enjoy each season of the agricultural year undisturbed. Baratz told her, however, that he and the other citizens of his kibbutz were "not only dreamers," but "also realists," who had "lived through many difficulties" and knew "that there are many more to come." They hoped to overcome all their problems with the help of their "many good friends in the world."[29] By the mid-1950s ER had proved herself one of the best of those friends.

ER visiting the memorial to Holocaust victims at the Zeilsheim DP camp in Germany, February 1946. (Reproduced by permission from the United States Holocaust Memorial Museum.)

Isaiah Bowman, geographer who advised FDR and ER, 1940. (FROM HOLMES I. MATTEE/ FERDINAND HAMBURGER ARCHIVES, SHERIDAN LIBRARY, JOHNS HOPKINS UNIVERSITY.)

ER with Justine Polier at an American Jewish Congress membership event, undated.
(Reproduced by permission from the American Jewish Historical Society.)

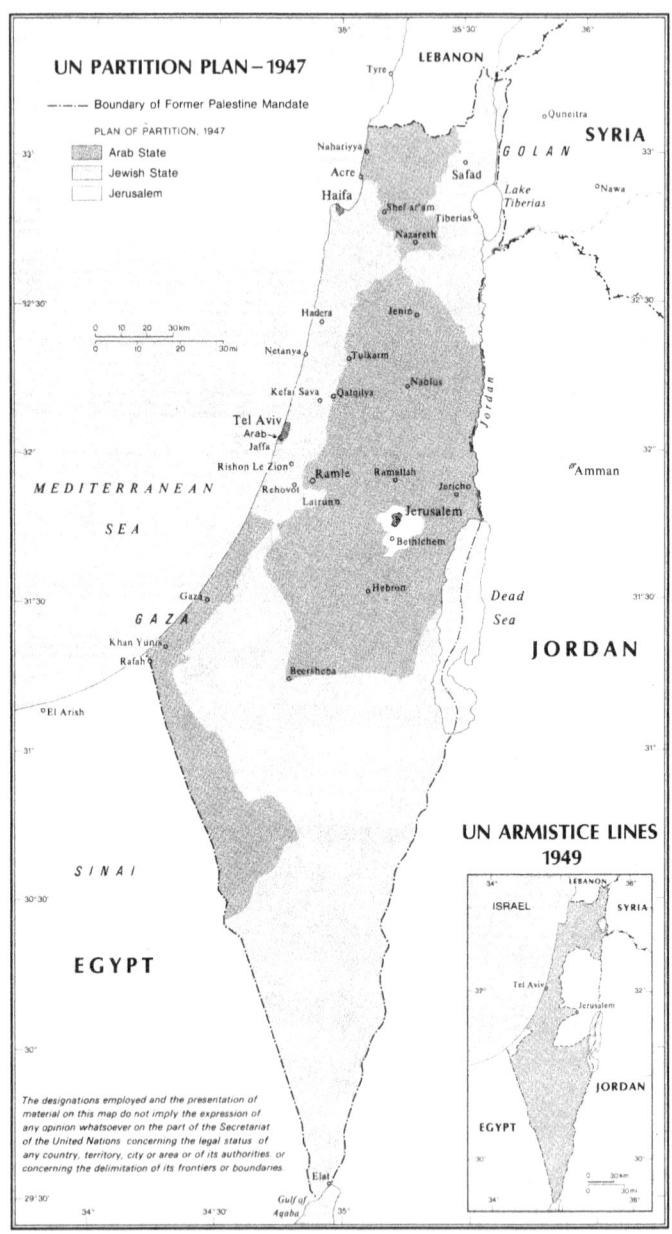

Map showing 1947 United Nations Partition Plan borders and 1949 UN armistice lines. (REPRODUCED BY PERMISSION FROM THE UNITED NATIONS DEPARTMENT OF PUBLIC INFORMATION.)

ER with Stephen Penrose, Jr., president of American University in Beirut, Lebanon, February 1952. (REPRODUCED BY PERMISSION FROM THE STEPHEN B. L. PENROSE, JR. PAPERS, WHITMAN COLLEGE AND NORTHWEST ARCHIVES.)

ER at Degania Alef with Joseph Baratz, who helped found the kibbutz in 1910. (REPRODUCED BY PERMISSION FROM THE DEGANIA A' ARCHIVE.)

ER visiting an ORT training school, Israel, February 1952. (Reproduced by permission from the Archives of the YIVO Institute for Jewish Research, New York.)

ER with Dr. K. J. Mann, director general of the Hadassah Medical Organization (second from left) and Julia Dushkin, member of the Hadassah Council in Israel, at a Hadassah medical facility in Beersheba, February 1952. (Courtesy of the FDR Library.)

ER and Trude Lash visiting with refugee girls in their room at the Women's League Hostel, Jerusalem, March 19, 1955. (COURTESY OF THE FDR LIBRARY.)

Trude Lash and ER visiting the Yuval Gad factory, producer of pipes to carry water to the Negev, March 1955. (COURTESY OF THE FDR LIBRARY.)

ER being greeted at the Pioneer Women's Agricultural School, Ayanot, March 1955. (Reproduced by permission from the Government Press Office, State of Israel/FDR Library.)

ER and Trude Lash flanking a portrait of Henrietta Szold, March 1955. (Courtesy of the FDR Library.)

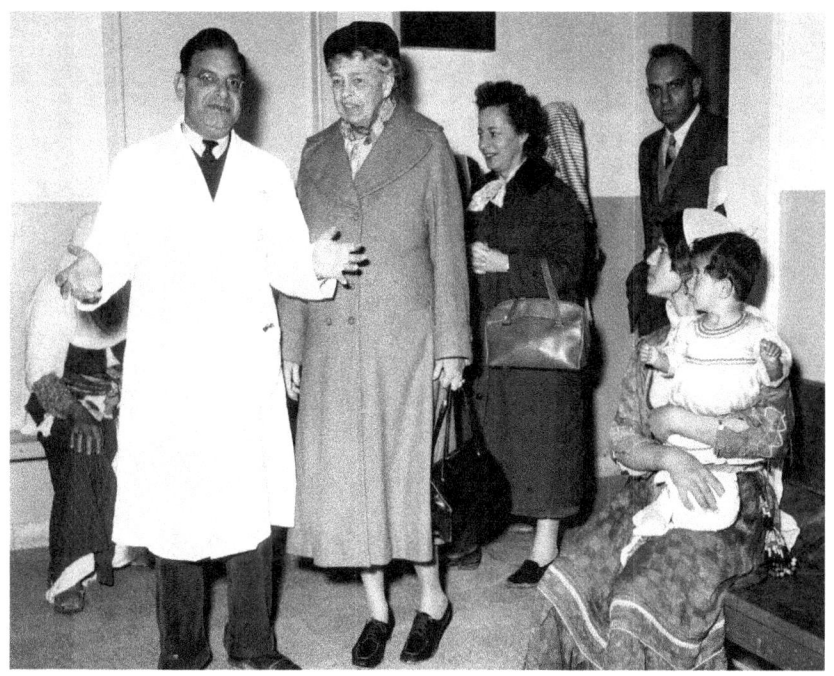

ER touring the health center at the Arab village of Baga-El-Gabya, 1959. (Reproduced by permission from the Government Press Office, State of Israel.)

ER visiting the Alonei Yitzhak Children's Village, March 1959. (Courtesy of the FDR Library.)

ER at the home of the immigrant woman she visited in 1952, 1955, and again in 1959 after the birth of her two children. (Reproduced by permission from the Government Press Office, State of Israel.)

ER and Moshe Kol speaking with home economics student at the Eleanor Roosevelt Youth Aliyah Day Centre, Beersheba, February 1962. (Courtesy of the FDR Library.)

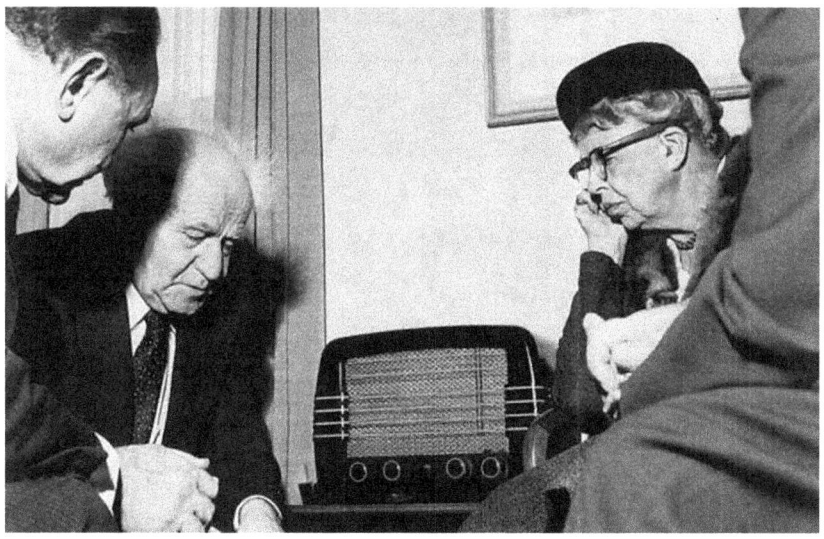

ER visiting with David Ben-Gurion in Jerusalem, March 1959. (Photograph by David Rubinger Reproduced by permission from the Government Press Office, State of Israel.)

ER and Golda Meir, 1949. (Photograph by Leo Rosenthal. Courtesy of the FDR Library.)

17

AMERICAN POLICY TOWARD ISRAEL IN THE 1950s

"Shortsighted beyond words"

From the time of the Balfour Declaration onward, many American Christians supported the establishment of a national home for the Jewish people in Palestine. They were also sympathetic to Israel after its founding as a state. The leading Christian organization that advocated for the establishment of a Jewish homeland was the American Christian Palestine Committee (ACPC), a group formed in 1946 from the merger of two earlier organizations. After the establishment of Israel, the ACPC worked in concert with the Israeli government and American Zionists to project a positive image of Israel to the American people. One of its leaders was Reinhold Niebuhr, Eleanor Roosevelt's colleague in the liberal anti-Communist organization Americans for Democratic Action, and its membership included many senators and congressmen. Among other activities, the ACPC organized study groups to visit Israel. Participants were encouraged to speak or write upon their return about what they had learned.[1]

Not all American Christians, however, agreed with the position of the ACPC or shared ER's joy at the founding of Israel. The State Department had objected to the UN partition plan and the establishment of Israel primarily for strategic reasons related to access to oil and the goal of preventing the Arab states from falling into the Communist orbit. Some influential American Christians opposed it for other reasons. They feared that American support for a Jewish state would jeopardize the work that American Protestant missionaries had been doing among Muslims and Christians throughout the Middle East for a century and put at risk the schools and other institutions, such as the American University of Beirut, the missionaries had founded. They also worried that in a Jewish state, Arab Christians would lose the status they enjoyed as a minority within a Muslim society. Some of the American Christians who were sympathetic to the Arab point of view had been engaged in missionary work in one way or another or were the children of missionaries and therefore had an emotional investment in the Arab world. They viewed the displacement of the Arabs and the taking of lands on which they had lived for many generations deeply troubling. Prior to the founding of Israel, *The Christian Century*, the leading mainstream Protestant magazine, favored a binational state, opposed massive Jewish immigration to Palestine, and regarded the UN partition plan as unjust to the Arabs. The magazine maintained its pro-Arab sympathies after Israel declared itself a state.

The sharpest American critic of Israel was the columnist Dorothy Thompson, whom ER had greatly admired in the 1930s and early 1940s for her outspoken opposition to Hitler and passionate advocacy on behalf of refugees fleeing Nazi persecution. At a Zionist convention in 1942, Thompson gave an ardent pro-Zionist speech in which she called for unrestricted Jewish immigration to Palestine. But after visiting Palestine in 1945, she concluded that the creation of a Jewish state would be an enormous mistake because it would lead to unending warfare. After this turnabout she became the most prominent American anti-Zionist and defender of the Palestinian Arabs in the United States, adopting a position diametrically opposed to ER's. As a result of her stance, the pro-Zionist editor of the *New York Post*, which had many Jewish readers, dropped Thompson's column in 1947 and Zionists smeared her as an antisemite.[2]

In 1951 Thompson founded the American Friends of the Middle East (AFME), which promoted a pro-Arab viewpoint to the American public by bringing Arab speakers to the United States, sending pro-Arab American speakers to the Middle East, organizing tour groups to Arab countries, and conducting a program of research and publication. AFME's publications included Stephen Penrose's speech to the World Council of Churches conference in Beirut in which he condemned the UN partition plan. AFME's sixty-three-member national council included eighteen prominent Protestant clergymen.[3] In 1952, Garland Evans Hopkins, who as associate editor of the *Christian Century* had accused Israel of failing to abide by the principles of the Universal Declaration of Human Rights (UDHR) in its treatment of the Arabs, took charge of directing AFME's work.[4] The central tenet of the organization was that Israel either had to become a predominantly Arab state like its neighbors in the region or "cease to exist." The AFME's aim was to persuade the American government to adopt a similar position. The Arabists in the State Department and the CIA, who shared similar views, gave the organization a foothold in the American government. In fact, it was revealed in 1967 that AFME received funding from the CIA.[5]

Both American Zionists and the Israeli government worried about the power of AFME and Dorothy Thompson to influence American public opinion against Israel. Thompson wrote about the conflict in the Middle East in her widely syndicated column

On the Record and lectured to church and women's groups and at other forums throughout the United States on Israel and on the Arab refugee problem. Writing to the Local Committees of the American Zionist Council (AZC) in 1951, Rabbi Jerome Unger, executive director of the AZC, warned that "given the weight her name carries," Zionists "must challenge her 'misstatements and hostile propaganda' wherever she appears" and ask that spokesmen sympathetic to Israel be invited to present their views to the same groups.[6]

Members of the American Christian Palestine Committee also worked to counteract criticism of Israel. In 1951, Karl Baehr, the executive secretary of the ACPC, warned the Israeli Office of Information in New York that some Christians were coming back from trips to Israel and the Middle East with a negative attitude toward Israel. "Christians return with admiration for what Israel has achieved," he wrote, "but, they conclude, all this has been accomplished at the expense of the Arabs. They conclude, as did Duke McCall [a Protestant clergyman] that Israel is an 'immoral miracle.'" Baehr recommended that Israel revise the information it gave visitors by informing them about Arab atrocities committed against Israelis and the oppression of Jews in Iraq, Yemen, and other Arab countries. He also suggested showing visitors areas damaged by the Arabs during the war and arranging interviews with wounded veterans rather than just showing off Israel's achievements.[7] Abe Harman, director of the Israeli Office of Information, agreed, and the Israeli ministry in charge of tourism took steps to expose Christian visitors to evidence of Arab aggression.[8]

In this struggle to sway American Christians in favor of Israel, ER's reputation as a humanitarian, her ability to reach a national audience through her My Day column, and her numerous speaking engagements made her enormously valuable to the ACPC, American Zionists, and the Israeli government. She made the case for Israel in her column, in speeches, and in her responses to letters she received from people critical of Israel. She often received letters from correspondents who felt she was insensitive to the rights of the Palestinian Arabs, sometimes from people who greatly admired her in other ways but were deeply disappointed by her position on the Arab-Israeli conflict. Two of her most prominent critics were women with whom she worked toward common goals in education and American refugee policy. One of them was Mossie Wyker, national president of United Church Women, who exercised considerable influence among Protestant Christian women. The other was Charl Ormond Williams, who as president of the National Educational Association was a leader among elementary and secondary educators. ER worried that these women would turn their constituencies toward the Arab point of view. She hoped that she could deepen their understanding of Israel and change their minds about the Arab-Israeli conflict.

Mossie Wyker was one of those Christians whom Karl Baehr had warned were returning from a visit to the Middle East with the view that Israel's accomplishments might indeed be a miracle but had been achieved at Arab expense. Writing to ER in May 1955, after visiting Egypt, Jordan, and Lebanon, but not Israel, and after rereading ER's *India and the Awakening East*, Wyker told ER that she found herself disagreeing with her for the first time. She had always trusted ER's "mature, objective judgment," but she could not share ER's view of the Zionist movement and was "more disturbed than I have ever been in my life":

> No matter how much good work the Jewish people may be doing in Israel, it seems to me it cannot justify the taking of land belonging to other people and giving it to the Jews. I have read, studied, listened for months—and after a visit in certain countries—I am still wondering.

ER replied that "The land was not taken, it was bought," and cited the Balfour Declaration. The buying of land in Palestine began after the declaration, ER said, and the UN partition plan "followed in logical sequence." The problem was the Arabs' refusal to accept the UN decision.

Wyker replied that the argument that the establishment of a Jewish state was the logical outcome of the Balfour Declaration did not satisfy the many Arab women with whom she had talked on her trip, women "whose homes and resources are still in Israel—and for which they have received no money from anyone." The women she spoke with resented America's support for Israel and Wyker wondered if this "tiny country" surrounded by Arab countries could possibly survive.[9] "Please don't think for a minute that Israel is not a permanent country," ER told Wyker. "The people have too much to live for to give it up, unless they are going to be exterminated by their Arab neighbors." ER was confident, given Israel's success in the 1948 war, that it could go on defending itself. Wyker told ER she remained "unconvinced."[10]

Charl Williams, president of the National Education Association, also had strong reservations about ER's position on Israel. As Williams traveled through Lebanon, Saudi Arabia, and Egypt in 1955 on her way to Jordan and Israel, she reported to ER that many of the people she spoke to complained "vehemently" that the Americans had "'thrown to the dogs' 40 million Arabs in their wholehearted support of 1 million Jews in Israel." Deeply disturbed by what she heard, Williams wondered "what will be the outcome."[11]

ER had provided Williams with letters of introduction to Israeli officials before Williams left on her trip. In addition, alarmed by the intensity of the sympathy Williams expressed for the Arab point of view, she asked Gideon Tadmor, the Israeli foreign affairs officer who had been her guide on her 1952 and 1955 trips to Israel, to pull out all the stops during Williams's tour of Israel so that she would emerge with a positive view of the country. Tadmor arranged for Williams to tour Hadassah institutions and Hebrew University, meet with leaders of the Ministry of Education, visit several schools, tour the Negev with officials of Youth Aliyah, and meet with the Haifa branch of the Israel-American Friendship League. Tadmor also made it possible for her to meet with David Ben-Gurion and to visit the homes of Moshe Kol and other prominent Israeli educators. ER was grateful for Tadmor's efforts.[12]

ER ALSO CAME INTO CONFLICT with the Eisenhower administration over her views on Israel. After Eisenhower's election, ER resigned from the Human Rights Commission, but her deep commitment to the success of the UN persisted. She volunteered her services to the American Association for the United Nations (AAUN), traveled the country to educate the public and generate grassroots support for the UN, helped establish new chapters of the AAUN, and defended the UN against attacks by Senator Joseph McCarthy and others. As she had done with President Truman, she urged Eisenhower to strengthen the UN by working through it rather than acting unilaterally, and she urged him to support Israel.

Eisenhower adopted a different policy toward the Middle East from that of his predecessor. Like many officials in the State Department, he and his advisors saw the region primarily in terms of the competition between the United States and the Soviet Union in the Cold War. Eisenhower and John Foster Dulles, his secretary of state, believed that free access to Middle Eastern oil was crucial to the economic well-being of Europe and its defense against Communist penetration. It was therefore extremely important to blunt the influence of the Soviet Union in the Middle East. Unlike Truman, Eisenhower had no influential Jews like David Niles in his administration, or Jewish friends like Eddie Jacobson, or strategists like Clark Clifford who had regarded prompt recognition of the new state of Israel as essential to Truman's reelection prospects in 1948. Eisenhower and Dulles believed it was vital to convince the Arabs that the United States was taking an even-handed approach to the region and that American policy was not being controlled by Israel or by influential Jewish lobbyists in the United States. Eisenhower's election provided an opening for the anti-Zionist American Council for Judaism and the American Friends of the Middle East to influence American policy, and they quickly established strong ties to Dulles's State Department and strengthened their ties to the CIA.[13]

Although ER, like Eisenhower and Dulles, believed in the need to contain Soviet influence and stop the spread of communism, she disagreed about the means of doing so. In April 1953, as it became clear that the new administration would take a different approach to the Middle East, ER expressed her concerns to Henry A. Byroade, assistant secretary of state for Near Eastern and South Asian Affairs. She agreed that the United States should treat Israel and the Arab states equally, but she worried that in seeking to be more evenhanded, the new administration would, in the end, penalize Israel unfairly. She did not think that Israel should receive less aid from the American government than the Arab states just because Israel received more funding from private donors in the United States. She pointed out that the United States was offering to finance the resettlement of refugees in Arab countries, while Israel was resettling about an equal number of Jewish refugees from North Africa, the Middle East, and elsewhere in Israel. She also felt that oil royalties paid to Arab states should be taken into account in considering the amount of aid those states should receive. Most importantly, ER said, Israel, unlike the Arab states, was a democracy, which upheld the principles of the free world, while the Arab states refused to recognize Israel or work with it toward the improvement of the whole region:

> I think we should in every way help the development projects and constructive work being done in the Arab states and yet we cannot forget the fact that the Arab states do not espouse the cause of the free world and that Israel does. If the Arab states would cooperate with Israel, they would go forward faster and some of Israel's difficulties would be solved.[14]

The following January, after the Eisenhower administration announced its intention to provide military assistance to the Arab states, but not to Israel, ER objected. While she understood the desire to show that the United States wanted the Arabs to be in a position to protect themselves against an attack by the Soviet Union, she told her My Day readers, providing arms to the Arabs was "a highly questionable policy." There was nothing to stop the Arabs from using the arms to attack Israel, she said, and that would lead to "a bitter war" in which the United States would "be forced to take a stand."[15]

In April, the United States concluded an arms deal with the pro-Western government of Iraq and continued to hold open the possibility of supplying other Arab states with weapons. But in September 1955, after Egypt balked at permitting an American advisory mission to enter Egypt as part of an arms deal, Egypt's president, Gamal Abdel Nasser, concluded a deal with the Russians to buy Czech weapons.[16] As Egypt began a military buildup, ER warned in My Day that the Israelis would begin to ask the question: "Have we a better chance of survival if we bring on a war before our neighbors are completely equipped to annihilate us?" This was particularly true given that Israel possessed "no direct guarantee of protection or of equipment which will give them equality with their Arab neighbors." She urged that the UN guarantee current borders and repeated her long-held belief that the UN needed to establish an international police force to keep the peace in the Middle East and other areas of conflict.[17]

TROUBLED BY NASSER'S INCREASINGLY THREATENING rhetoric against Israel after the Czech-Egyptian arms agreement and by the perception of Israel as an "aggressor nation," ER's Israeli friend Joseph Baratz pleaded with ER to raise her voice against "this slander":

> How did it happen that we, a people who are attacked day by day, are now termed by others a monstrous "aggressor"? Ever since the Arab states declared war on us as a result of the United Nations decision, we have been exposed to non-stop attack.[18]

The portrayal of Israel as an aggressor nation was propaganda, ER replied, and the "rather extensive propaganda machine" the Arabs had in the United States made it hard to combat. She was no doubt thinking about the activities of Dorothy Thompson, the AFME, and the American Council for Judaism, whose newsletters, pamphlets, news releases, and speakers sought to get pro-Arab views before the American public.[19] In September 1955, *Time* had published a flattering cover story on Nasser and in November reprinted an editorial from the anti-Zionist *Jewish Newsletter* blaming Zionist leaders for creating "hysteria" about Israel among American Jews. ER promised Baratz that she would "redouble" her "efforts to have Israel better understood," but she did not think she could be very effective with the Democrats out of power.[20]

In January 1956 ER fulfilled her pledge. She pressed the Eisenhower administration to act more decisively to defend Israel and to send a clearer message to the Arab states. After Czechoslovakia and the Soviet Union began supplying arms to Egypt, Israel Goldstein, president of the American Jewish Congress (AJC), wrote to ER asking her to respond to the "ominous developments in the Middle East" by signing a statement outlining the situation and calling on the United States government to supply defensive weapons to Israel. It also urged the United States to negotiate treaties with Israel and any of its Arab neighbors willing to cooperate that guaranteed their current borders against alteration by military force.[21] ER did not sign the statement, but a few days later Justine Polier, as national vice president of the AJC, sent ER a redrafted version of the statement and urged her to sign it and to invite several other prominent non-Jews to do so as well. Polier felt that a letter signed by a small number of well-known Gentile leaders would carry more weight than a letter signed by many Americans. At Polier's suggestion, ER recruited former president Truman and Walter Reuther, vice president of the American Federation of Labor and Congress of Industrial Organizations (AFL-CIO), to sign the statement with her.[22]

ER released the statement on January 29, 1956, the day before British prime minister Sir Anthony Eden arrived in the United States to confer with Eisenhower and Dulles about the Middle East and other matters. The statement warned that the "border clashes" between Arabs and Israelis that were recurring "with increasing frequency" might "at any time erupt into war," a war that might then "spread far beyond the Middle East." It asserted that the United States had the responsibility to do everything possible to prevent such a course of events. The statement contained many of the arguments ER often made in My Day, in speeches, and in her responses to letters criticizing her position on the Israeli-Arab conflict, thus reflecting the congruence of her views with those of most of her Jewish friends, including Polier: (1) the State of Israel was "a great and irrevocable historic fact," (2) it was the "practical expression" of a policy supported by the American government ever since World War I, (3) Israel had shown "how the desert can be transformed by human skill and perseverance," and (4) if there were peace, Israel could share its skills and experience with the whole Middle East, thus helping "the region to achieve a new flowering, unparalleled since Biblical days." As to the Arab refugees, the statement argued that Israel could not "economically or politically afford to admit more than a small number." The "vast Arab Lands" offered a "far more promising" area for the resettlement of the refugees than Israel possibly could. The statement urged the American government to furnish "the defensive arms needed by Israel to protect itself against any aggression made possible or incited by the introduction of Communist arms." ER told the press that she would have preferred that neither side acquire arms, but since the Communist nations had furnished arms to Egypt, Israel needed arms in order to right the balance in the region.[23] As ER had done repeatedly since the adoption of the partition plan by the UN, the statement advocated that the United States adopt "an unequivocal policy in regard to the Middle East," for the signers believed that the lack of a definite policy in the past had encouraged the Arabs in their rejection of Israel's right to exist.[24]

After the statement appeared in the press, Baratz wrote ER to say that he had seen it in the *New York Times*. He had also seen an ad by the American Friends of the Middle East (AFME), signed by Dorothy Thompson and other officers of the organization. The AFME ad warned that furnishing arms to Israel would begin an arms race between Israel and the Arab states that would only increase tensions. AFME argued that "the conviction that America could be counted on under all circumstances" had encouraged Israel to act aggressively and remain intransigent. Baratz told ER that he was "confident that most people in the United States will grasp the difference in the nature and quality of the two statements." He and other Israelis hoped that people in the free world would "understand who is the attacker, we or those who each day proclaim their intention to destroy the State of Israel."[25]

As tensions increased in the Middle East, ER continued to challenge American policy. "If we made arrangements for an airfield in Saudi Arabia," she asked in February, "was it not strange that we also did not make arrangements for one in Israel?" Such actions did not seem to her to jibe with the Eisenhower administration's professed desire to remain neutral.[26] Eisenhower and Dulles, however, continued to resist the calls by Jewish groups and their supporters to provide defensive arms to Israel.

ON JULY 26, 1956, AFTER the United States withdrew an offer to provide financial assistance for the construction of the Aswan Dam, Nasser nationalized the Suez Canal Company, a jointly owned British and French enterprise. Fearing that the British and French governments might attack Egypt and weaken American influence with the Arabs by drawing the United States into an imperialist enterprise, Eisenhower dispatched Dulles to London to counsel restraint. The British, French, and Israelis, however, began making secret plans to invade the Sinai and take back the canal. The Israelis were motivated by their feeling that the United States was not addressing their concerns about the frequent raids along its borders by Arab guerrillas, the Egyptian blockade of the Straits of Tiran, which controlled the passage from the Gulf of Aqaba to the Red Sea, and the Czech-Russian arms deal with Egypt.[27] They had also concluded, as ER had warned they might, that they needed to act to prevent Egypt from completing its military buildup, at which point they expected Nasser to carry out his threat to attack Israel.[28]

On October 29, 1956, Israel invaded the Sinai Peninsula, driving to within ten miles of the Suez Canal. The United States immediately introduced a resolution in the UN Security Council demanding that Israel withdraw and calling on other nations to refrain from entering the conflict or providing assistance to Israel. Eisenhower felt that the Tripartite Agreement signed by the United States, Britain, and France in 1950 during the Truman administration committed the United States to coming to the aid of either side in the Arab-Israeli conflict if attacked by the other. He also wished to make American opposition to colonialism clear and feared that if the United States did not act, the Russians might become involved. He was willing to risk alienating supporters of Israel and his reelection chances, if those were the consequences of taking a stand against America's old allies. ER was aghast: "It could not be possible that we would present such a resolution, knowing that we would find ourselves lined up with the Soviet Union and the dictator of Egypt, against Great Britain and France and the only democratic country in the Near East—Israel!"[29]

The British and French vetoed the resolution and issued an ultimatum demanding that the Israelis and Egyptians withdraw their forces ten miles to each side of the canal within twelve hours. After the Egyptians refused to obey, the British and French bombed their airfields. On November 2, the United States took the matter to the UN General Assembly, which immediately passed an American resolution calling for a ceasefire and withdrawal of Israeli forces from the Sinai. The resolution urged all parties to respect the armistice lines between Israel and the Arab states and called for the Suez Canal to be cleared of the ships sunk by the Egyptians and reopened with freedom of navigation restored once a ceasefire went into effect.[30] On November 5, the UN General Assembly voted to adopt a Canadian proposal to create a UN police force to supervise a ceasefire in the Middle East.[31] That same night, British and French forces landed troops in the canal zone, ostensibly to protect the canal. The United

States joined the USSR and the UN in condemning the aggression. By this time the Israelis, who had taken control of Gaza and the entire Sinai, had agreed to a ceasefire. The invasion finally came to a stop on November 6 after the United States persuaded the British and the French to cease operations.[32]

Although ER felt strongly that international disputes should be settled at the UN and not by unilateral military action, she believed that in this case, the danger Israel faced justified the action it took. America's condemnation of Israel disturbed her. She was glad, however, that the UN would now create a peacekeeping force. The United Nations Emergency Force, which was created to ensure the withdrawal of Israel, French, and British forces from Egyptian territory and then to act as a buffer between Israeli and Egyptian forces, was the first armed peacekeeping force established by the UN. ER and other leaders of the AAUN, for which she now served as chairman of the Board of Governors, issued a statement praising its creation and pointing out that the AAUN had "long advocated that an international force guarantee the security of the armistice line between Israel and the Arab States."[33] In a My Day column a few weeks later, ER urged that the UN deploy "a real military force and of sufficient size to constitute a power that would enforce all U.N. decisions." If it were merely "a token police force, with no ability to enforce the will of the majority in the U.N.," that would create "a real dilemma."[34] But while the UN created police forces that acted as buffers between nations in conflict and monitored compliance with the terms of UN resolutions, neither then nor later did it create a military force to enforce its decisions with the sort of muscle ER advocated.

On November 7 Eisenhower, who had been reelected easily the day before, threatened further UN resolutions against Israel and an end to American governmental and private assistance if Israel did not withdraw from the Sinai. He also warned of possible attacks on Israel by "volunteers" from the Soviet Union. As a result, Ben-Gurion agreed to withdraw Israeli forces from the Sinai as soon as a UN force was ready to move into the area. Under continued pressure from the United States, Britain and France also yielded to American pressure, pulling their troops out of the canal zone by the end of December.[35]

Israel, however, put off the date of its withdrawal while it sought assurances that the Egyptians would not reoccupy the Sinai and resume raids across Israel's border. It also lobbied hard to win sympathy for its position from influential Americans, leaders of Congress, and members of the American Jewish community, some of whom had been skeptical of Israeli actions. ER was one of those who raised her voice, speaking passionately on behalf of Israel.

In January 1957, as the UN continued to demand that Israel withdraw from the Sinai without any guarantees from Egypt that raids on Israel would cease, ER protested in her My Day column. Israel was America's friend, she said, and she found "it difficult to understand just why we should make life so difficult for them" after Israel had acknowledged that they should have gone to the UN first before invading Sinai. From the beginning of its existence, she said, Israel had been "willing to sit down and discuss with the Arab states how their difficulties can be best resolved," but the Arab nations "have never been willing to recognize the existence of Israel." It was true that Israel was willing to negotiate, but it insisted that any resolution of the Arab refugee problem would have to come after a peace agreement that assured its security. The Arabs refused to negotiate a peace agreement until the refugee issue was resolved.[36]

Israel's effort during the opening months of 1957 to shift American opinion more toward its point of view achieved some success. The Democratic and Republican leaders of the Senate, Lyndon Johnson (D-TX) and William Knowland (R-CA), questioned the Eisenhower administration's tough stance toward Israel, and Congress did not agree to issue a statement demanding Israeli withdrawal. In the face of this opposition, Eisenhower went on radio and TV on February 20 to make his case to the American people. His unequivocal rejection of Israeli justifications for its actions and his statement that the UN would have no choice but to put maximum pressure on Israel if it did not obey UN resolutions—a clear indication that the United States would support the imposition of sanctions—angered ER. There could be no peace, she said, if Israel did not receive guarantees that the UN peacekeeping forces would occupy the Gaza Strip and protect Israel's access to the Gulf of Aqaba. Israel could not risk "being wiped off the face of the earth."[37]

Eisenhower's statement on February 20, however, convinced the Israelis that they would have to withdraw. On March 1, Israel's foreign minister, Golda Meir, announced that Israel agreed to do so under two conditions: that the UN force stay in Sinai and that Israel would act in self-defense under Article 51 of the Charter if the free passage of Israeli ships in the Gulf of Aqaba were prevented.[38]

After Israel agreed to withdraw, Joseph Baratz wrote to ER from Degania in "a state of deep depression" about the way the American State Department had treated Israel. Neither all of Israel's political parties nor all the Israeli people had greeted the agreement that was finally reached with enthusiasm, Baratz told her. It took ER almost a month to answer Baratz's letter because she felt that "my country has behaved so very badly and I hated to admit it." She felt that the United States had "been shortsighted beyond words" in not firmly backing Israel and that "the fear that Israel may have to go to war to get her real security is to me a terrible failure on the part of the US."[39]

AFTER THE SUEZ CRISIS and after an effort to build up King Saud of Saudi Arabia as a counterbalance to Nasser yielded little result, the Eisenhower administration pursued what became known as the Eisenhower Doctrine. The goal was to establish bilateral relationships with Arab countries by offering economic and military aid, reduce Nasser's influence in the area, and prevent Communist inroads into the Middle East. Rather than seek a solution to the Arab-Israeli conflict or become embroiled in other regional conflicts, the idea was to concentrate on resisting the threat of Communism whether in the form of subversion engineered by Russia or the development of internal Communist movements.[40]

ER did not think the Eisenhower Doctrine had much merit, she told her young friend Gus Ranis, and would have preferred that the United States "have a little more courage" and adopt a clear policy that the Suez Canal would be open to ships from all nations and that Israel would "exist in peace."[41] Although she believed American oil interests in the Middle East heavily influenced American policy, she knew that Eisenhower would say that he was acting to prevent the Arab nations from depending on the Soviet Union for assistance. "I disagree completely with the way he has been trying to do this," she told another correspondent. The United States should deal plainly with Nasser even at the risk of him turning to the Soviet Union, although she could see why the president might think that "too great a responsibility for the government to take."[42]

After Eisenhower's election in 1952, Israelis worried that without Truman's support, Israel might be forced to return to the partition borders drawn by the UN in 1947, admit thousands of angry Arab refugees, and give up a large part of Jerusalem. By 1960, however, despite Eisenhower's policy of evenhandedness in the Arab-Israeli conflict and strong stand against the Israeli invasion of the Sinai, the territory Israel controlled remained the same, the Arab refugees had not returned, and Israel's credibility as a nation had increased. ER had no influence on the policy of the Eisenhower administration, but her forceful advocacy had helped make the new nation's case to the American people and earned the gratitude of Israel's leaders.[43]

18

A SPECIAL BOND WITH ISRAEL

"There is no country as exciting as Israel"

By the time Eleanor Roosevelt returned to Israel in 1959, she had both deepened her commitment to the new nation and cemented her role as its most prominent Gentile defender in the United States. She had protested the sale of weapons to Arab countries, unsuccessfully advocated the sale of defensive weapons to Israel, defended Israel's 1956 incursion into the Sinai, and criticized the Eisenhower Doctrine. ER loved to be needed, and Israel needed strong voices in the United States to establish its legitimacy and help it acquire the resources necessary for its survival. Closely connected to the American Jewish community and widely admired by Americans of many backgrounds, ER was in a unique position to meet that need. Her syndicated daily column, speaking engagements, and radio and TV appearances enabled her to reach large numbers of Americans.

Beginning with her visit to the training center at Cambous for Moroccan Jewish children on their way to Israel, ER had taken a special interest in the well-being of Moroccan Jews. In 1956 she intervened with the sultan of Morocco on behalf of over 6,000 Jews seeking to emigrate to Israel. In 1959 she appealed to him to restore postal communication between his country and Israel, and in 1961 she again asked him to ease emigration restrictions. In 1957 ER traveled to Morocco to express her support for its Jewish community. When she discovered that Morocco was on the brink of famine, she lobbied for American aid to provide food to all Moroccans and brought Moroccan leaders and officials of the Joint Distribution Committee (JDC) together at her home in New York in an effort to promote their cooperation.[1]

ER had also become a valued resource for Youth Aliyah, serving as a highly effective fundraiser for the organization in Great Britain, Mexico, Canada, and the United States. She was so important to Moshe Kol and the other leaders of Youth Aliyah and

Hadassah that they postponed Youth Aliyah's 1959 world conference in Jerusalem, at which they would celebrate the organization's twenty-fifth anniversary, to make it possible for ER to attend.[2]

On her 1959 trip to Israel ER traveled with her teenage granddaughter, Nina Roosevelt. Before going to Israel, ER and Nina visited Iran, where ER's daughter Anna was living at the time with her husband, Dr. James A. Halsted, a Fulbright professor. Halsted was assisting in the establishment of a medical school at Shiraz University. In Tehran ER toured schools, hospitals, and other institutions. The people of Iran were largely illiterate at the time and the need for education and economic development was great. ER discussed the country's needs with representatives of the UN technical assistance program, the American Point 4 program, and the Joint Distribution Committee, all of which were managing projects to improve conditions in the country.

There was still a substantial Jewish population in Iran, although some Jews had already gone to Israel. At Moshe Kol's suggestion ER visited the Jewish ghetto in Shiraz, where she rated the housing worse than the lowest standard of housing in the United States.[3] A family of eight or ten lived in one windowless room with a charcoal brazier for cooking and heating and no sanitary facilities. Most of the Jewish men were peddlers. Twenty to 30 percent of the population in the Jewish quarter were Muslims, which meant, ER was glad to see, that programs to improve conditions in the area benefited Muslims as well as Jews.[4] ER also had lunch with the shah and attended a dinner in her honor with the American ambassador, Iranian officials, and foreign diplomats.[5]

After leaving Iran, ER and Nina flew to Israel, where ER's itinerary included visits to Youth Aliyah and Hadassah facilities, housing and factory sites, meetings with Israeli and American officials, and a visit to Jerusalem's Old City to attend Easter service. ER's days in Israel were, as usual, very busy and reflected her numerous ties to the nation and its people. She continued to take a keen interest in Youth Aliyah's innovative approaches to educating and assimilating immigrant children. She visited the Alonei Yitzhak Children's Village, where the children lived in group houses without an adult counselor and spent three to four hours a day raising vegetables and poultry, working in the kitchen, and keeping the buildings clean, in addition to studying in school. It seemed to ER "a pretty strenuous schedule," given the ages of the children, but they "looked healthy and strong" and she recognized that since it was "the object of the village to teach the children how to live and to be useful citizens," the combination of rigorous physical activity and study served this goal.[6]

In Haifa ER was impressed with Israel's Institute of Technology (the Technion), which was becoming known as Israel's MIT. At Tiberias she enjoyed seeing the Sea of Galilee by moonlight and later dined at Degania with Joseph and Miriam Baratz. In Tel Aviv she watched the children's Purim parade as a guest of the mayor. In Eilat, Israel's port city on the Red Sea, she observed the town's developing diamond and precious stone-cutting industry and then toured a kibbutz out in the Negev. There she found a band of eighty young people, who, she said, were "making the desert bloom. I literally mean bloom." The members of the kibbutz grew flowers, tomatoes, and onions with water drawn from a deep well and raised cattle, sheep, and poultry. ER admired the "spirit and determination" of these pioneering youth, which she felt was exemplified by the way they rushed to their fields during an attack by locusts, spraying and flailing to death enough of the insects to save their crops.[7]

In Beersheba ER and Nina attended the dedication of the Eleanor Roosevelt Youth Aliyah Day Centre, which, like the Alonei Yitzhak Children's Village, was adapted to meeting a special educational need. This center provided education and vocational training to immigrant teenagers age fourteen to seventeen, who needed to learn Hebrew as fast as they could and, often, to catch up on their studies because of the poor education they had received in their countries of origin.

ER was impressed with the rapid growth of Beersheba, which she had first seen in 1952 when 20,000 people lived there. Now the population had more than doubled to 42,000 and there were six factories instead of two. To provide a personal measure of the town's development, ER told her My Day readers about a young man and woman whom she met on her first visit just after they had arrived as immigrants. The couple lived at that time in a two-bedroom house. When she returned three years later, the man was happy because he had a lot of work as a carpenter, but the man and woman felt "there was a shadow in the house" because they had no children. Now, in 1959, she asked to see them again and found "to my joy" that they had two children and the man was adding two and a half rooms to their house in his spare time.[8]

In Jerusalem, she met with Dr. K. J. Mann, director general of the Hadassah Medical Organization, who, on an earlier trip, had shown her the temporary facilities used by Hadassah's University Hospital after the Arabs had driven the Jews off Mount Scopus in 1948. Now he proudly showed her the new Medical Center at Ein Kerem. The facility, he told her, was being completed with funds raised by "our wonderful Hadassah ladies in America" to house Hadassah's medical care and teaching programs.[9] ER also attended the dedication of the Eleanor Roosevelt Chair of the History and Philosophy of Science at Hebrew University, spoke at the conference marking the twenty-fifth anniversary of Youth Aliyah, and went to the dedication of the Youth Center for Handicapped Children, which was being named in honor of her friend Vera Weizmann, Chaim Weizmann's widow. On the way to Tel Aviv she stopped at Sarafand Hospital to visit the Rehabilitation Center for Post-Polio Children given to the hospital by the Canadian Hadassah organization and named for ER.[10]

Before arriving in Israel, ER had been invited by Hasan-El-Kaatib, the Muhafez (guardian) and military governor of Jerusalem's Old City, to attend the Easter Sunday service at the Church of the Holy Sepulchre on March 29. She was to be seated in a place of honor by his side. When ER's visit became public, the Palestinian Arab newspaper *Falastin* vehemently attacked the Jordanian government for granting permission to ER to cross into Jordanian-held Jerusalem, calling her "the greatest enemy of Arab peoples in the world." As a result, the Jordanian government considered withdrawing permission. The American consulate, which sent a telegram to Acting Secretary of State Christian Herter in Washington expressing fear that there might be a "good chance of stones, name-calling, unpleasant incidents in fairly long, crowded walk from automobile road to Holy Sepulchre," also debated calling off her visit. The consulate expected that the Muhafez would contract a "diplomatic illness" rather than be seen at a public ceremony attended largely by Arab Christians, many of them refugees. Instead, the Muhafez urged the acting prime minister of Jordan to allow the visit to go forward on the grounds that canceling ER's visit would damage King Hussein's diplomatic efforts. Hussein and the Jordanian prime minister, Samir el-Rifai, were on a mission to the United States at the time to obtain foreign aid. The Muhafez also argued that it was important to persuade humanitarians like ER to recognize that Arabs, too, deserved their concern and would welcome their friendship. He assured the American consulate that he was planning to go to unusual lengths to ensure that no incident occurred during ER's visit. With these assurances, the consulate allowed the visit to go ahead.[11]

The event went smoothly, and the consulate reported afterward that the Jordanian government had taken the most extreme measures to protect ER from physical harm or embarrassment. It had forbidden further attacks in the press and issued a false press statement on March 27 that ER was not coming. The head of Jerusalem's criminal investigation department rode in the car with ER and the consul general. A Land Rover with an armed patrol followed the car. Each of the participants in the Easter ceremony was individually screened. The consulate praised Hasan-El-Kaatib for "his soundness in forestalling ill-considered slanging matches as a tactic in the Arab-Israel disagreement."[12] ER herself enjoyed the visit and the American consul, who was fluent in Arabic, told her that he repeatedly heard the word "welcome" as she walked from the services through the streets to a waiting car. At a reception at the American consulate following the service, she spoke with the governor and mayor of Arab Jerusalem about the refugee issue and Jordan's problems.

After the reception, ER wrote in My Day that the refugee situation would grow progressively worse. Although she understood that the refugees were now being permitted to work, "resettlement and some kind of reparations paid are the only real solutions, and the problem should be faced and settled through the United Nations as soon as possible."[13]

ON HER FLIGHT OUT OF ISRAEL, ER tried, once again, to identify what made the atmosphere of Israel so different from that of Iran and Israel's Arab neighbors. She had concluded at the end of her visit to the Arab countries on her first trip to the Middle East that people did not seem to enter into government service in order to serve their country, but for private gain, and felt completely justified in doing so. She formed a similar opinion about Iran in 1959 when she said that it was an absence of a sense of "community responsibility" that held it back.[14] The concept of community responsibility and active citizenship was, of course, at the very heart of her own political philosophy, which she had preached in the 1930s. In Israel, she found this ideal fulfilled in the responsibility the nation took for all the immigrants streaming into the country and, especially, through its cooperative communities: the kibbutzim, moshav, and youth villages.[15]

Although she was disappointed by what she perceived as a lack of civic commitment among the Iranians and Arabs, she was far from indifferent to their needs. In regard to the Arabs living within Israel, she expressed the hope to her Israeli hosts that the Arabs would be given equal rights with the nation's Jewish citizens. In early 1959, after the American Friends Service Committee expressed concern to ER that the Israeli government was violating the rights of the Arabs living in Acre, ER asked Gideon Tadmor, the foreign affairs officer who served as her guide on earlier trips to Israel, for information on the status of Israel's Arab citizens. Tadmor told her that, with the exception of border regions where Israel imposed restrictions because of the "unilateral state of war," the policy of the Israeli government was to grant Israeli Arabs the same rights as Jews. He hoped that when she visited Israel that spring, she would have a chance to observe for herself "the achievements and progress" of Israel's Arab citizens and said he would help arrange opportunities to do so.[16]

When ER was in Israel in April, Tadmor did make it possible for her to find out more about the conditions under which Israel's Arab citizens lived. She visited the Arab village of Baqa-al-Garbya, where she toured a new canning plant that put up oranges and sauerkraut. The conditions in the Arab villages were "being improved quite rapidly," she reported in My Day. She delved somewhat deeper during a long talk with an Arab high school teacher in Acre who gave her insight into the grounds of Arab dissatisfaction. It was "obvious," she reported in My Day, "that the Arabs living in Israel are not very happy." She recognized that "it must be very hard on [the Arabs] not to be able to visit with ease and freedom their families and friends just across a border." Nevertheless, she thought it was "only natural in a country that is surrounded by unfriendly Arab countries" for the Israeli government to impose certain restrictions on its Arab population and to hesitate to grant "more freedom of movement than is at present permitted."[17]

In most cases, it was true that the Arabs who remained in Israel were better off than those who had fled or been expelled and now languished in refugee camps, but they were far from being treated equally with Israel's Jewish citizens, despite the Israeli government's pledge to do so. The Arab citizens of Israel remained under military rule until 1966 and they have remained second-class citizens. Although ER recognized that the Israeli Arabs were "not very happy," she did not look into the issues of property rights, access to education, employment, mobility, identification papers, and intimidation by police and judicial authorities with which they, like suspect minorities elsewhere, had to contend.[18] For her, Israel was all about dynamic economic and social change, and she was content to believe, as Tadmor and the Israeli government no doubt wanted her to believe, that conditions were improving for the Arabs as well as the Jews and would continue to do so.

Although the divide between Israel and its neighbors appeared unbridgeable, Israel itself continued to inspire ER: "Israel was more exciting than ever," she wrote to Henry Morgenthau III after she returned home. She was struck by how much the country had changed—"I felt more growth had taken place in four years than I thought was possible"—and by the contrast between Israel and the other countries in the region: "There is no country as exciting as Israel but I am awfully glad that Nina and I saw Iran first because it sharpened the contrast for her enormously."[19]

SOME OF THE DEEPEST BONDS that connected ER to Israel, which grew stronger over time, were her relationships with Israel's leaders, especially David Ben-Gurion and Golda Meir. These relationships, nourished by their visits with each other both in Israel and the United States, were built on the appreciation of the Israeli leaders for ER's ardent support of Israel and her admiration for their dynamic leadership. Because they did not always get the backing they desired from the Eisenhower administration, the Israeli leaders especially valued her support. They appreciated ER's public criticism of her own government during the Suez Crisis, her advocacy of military and economic aid to Israel, and all the other ways she had supported the cause of the new nation.

But ER's relationships with Ben-Gurion, Golda Meir, and other Israeli leaders were not merely political. As her devotion to Israel deepened, these relationships became warm and personal. "You looked wonderfully well and full of spirits," she told Ben-Gurion after her 1959 visit, "and there is no one in Israel who does not depend on you for inspiration. Just seeing you is a great inspiration to me, and I was glad to have my granddaughter have this opportunity also."[20] To Golda Meir she expressed her joy in seeing her several times during her 1959 trip and characteristically expressed embarrassment, as well as gratitude, at the "great generosity" of the Israeli government in making her its guest: "I don't think it is right because I can and should pay my own way but at every hotel where I tried to pay my bill they insisted that the Foreign Office had told them that they wanted to take care of it and they would not take my money. All I can say is thank you."²¹ During ER's final illness in the fall of 1962, Meir sent a telegram to ER wishing her a "speedy recovery" and telling her that she felt her absence at an event in Meir's honor that ER was unable to attend "with all my heart." One sign of the intimacy of the friendship between the two women was that Meir addressed ER in the telegram as "Dear Eleanor." Very few people did.²²

ER believed that Israel was blessed with an unusually gifted group of leaders. When Ambassador Abba Eban, another Israeli leader ER became very fond of, was returning to Israel, ER told Meir that she would miss him and added: "it seems to me that you are among the few countries that actually have more men and women capable of leadership than you absolutely need. That is why, I think, you accomplish the impossible."²³ It was this leadership that helped generate the excitement and sense of purpose she repeatedly encountered during her visits. Ben-Gurion, especially, inspired her. "His eyes snap as though he were a young man when he is talking about something he is vitally interested in," she wrote after visiting him in Jerusalem in 1959, "and he gives you a feeling of resourcefulness, courage and flexibility in his thinking, which is quite extraordinary."²⁴ These qualities helped him inspire the young "to leave well established, easy living in an old kibbutz or a good job" and "face the incredible hardships" of building a new kibbutz in the Negev.²⁵

ER's relationship with Joseph Baratz was another one of the warm friendships with Israeli leaders that bound ER closely to Israel's land and people. Because of the attack by Syria that kibbutz Degania had repelled during the 1948 war and the periodic harassment by Syrian forces it had suffered since then, Baratz was keenly aware of Israel's vulnerability. But while Baratz expressed the anxieties that he and other Israelis felt about Israel's continually besieged position and their uncertainty about whether they had America's full support, he also wrote to ER with confidence about Israel's growth and prospects. The average Israeli wanted to know "one thing," he wrote in the summer of 1958, namely, "What is our fate to be in all this political muddle?" But in the daily life of Israel, he told ER, "you would feel none of this anxiety." Life in Israel was "accented by dynamic growth, development and building everywhere—no where has there been a lull. Neither has the stream of tourists been hindered. I like to see in this a good omen for our country." Baratz often turned after a discussion of the "troubled waters with the Syrians" or other political concerns to the rhythms of ordinary life in the small agriculture community that he headed: "We celebrate Chanukka—the Festival of Lights, marking the Maccabee victories of old," he wrote to her in December 1958. "We enjoy our children and our children's children, and life follows its course in well known furrows."²⁶

The common interest Baratz and ER shared in Youth Aliyah formed an important bond between them. On the twenty-fifth anniversary of the founding of Youth

Aliyah, Baratz told ER that her name "appears again and again like a silver thread in the weaving of this particular piece of history." He himself was proud of the contribution Degania made to the growth of Israel through Youth Aliyah. The boys and girls from Youth Aliyah "who were educated in Degania," he told ER, "are today settled in agricultural settlements through-out the length and breadth of the country, and they have played no small part in the development of the country."[27]

ER'S VISITS TO ISRAEL WERE not primarily for pleasure, although she took great delight in her interactions with the people she met. As World Patron of Youth Aliyah, ER felt that the purpose of her trips was to gather information and stories that would make her a more effective spokesperson for the organization she represented and for Israel. In preparing for her 1962 trip, she told Golda Meir that she wanted to return to the United States with "a good comparison" between places she had seen before and their current state so that she could "speak with greater force on the subject of development."[28] After her 1962 trip, she assured President Yitzhak Ben-Zvi that she would remember the things he had said to her and "see if I can make them better understood at home."[29]

For the most part, ER continued to let Youth Aliyah, Hadassah, and the Israeli government show her whatever served their public relations purposes. Her expression of concern in 1959 about the report she had received about the Israeli government's possible violation of Arab rights in Acre was an exception. Even then, Tadmor selected the Arab village and the high school teacher to whom she spoke. Often ER was happy to amplify the message the Israeli government wished to convey to the American public. Tadmor regularly provided ER with information and suggestions to use in her My Day column, in speeches, or in answering questions about Israel put to her by her correspondents as part of his government's efforts to counteract Arab propaganda in the United States. Sometimes, as when the Moroccan government cut off all postal communication between Moroccan Jews and their kinsmen in Israel, he also asked for her help in resolving a diplomatic issue. "It seems to me," he apologized in a letter to her in 1959, "that whenever I write to you there is something which we would like you to do for us."[30]

When ER was planning to return to Israel in late February 1962, ER asked Golda Meir for a car and a guide as well as help in choosing what she should see: whatever "you feel are valuable would be perfectly acceptable to me." She had a few specific requests: a stop for lunch in Degania, an overnight stay in Safed, which she heard had become an art center, perhaps a visit to the port city of Eilat on the Red Sea, an overnight stay in Beersheba, and a visit to the children's villages. Finally, on the last day, she wanted to go to Jerusalem.[31]

On this, her fourth and last trip to Israel, ER was accompanied by her secretary, Maureen Corr, and Edna Gurewitsch, the wife of David Gurewitsch, who had traveled with her on her first trip. ER was pleased with the arrangements the Israeli foreign office made for her, including the assignment once again of Gideon Tadmor as her guide and the provision of a car.[32] She again visited Youth Aliyah training facilities, schools, immigrant villages, Hadassah medical facilities, Hebrew University, and the Degania kibbutz. When she visited Beersheba for the fourth time, she was again amazed by the new houses and new industries built or in the process of being built and by the greening of the surrounding desert by the water that was being piped in from the north. Beersheba's population had now grown to 50,000. She stopped at the Eleanor Roosevelt Youth Aliyah Day Centre that she and Nina had visited three years before and found that it was meeting the need to educate older children who came from countries with poor schools and were too old to attend Israeli primary schools.[33]

Beersheba had become her "yardstick in Israel," she reported, where she "could easily see the great changes that come about year by year." Many problems remained because of the surge in population—not enough housing, not enough space in schools and hospitals—"but the building was going on fast enough to give everyone hope." A new Youth Aliyah camp provided training while more schools were being built to take the pressure off schools running double shifts. Beersheba was one of the "miracles" of Israel, ER wrote in an article for *Hadassah Magazine*, and instilled in her a "feeling of vigor, of growth, of being on the move."[34]

OVER THE YEARS, ER OBSERVED how Youth Aliyah had to adapt its ways of organizing immigrant communities and its training methods to meet the particular needs of different groups of young immigrants as they entered Israel. Although she admired all the ways Youth Aliyah sought to assimilate the newcomers, she did express some awareness of the pain that immigrant families experienced in shedding their cultural traditions. Israeli leaders had originally thought that immigrants from various countries should be placed all together in one town to encourage their integration into one people, but this created problems. The shock of rapid acculturation could be too great, particularly for the families from North Africa and the Middle East who had acquired the cultural habits of the countries in which they had lived for centuries. As a result, Youth Aliyah made some effort to mitigate the effects. On her 1962 trip, ER visited an experimental immigrant community called Kiryat Gat that took a different approach. In this settlement, the Israelis placed immigrants from each country in separate villages not far from a central town that provided secondary schools, medical and social services, and better-stocked stores than the ones in the villages, plus cultural facilities, such as movie theaters. That way the immigrant families could maintain in their own village some of the customs they were used to, while all the children went to the same secondary school in the central town and the parents went to town occasionally to take advantage of the resources not available in the villages. The idea was that as the children grew together in the schools, their parents would also be drawn together. "The process of amalgamation would be slower," ER explained in My Day, "but in the end it would be less painful than throwing them all together at the start in one place." The head of agricultural services at Kiryat Gat told her that the plan did not succeed completely but he thought it worked better than the old way of doing things. During her visit to Israel with ER in 1955, Trude Lash had noted "the willingness" of Youth Aliyah workers "to face mistakes and search for better ways of doing things."[35] For ER, who never lost her faith in the "bold, persistent experimentation" advocated by FDR at the outset of the New Deal, the spirit of innovation that inspired experiments like Kiryat Gat in organizing communities, educating children, and absorbing immigrants was an important element of Israel's appeal.[36]

As Charles Segal, Hadassah's director of public relations, explained to ER, each new group of immigrant children had different needs and required a different educational program. The first group were survivors of the Holocaust, children who "had been scarred mentally—and some physically—by the ordeals they had endured." Their rehabilitation "required delicate psychological handling." The second group were the children from Morocco and other North African and Middle Eastern countries, most of whom were completely lacking in education and were therefore unprepared for Israeli schools. They required special programs to help them catch up with their peers and deal with the psychological stress of being so out of step with Israeli children. A majority of the children in the third group, which was now arriving from Eastern Europe, had begun secondary education but had to learn a new set of values. Many of them had been unaware of their Jewishness before they left for Israel and the realization that they were Jews came as a shock. Their teachers and propagandists in the Communist countries from which they came had tried to indoctrinate them in Communist ideology and, being aware of this, the children had grown skeptical of what teachers told them. To get around this, Segal told ER, Youth Aliyah took them to places in Israel where they could see for themselves how democracy worked, rather than telling them about it.[37]

Three years before, at Hadassah's celebration in New York of the twenty-fifth anniversary of Youth Aliyah, ER had spoken of the challenges Youth Aliyah met with each of these groups of children. ER felt that the last group, which had to learn democratic values as they shed the Communist ideas they had been taught, represented the biggest challenge. She expected that their indoctrination in Communism was "a very thorough indoctrination," because its model came from the Soviet Union, and the Youth Aliyah educators would "find great difficulty in changing the trend of thought," but she was "equally sure that the experienced, dedicated people who have accomplished miracles for all the children that have come before will be able to do it again."

In her speech, ER expressed her wonderment at what Youth Aliyah had accomplished in the past. When she first saw the children who had survived the Holocaust in the displaced person (DP) camps in Germany in 1946, she thought "it would be impossible to bring these children back to normal, happy people, and yet later in Israel I saw what had been done." She met some of the children who had been in the camps who were now grown up and living happy, productive lives as citizens of Israel. She marveled at how the Youth Aliyah workers had managed to help the children put the horrors of the camps in Germany in the past by giving them love, but also by communicating to them their own excitement in building a new country. The reason for Youth Aliyah's success, she believed, lay in its ability to make the children feel part of something momentous: "You manage to give the children the feeling that they are needed; not that they are a burden, not that they are receiving charity, but they are needed! They are the people who are going to build Israel."[38]

ER herself felt intensely proud of being part of what she regarded as a great historical event: the spiritual transformation of children broken by the horrors they had endured. "There can be no greater happiness," she whispered to Moshe Kol during a fundraising event for Youth Aliyah in Great Britain, "than seeing this miracle of resurrection realized, and I myself taking part in it."[39]

CONCLUSION

Eleanor Roosevelt's commitment to Israel originated in her efforts before, during, and after World War II to find homes for the victims of Nazi persecution. The national home that Israel provided for thousands of Jews relieved some of the grief she felt at her limited success in persuading the American public, her husband, and the State Department to admit more refugees into the United States in the 1930s and 1940s. It made more bearable her feeling, reported by Moshe Kol and Ruth Gruber, that more should have been done to rescue Jews during the Holocaust. After the failure of the Wagner-Rogers bill, the frustration of trying get the State Department to issue more visas, the stubborn resistance of Congress to admitting more refugees after the war, the harsh policy of Great Britain in blocking immigration to Palestine, and the Arab rejection of the UN partition plan, ER saw in the establishment of Israel an opportunity, at last, for large numbers of Jewish refugees to rebuild their lives in a place where they were both wanted and needed. "One of the most compelling reasons for the existence of Israel," she said in 1956, "is the fact that it is the only sure haven for the Jewish people. In troubled times, when they are the first to suffer, it is essential for them to have their own country of refuge."[1]

ER's bond with Israel also grew out of her special concern for the well-being of children. Her support for the Wagner-Rogers bill, her involvement with the United States Committee for the Care of European Children, her efforts to help rescue 5,000 Jewish children from unoccupied France, her initial association with Youth Aliyah in 1940, and the active role she played as World Patron of Youth Aliyah drew her deeply into the work of rescuing and rehabilitating Jewish children. She saw in the "beautiful radiant faces" of children she encountered at the Youth Aliyah training centers in

Israel a sign that Youth Aliyah's programs were succeeding in transforming the shattered lives of children who had experienced the trauma of war, concentration camps, antisemitism, or extreme poverty.

To many Jews, the establishment of Israel, coming so soon after the Holocaust, seemed miraculous. Its significance went far beyond the need to create a haven for Holocaust survivors; it was the realization of a dream dating back to biblical times whose fulfillment they prayed for in their liturgy. As ER said of the children being prepared by Youth Aliyah for citizenship in the reborn nation:

> They know that in Israel there is something for them that meets the longing of their people over thousands of years. They have finally found a homeland where they are free under their own government in which they participate and which gives them a sense of loyalty and devotion.[2]

ER shared in this sense of fulfillment and in the excitement of Israelis about their future, both as a player in the political struggle for the establishment of Israel and as a warmly engaged personal actor in Israel's growth as a nation.

ER's bond with Israel also grew out of the warm relationship she developed with American Jews during the 1930s and 1940s. She spoke at Hadassah, ORT, and UJA meetings, at synagogues, and in other venues. She partnered with American Jews in addressing issues she cared deeply about, including refugees, religious tolerance, the civil rights of African Americans, child welfare, public health, and human rights. In addition, Israel seemed to be practicing on a large scale the values that she shared with the Quaker leader Clarence Pickett and promoted in the United States in the 1930s: the ideals of active citizenship, cooperative community-building, rural revitalization, and the provision of resources to people in need so that they could build their own futures. Like Henrietta Szold, ER had been inspired by the leaders of the settlement house movement in the early years of the twentieth century and they had pointed her in the direction her activist career would follow. In many ways, ER's devotion to Israel was the culmination of that career.

ER was, without doubt, one of the great humanitarians of the twentieth century. She worked tirelessly to relieve suffering and uphold human rights. She moved far ahead of her contemporaries in her attitudes toward African Americans and Jews and, more significantly, in her relationships with them. As an anticolonialist, she took a keen interest in the developing nations that were freed after World War II. Nevertheless, the society in which she lived, the perspectives of the people she was closest to, and her personal experience limited her understanding of cultures with which she was unfamiliar. Her strongly Western perspective on the world was evident in the paternalistic and demeaning attitudes she expressed toward the Arabs, attitudes widespread in

Western society and rooted in the cultural representations of the Muslim world that Edward Said has termed "Orientalism." Like most Americans of her time, she had no knowledge of Arab culture or appreciation for its traditions. As the historian Michelle Mart writes: "The image of Arab Muslims is part of a long-standing European narrative that stigmatized the 'Orient' as outside the bounds of Western culture."[3] ER's unbridled enthusiasm for what the Jews were accomplishing existed behind cultural blinders that prevented her from fully recognizing the very different reality experienced by the Palestinian Arabs.

ER was critical of Great Britain's colonialist policies and, in the case of Palestine, she regarded Britain's efforts to prevent Jewish immigration and to suppress Jewish resistance to its rule as yet another manifestation of imperialism. Viewing the Palestinian Jews as an oppressed population fighting the British for their freedom made it easier for her to discount the fact that most of the Jews in Palestine were European settlers whom the Arabs increasingly resented for expanding their settlements on what had been Arab land. Whether or not one believes, as ER did, that the UN vote to partition Palestine into Jewish and Arab states was the only realistic solution to the conflict given the presence by 1947 of over 500,000 Jews in Palestine and the passionate commitment of both parties to fight for their cause, the contrast between ER's deep humanitarian response to the crisis of the Jews and her hard pragmatic response to the plight of the Arabs is troubling.[4]

ER did not seem to recognize that the establishment of Israel was a case in which the achievement of human rights for one people collided with the human rights of another people. She ignored or downplayed the fact that the Jews had expelled many Arabs or terrorized them into fleeing and then destroyed their villages so that they had no homes to return to. To the Jews (and to ER), the 1948 war with the Arabs was the "War of Independence." To the Arabs, the establishment of Israel was "Al Nakbar" ("the Catastrophe").

What is most striking about ER's views on the establishment of Israel is the absence of doubt. There is no indication that she wrestled with the moral complexity of the struggle between the Arabs and the Jews or grasped the Arabs' profound experience of dispossession. Durward Sandifer, who was Eleanor Roosevelt's principal State Department adviser when she served on the American delegation to the UN in 1948, said to Joseph Lash in describing ER's attitude during and after the debate over the UN partition plan for Palestine: "She impressed me as having an open mind on every other subject than Palestine. She was not open to persuasion on that issue."[5] Sandifer, who opposed the creation of a Jewish state like nearly all his colleagues in the State Department, thought that ER was "a person with a great capacity for growth." She "was always searching for new ideas," and in absorbing them and "making them her own, she grew. . . . That's what made the Palestine case stand out as a maverick."

Perhaps because ER had an optimistic view of history, she did not perceive that precisely because of their success, the Jews had locked themselves into a tragic embrace with the Arabs from which it would not be easy to free themselves. She sympathized with the suffering of the Palestinian Arab refugees and advocated for aid to help them begin new lives elsewhere. However, she did not believe that the situation in which they found themselves resulted from the infliction of injustice upon them by the Jews or the UN. It was, she thought, the consequence of a conflict the Arabs had themselves initiated in defiance of the UN. They had lost. Now, she believed, they should move on. The UN and the Arab states, with some financial compensation from Israel for the property the refugees had left behind, needed to take responsibility for resettling elsewhere those Arabs who had been displaced.

Throughout her public life ER exhibited a combination of idealism and political realism in her approach to the world. While a great humanitarian and champion of human rights, she was also a pragmatist who recognized that solutions to complex political problems were unlikely to satisfy all sides or even satisfy one side completely. Difficult choices had to be made, and made decisively, in order to move forward. The UN partition plan for Palestine was one of those imperfect solutions. She was not originally in favor of the creation of a Jewish state, but once the partition plan was adopted, ER backed it passionately. She became immune to arguments on the Arab side of the conflict. She no longer expressed the concerns she voiced in 1946 about Arab opposition to massive Jewish settlement or the doubts sown by Isaiah Bowman and his warning that seeking to build a Jewish state in Palestine would lead to ongoing conflict. Nor did she express concern about the fact that the partition plan deprived the majority population of Palestine of the right to choose their own government through free elections. That right was now among the provisions of the Universal Declaration of Human Rights (UDHR), whose drafting and acceptance by the UN she had worked hard to achieve. It reads, "The will of the people shall be the basis of the authority of government; this shall be expressed in periodic and genuine elections which shall be by universal and equal suffrage and shall be held by secret vote or by equivalent free voting procedures."[6] Whatever the merits of the partition plan as a way to settle the conflict, it was imposed by the nations that made up the UN, not voted on by the inhabitants of Palestine, the great majority of whom were Arabs.

Once Israel was established, ER's position on the Cold War played a role in her defense of its existence. She thought the most effective response to the efforts of the Soviet Union to spread Communism throughout the developing world was not military aid but economic aid and the nurturing of democratic institutions. Israel, she believed, served as an example to the entire developing world of how a democracy could create thriving agricultural and industrial enterprises while meeting the essential needs of all its citizens for food, housing, education, and health care.

ER did have misgivings about some of Israel's policies toward its minorities and about the power exerted by the Orthodox religious parties in such areas as state support for religious schools and Sabbath laws, but she regarded these problems as likely to be resolved in time. When her friend Charl Williams, with whom she disagreed on other issues related to Israel, complained in 1958 about the Sabbath restrictions imposed in Israel at Orthodox insistence, ER shared her friend's annoyance but added that she "would not mind this so much as interference in actual government." She told Williams that the Israeli leaders "felt so far that they were not strong enough to stand an actual showdown" with the religious parties, "but it will have to come."[7]

ER found much to admire about the Israel of her day, especially in the vitality of its people. For her, contributing to a cause larger than oneself, as the citizens of Israel were doing, was an especially invigorating form of "self-expression." In *Tomorrow Is Now*, a book she was working on at the time of her death in 1962, ER wrote:

> The building of a new nation is one of the most inspiring activities that man can know, activating everyone from the smallest child to the oldest grandfather. This particular excitement of self-expression can be seen best, perhaps, today in the state of Israel. There you see everyone working, stirred by participation in a common cause for a single goal.[8]

ER felt that she too contributed to the building of Israel, and she shared in the excitement of its rapid growth. She loved being part of the communal effort to ensure Israel's survival in her role as World Patron of Youth Aliyah, as a speaker and writer about Israel in the United States, and as a fundraiser for Hadassah. Israel's success validated her commitment to its welfare. And, as a prominent defender of both Israel and human rights, she helped affirm Israel's legitimacy as a nation.

ACKNOWLEDGMENTS

I FIRST BEGAN THINKING about the subject of this book while I served as associate editor for the Eleanor Roosevelt Papers Project at George Washington University. I am grateful to Allida Black, who directed the project, for inviting me to join her staff after my retirement from the Roosevelt Institute and for sharing her great knowledge of Eleanor Roosevelt with me and the other participants in the editing of ER's postwar papers.

Thanks to the Franklin and Eleanor Roosevelt Institute for granting me two Arthur M. Schlesinger Jr. Fellowships at the beginning of my research, which enabled me to make a research trip to Israel. I also want to take this opportunity to thank William J. vanden Heuvel, retired president of the institute, and Fredrica Goodman, my mentor when I served as executive director, for drawing me into the world of the Roosevelts in the first place. I have many good memories of our working together.

The Department of History at Smith College appointed me to the position of research associate for several years, which gave me access to the Smith Library and to its online databases. When I was living in Providence some years back, the Brown University History Department extended similar privileges to me. I greatly appreciate their providing access to these resources, which were crucial to my work.

I benefited from the expertise of many archivists during my research. I am particularly indebted to the staff of the Franklin D. Roosevelt Presidential Library and Museum in Hyde Park, where I spent many hours. Special thanks to Kirsten Carter, the supervisory archivist; Robert Clark, the former supervisory archivist; Virginia Lewick; Matthew Hanson; Alicia Vivona; and Mark Renovitch. Herman Eberhardt, supervisory curator of the museum, was also helpful in tracking down some items.

Cynthia Koch, former director of the library, provided much encouragement along the way, and she and her husband, Eliot Werner, sometimes sustained me with their hospitality during research forays to Hyde Park. My dear friends Ralph Arlyck and Elisabeth Cardonne Arlyck also warmly welcomed me to their home when I was conducting research at the library.

I am grateful to the staff of the National Archives II in College Park, Maryland, for assistance in searching the papers of the Department of State (not easy to navigate on your own!) and the staff at the Center for Jewish History (CJH) in New York City. Susan Woodland, head of the Hadassah Archives when I conducted research at the CJH, was especially helpful in directing me to material relevant to my subject, as was Don Davis at the American Friends Service Committee Archives in Philadelphia. Both the Hadassah Archives and the AFSC Archives furnished me with material not mined by other scholars.

I am thankful to the archivists of the Manuscript Division of the Library of Congress, the Rare Book and Manuscript Library at Columbia University, the Schlesinger Library on the History of Women in America, the Joint Distribution Committee (JDC) Archives in New York City, the Social Welfare History Archives at the University of Minnesota, the Northwest and Whitman College Archives, and the M. E. Grenander Department of Special Collections and Archives at the State University of New York, Albany, for their assistance with my research in their collections.

I am grateful for the assistance of the archivists at the Israel State Archives and the Central Zionist Archives in Israel and for the help of Boaz Levtov, now lecturer and head of the Department of History and the Time Tunnel Project at Beit Berl College. Dr. Levtov helped me search those two archives and, sitting at my side, provided the gist of documents that were in Hebrew. Thanks also to Tamar Shadur, who later reviewed the Hebrew documents with me to determine what might be useful to my project. I am also indebted to Yael Haran and other members of the Degania Alef archives staff for their help in accessing records of Eleanor Roosevelt's four visits to Degania and to Ron Shapiro, Joseph Baratz's grandson, for sharing family photos with me and welcoming my interest in his grandfather's legacy.

Jonathan Sarna and Jody Myers provided helpful advice at several points during my research and preparation of the book for publication. Thanks also to Suzy Groden, who read an early draft of the first half of the book and made constructive suggestions.

David Woolner, my successor as executive director of the Roosevelt Institute and now the institute's senior fellow and resident historian in Hyde Park, read and provided feedback on a rough draft of the early chapters. He also put me in touch with Richard Breitman at American University. Professor Breitman's thoughtful comments on the early chapters were enormously helpful to me in finding the direction the book would eventually take.

Ken Schoen, the owner of Schoen Books in South Deerfield, MA, who has a gift for connecting people with each other, put me in touch with Kathy, Tom, and Peter Pfister; sent or alerted me to relevant books, articles, and reviews; and cheered me along the way. He wishes I had finished the book a long time ago ("This is important, John! Get it done!"). Well, it is finally done. Thank you, Ken, for your friendship and enduring support!

I am greatly indebted to Mary Jo Binker, one of my former colleagues at the Eleanor Roosevelt Papers Project, for directing me to important secondary sources and for her excellent suggestions for improving the postwar chapters of the book. Her knowledge and insight, acquired from many years of editing ER's public papers, as well as her enthusiasm for my topic, made her an ideal sounding board as I revised my manuscript.

Tom, Kathy, and Peter Pfister, who were researching and writing an account of the extraordinary lives of their parents while I was working on my project, generously shared documents in their collection of family papers with me. Their book, *Eva & Otto: Resistance, Refugees, and Love in the Time of Hitler* (Purdue University Press, 2020), is a moving account of their parents' anti-Nazi activities and devotion to each other. It is a testimony to the Pfisters' resourcefulness and persistence in researching their parents' story.

I am grateful to Nancy Roosevelt Ireland, trustee of Eleanor Roosevelt's literary estate, for permission to quote from ER's published writings. I am also grateful to McIntosh & Otis and the Special Collections Research Center at Syracuse University for permission to quote from Dorothy Thompson's column, "To a Jewish Friend"; to Hadassah for granting me permission to quote from documents generated by Hadassah officials; to Dr. Alexander Matthews for permission to quote from the correspondence of Martha Gellhorn with Eleanor Roosevelt; to James Fry, Varian Fry's son, for permission to quote from Varian Fry's correspondence and reports; and to Marnie Mueller for permission to quote from the correspondence of her grandmother, Sarah Siegel, with Eleanor Roosevelt.

I am very grateful to Justin Race, my editor at Purdue University Press, for his guidance, patience, and support during the process of preparing the manuscript for publication and to the rest of the PUP staff: Susan Wegener for facilitating my acquisition of photos and permissions, Katherine Purple and Kelley Kimm for guiding me through the copyediting and production process, Christopher Brannan for his splendid cover design, and Bryan Shaffer and Matthew Mudd for their help with marketing.

My sons, Will and Jack, have been a source of support, companionship, and love during the dozen years I have devoted to this project. It has been a pleasure to see them discover their vocations and become expert in their work during this time.

Finally, I would like to thank my wife, Jane Myers, for her keen interest in this project, for her love, and for sustaining me in so many ways. She read every chapter of the manuscript with a critical eye, read revisions of every chapter, and helped me think through difficult issues. It is a better book because of her.

NOTES

INTRODUCTION

1. See for example, David S. Wyman, *Paper Walls: America and the Refugee Crisis, 1938–1941* (New York: Pantheon Books, 1968, rpt. 1985); Henry L. Feingold, *The Politics of Rescue: The Roosevelt Administration and the Holocaust, 1938–1945* (New York: Holocaust Library, 1970); David S. Wyman, *Abandonment of the Jews: America and the Holocaust, 1941–1945* (New York: New Press, 2007); Richard Breitman and Alan M. Kraut, *American Refugee Policy and European Jewry, 1933–1945* (Bloomington: Indiana University Press, 1987); Monty Noam Penkower, *The Holocaust and Israel Reborn* (Urbana: University of Illinois Press, 1994); Verne Newton, ed., *FDR and the Holocaust* (New York: St. Martin's Press, 1996); William D. Rubinstein, *The Myth of Rescue* (London: Routledge, 1997); David S. Wyman and Rafael Medoff, *A Race Against Death: Peter Bergson, America, and the Holocaust* (New York: New Press, 2002); Richard Breitman and Allan J. Lichtman, *FDR and the Jews* (Cambridge, MA: Harvard University Press, 2013).
2. See Joseph Lash, *Eleanor and Franklin* (New York: W. W. Norton, 1971) and *The Years Alone* (New York: W. W. Norton, 1972); Doris Kearns Goodwin, *No Ordinary Time* (New York: Simon & Schuster, 1994); Penkower, "Eleanor Roosevelt and World Jewry," in *The Holocaust and Israel Reborn* (1994); Blanche Wiesen Cook, *Eleanor Roosevelt, Vol. 2: The Defining Years, 1933–1938* (New York: Viking, 1999); and *Eleanor Roosevelt, Vol. 3: The War Years and After, 1939–1962* (New York: Viking, 2016). Beginning in 1909, ER signed letters to FDR, "ER." Allida Black in *Casting Her Own Shadow* (New York: Columbia University Press, 1996) and Blanche Cook in her biography of Eleanor Roosevelt also adopted this usage. It puts ER on the same playing field as FDR and avoids any confusion.

3. Doris Fleeson to ER, August 31, 1949; Folder: Fleeson, Doris; Correspondence 1945–1952; Eleanor Roosevelt Papers (hereafter: ERP); FDR Library (hereafter: FDRL).
4. Joseph Lash, *Eleanor Roosevelt: A Friend's Memoir* (New York: Doubleday, 1964), 134.
5. The best account of ER's relationship to Israel is Michelle Mart, "Eleanor Roosevelt, Liberalism, and Israel," *Shofar* 24, no. 3 (Spring 2006): 58–89. Mart places special emphasis on ER's perception of Israel as "the liberal ideal of a modern, progressive state" and on the role of ER's Jewish friends in accounting for ER's attachment to Israel.
6. Quoted in Lash, *Eleanor and Franklin*, 135, 214. Lash reports that the 1907 Columbia Law School roster listed 21 Jewish names out of 74 members of the graduating class.
7. Leonard Dinnerstein, *Antisemitism in America* (New York: Oxford University Press, 1994), 81.
8. Quoted by Dinnerstein in *Antisemitism*, 95.
9. See Dinnerstein, *Antisemitism*, chap. 7, "Antisemitism at High Tide: World War II (1939–1945)"; Sonja Schoepf Wentling and Rafael Medoff, *Herbert Hoover and the Jews: The Origins of the "Jewish Vote" and Bipartisan Support for Israel* (Washington, DC: The David S. Wyman Institute for Holocaust Studies, 2012), 67.
10. Oral history interview with Henry Morgenthau III conducted by Emily Williams, November 9, 1978, 74–76; Eleanor Roosevelt Oral History Transcripts; FDRL.
11. Interview with Henry Morgenthau III conducted by the author, May 1, 2008.
12. Henry Morgenthau III, *Mostly Morgenthaus* (New York: Ticknor & Fields, 1991), 274.
13. Henry Morgenthau Jr., "Address of Henry Morgenthau, Jr. before a meeting of the Federation of Brotherhoods of the Temples and Synagogues of Baltimore," December 20, 1936, 2–4, 9–11, enclosed in Elinor Morgenthau to ER, July 29, 1938; Folder: Morgenthau Family; Personal Letters 1938; ERP; FDRL.

CHAPTER 1

1. Beginning with FDR's second term in 1937, the inauguration of American presidents was moved from March 4 to January 20.
2. McDonald's diary, April 3, 1933, *Advocate for the Doomed: The Diaries and Papers of James G. McDonald, 1932–1935*, ed. Richard Breitman, Barbara McDonald Stewart, and Severin Hochberg (Bloomington: Indiana University Press, 2007), 36. Hereafter cited as Breitman, Stewart, and Hochberg, *AD*.
3. McDonald's diary, April 3, 1933, Breitman, Stewart, and Hochberg, *AD*, 28.
4. Quoted by editors in Breitman, Stewart, and Hochberg, *AD*, 48.
5. McDonald's diary, April 28, 1933, Breitman, Stewart, and Hochberg, *AD*, 59.
6. McDonald to ER, May 4, 1933; Folder 47: Eleanor Roosevelt; Box 3; James G. McDonald Papers, Rare Book & Manuscript Library, Columbia University. Hereafter: McDonald Papers, Columbia.

7. "The Larger Question," *New York Times*, March 30, 1933, 16. Hereafter: *NYT*.
8. "1,200 Clergymen Sign Nazi Protest," *NYT*, May 26, 1933, 13.
9. Catt to Manus, April 25, 1933; Carrie Chapman Catt Papers on microfilm, Box 6/Reel 4, Library of Congress. Hereafter: Catt Papers.
10. "Protest of 9,000 Non-Jewish Women against the treatment of Jews in Germany," Broadside; Political/1–156; American Jewish Historical Society, Center for Jewish History. Hereafter: AJHS.
11. Richard Breitman and Allan J. Lichtman, *FDR and the Jews* (Cambridge, MA: Harvard University Press, 2013), 62–63. Hereafter: Breitman and Lichtman, *FDR and the Jews*.
12. "Mrs. Catt Gets 1933 American Hebrew Medal," *New York Herald Tribune*, November 24, 1933, 23. Hereafter: *NYHT*.
13. Blanche Wiesen Cook, *Eleanor Roosevelt, Vol. 2: The Defining Years, 1933–1938* (New York: Viking, 1999), 122–23.
14. Hamilton to Addams, July 1, 1933, quoted in Cook, *Eleanor Roosevelt, Vol. 2*, 127.
15. Cook, *Eleanor Roosevelt, Vol. 2*, 124.
16. "Roosevelt Asked to Aid Refugees," *NYT*, September 11, 1933, 10.
17. "Nazis 'Convicted' of World 'Crime' By 20,000 in Rally," *NYT*, March 8, 1934, 1; Catt to Rosa Manus, March 16, 1934; Catt Papers, Box 6/Reel 4. Neither the *New York Times* nor the *New York Herald Tribune* article on the event contain a reference to ER having been there.
18. Cook, *Eleanor Roosevelt, Vol. 1: The Early Years, 1884–1933* (New York: Viking, 1992), 364; Melissa R. Klapper, "'Those by Whose Side We Have Labored': American Jewish Women and the Peace Movement between the Wars," *Journal of American History* 97, no. 3 (December 2010), 650.
19. Editors' note, Breitman, Stewart, and Hochberg, *AD*, 77–78.
20. McDonald's diary, October 16, 1933, Breitman, Stewart, and Hochberg, *AD*, 128.
21. McDonald's diary, October 17 and 26, 1933, Breitman, Stewart, and Hochberg, *AD*, 130, 133.
22. McDonald's diary, December 25, 1933, Breitman, Stewart, and Hochberg, *AD*, 231.
23. McDonald to ER, December 15, 1934; Folder 47: Eleanor Roosevelt; Box 3; McDonald Papers, Columbia.
24. McDonald's diary, December 17, 1934, Breitman, Stewart, and Hochberg, *AD*, 579; Scheider [Malvina Thompson] to McDonald, December 20, 1934; Folder 47: Eleanor Roosevelt; Box 3; McDonald Papers, Columbia.
25. McDonald was probably referring to President Benjamin Harrison's protest against Russia's treatment of its Jewish citizens in 1891 and to President Theodore Roosevelt's personal letter to the czar protesting the pogrom at Kishinev in 1903.
26. McDonald to ER, July 24, 1935; ER to McDonald, August 2, 1935; Breitman, Stewart, and Hochberg, *AD*, 788–89.

27. "Text of Resignation of League Commissioner for German Refugees," *NYT*, December 30, 1935, 12.
28. McDonald to ER, January 8, 1936; J. M. Helm to McDonald, February 5, 1936; Folder 47: Eleanor Roosevelt; Box 3; McDonald Papers, Columbia.
29. *Refugees and Rescue: The Diaries and Papers of James G. McDonald, 1935–1945*, ed. Richard Breitman, Barbara McDonald Stewart, and Severin Hochberg (Bloomington: Indiana University Press, 2009), 111. Hereafter: Breitman, Stewart, and Hochberg, *Refugees and Rescue*.
30. "Jews! Jews! Jews Everywhere," flyer, OF 76C, FDRL. According to FDR Library records, this flyer was dropped by airplane over Los Angeles by an unknown anti-Communist organization. A concerned citizen in LA sent it to the White House.
31. "We're For Roosevelt," Editorial, *Washington Jewish Review*, October 30, 1936; Folder: Eleanor Roosevelt, 1936; PPF2; FDR Papers, FDR Library. Hereafter: FDRL.
32. In 1937, for example, she canceled a speech at a country club in Lancaster, Pennsylvania when she learned that it excluded Jews. Cook, *Eleanor Roosevelt, Vol. 2*, 557.
33. Florence Rothschild, "The Mistress of the White House," *Wisconsin Jewish Chronicle*, March 9, 1934; clipping enclosed in Solomon Levitan to Louis Howe, March 12, 1934; Folder: Eleanor Roosevelt, 1934; PPF2; FDR Papers, FDRL.
34. "Mrs. Roosevelt Calls Poverty in U.S. Disgrace: Appeals for Co-operative Work in Interest of Welfare at Zionist Dinner," *NYHT*, October 17, 1934, 13. See also Cook, *Eleanor Roosevelt, Vol. 2*, 322–23.
35. "Mrs. Roosevelt Calls Poverty in U.S. Disgrace," 13.
36. ER to Elinor Morgenthau, August 26, 1935; Folder: Correspondence with Eleanor Roosevelt 1935; Elinor Morgenthau Papers; FDRL. In 1937, ER spoke about "Public Health" on a national Hadassah broadcast, while James McDonald addressed the "Challenge of the Refugee Problem." "Purim Marked by Hadassah in U.S. Broadcasts," *NYHT*, February 26, 1937, 12. After Germany annexed Austria in 1938 ER wrote to Elinor Morgenthau: "Isn't this Austrian situation terrible and Spain is pretty depressing too I think." ER to EM, March 17, 1938; Folder: Elinor Morgenthau Correspondence: Transcripts of Correspondence with Eleanor Roosevelt; Elinor Morgenthau Papers; FDRL.
37. Cook, *Eleanor Roosevelt, Vol. 2*, 329; Rothschild, "The Mistress of the White House."

CHAPTER 2

1. See Blanche Wiesen Cook, *Eleanor Roosevelt, Vol. 2: The Defining Years, 1933–1938* (New York: Viking, 1999), 130–31; Clarence Pickett to ER, August 14, 1933; General Files 1933–37, American Friends Service Committee Archives, Philadelphia, PA. Hereafter: AFSC Archives.
2. "Mrs. Roosevelt's Radio Talk—Westtown School," April 25, 1935; General Files 1935, Comms and Orgs, AFSC Archives.

3. ER to Alice Davis, August 24, 1933; General Files 1933–37, AFSC Archives.
4. Joseph P. Lash, *Eleanor and Franklin* (New York: W. W. Norton, 1971), 391–96.
5. "Clarence E. Pickett's Journal," September 22, 1934; AFSC Archives. Hereafter: Pickett's Journal.
6. Emma Bugby, "Mrs. Roosevelt Gets 105,000 Letters in Year," *New York Herald Tribune* (*NYHT*), March 3, 1935.
7. "Mrs. Roosevelt's Radio Talk—Westtown School."
8. "Mrs. Roosevelt's Radio Talk—Westtown School."
9. "Radio Statement for American Friends Service Committee," November 13, 1949 in Allida Black, Mary Jo Binker, Christopher Brick, Robert P. Frankel Jr., and Christy Regenhardt, et al., eds., *The Eleanor Roosevelt Papers, Vol. 2: The Human Rights Years, 1949–1952* (Charlottesville, VA: University of Virginia Press, 2012), 239–40.
10. "Mrs. Roosevelt's Radio Talk—Westtown School."
11. Grace Rhoads Jr. to Robert A. Ashworth, April 27, 1934; General Files 1933–37, AFSC Archives.
12. Pickett, "A Quaker Looks at Modern Judaism" (1949); General Files 1933–37, AFSC Archives.
13. Thompson to Pickett, January 8, 1937; Pickett to Thompson, January 6, 1937; General Files 1933–37, AFSC Archives.
14. McDonald diary, February 21, 1934, *Advocate for the Doomed: The Diaries and Papers of James G. McDonald, 1932–1935*, ed. Richard Breitman, Barbara McDonald Stewart, and Severin Hochberg (Bloomington, IN: Indiana University Press, 2007), 300. Hereafter: Breitman, Stewart, and Hochberg, *AD*. Pickett also discussed the idea with J. C. Hyman of the Jewish Joint Distribution Committee. Hyman to Pickett, January 24, 1934; General Files 1933–37, AFSC Archives.
15. Pickett to McDonald, March 3, 1934; General Files 1933–37, AFSC Archives.
16. McDonald diary, March 6 and March 17, 1934, Breitman, Stewart, and Hochberg, *AD*, 313, 322.
17. McDonald to Pickett, March 19, 1934; General Files 1933–37, AFSC Archives.
18. Pickett, "To Our Friends," June 1934, 6; Folder: Pickett, Clarence; Correspondence with Government Departments 1934; Eleanor Roosevelt Papers (hereafter: ERP); FDR Library (hereafter: FDRL).
19. Pickett to M. L. Wilson, June 18, 1934; General Files 1933–37, AFSC Archives; Pickett to M. L. Wilson, June 18, 1934 and enclosure: "Memorandum of conversation with President Roosevelt on Friday, June 15"; General Files 1933–37, AFSC Archives; Pickett's Journal, October 28, 1938; AFSC Archives.
20. McDonald to Pickett, August 30, 1934; General Files 1933–37, AFSC Archives.
21. McDonald, current affairs lecture, Chautauqua, NY, July 10, 1933, Breitman, Stewart, and Hochberg, *AD*, 76. See also, AD, 140n7, 140–43.
22. Minutes of the American Christian Committee for German Refugees, May 11, 1934;

General Files 1933–37, AFSC Archives; "All Faiths Move to Aid Refugees," *New York Times* (*NYT*), May 22, 1934.

23. Frank Ritchie, "German Refugees and American Christians" (Draft); General Files 1935, Comms and Orgs, AFSC Archives. Underlining is Ritchie's.

24. Draft of letter to be signed by clergymen appealing for $400,000 for non-Aryan refugees, 1935; General Files 1935, Comms and Orgs, AFSC Archives.

25. Ritchie to Pickett, February 3, 1936; General Files 1933–37, AFSC Archives; "Move Here to Aid Exiled Christians," *NYT*, February 28, 1936.

26. Harry Emerson Fosdick to FDR, November 7, 1936; General Files 1933–37, AFSC Archives; "Drive to Seek Aid for German Exiles," *NYT*, October 7, 1936.

27. Pickett's Journal, November 7, 1936; Pickett to ER, telegram, November 12, 1936; General Files 1933–37, AFSC Archives.

28. Stephen Early, Memorandum for Miss Le Hand quoting a memorandum from Acting Secretary R. Walton Moore, November 13, 1936; PPF, 133; FDR Papers, FDRL.

29. Ritchie to Pickett, November 17, 1936; General Files 1933–37, AFSC Archives.

30. Lash, *Eleanor and Franklin*, 428.

31. Pickett to ER, November 13, 1936; General Files 1933–37, AFSC Archives.

32. Eleanor Roosevelt, "My Day, December 2, 1936," The Eleanor Roosevelt Papers Digital Edition (2017), https://erpapers.columbian.gwu.edu/browse-my-day-columns. Hereafter: ER, My Day.

33. Pickett to Ritchie, December 8, 1936; Ritchie to Pickett, December 10, 1936; General Files 1933–37, AFSC Archives.

34. For expressions of the frustration McDonald and Fosdick felt about how "impossibly difficult" it was to "make Christian people shoulder practical responsibility" for Christian refugees, see James G. McDonald and Harry Emerson Fosdick, *Addresses on Modern Christian German Martyrs* (New York: American Christian Committee for German Refugees, [1937]).

35. Pickett to Ritchie, November 1, 1937; General Files 1933–37, AFSC Archives.

36. ER, "Because the War Idea is Obsolete" (1935), in Allida M. Black, *Courage in a Dangerous World: The Political Writings of Eleanor Roosevelt* (New York: Columbia University Press, 2000), 84.

37. For an in-depth discussion of ER's work with Lape, Read, Catt, Addams, and Wald, see Cook, *Eleanor Roosevelt, Vol. 2*.

38. "National Drive for Peace Will Begin April 21," *NYHT*, March 1, 1936, 23.

39. Quoted in Cook, *Eleanor Roosevelt, Vol. 2*, 330.

40. Quoted in Cook, *Eleanor Roosevelt, Vol. 2*, 312.

41. Pickett, "To Our Friends," June 1934, 1; Folder: Pickett, Clarence; Correspondence with Government Departments 1934; ERP; FDRL.

42. "The Outlook for Peace," Speech to Tenth Conference on the Cause and Cure of War,

Washington, DC, January 22–25, 1935; Folder: Eleanor Roosevelt 1935; ERP, FDRL.
43. Eleanor Roosevelt, *This Troubled World* (New York: H. C. Kinsey, 1938), 1, 28, 14–15, 32–33. ER dedicated the book to Carrie Chapman Catt.
44. *This Troubled World*, 17, 44–45, 47.

CHAPTER 3

1. Caroline Moorehead, *Gellhorn: A Twentieth-Century Life* (New York: Henry Holt, 2003), 80–83.
2. Gellhorn to ER, n.d. Written on board the *Queen Mary* before April 24, 1938; Folder: Gellhorn, Martha; Personal Letters 1937; Eleanor Roosevelt Papers (hereafter: ERP); FDR Library (hereafter: FDRL).
3. Martha Gellhorn, Introduction to *Eleanor Roosevelt's My Day: Her Acclaimed Columns 1936–1945*, ed. Rochelle Chadakoff (New York: Pharos Books, 1989), xii.
4. Richard Breitman and Allan J. Lichtman, *FDR and the Jews (Cambridge, MA: Harvard University Press, 2013)*, 102.
5. Cable from Cordell Hull to American Embassy, London, March 23, 1938; Folder: Treasury Department; Welles Papers; FDRL.
6. Richard Breitman, Barbara McDonald Stewart, and Severin Hochberg, eds., *Refugees and Rescue: The Diaries and Papers of James G. McDonald, 1935–1945 (Bloomington: Indiana University Press, 2009)*, 127–30. Among others attending the conference were Sumner Welles, Bernard Baruch, Henry Morgenthau Sr., and Rabbi Stephen Wise.
7. Rose Schneiderman to ER, April 14, 1938; Folder: Schneiderman, Rose; Personal Letters 1938; ERP; FDRL.
8. Pickett's Journal, April 14–15, 1938; AFSC Archives.
9. Neil Smith, *American Empire: Roosevelt's Geographer and the Prelude to Globalization* (Berkeley: University of California Press, 2003), 295, *304–15*. See Smith for a discussion of Bowman's antisemitism.
10. Sumner Welles, *Palestine's Rightful Destiny* (New York: American Christian Palestine Committee, 1946).
11. Pickett's Journal, July 12 and September 5–6, 1938; AFSC Archives; Pickett, *For More Than Bread* (Boston: Little, Brown, 1953), 125–26.
12. Pickett's Journal, September 1–2, 1938; AFSC Archives.
13. Pickett's Journal, October 28, 1938; AFSC Archives.
14. Pickett's Journal, November 9, 1938; AFSC Archives; Pickett to Lilly Pickett, November 10, 1938; General Files 1938–41, AFSC Archives.
15. Pickett, *For More Than Bread*, 133.
16. Gellhorn to ER, October 19, 1938, and attached report: "Anti-Nazi Refugees in Czechoslovakia," 8; ER to Gellhorn, November 15, 1938; Folder: Gellhorn, Martha and Edna; Personal Letters 1938; ERP; FDRL.

17. "The Five Hundredth Press Conference," November 15, 1938. *Public Papers and Addresses of Franklin D. Roosevelt*, 1938 Volume (New York: Macmillan, 1941), 597.
18. Schneiderman to ER, November 18, 1938; Folder: Schneiderman, Rose; Personal Letters 1938; ERP; FDRL.
19. Lorena Hickok, *Empty Without You: The Intimate Letters of Eleanor Roosevelt and Lorena Hickok*, ed. Rodger Streitmatter (New York: Free Press, 1998), 212.
20. Peter Kurth, *American Cassandra: The Life of Dorothy Thompson* (Boston: Little, Brown, 1990), 232, 282.
21. "To a Jewish Friend," On the Record, November 14, 1938; Box 96, Dorothy Thompson Papers, Syracuse University.
22. My Day, November 15, 1938.
23. ER to Thompson, November 16, 1938; Folder: Th–To; Personal Letters 1938; ERP; FDRL.
24. ER to Thompson, February 28, 1939; Folder: Thompson, Dorothy; Personal Letters 1939; ERP; FDRL.

CHAPTER 4

1. For an insightful discussion of the paradox that Jews were ardently seeking a nation state of their own at a time when Western democracies were seeking to build an international order as an antidote to ardent nationalism, see Michael N. Barnett, *The Star and the Stripes: A History of the Foreign Policies of American Jews* (Princeton: Princeton University Press, 2016), 126–27.
2. H. G. Wells, "The Future of the Jews," *Liberty* 15 (December 24, 1938).
3. McDonald diary, November 21, 1933, Richard Breitman, Barbara McDonald Stewart, and Severin Hochberg, *Advocate for the Doomed: The Diaries and Papers of James G. McDonald, 1932–1935* (Bloomington: Indiana University Press, 2007), 182. Hereafter: Breitman, Stewart, and Hochberg, *AD*.
4. Levin to Louis M. Fushan, June 1, 1934; Fushan to Levin, 3 July 1934; Phi Epsilon Pi Papers, I-76, Box 13; American Jewish Historical Society. Hereafter: AJHS.
5. ER's use of the word "race" here rather than "people" and "racial" elsewhere are problematic in the context of Nazi theories about the Jews, but it is clear that she regarded Jews, as she did African Americans, as in no way inferior to other people.
6. ER expressed this view in a more shocking manner in a letter written just after the Nazi invasion of Poland to her German friend, Carola Schaeffer-Bernstein. "I realize quite well," she told Carola, "that there may be a need for curtailing the ascendency of the Jewish people, but it seems to me it might have been done in a more humane way by a ruler who had intelligence and decency." At the advice of Sumner Welles, who feared possible diplomatic repercussions and danger to ER's friend, ER did not send this letter. ER to Carola Schaeffer-Bernstein, September 6, 1939; Folder: Benh–Bez;

7. "Mrs. Roosevelt Answers Mr. Wells on the Future of the Jews," *Liberty* 15 (December 31, 1938).
8. George Carlin to ER, December 21, 1938; Folder: United Feature Syndicate; Personal Letters 1938; ERP; FDRL.
9. Rabbi Louis Swichkow to ER, January 10, 1939; ER to Swichkow, January 16, 1939; Folder: Stu–Sz 1939; ERP, FDRL.
10. See, for example, "Religious Join in Crusade Against Hate," *Washington Post*, Jan. 14, 1940, B3 and "Mrs. Roosevelt to Lead Panel . . . ," *Washington Post*, Jan. 16, 1940, 3.
11. For consistency, "NCCJ" will be used throughout to refer to the National Conference of Jews and Christians and its successor, the National Council of Christians and Jews.
12. Benny Kraut, "Towards the Establishment of the National Conference of Christians and Jews: The Tenuous Road to Religious Goodwill in the 1920s," *American Jewish History* 77, no. 3 (March 1988): 410–12.
13. Dr. S. Parkes Cadman, *New York Herald Tribune* (*NYHT*), November 13, 1932, SM, 10.
14. "Report on Current Work," *Opinion*, April 10, 1933; National Conference of Christians and Jews Records, Box 1, Correspondence 1930–33, NCCJ Collection, University of Minnesota Libraries. Hereafter: NCCJ Collection.
15. "Report on Current Work."
16. The three men were Rev. Everett R. Clinchy; Father John Elliot Ross, a professor of religion at the University of Iowa; and Rabbi Morris S. Lazaron of Baltimore. "The Pilgrimage Team of the National Conference Continue Their Tour," *Information Bulletin* of the NCJC, January 1934; NCCJ Records, Box 10, Folder 19, NCCJ Collection.
17. Robert A. Ashworth's "Can Protestants, Catholics and Jews Cooperate?," *Christian Century*, January 26, 1938.
18. Clinchy to James N. Rosenberg, October 24, 1938; Everett R. Clinchy Papers, Correspondence with Individuals and Organizations, 1928–1978, Box 13, NCCJ Collection.
19. The commandments were:
    1. I will repudiate the idea that those who disagree with me are not good Americans.
    2. I will not allow racial or religious differences to determine my vote.
    3. I will appreciate what others than my own group have done to make America great.
    4. I will try to understand the background of those of other religious loyalties.
    5. I will help to create mutual respect and trust between members of different religious and racial groups.
    6. I will cooperate heartily with those of other faiths in the work for the common good.

7. I will always protest when those of other faiths are defamed.
8. I will not be misled by false doctrines of race nor claim superiority to others on the ground of race alone.
9. I will apply the Golden Rule to those of all races and religions and treat them as I should like to be treated.
10. I will pray for those of other faiths than my own and prize other[s'] prayers for myself.

My Day, February 15, 1940.

20. "Keepers of Democracy," *Virginia Quarterly Review*, Winter 1939, rpt. *Courage in a Dangerous World*, ed. Allida M. Black (New York: Columbia University Press, 2000), 118; "Intolerance," *Cosmopolitan*, February 1940, rpt. *Courage in a Dangerous World*, 121, 124.
21. My Day, April 14, 1939.
22. "Mrs. Roosevelt Asks Women Aid New Deal," *New York Times* (*NYT*), July 26, 1933, 5.
23. "Mrs. Roosevelt Asks Revival of Religion," *NYT*, October 14, 1933, 16.
24. "What Religion Means to Me," *Washington Jewish Review*, October 30, 1936, 1, 4; rpt. from *Forum Magazine*; Folder: Roosevelt, Eleanor; PPF2; FDR Papers, FDRL.
25. Eleanor Roosevelt, *The Moral Basis of Democracy* (New York: Howell, Soskin & Co., 1940), 52–53, 70.
26. Oral history interview with Justine Polier conducted by Thomas F. Soapes, September 14, 1977, 20; Eleanor Roosevelt Oral History Transcripts; FDRL. Hereafter: Polier OH.
27. Pickett, "Christianity in Action: Experiments in Social Regeneration," October 1938; Clarence Pickett's Speeches 1938–49, American Friends Service Committee Archives. Hereafter: AFSC Archives.
28. Beth Campbell, "Mrs. Roosevelt Is on Stump for New Brand of Citizenship," *Richmond Times-Dispatch*, May 15, 1938. ERP, FDRL; *The Moral Basis of Democracy*, 68.
29. *The Moral Basis of Democracy*, 12–14.
30. Mary Hoxie Jones to Katherine Theobald, November 27, 1940; General Files 1940, Comms and Orgs to Individuals, AFSC Archives.

CHAPTER 5

1. Harvard Sitkoff, *New Deal for Blacks: The Emergence of Civil Rights as a National Issue. Volume 1: The Depression Decade* (New York: Oxford University Press, 1978), 269.
2. White to ER, April 20, 1934; Folder: White, Walter; Personal Letters 1934; Eleanor Roosevelt Papers (hereafter: ERP), FDR Library (hereafter: FDRL).
3. "To the Honorable Franklin D. Roosevelt, President of the United States," December 27, 1934; Folder: White, Walter; Personal Letters 1934; ERP, FDRL. The other senators who signed the statement were: C. Douglas Buck (Delaware), William A. Comstock

(Michigan), Frank D. Fitzgerald (Michigan), A. Harry Moore (New Jersey), Harold G. Hoffman (New Jersey), and Tom Moodie (North Dakota).

4. Joseph P. Lash, *Eleanor and Franklin (New York: W. W. Norton, 1971)*, 517–18; Blanche Wiesen Cook, *Eleanor Roosevelt, Vol. 2: The Defining Years, 1933–1938* (New York: Viking, 1999), 245–46.

5. "Mrs. Roosevelt Urges Negroes to Higher Life," *New York Herald Tribune* (hereafter *NYHT)*, December 13, 1935, 16.

6. ER to FDR, memorandum, March 4, 1937; White, Walter; Personal Letters 1934; ERP, FDRL.

7. Walter White to FDR, December 23, 1938 (copy sent to ER); ER to White, January 3, 1939; Folder: White, Walter; Personal Letters 1938; ERP, FDRL.

8. For statistics on the use of the German-Austrian quota, see David S. Wyman, *Paper Walls: America and the Refugee Crisis, 1938–1941* (New York: Pantheon Books, 1985), 220–22.

9. Richard Breitman and Alan M. Kraut, *American Refugee Policy and European Jewry, 1933–1945* (Bloomington: Indiana University Press, 1987), 7–8, 33, 46–50; Richard Breitman and Allan J. Lichtman, *FDR and the Jews (Cambridge, MA: Harvard University Press, 2013)*, 74, 94–95.

10. Field, who was the grandson of the founder of the Marshall Field department store in Chicago, was an investment banker, newspaper publisher, and heir to the family fortune. Levy was the sister of Lessing J. and William Rosenwald. The three of them were heirs to the Sears, Roebuck fortune.

11. Pickett's Journal, February 19, 1939; American Friends Service Committee (AFSC) Archives; Justine Polier, "As I Knew Mrs. Roosevelt," *The Petal Paper* 10, no. 3 (January 1963); Folder 574, Articles, reports, speeches, re: juvenile justice and child welfare, 1963: Eleanor Roosevelt; Justine Wise Polier Papers, Schlesinger Library. Hereafter: Polier Papers.

12. ER to Polier, January 4, 1939; Folder: Pl-Po; Personal Letters 1939; ERP; FDRL.

13. A group of representatives of Christian Churches of America, "Providing for German Children in America," January 10, 1939, Folder 452: Non-Sectarian Foundation for Refugee Children; Polier Papers.

14. "The Wagner-Rogers Bill for Refugee Children"; Folder 452: Non-Sectarian Foundation for Refugee Children file; Polier Papers. Statement issued by Polier and other members of the group that initiated the bill after its introduction.

15. Pickett to ER, January 16, 1939; Folder: Pickett, Clarence; Correspondence with Government Departments 1939; ERP; FDRL.

16. Moffat to Welles, January 27, 1939; Folder: 1939 Thompso–Tu; Welles Papers; FDRL.

17. "Mrs. Roosevelt Asks U.S. Admit Child Refugees: Urges Wagner Bill's Passage," *NYHT*, February 14, 1939, 6.

18. "Aiding Refugee Children," Richmond *Times Dispatch*, editorial, February 15, 1939; Folder 452, Non-Sectarian Foundation for Refugee Children; Polier Papers.
19. Pickett's Journal, February 17, 1939; AFSC Archives.
20. Message from Marion Kenworth to Justine Polier, n.d. Folder 452, Non-Sectarian Foundation for Refugee Children, Polier Papers.
21. ER to Polier February 28, 1939; Folder: Pl–Po; Personal Letters 1939; ERP; FDRL.
22. Press release containing Pickett's announcement of the formation of the Non-Sectarian Committee for German Refugee Children, March 2, 1939; Folder: I–Je; Personal Letters 1939; ERP; FDRL.
23. "Admission of German Refugee Children," Hearings before the Committee on Immigration and Naturalization, House of Representatives, Seventy-sixth Congress, First Session, on H.J. Res. 165 and H.J. Res. 168, May 24, 25, 31 and June 1, 1939, 267–68, 185.
24. "Admission of German Refugee Children," Joint Hearings before a Subcommittee of the Committee on Immigration, United States Senate and a Subcommittee of the Committee on Immigration and Naturalization, House of Representatives, Seventy-sixth Congress, First session on SJ. Res. 64 and H.J. Res. 168, April 20, 21, 22, and 24, 1939, 164.
25. Polier OH, 16.
26. *Fortune*, 19 (April 1939), 102–103.
27. Wyman, *Paper Walls*, 91.
28. Pickett to ER, January 16, 1939; Folder: Pickett, Clarence; Correspondence with Government Departments 1939; ERP; FDRL; Gerald Holton, "The Grand Wake for Harvard Indifference," *Harvard Magazine*, September/October 2006.
29. Thompson to Welles, January 24, 1939; Messersmith to Welles, January 26, 1939; Welles to Pierrepont Moffat, January 26, 1939; Moffat to Welles, January 27, 1939; Copy of Welles to Thompson, January 30, 1939; Folder: 1939 Thompson–Tu; Welles Papers; FDRL.
30. Pickett to Hull, March 13, 1939; Perkins to ER, March 15, 1939; Folder: Pickett, Clarence; Correspondence with Government Departments 1939; ERP; FDRL.
31. Hull to ER, April 6, 1939 with enclosed copy of response to Pickett; A. M. Warren, Chief, Visa Div., to Pickett, April 3, 1939; Folder: Hull, Cordell; Personal Letters 1939; ERP; FDRL.
32. Intercollegiate Committee to Aid Student Refugees, "Summary of Progress, January to June, 1939," document attached to Ingrid Warburg to Elinor Morgenthau, June 6, 1939; Folder: Wan–Wat; Personal Letters 1939; ERP; FDRL.
33. My Day, August 30, 1939.
34. Holton, "The Grand Wake for Harvard Indifference."

CHAPTER 6

1. Pickett's Journal, September 14, 1939; November 6, 1939; American Friends Service Committee (AFSC) Archives.
2. Pickett to Rabbi Henry Cohen, William Allen White, Owen D. Young, Robert Hutchins, March 13, 1940; Pickett to Marion Kenworthy, December 4, 1939; Pickett to Agnes King Inglis, May 3, 1940; Owen R. Lovejoy, "Request to the Allocations Committee of the Children's Crusade on Behalf of the Non-Sectarian Foundation for Refugee Children," n.d.; Folder 452, Non-Sectarian Foundation for Refugee Children, Polier Papers; Pickett to ER, May 3, 1940; Folder: Pickett, Clarence, Apr.–July 1940; Correspondence with Government Departments 1940; Eleanor Roosevelt Papers (hereafter: ERP); FDR Library (hereafter: FDRL).
3. Caroline O'Day to ER, June 14, 1940; Folder: O'Day, Caroline; Personal Letters 1940; ERP; FDRL.
4. Pickett's Journal, June 16, 1940; AFSC Archives.
5. Eric Biddle, "Report of the Executive Director to the Board of Directors—January 1941," enclosed in Katherine Lenroot to ER, January 21, 1941; Folder: Lenroot, Katherine; Correspondence with Government Departments 1941; ERP; FDRL.
6. Biddle, "Report of the Executive Director."
7. Joseph Alsop to ER, July 3, 1940; ER to Alsop, July 7, 1940; Folder: Alsop, Joseph; Personal Letters 1940; ERP; FDRL.
8. In her thank-you note to Alsop, ER wrote: "I thought the script excellent and, while I felt guilty at making you write it, I am so glad you did, as it was so much better than I could have done"; ER to Alsop, July 7, 1940.
9. "Mrs. Roosevelt Wants Red Tape Cut on Refugees: Thousands Ready to Take British Children Stopped by Quota Laws, She Says," *New York Herald Tribune* (hereafter: *NYHT*), July 7, 1940, p. 10.
10. My Day, July 13, 1940.
11. Sophonisba Breckinridge to Hull, July 9, 1940, RG59, 811.111 Refugees/168, NARA.
12. Richard Flournoy to James Dunn, Julian Harrington, and Eliot Coulter, July 10, 1940, RG59, 811.111 Refugees/168, NARA.
13. Hull to Sophonisba Breckinridge, July 11, 1940, RG59, 811.111 Refugees/168, NARA.
14. Drew Pearson and Robert S. Allen, "State Department Blocking Young War Refugees. Career Men for Some Strange Reason, Refuse to Let British Children In," Washington Merry-Go-Round, July 8, 1940, RG59, 811.111 Refugees/160, NARA.
15. "Roosevelt Denies Refugee Red Tape," *New York Times* (hereafter: *NYT*), July 10, 1940, 9.
16. American Embassy [Ambassador Kennedy] to President and Secretary of State, July 10, 1940, RG59, 811.111 Refugees/160, NARA.
17. Memorandum for files, Visa Division, July 11, 1940, RG59, 811.111 Refugees/151, NARA.

18. Hull to Embassy, London, July 11, 1940. RG59, 811.111 Refugees/150 A, NARA.
19. "U.S. Removes Curb on Child Refugees," *NYT*, July 14, 1940, 1, 22.
20. "British Delay Plan on Child Refugees," *NYT*, July 17, 1940, 19.
21. "The Bombers Are Coming," August 1940, 5; Folder: Inglis, Agnes; Refugee Letters 1940; ERP; FDRL.
22. "Nazis Assail U.S. on Mercy Ship Law," *NYT*, August 30, 1940, 8.
23. "U.S. Committee Halts Drive for Child Refugees," *NYHT*, October 8, 1940, 11.
24. For a detailed account of how the USCCEC operated, see Michal Ostrovsky, "'We Are Standing By': Rescue Operations of the United States Committee for the Care of European Children," *Holocaust and Genocide Studies* 29 (Fall 2015), 230–50; Biddle, "Report of the Executive Director," 12–14.
25. Pickett's Journal, November 1, 1940; AFSC Archives.
26. Pickett's Journal, November 2, 1940; AFSC Archives; Ernst Papanek (with Edward Linn), *Out of the Fire* (New York: William Morrow, 1975), 244–47, 250–51.
27. USCCEC, "Plan for Evacuation of Children from France in Relation to the Problem of Securing Admission of Such Children into the United States," n.d. (ca. November 1940); General Files 1941, Comms and Orgs, AFSC Archives.
28. Pickett's Journal, November 9, 1940; AFSC Archives.
29. Pickett's Journal, November 11, 1940; memorandum from Pickett to Mary Rogers, et al., November 12, 1940; General Files 1940, Comms and Orgs, USCCEC file; Pickett's Journal, November 11, 1940; AFSC Archives.
30. Memorandum from Pickett to Mary Rogers, et al., November 12, 1940.
31. USCCEC, "Administrative Report of the Activities of the USCCEC," February 22, 1941, 45; Folder: U.S. Committee for Care of European Children; Refugee Letters 1941; ERP; FDRL.
32. USCCEC, untitled press release, June 20, 1941; Folder: U.S. Committee for Care of European Children; Refugee Letters 1941; ERP; FDRL; "25 Child Refugees In on Liner," *NYHT*, December 24, 1940; "119 Child Refugees Here From Lisbon," *NYT*, June 22, 1941, 19. Some of the children who arrived on June 21, 1941 were probably among the group of 350 children smuggled out of Germany, Czechoslovakia, and Poland by Ernst Papanek that the USCCEC had first discussed on November 1, 1940. Reports on the number of children who arrived varied.
33. Ostrovsky, "'We Are Standing By,'" 240, n72.
34. Pickett's Journal, June 17, 1941; AFSC Archives.
35. Troper to ER, June 7, 1941, copy enclosed in Robert Lang to ER, June 20, 1941; Folder: U.S. Committee for Care of European Children; Refugee Letters 1941; ERP; FDRL.
36. Marshall Field, "Our Job *Now*" in "Our Job Goes On: Rescue *and* Refuge," USCCEC brochure, ca. June 1941, 1, 5; General Files, 1941, Comm and Orgs, USCCEC file, AFSC Archives.

37. ER to Norman Davis, January 30, 1941; Folder: Davis, Norman; Personal Letters 1941; ERP; FDRL.
38. Marshall Field to ER, July 21, 1941; Field to ER, August 26, 1941; Folder: Field, Marshall; Personal Letters 1941; ERP; FDRL; "Child Refugees' Plight Is Told in Plea for Funds," *NYHT*, September 11, 1941, 3.
39. "Conquered Youth Held Aim of Nazis," *NYT*, September 11, 1941, 6.
40. "Child Refugees Tell of Seeing Parents Starve," *NYHT*, September 25, 1941.
41. "$200,000 Collected for Children," *NYT*, November 10, 1941, 17; Marshall Field to USCCEC, October 10, 1941; Folder: U.S. Committee for Care of European Children; Refugee Letters 1941; ERP; FDRL; Pickett's Journal, October 31, 1941; AFSC Archives; "45 War Waifs in From Europe With Tales of Hunger and Woe," *NYHT*, September 3, 1941, 21.

CHAPTER 7

1. Karl Frank to ER, June 15, 1940; ER to Frank, June 21, 1940; Folder: Fr–Fu; Personal Letters 1940; Eleanor Roosevelt Papers (hereafter: ERP); FDR Library (hereafter: FDRL); Joseph P. Lash, *Eleanor Roosevelt: A Friend's Memoir* (New York: Doubleday, 1964), 112–13. For background on Karl Frank and the origins of the Emergency Rescue Committee, see Terence Renaud, "'This is our Dunkirk': Karl B. Frank and the Politics of the Emergency Rescue Committee" (2009), http://terencerenaud.com/The_Politics_of_the_ERC_FINAL.htm#_ftnref7 and "The German Resistance in New York: Karl B. Frank and the New Beginning Group, 1935–45" (2007), http://terencerenaud.com/german_resistance.htm.
2. ER to A. A. Berle Jr., June 25, 1940; Berle to ER, June 26, 1940; Folder: Berle, Adolf A.; Personal Letters 1940; ERP; FDRL.
3. ER to Sumner Welles, July 2, 1940; Welles to ER, July 5, 1940; Folder: Welles, Sumner; Correspondence with Government Departments 1940; ERP, FDRL.
4. The exploits of the Scarlet Pimpernel would have been fresh in people's minds in Varian Fry's time. The Scarlet Pimpernel was the hero of an immensely popular play (1903) and later novel (1905) of that name. A precursor to Batman, Superman, and other superheroes, he lived in disguise as a wealthy, foppish English nobleman named Sir Percy Blakeney. As the Scarlet Pimpernel he secretly rescued French noblemen from the guillotine during the French Revolution. A Hollywood film version of *The Scarlet Pimpernel*, starring Leslie Howard, appeared in 1934 and a radio drama with Howard and Olivia de Havilland followed in 1938.
5. Varian Fry to ER, June 27, 1940; Folder: Fr–Fu; Personal Letters 1940; ERP; FDRL.
6. ER wrote "FDR What about this?" in pencil on Fry's June 27 letter; Memorandum from FDR to ER, July 3, 1940; ER to Fry, July 8, 1940; Folder: Fr–Fu; Personal Letters 1940; ERP; FDRL.

7. Frank to ER, July 17, 1940; Frank to ER, August 15, 1940; Folder: Fr–Fu; Personal Letters 1940; ERP; FDRL.
8. George Warren to ER, June 29, 1940; Folder: Sm–Z; Refugee Letters 1940; ERP, FDRL.
9. Richard Breitman and Alan M. Kraut, *American Refugee Policy and European Jewry, 1933–1945* (Bloomington: Indiana University Press, 1987), 129.
10. David S. Wyman, *Paper Walls: America and the Refugee Crisis, 1938–1941* (New York: Pantheon Books, 1985), 138–40; Breitman and Kraut, *American Refugee Policy*, 129.
11. Mildred Adams to Thompson, July 30, 1940; Adams to Thompson, August 7, 1940; Folder: A–B; Refugee Letters 1940; ERP; FDRL.
12. Sheila Isenberg, *A Hero of Our Own: The Story of Varian Fry* (New York: Random House, 2001), 12, 5; *The Encyclopedia of the Righteous Among the Nations*, ed. Israel Gutman (Jerusalem: Yad Vashem, 2007); "Editor Describes Rioting in Berlin," *New York Times* (hereafter: *NYT*), July 17, 1935, 4.
13. Pierre Sauvage, "Varian Fry in Marseille," http://www.varianfry.org/sauvage_fry_oxford_en.htm#_edn40. There is no completely reliable account of Fry's mission to France. It is not true, for example, as Sauvage states, that ER "returned to the 'thunderous' silence, as Blanche Wiesen Cook has characterized it, that she had displayed about Nazi persecution in the 30s" after the fall of 1940. Sauvage is correct when he says that ER was not "spearheading the rescue effort" or acting as Fry's "emissary," but she remained active in supporting Fry's activities, particularly by pressuring Welles to act on particular cases, passing on Fry's reports to Welles and the president, and expressing her concern about Fry's safety, as the rest of this and subsequent chapters demonstrate.
14. Wyman, *Paper Walls*, 137. "German" meant anyone from Germany or countries occupied by Germany, including Austria and Czechoslovakia.
15. Sauvage, "Varian Fry in Marseille"; Wyman, *Paper Walls*, 150–51.
16. Wyman, *Paper Walls*, 168.
17. Department of State telegram to U.S. Consulate, Marseille, Sept. 18, 1940; quoted in Isenberg, *A Hero of Our Own*, 85.
18. Varian Fry, *Assignment: Rescue* (New York: Four Winds Press, 1968), 215. Fry's memoir was originally published as *Surrender on Demand* (1945). See also Wyman, *Paper Walls*, 168, and Ronald Weber, *The Lisbon Route* (Lanham, MD: Ivan R. Dee, 2011), 57, 73. Mordecai Paldiel, *Diplomatic Heroes of the Holocaust* (Jersey City, NJ: KTAV Publishing House, 2007) mentions Bingham briefly, 203–4.
19. Richard Breitman and Allan J. Lichtman, *FDR and the Jews* (Cambridge, MA: Harvard University Press, 2013), 314.
20. See Blanche Wiesen Cook, *Eleanor Roosevelt, Vol. 3: The War Years and After, 1939–1962* (New York: Viking, 2016), 81–82.
21. McDonald to Stephen Wise, September 10, 1940; Folder: 165; Box 5; McDonald Papers, Columbia.

22. Eliot B. Coulter, Acting Chief, Visa Division, to ER, September 19, 1940; Folder: Welles, Sumner; Correspondence with Government Departments 1940; ERP; FDRL; Breitman and Lichtman, *FDR and the Jews*, 170; Minutes of Fortieth Meeting of the President's Advisory Committee on Political Refugees, September 12, 1940; Folder 64; Box 32; McDonald Papers, Columbia; Richard Breitman, Barbara McDonald Stewart, and Severin Hochberg, *Refugees and Rescue: The Diaries and Papers of James G. McDonald, 1935–1945* (Bloomington: Indiana University Press, 2009), 208–10; Stephen J. Morewitz, "The Saving of the S.S. *Quanza*," *William and Mary Magazine* (Summer 1991). The number of refugees aboard the *Quanza* varies in different accounts. Coulter in his letter to ER of September 19 refers to eighty-one passengers.

23. Stephen Wise to Otto Nathan, September 17, 1940. Quoted in Breitman, Stewart, and Hochberg, *Refugees and Rescue*, 209; Henry L. Feingold, *The Politics of Rescue: The Roosevelt Administration and the Holocaust, 1938–1945* (New York: Holocaust Library, 1970), 144.

24. ER to Welles, September 6, 1940; Folder: Welles, Sumner; Correspondence with Government Departments 1940; ERP; FDRL; Frank to ER, September 20, 1940; Folder: Kingdon, Frank; Refugee Letters 1940; ERP, FDRL.

25. Quoted in Wyman, *Paper Walls*, 143.

26. Wyman, *Paper Walls*, 143–45; Breitman and Kraut, *American Refugee Policy*, 129–31; Breitman, Stewart, and Hochberg, *Refugees and Rescue*, 210–12. For an in-depth discussion of the effect that the fear of subversion had on FDR and other policy makers, see Breitman and Lichtman, *FDR and the Jews*, 161–83.

27. Frank to ER, September 23, 1940; Folder: Welles, Sumner; Correspondence with Government Departments 1940; ERP; FDRL.

28. Long to Welles, September 30, 1940; Folder: Roosevelt, Eleanor 1940; Office Correspondence 1920–1943; Welles Papers; FDRL; Welles to ER, October 1, 1940; Folder: Welles, Sumner; Correspondence with Government Departments 1940; ERP; FDRL.

29. Minutes of the Forty-First Meeting of the President's Advisory Committee on Political Refugees, October 30, 1940; Folder 64: Box 32; McDonald Papers, Columbia.

30. ER to FDR, September 28, 1940. Quoted in Breitman and Kraut, *American Refugee Policy*, 131.

31. Memorandum for the Under-Secretary of State, October 2, 1940; quoted in Breitman, Stewart, and Hochberg, *Refugees and Rescue*, 216; Breitman and Kraut, *American Refugee Policy*, 236–39, 131–32; Wyman, *Paper Walls*, 145. FDR's meeting with Long was on October 3.

32. Minutes of the Forty-First meeting of the President's Advisory Committee; Breitman and Lichtman, *FDR and the Jews*, 174.

33. McDonald to ER, October 10, 1940; Folder: Eleanor Roosevelt; Box 3; McDonald Papers; Columbia.

34. McDonald to Felix Frankfurter, October 10, 1940; Folder: Felix Frankfurter; Box 2; McDonald Papers, Columbia.
35. Pickett's Journal, November 11, 1940; AFSC Archives; Breitman, Stewart, and Hochberg, *Refugees and Rescue*, 131–33; Breitman and Lichtman, *FDR and the Jews*, 174.
36. Breitman and Kraut, *American Refugee Policy*, 133; McDonald to ER, October 24, 1940; Folder: Mc; Correspondence with Government Departments 1940; ERP; FDRL.
37. Breitman and Kraut, *American Refugee Policy*, 133–36; Pickett's Journal, May 5, 1942; AFSC Archives.
38. Memorandum from ER to FDR, October 1, 1940; Memorandum from FDR to ER, October 2, 1940; Folder: Vogl, Edith; Personal Letters; 1940; ERP; FDRL.
39. The Vogls were the mother and sister of Dr. Edith Vogl, a Christian, who had come to the United States as a Czech representative to the World Youth Conference at Vassar College in 1938. There she met ER. ER became her advocate, pressed the visa cases of her mother and sister with the State Department, and subsidized the teaching job Pickett found for Dr. Vogl at Keuka College.
40. Frank Kingdon to ER, October 4, 1940; Folder: Kingdon, Frank; Refugee Letters 1940; ERP, FDRL.
41. Gene D. Phillips, *Some Like It Wilder*. Bohumil was Lustig's Czech name. He had apparently adopted the name Hans after moving to Berlin. According to the Sousa Mendes Foundation, Jan/Bohumil Lustig (37) and his wife Charlotte (43) were issued Portuguese visas in Bordeaux with the help of the Portuguese consul, Aristides de Sousa Mendes, a Catholic descended from Marranos (Jews compelled to convert to Christianity in the fifteenth century). They had reached Figueira da Foz, Portugal, by July 1940; then sailed from Portugal to New York in November. Mendes provided about 30,000 people who were fleeing the Nazis with Portuguese visas, according to the Mendes Foundation, which is directed by descendants of some of the visa recipients. For defying the instructions of his government, he was recalled to Lisbon and fired from diplomatic service. He died impoverished in 1954. He is honored for his rescue efforts at the Yad Vashem memorial in Israel. http://sousamendesfoundation.org/gutwirth-hartogs-lustig. For information on Mendes, see Paldiel, *Diplomatic Heroes of the Holocaust*, 71–87.
42. Copy of Hans Lustig letter to "My dear C.," September 13, 1940, enclosed with Frank Kingdon to ER, October 4, 1940; Folder: Kingdon, Frank; Refugee Letters 1940; ERP, FDRL.
43. Kingdon to ER, October 4, 1940; Folder: Kingdon, Frank; Refugee Letters 1940; ERP, FDRL.
44. Long to FDR, October 11, 1940 with attachment: "Memorandum for Mrs. Roosevelt"; Folder: Kingdon, Frank; Refugee Letters 1940; ERP, FDRL.
45. Wyman, *Paper Walls*, 173. The colleagues were Adolf A. Berle Jr. and James C. Dunn; Feingold, *The Politics of Rescue*, 142.

46. "Memorandum for Mrs. Roosevelt," October 11, 1940; Thompson to Kingdon, October 22, 1940; Folder: Kingdon, Frank; Refugee Letters 1940; ERP, FDRL; Henry Koster and Irene Kahn Atkins, *Henry Koster* (Metuchen, NY: Scarecrow Press, 1987), 35. Another case in which ER intervened successfully was that of Dr. Vera Lachmann, a gifted educator who headed a school in Berlin for Jewish and non-Aryan Christians from 1933 until the Nazis shut it down in 1939. See Cook, *Eleanor Roosevelt, Vol. 3*, 221–24.
47. Martha Gellhorn to ER, October 24, 1940; ER to Gellhorn, November 8, 1940: Folder: Gellhorn, Edna & Martha; Personal Letters 1940; ERP; FDRL.
48. Joseph Alsop and Robert Kintner, "U.S. Problem With Axis Consuls Enmeshed in Capital's [*sic*] Red Tape," *New York Herald Tribune* (hereafter: *NYHT*), November 25, 1940, 2.
49. Breitman and Kraut, *American Refugee Policy*, 121, 237–40.
50. Memorandum from FDR to ER, October 16, 1940; Folder: Welles, Sumner; Correspondence with Government Departments 1940; ERP; FDRL.
51. Ingrid Warburg to ER, December 4, 1940; Folder: War–Way; Personal Letters 1940; ERP; FDRL.
52. ER to Welles, December 11, 1940; Welles to ER, December 13, 1940; Folder: Welles, Sumner; Correspondence with Government Departments 1940; ERP; FDRL. The draft of the letter has Breckinridge Long's initials at the bottom. RG59, 811.111 Refugees/771, NARA.
53. Thompson to Welles, December 16, 1940; Folder: Welles, Sumner; Correspondence with Government Departments 1940; ERP; FDRL; Jay Allen, "Strictly Confidential," Lisbon, November 15, 1940, 4; enclosed in Warburg to ER, December 4, 1940.
54. Memorandum from ER to FDR, December 10, 1940; Folder: War–Way; Personal Letters 1940; ERP; FDRL. An accompanying note read: "For the President to Read: See Mrs. Roosevelt's note."
55. Warburg to ER, December 14, 1940; Folder: War–Way; Personal Letters 1940; ERP; FDRL.
56. Welles to ER, December 11, 1940; Folder: Welles, Sumner; Correspondence with Government Departments 1940; ERP; FDRL.
57. Memorandum from FDR to ER, December 18, 1940; Folder: War–Way; Personal Letters 1940; ERP; FDRL.
58. Reports from Fry in Marseille to the ERC, October 27 and 31, 1940; Folder: War–Way; Personal Letters 1940; ERP; FDRL.
59. Frank Kingdon to "Dear Friend," December 17, 1940; Folder: Kingdon, Frank; Refugee Letters 1941; ERP; FDRL.
60. Kingdon to ER, February 20, 1942; ER to Kingdon, March 26, 1941; Folder: Kingdon, Frank; Refugee Letters 1942; ERP; FDRL.
61. Warburg and Kingdon to ER, May 2, 1941; Folder: Kingdon, Frank; Refugee Letters 1941; ERP; FDRL.
62. My Day, December 21, 1940.

CHAPTER 8

1. "A Group of Refugees, Trapped in the Unoccupied Part of France. Some in Switzerland," n.d., signed by Dr. Anna Stein; Folder: Welles, Sumner; Correspondence with Government Departments 1940; Eleanor Roosevelt Papers (hereafter: ERP); FDR Library (hereafter: FDRL). The twelve people were: Erich Lewinski, Hans Kakies, Erna Blencke, Eugen Albrecht, Gisela Peiper, Frieda Timmerman, Otto Pfister, Nora Block, Herta Walter (sister of Block), Irmgard Amelung, and Rene and Johanne Bertholet.
2. Tom, Kathy, and Peter Pfister, *Eva & Otto: Resistance, Refugees, and Love in the Time of Hitler* (West Lafayette, IN: Purdue University Press, 2020), 193–94. Like ER, Hill had been active in the Consumer's League and, in the 1930s, assisted ER in assessing the needs of people in the Buffalo area who wrote to ER for help. Hill founded the Wellesley Summer Institute for Social Progress in the early 1930s and directed it for twenty-five years.
3. Pfister, *Eva & Otto*, 177; Paul Benjamin to George Warren, March 12, 1941; Pfister Family Papers. I am very grateful to the children of Eva Lewinski and Otto Pfister for sharing this and other documents in their possession with me.
4. Benjamin was an official at the Buffalo Welfare Department. Pfister, *Eva & Otto*, 204.
5. The two that would be expedited were those of Otto Pfister and Nora Block. Welles to Thompson, December 30, 1940; Folder: Welles, Sumner; Correspondence with Government Departments 1940; ERP; FDRL.
6. ER to Welles, December 30, 1940; Folder: Welles, Sumner; Correspondence with Government Departments 1940; ERP; FDRL; Welles to Long, December 31, 1940, RG59, FW 811.111 Refugees/773, NARA.
7. Welles to ER, January 2, 1941; Folder: Welles, Sumner; Correspondence with Government Departments 1940; ERP; FDRL.
8. Pfister, *Eva & Otto*, 209–11, 239–51.
9. Eva Lewinski, "Conference with Mrs. Roosevelt, December 27, 1940, White House," memorandum of conversation, January 1941; quoted in Pfister, *Eva & Otto*, 204–7 and reproduced in *Eva and Otto: America's Vetting and Rescue of Political Refugees during World War II* (Los Angeles: Pfisters, 2017), 132–33.
10. "Aid 2,000 Refugees to Leave War Zone," *NYT*, December 19, 1940, 16.
11. "Recruits for Democracy," *NYT*, December 20, 1940, 24.
12. Lewinski, "Conference with Mrs. Roosevelt."
13. Polier OH, 19. The discussion of Long took place in early 1943. Polier said in her oral history interview that "Something came up and [ER] said about either Welles or Breckinridge [Long]—I cannot remember which—'Franklin, you know he's a fascist.'" Given ER's friendship with Welles, which continued long after the war, his sympathy with refugees, his efforts to persuade Latin American nations to take in Jewish refugees, and his willingness to look into individual refugee cases, it would defy all the evidence to think that she was referring to him.

14. Lewinski, "Conference with Mrs. Roosevelt."
15. Pfister, *Eva & Otto*, 207.
16. Paul Benjamin to ER, December 31, 1940; Folder: Welles, Sumner; Correspondence with Government Departments 1941; ERP; FDRL.
17. "Group to Ask Conference on Refugee Visas," news clip, Buffalo *Courier-Express*, January 6, 1941; Folder: Welles, Sumner; Correspondence with Government Departments 1941; ERP; FDRL.
18. Benjamin Carter Hett, *Crossing Hitler: The Man Who Put the Nazis on the Witness Stand* (New York: Oxford, 2008), 20–24.
19. Jon Kelly, "Hans Litten: The Man Who Annoyed Adolf Hitler," *BBC News Magazine*, August 19, 2011. http://www.bbc.com/news/magazine-14572578; Hett, *Crossing Hitler*, 93.
20. My Day, September 17, 1940. Rainer's full name was Karl Reinhard Litten. See My Day, September 23, 1940.
21. "Suggested Introduction," Robert E. Sherwood Papers, Houghton Library, Harvard University, Box 1470. The playwright and speechwriter for FDR, Robert Sherwood, drafted the script ER used in preparing her prologue to the film. Unfortunately, copies of *Pastor Hall* are not easily obtainable. A copy with ER's prologue could not be found.
22. Ernest Simmel to ER, December 31, 1940; Folder: Welles, Sumner; Correspondence with Government Departments 1940, ERP, FDRL. For a fuller account of the film, see Blanche Wiesen Cook, *Eleanor Roosevelt, Vol. 3: The War Years and After, 1939–1962* (New York: Viking, 2016), 316–19.
23. Welles to ER, December 31, 1940; Folder: Kingdon, Frank; Refugee Letters 1941; ERP; FDRL.
24. In May, Ingrid Warburg wrote to Tommy about the Litten case: "Governor Lehman, who is also interested in this case, asked us what exactly is lacking." She said he would be glad to help. Warburg to Thompson, May 21, 1941; Folder: Warburg, Ingrid; Refugee Letters 1940; ERP; FDRL.
25. Welles to ER, December 31, 1940; Folder: Kingdon, Frank; Refugee Letters 1940; ERP; FDRL.
26. Welles to ER, April 2, 1941; ER to Welles, April 7, 1941; Welles to ER, April 9, 1941; ER to Welles, May 14, 1941; Folder: Welles, Sumner; Correspondence with Government Departments 1941; ERP; FDRL; Welles to ER, May 17, 1941; Folder: Kingdon, Frank; Refugee Letters 1941; ERP; FDRL.
27. Warburg to Thompson, August 8, 1941; Folder: Warburg, Ingrid; Personal Letters 1941; ERP, FDRL; ER to Welles, August 15, 1941; Folder: Welles, Sumner; Correspondence with Government Departments 1941; ERP; FDRL; Warburg to Thompson, August 19, 1941; Irmgard Litten to ERC, August 6, 1941; Folder: Warburg, Ingrid; Personal Letters 1941; ERP, FDRL; Long to ER, September 3, 1941; Folder: Welles, Sumner; Correspondence with Government Departments 1941; ERP; FDRL; Long to ER,

September 18, 1941; Folder: Li–Ly; Correspondence with Government Departments 1941; ERP; FDRL.
28. Thomas Blubacher, "Rainer Litten," in Andreas Kotte (Hg.): *Theaterlexikon der Schweiz*, Chronos Verlag Zürich 2005, Band 2, S. 1119–1120, Theaterlexikon der Schweiz online, http://tls.theaterwissenschaft.ch/wiki/Rainer_Litten.
29. Welles to ER, January 10, 1941; Folder: Welles, Sumner; Correspondence with Government Departments 1941; ERP; FDRL.
30. McDonald to ER, February 5, 1941; Folder: McDonald, James G.; Personal Letters 1941; ERP, FDRL.
31. ER to McDonald, March 2, 1941; McDonald to ER, March 5, 1941; Folder: McDonald, James G.; Personal Letters 1941; ERP, FDRL.
32. Memorandum from ER to Welles, February 21, 1941; Welles to ER, February 22, 1941; Folder: Welles, Sumner; Correspondence with Government Departments 1941; ERP; FDRL; Breckinridge Long, memorandum of conversation, February 21, 1941; Welles to ER, February 22, 1941; Folder: FL–Fu 1941; Office Correspondence 1920–1943; Welles Papers, FDRL.
33. Pierre Sauvage, "Varian Fry in Marseille." http://www.varianfry.org/sauvage_fry_oxford_en.htm.
34. Warburg to ER, March 7, 1941; Folder: Warburg, Ingrid; Personal Letters 1941; ERP, FDRL.
35. Fry to ERC, January 24, 1941, 3–5, 10; enclosed with Warburg to ER, March 7, 1941.
36. ER to Eileen Fry, May 13, 1941; Folder: Fo–Fy; Personal Letters 1941; ERP; FDRL.
37. David S. Wyman, *Paper Walls: America and the Refugee Crisis, 1938–1941* (New York: Pantheon Books, 1985), 148, 197.
38. Pickett's Journal, June 9, 1941; June 17, 1941; American Friends Service Committee (AFSC) Archives.
39. Albert Einstein to ER, July 26, 1941; PPF 7177, FDR Papers, FDRL. See also: Einstein Archives Online, Archival Call Number: 124–158.
40. Memorandum from PACPR to Mr. President, September 4, 1941; Folder 65: Geo Warren 1941; Box 32; McDonald Papers, Columbia.
41. Richard Breitman, Barbara McDonald Stewart, and Severin Hochberg, *Refugees and Rescue: The Diaries and Papers of James G. McDonald, 1935–1945* (Bloomington: Indiana University Press, 2009), 255–56; "Fifty-First meeting of the President's Advisory Committee on Political Refugees," December 2, 1941; Folder: 65; Geo Warren 1941; Box 32; McDonald Papers, Columbia.
42. Joseph Lash to members of the executive committee of the International Student Service, May 7, 1941; Folder: Lash, Joseph P.; Personal Letters 1941; ERP; FDRL.
43. ER to Louis Weiss, July 3, 1941; ER to Weiss, October 9, 1941; Folder: We–Wh; Personal Letters 1941; ERP; FDRL; Trude Lash to Thompson, October 24, 1941; Trude

Lash to ER, November 19, 1941; Folder: Pratt, Mrs. Eliot; Personal Letters 1941; ERP; FDRL.

44. Joseph Lash to ER, October 6, 1941; Folder: Welles, Sumner; Correspondence with Government Departments 1941; ERP; FDRL.
45. Welles to Warren, October 24, 1941; Folder: Roosevelt, Eleanor 1941; Office Correspondence 1920–1943; Welles Papers, FDRL; Welles to Thompson, October 17, 1941; Folder: Welles, Sumner; Correspondence with Government Departments 1941; ERP, FDRL.
46. Welles to ER, October 30, 1941; ER to Welles, November 6, 1941; Folder: Welles, Sumner; Correspondence with Government Departments 1941; ERP; FDRL.
47. "Fry Says Nazis Kidnap German Exiles in Lisbon," *NYHT*, November 3, 1941, 3A.
48. Kingdon to ER, October 14, 1941; Thompson to Kingdon, October 17, 1941; Kingdon to ER, October 25, 1941; ER to Kingdon, October 27, 1941; Folder: Kingdon, Frank 1941; Refugee Letters 1941; ERP; FDRL.

CHAPTER 9

1. David S. Wyman, *Paper Walls: America and the Refugee Crisis, 1938–1941* (New York: Pantheon Books, 1985), 5.
2. Claims about the number of Jews entering the country and about their taking jobs away from native-born Americans were often grossly exaggerated. The flyer dropped from an airplane over LA at the time and sent to the White House proclaimed that "OVER ¼ MILLION EUROPEAN JEWS ARE NOW COMING TO THE UNITED STATES TO THROW WHITE AMERICAN WORKERS OUT OF JOBS." "Jews! Jews! Jews Everywhere;" OF 76C; FDR Papers; FDR Library (hereafter: FDRL).
3. Pickett's Journal, August 19, 1936; AFSC Archives. The National Coordinating Committee included among its members Pickett, Professor Joseph Chamberlain of Columbia, its founder, James McDonald's former assistant Norman Bentwich, William Rosenwald, Felix Warburg, and Joseph Hyman.
4. Richard Breitman and Alan Kraut write that "the increase in European immigration to the United States was dramatic." The 6,978 visas issued under the German quota in fiscal 1936, for example, jumped to 20,301 in fiscal 1938. Breitman and Kraut, *American Refugee Policy and European Jewry, 1933–1945* (Bloomington: Indiana University Press, 1987), 50.
5. ER to Pickett, December 17, 1938; Pickett to ER, December 21, 1938; Folder: Pickett, Clarence; Correspondence with Government Departments 1938; Eleanor Roosevelt Papers (hereafter: ERP); FDRL; My Day, July 22, 1939.
6. American Jewish Congress House fundraising brochure, NYC, 1940; Folder: Wise, Mrs. Stephen; Personal Letters 1940; ERP; FDRL.
7. Catt to ER, May 3, 1940; ER to Catt, May 6, 1940; Folder: Catt, Carrie Chapman;

Personal Letters 1940; ERP, FDRL; My Day, June 25, 1940; My Day, July 3, 1940.
8. "Recital by Elman for Refugees Held," *New York Times* (*NYT*), January 22, 1939, 34; My Day, January 23, 1939.
9. Julian M. Pleasants, *Buncombe Bob: The Life and Times of Robert Rice Reynolds* (Chapel Hill: University of North Carolina Press, 2000), 98–100.
10. Pickett to ER, May 29, 1939; Folder: Pickett, Clarence; Correspondence with Government Departments 1939; ERP; FDRL.
11. My Day, July 19, 1939. *Today's Refugees, Tomorrow's Citizens: A Study of Americanization* by Gerhart Saenger (New York: Harper & Brothers, 1941), reviewed in *The Nation*, August 2, 1941, came to conclusions similar to those in *Refugee Facts* about the net numbers of immigrants and their contributions to the American economy.
12. "Mrs. Roosevelt Urges a Drive to Make U.S. Democracy Work," *New York Herald Tribune* (*NYHT*), October 25, 1939, 18.
13. ER, "The Back-Log of Defense," typescript, Herald Tribune Forum, October 22, 1940; Folder: Meloney, Mrs. William B.; Personal Letters 1940; ERP; FDRL.
14. My Day, May 21, 1941.
15. "Mrs. Roosevelt Asks Merger of N.Y.A., C.C.C." *NYHT*, November 3, 1941, 3A. $18 would be approximately $328 in 2020 dollars.
16. "Lindbergh Accuses Jews of Pushing U.S. to War," September 11, 1941; Jewish Virtual Library, https://www.jewishvirtuallibrary.org/lindbergh-accuses-jews-of-pushing-u-s-to-war.
17. S. M. Cartwell to ER, October 16, 1941; ER to Cartwell, October 22, 1941; Folder: Ca: Personal Letters 1941; ERP; FDRL.
18. "Phew!," *PM*, January 27, 1944; Dr. Morton Greenwald to ER, n.d., handwritten note on clipping from *PM*; ER to Dr. Greenwald, February 8, 1944; Folder: Gra–Gre; Personal Letters 1944; ERP; FDRL.
19. My Day, June 19, 1943.
20. James Waterman Wise to ER, July 31, 1942; "*Why* AMERICAN UNITY." Prospectus for *American Unity: A Monthly Manual of Education*, Issued by Council Against Intolerance in America; ER, "For American Unity," Folder: Wi; Personal Letters 1942; ERP; FDRL; "'Where Do Human Rights Begin': Remarks at the United Nations," March 27, 1953, in *Courage in a Dangerous World: The Political Writings of Eleanor Roosevelt (New York: Columbia University Press, 2000)*, ed. Allida M. Black, 190.

CHAPTER 10

1. Varian Fry to ER, August 27, 1942, enclosed in ER's Administrative Officer, Social Correspondence to Sumner Welles, September 12, 1942; memorandum dated August 26, 1942, enclosed with Fry to ER, August 27, 1942; ER's Administrative Officer for Social Correspondence to Welles, September 12, 1942; Folder: Welles, Sumner;

Correspondence with Government Departments 1942; Eleanor Roosevelt Papers (hereafter: ERP); FDR Library (hereafter: FDRL).

2. Welles to ER, September 22, 1942; Folder: Welles, Sumner; Correspondence with Government Departments 1942; ERP; FDRL; "U.S. Protested to Vichy On Deporting Alien Jews: Most Vigorous Action Possible Taken, Welles Letter Reveals," *New York Herald Tribune (hereafter: NYHT)*, September 5, 1942, 3.

3. Flora McPherson to ER, July 8, 1942; Archibald MacLeish to ER, September 1, 1942; Folder: Welles, Sumner; Correspondence with Government Departments 1942; ERP; FDRL.

4. "U.S. Women Cheer Sisters in Poland," *New York Times* (hereafter: *NYT*), September 24, 1942, 12.

5. My Day, September 25, 1942.

6. Jacob Blaustein, "Tribute to Mrs. Roosevelt;" Folder: ER and Hadassah Memorials 76–2; Small Collections: Hadassah; FDRL.

7. "Princesses Give Up Dolls," *NYT*, May 6, 1942, 22.

8. "39 European Children in U.S. to Seek New Life," *NYHT*, July 31, 1942, 15.

9. Georges Thelin, International Save the Children Union; Evelyn Fox, World's YWCA; and Donald Lowrie, World's Committee YMCA to ER, telegram, August 31, 1942; Folder: U.S. Committee for the Care of European Children; Refugee Letters 1942; ERP; FDRL.

10. ER to Norman Davis, September 4, 1942; Folder: Davis, Norman; Personal Letters 1942; ERP; FDRL.

11. Minutes of the Fifty-Fifth Meeting of the President's Advisory Committee on Political Refugees, September 9, 1942; Folder 66: George Warren; Box 33; McDonald Papers, Columbia.

12. McDonald to ER, September 14, 1942; Folder: McDonald, James; Personal Letters 1942; ERP; FDRL.

13. USCCEC, "Plans Rescue of 1,000 Refugee Children: U.S. Committee Seeks to Save Boys and Girls Left in Southern France when Parents were Deported," press release (revised draft), n.d., enclosed in Margaret Frawley to Maxwell Hahn, September 17, 1942; General Files 1942: Comms & Orgs to Individuals; AFSC Archives; ER to Norman Davis, telegram, ca. September 4, 1942: Folder: Field, Marshall; Personal Letters 1942; ERP; FDRL.

14. Memorandum from George Warren to PACPR, October 16, 1942; Folder: George Warren; Box 3; McDonald Papers, Columbia; McDonald to Welles, September 25, 1942, Folder: Sumner Welles; Box 5; McDonald Papers, Columbia.

15. Welles to McDonald, October 2, 1942; Folder: McDonald, James 1942; Office Correspondence 1920–1943; Welles Papers; FDRL.

16. "Report on the activities of the Toulouse delegation," December 14, 1942, 2; General

Files, Foreign Service France: Relief + Refugees Marseilles, Letters & Cables to, 1942; AFSC Archives; Michal Ostrovsky, "'We Are Standing By': Rescue Operations of the United States Committee for the Care of European Children," *Holocaust and Genocide Studies* 29 (Fall 2015): 243–44; Wilfrid Fleisher, "Haven Offered to Children of French by U.S." *NYHT*, October 8, 1942, 2; "Welles Reports Accord Is Near in Martinique," *NYHT*, October 16, 1942, 10.

17. "U.S. Committee to Bring French Children Here," *NYHT*, October 9, 1942, 3; "Refugee Aid Planned," *NYT*, October 9, 1941.
18. "France to Send US Jewish Children," *NYT*, October 15, 1942, 11.
19. Richard Breitman and Alan M. Kraut, *American Refugee Policy and European Jewry, 1933–1945* (Bloomington: Indiana University Press, 1987), 162–64.
20. Field to ER, November 30, 1942; Texts of Bennet Schauffler cables, November 25 and 27, 1942; Folder: USCCEC 1942; Refugee Letters 1942; ERP; FDRL. See also, "Vichy Lets 5,000 Young Refugee Jews Go to U.S.," *NYHT*, October 15, 1942, 5.
21. My Day, May 14, 1943.
22. Robert Lang to Louis Weiss, April 28, 1943; Folder: USCCEC 1942; Refugee Letters 1942; ERP; FDRL.
23. Thompson to Welles, May 20, 1943: Folder: Welles, Sumner; Correspondence with Government Departments 1943; ERP; FDRL.
24. Welles to Thompson, May 28, 1943, RG59, 811.111 Refugee Children/159, NARA.
25. Kathryn Close, *Transplanted Children: A History* (New York: United States Committee for the Care of European Children, 1953), 28, 68; Maurice R. Davie, *Refugees in America: Report of the Committee for the Study of Recent Immigration from Europe* (New York: Harper & Brothers, 1947), 210–1; Stephen Becker, *Marshall Field III: A Biography* (New York: Simon and Schuster, 1964), 186–87, 471.
26. Close, *Transplanted Children*, 69.
27. The White House officially announced Sumner Welles's resignation on September 26, 1943, but he was virtually out by August of that year.
28. For a full account of the rivalry within the State Department and Welles's resignation, see Irwin F. Gellman, *Secret Affairs: Franklin Roosevelt, Cordell Hull, and Sumner Welles* (Baltimore: Johns Hopkins University Press, 1995), 308–17.
29. Memorandum from Welles to Avra Warren, November 18, 1941: Folder: Roosevelt, Eleanor, 1941; Office Correspondence 1920–1943; Welles Papers, FDRL.
30. Irving Gellman says FDR gave Welles responsibility for refugee issues, Gellman, *Secret Affairs*, 229.
31. Minutes of PACPR Dinner Meeting, October 14, 1940; Folder: 46; Joseph Chamberlain Papers, YIVO, quoted by Breitman and Kraut, *American Refugee Policy*, 133.
32. Richard Breitman and Allan J. Lichtman, *FDR and the Jews* (Cambridge, MA: Harvard University Press, 2013), 8–9.

33. Gellman, *Secret Affairs*, 84. Gellman's observations about Welles's character help explain his behavior during the refugee crisis, but Gellman devotes only two sentences to ER's interactions with Welles on refugee matters and does not discuss Welles's response to the efforts of the ERC and the USCCEC. Gellman says, incorrectly, that appeals went from Jewish leaders to ER, to FDR, and then to Welles, "who was known to be sympathetic. When Welles did not respond quickly, the First Lady prodded him into action." The appeals to ER arrived from various sources, often from the ERC, the USCCEC, and those needing assistance. Usually ER sent visa cases or complaints about the visa process directly to Welles, not to the president. Gellman, *Secret Affairs*, 229.
34. Breitman and Lichtman, *FDR and the Jews*, 205–206. David Wyman says, "Welles's reaction to the Holocaust remains an enigma. On many occasions, he cooperated with Jewish leaders and seemed on the point of forcing middle-level officials to act. But he seldom followed through." The record of his response to ER's pressure bears out this judgment. David S. Wyman, *Abandonment of the Jews: America and the Holocaust, 1941–1945* (New York: New Press, 2007), 190–91.
35. "We are going to have a good and, I hope, understanding talk with Welles, whom we have reason to trust, as against Long, who is chiefly a friend of the Skipper," Wise wrote to Otto Nathan on September 17, 1940. Quoted in Richard Breitman, Barbara McDonald Stewart, and Severin Hochberg, eds., *Refugees and Rescue: The Diaries and Papers of James G. McDonald, 1935–1945* (Bloomington: Indiana University Press, 2009), 210. Clarence Pickett and the columnist Drew Pearson also perceived Welles as sympathetic to Jewish and non-Jewish refugees and not an obstructionist.
36. Breitman and Lichtman, *FDR and the Jews*, 174.
37. Sumner Welles, "Welles Urges Action by Nations On Post-War Refugee Problem," *NYHT*, August 30, 1944, 15. As Breitman and Lichtman point out, Welles "was the only prominent State Department official to whom Jewish issues mattered significantly after he left office." Breitman and Lichtman, *FDR and the Jews*, 308.
38. Benjamin Welles, *Sumner Welles: FDR's Global Strategist* (New York: St. Martin's Press, 1997), 231–32.

CHAPTER 11

1. Richard Breitman and Alan M. Kraut, *American Refugee Policy and European Jewry, 1933–1945* (Bloomington: Indiana University Press, 1987), 148–51, 157.
2. The *New York Times*, for example, published an article headlined: "SLAIN POLISH JEWS PUT AT A MILLION: One-third of number in Whole Country Said to Have Been Put to Death by Nazis," *NYT*, November 26, 1942, 16. The news did not appear on or even close to the front page, however.
3. My Day, December 5, 1942. ER wrote the column on December 3.

4. Richard Breitman and Allan J. Lichtman, *FDR and the Jews* (Cambridge, MA: Harvard University Press, 2013), 198–99, 201–2.
5. "Memorandum to the President of the United States," December 8, 1942. Printed in the *Congress Weekly* 9 (December 11, 1942). The delegation consisted of Marcie Wertheim, president, American Jewish Committee; Dr. Stephen S. Wise, president, American Jewish Congress; Henry Monsky, president, B'nai B'rith; Adolph Held, president, Jewish Labor Committee; Israel Goldstein, president, Synagogue Council of America; and Rabbi Israel Rosenberg, chairman, Union of Orthodox Rabbis.
6. "Roosevelt Tells Jews Nazis Will Get Accounting," *New York Herald Tribune* (hereafter: *NYHT*), December 9, 1942, 5.
7. "11 Allies Condemn Nazi War on Jews," *NYT*, December 18, 1942, 1; Breitman and Kraut, *American Refugee Policy*, 159–60.
8. Stephen Wise to ER, December 10, 1942; ER to Wise, December 28, 1942; Folder: Wise, Stephen; Personal Letters 1942; Eleanor Roosevelt Papers (hereafter: ERP); FDR Library (hereafter: FDRL).
9. Stephen Wise to ER, February 16, 1943; ER to Wise, February 18, 1943; ER to Wise, December 28, 1942; Folder: Wi; Personal Letters 1943; ERP; FDRL.
10. "Save Doomed Jews, Huge Rally Pleads: United Nations Must Halt Nazi Murders Now," *NYT*, March 2, 1943, 1.
11. My Day, June 8, 1944.
12. My Day, April 14, 1943; Monty Noam Penkower, "In Dramatic Dissent: The Bergson Boys," in *The Holocaust and Israel Reborn* (Urbana: University of Illinois Press, 1994), 67–68.
13. Irwin Greenberg to ER, June 14, 1943; ER to Greenberg, June 19, 1943; Folder: Gr–Gu; Personal Letters 1943; ERP; FDRL.
14. Max Lerner to ER, July 17, 1943, telegram; ER to Lerner, July 23, 1943; Folder: Le; Personal Correspondence 1943; ERP; FDRL.
15. Blanche Wiesen Cook, *Eleanor Roosevelt, Vol. 3: The War Years and After, 1939–1962* (New York: Viking, 2016), 475; Bergson to ER, August 11, 1943 with enclosures; FDR to Thompson, August 16, 1943; Folder: Be; Personal Letters 1943; ERP; FDRL. Bergson said in an interview with David Wyman in 1973 that he met with ER three or four times. See David S. Wyman and Rafael Medoff, *A Race Against Death: Peter Bergson, America, and the Holocaust* (New York: New Press, 2002), 137–39.
16. My Day, August 13, 1943.
17. Michael Barnett writes that the Zionists who settled in Palestine held a similar view of Jews in the diaspora: "forced to play the victim," the Jews in exile had "become a cowering, cowardly, passive and obsequious people." Zionism, they believed, would turn them into proud, active, confident men and women. Barnett, *The Star and the Stripes: A History of the Foreign Policies of American Jews* (Princeton: Princeton University Press, 2016), 150–51.
18. My Day, August 13, 1943.

19. ER, "For American Unity," in *American Unity: A Monthly Manual of Education*, Issued by Council Against Intolerance in America, 1942; Folder: Human Rights; Topical Files; ERP; FDRL.
20. Penkower, "In Dramatic Dissent," 71–73; Breitman and Lichtman, *FDR and the Jews*, 228–29; see also, Deborah E. Lipstadt, *Beyond Belief: The American Press and the Coming of the Holocaust* (New York: Free Press, 1986), 200–201, 224–25.
21. Breitman and Lichtman, *FDR and the Jews*, 233–36.
22. Rebecca Erbelding, *Rescue Board: The Untold Story of America's Efforts to Save the Jews of Europe* (New York: Doubleday, 2018), 57.
23. Breitman and Lichtman, *FDR and the Jews*, 266–67; "Text of the Statement by Roosevelt," *NYT*, March 25, 1944, 4.
24. Breitman and Lichtman, *FDR and the Jews*, 289–90, 294.
25. My Day, September 22, 1944.
26. Ruth Gruber, *Haven: The Dramatic Story of 1,000 World War II Refugees* (New York: Three Rivers Press, 2000), 186–87.
27. Joseph Smart to ER, October 12, 1944; Folder: Sm–Sn; Personal Letters 1944; ERP; FDRL.
28. ER to Arthur Ernst, March 12, 1945; Folder: E; Personal Letters 1945; ERP, FDRL.
29. Sharon R. Lowenstein, *Token Refuge: The Story of the Jewish Refugee Shelter at Oswego, 1944–1946* (Bloomington, IN: Indiana University Press, 1986), 122–137.
30. The questioner was Dr. Herzl Rosenblum, editor of the Hebrew-language newspaper *Yediot Achronot*. Moshe Kol, "I Remember Eleanor Roosevelt," from *Youth Aliyah Bulletin*, November 1963, 6; Folder: ER and Hadassah Memorials 76-2; Small Collections: Hadassah; FDRL.
31. Ruth Gruber, *Inside of Time: My Journey from Alaska to Israel* (New York: Carroll & Graf, 2003), 351.

CHAPTER 12

1. Zionism means different things to different people. I am using it in its historical sense as A. B. Yehoshua defines it in an article in *Haaretz*: "A Zionist is a person who desires or supports the establishment of a Jewish state in the Land of Israel, which in the future will become the state of the Jewish people. This is based on what Herzl said: 'In Basel I founded the Jewish state.'" A. B. Yehoshua, "Defining Zionism: The Belief That Israel Belongs to the Entire Jewish People," *Haaretz*, May 21, 2013, 56. http://www.haaretz.com/opinion/defining-zionism-the-belief-that-israel-belongs-to-the-entire-jewish-people.premium-1.525064.
2. Howard M. Sachar, *A History of Israel from the Rise of Zionism to Our Time*, 3rd ed. (New York: Knopf, 2007), 189.
3. Richard Breitman and Alan M. Kraut, *American Refugee Policy and European Jewry, 1933–1945* (Bloomington: Indiana University Press, 1987), 99; Richard Breitman and

Allan J. Lichtman, *FDR and the Jews* (Cambridge, MA: Harvard University Press, 2013), 92. There were Arab revolts over Jewish immigration and land acquisition in Palestine in 1929 and during the years 1936–39.

4. Breitman and Lichtman, *FDR and the Jews*, 119; Stephen Wise to FDR, telegram, October 6, 1938; Marvin E. McIntyre to Wise, telegram, October 12, 1938; PPF 3292, Rabbi Stephen Wise; FDR Papers; FDR Library (hereafter: FDRL).

5. The name "ORT" originated as an acronym for the Russian words Obshestvo Remeslennogo zemledelcheskogo Truda (The Society for Trades and Agricultural Labour).

6. Emily M. Rosenstein, Rebekah Kohut, and Rose Schneiderman, Women's American ORT to ER, March 26, 1937; Rosenstein to ER, December 16, 1937; ER statement enclosed in Rosenstein to ER, April 23, 1937; Folder: Schneiderman, Rose; Personal Letters 1937; Eleanor Roosevelt Papers (hereafter: ERP); FDRL.

7. ER to Rosenstein, December 16, 1937; Folder: Schneiderman, Rose; Personal Letters 1938; ERP; FDRL.

8. Rose Schneiderman to ER, April 14, 1938; Folder: Schneiderman, Rose; Personal Letters 1938; ERP; FDRL.

9. George Summerlin, chief of protocol, Department of State, to Malvina T. Scheider (Thompson), April 23, 1938, with reference to Scheider's memo of April 20, 1938 regarding Schneiderman's letter of April 14, 1938; Folder: Schneiderman, Rose; Personal Letters 1938; ERP; FDRL.

10. ER to Schneiderman, April 25, 1938; Schneiderman to ER, May 18, 1938; ER to Schneiderman, May 19, 1938; Scheider (Malvina Thompson) to Schneiderman, September 4, 1938; Schneiderman to ER, December 12, 1938; Folder: Schneiderman, Rose; Personal Letters 1938; ERP; FDRL.

11. My Day, December 8, 1938.

12. ER, "Sixty Years of Constructive ORT Work," *ORT Economic Bulletin* (November–December 1940): 1–2; My Day, November 20, 1940.

13. My Day, November 11, 1941; Schneiderman to ER, February 7, 1942; ER to Schneiderman, February 12, 1942; Folder: Schneiderman, Rose; Personal Letters 1942; ERP; FDRL; Thompson to Schneiderman, January 11, 1943; Folder: Schneiderman, Rose; Personal Letters 1943; ERP; FDRL.

14. Marc Lee Raphael, *A History of the United Jewish Appeal, 1939–1982* (Providence, RI: Scholars Press, 1982),1, 13.

15. Raphael, *History of the United Jewish Appeal*, 16–17.

16. Adele Levy to ER, November 27, 1944; Folder: Levi, Mrs. David: Personal Letters 1944; ERP; FDRL.

17. My Day, February 16, 1945.

18. "The German Youth Aliyah," *Palestine*, January 5, 1938, no identified author; Folder: 34/Events and clippings; RG1, Box 7; Hadassah Archives, Center for Jewish History, NYC. Hereafter: HA.

19. Mira Katzburg-Yungman, *Hadassah: American Women Zionists and the Rebirth of Israel* (Oxford: Littman Library of Jewish Civilization, 2002), 14, 26–27.
20. Erica B. Simmons, *Hadassah and the Zionist Project* (New York: Rowman & Littlefield, 2006), 9–14.
21. Zohar Segev, "From Philanthropy to Shaping a State: Hadassah and Ben-Gurion, 1937–1947," *Israel Studies* 18 (Fall 2013): 133–57. It is interesting to note that Szold and Rose Jacobs, a two-time national president of Hadassah, both favored a binational state in which Jews and Arabs would live peacefully together. They feared that in a Jewish state the Arabs would feel excluded and not have equal rights. Segev, "From Philanthropy to Shaping a State," 143.
22. Joyce Antler, *The Journey Home: Jewish Women and the American Century* (New York: Free Press, 1997), 107.
23. "Mrs. Roosevelt Calls Poverty in U.S. Disgrace: Appeals for Co-operative Work in Interest of Welfare at Zionist Dinner," *New York Herald Tribune* (*NYHT*), October 17, 1934. In 1937 she again spoke on the topic of public health as part of a national Hadassah broadcast marking the organization's twenty-fifth anniversary. "Purim Marked by Hadassah in U.S. Broadcasts," *NYHT*, February 26, 1937.
24. My Day, June 2, 1938.
25. Hadassah, "Mrs. Roosevelt Lauds Project for Removing Refugee Children to Palestine," June 3, 1938; Folder: 33; RG1, Box 7; HA.
26. My Day, October 13, 1938. Junior Hadassah was Hadassah's division for young women. It had taken over financial responsibility for the Meir Shfeyah Children's Village in 1925.
27. Statement by Nell Ziff at reception honoring ER, February 13, 1940; Folder: 13; RG1, Box 9; HA.
28. "Mrs. Roosevelt Receives a Gift from Palestine," *NYHT*, February 14, 1940, 16; Folder: 34; RG1, Box 7; HA.
29. "Reported by Mrs. Pool" to National Board of Youth Aliyah, February 14, 1940, 2; "Children Make Book for Mrs. Roosevelt," newsclip, February 1940 (newspaper unknown); Folder: ER and Hadassah 76–2; Small Collections: Hadassah; FDRL.
30. Marian [Mrs. David] Greenberg to ER, December 1, 1938; "Rescue the Children! through Youth Aliyah," Hadassah illustrated pamphlet; ER to Marian Greenberg, December 10, 1938; Folder: Gr–Gu; Personal Letters 1938; ERP; FDRL.
31. Tourover to Marian Greenberg, December 21, 1939; Folder 1; RG7; Denise Tourover Ezekiel Papers, 1936–81; HA; "Report on Conference with Mrs. Franklin D. Roosevelt, at the White House, Jan. 10/1940"; Elinor Morgenthau to Pool, January 20, 1940; Folder 21; RG1, Box 5B; HA.
32. Greenberg to Szold, April 18, 1940; Folder 21; RG1, Box 5B; HA. In September 1942 the Youth Aliyah Advisory Committee letterhead listed as its members: Mrs. Franklin D. Roosevelt, Mrs. Louis Brandeis, Mrs. Dorothy Canfield Fisher, Henry Monsey,

Clarence E. Pickett, Lewis L. Strauss, Oswald Garrison Villard, Senator Robert F. Wagner, George L. Warren, and Dr. Stephen S. Wise. Mrs. Herbert H. Lehman, Mrs. Henry Morgenthau Jr., Mrs. Roger F. Straus, and Mrs. Felix M. Warburg were listed as honorary chairmen.

33. Greenberg to ER, May 7, 1940; Folder 21; RG1, Box 5B, HA.
34. "Report on Conference with Mrs. Franklin D. Roosevelt, at the White House, Jan. 10/1940;" Folder 21; RG1, Box 5B; HA.
35. Irwin H. Greenberg to ER, June 14, 1943; ER to Irwin H. Greenberg, June 19, 1943; Folder: Gr–Gu; Personal Letters 1943; ERP; FDRL.
36. Rose Luria Halprin to ER, November 26, 1943; "The Absorptive Capacity of Palestine," report prepared by the Post-War Planning Committee of the American Zionist Emergency Council; FDR to ER, December 14, 1943; Folder: Haa–Han; Personal Letters 1943; ERP; FDRL.
37. Isaiah Bowman to ER, January 24, 1944; Bowman, "Memorandum to Mrs. Roosevelt," January 24, 1944; Typed note on thank note from ER to Bowman, January 28, 1944; Folder: Bo; Personal Letters 1944; ERP; FDRL.
38. Jewish Virtual Library, https://www.jewishvirtuallibrary.org/jsource/History/struma.html. The number of casualties varies in different accounts.
39. Polier to ER, March 8, 1942; Folder: Welles, Sumner; Correspondence with Government Departments 1942; ERP; FDRL; "Memorandum on the Sinking of the Refugee Ship 'Struma' and Similar Earlier Disasters," March 1942, probably prepared by the World Jewish Congress; Folder: Roosevelt, Eleanor, January–June 1942; Office Correspondence 1920–1943; Welles Papers; FDRL.
40. ER to Welles, March 9, 1942; Welles to ER, March 12, 1942; ER to Welles, March 13, 1942; Folder: Welles, Sumner; Correspondence with Government Departments 1942; ERP; FDRL.
41. Polier OH, 18–19.
42. In a letter to Carl Spaeth, American member of the Emergency Advisory Committee on Political Defense, Welles wrote: "While obviously you and I know that Axis agents frequently are sent out by the German Government among Jewish refugees who are proceeding to the Western Hemisphere, every effort should of course be made from the standpoint of humanity, to prevent innocent refugees from being treated unjustly because of this fact." Welles to Spaeth, May 25, 1942; Folder: Spaeth, Carl B., 1942; Office Correspondence 1920–1943; Welles Papers, FDRL.
43. Welles to ER, March 14, 1942; Folder: Welles, Sumner; Correspondence with Government Departments 1942; ERP; FDRL.
44. Welles to Ray Atherton, March 16, 1942; Atherton to Welles, March 17, 1942, RG59, 819.857/111 and FW819.857/111; Welles to Myron Taylor, March 30, 1942, RG59, 819.857/112A; Welles to Atherton, March 19, 42, RG59, FW819.957/112, NARA.

45. Welles to ER, March 18, 1942, enclosing "Paraphrase of Telegram" from the American Embassy in London, March 16, 1942, which quotes the text of a memo received from the British Foreign Office re: the *Struma*; Folder: Welles, Sumner; Correspondence with Government Departments 1942; ERP; FDRL.
46. Tamar de Sola Pool and Gisela Warburg to ER, February 19, 1943; Folder: 2; RG7; Denise Tourover Ezekiel Papers, HA. For an account of Hadassah's resourceful campaign to rescue these children, see Report by Denise [Mrs. Raphael] Tourover, "Re: Teheran Children, 1942–43," given at Youth Aliyah Committee Meeting, August 21, 1958, 4–5; Folder: 2; RG7; Denise Tourover Ezekiel Papers.
47. Will Rogers Jr. to ER, April 17, 1944; ER to Rogers, April 21, 1944; Folder: Roc–Roo; Personal Letters 1944; ERP; FDRL.
48. Kirchwey to ER, October 2, 1944; ER to Kirchwey, October 4, 1944; Folder: Kirchwey, Freda; Personal Letters 1944; ERP; FDRL.
49. Breitman and Lichtman, *FDR and the Jews*, 259.
50. "U.S. Presidential Elections: Jewish Voting Record (1916–Present)," http://www.jewishvirtuallibrary.org/jewish-voting-record-in-u-s-presidential-elections.
51. J. Litner (Mrs. Erwin) to ER, March 6, 1945; ER to J. Litner, March 16, 1945; Folder: Le–Ly; Personal Letters 1945; ERP; FDRL.

CHAPTER 13

1. *The Autobiography of Eleanor Roosevelt* (New York: Da Capo Press, 1992), 303.
2. Memorandum of Press Conference Held by Mrs. Eleanor Roosevelt, January 3, 1946, Allida Black, John F. Sears, and Mary Jo Binker, eds., *The Eleanor Roosevelt Papers, Vol. 1: The Human Rights Years, 1945–1948* (Detroit, MI: Thomson Gale, 2007), 185. Hereafter: *ER Papers*, vol. 1.
3. S. J. Woolf, "The New Chapter in Mrs. Roosevelt's Life," *New York Times* (*NYT*), December 15, 1946, SM8. A 1945 portrait of ER by Woolf is in the National Portrait Gallery.
4. ER to Joseph Lash, February 13, 1946; *ER Papers*, vol. 1, 248.
5. My Day, February 16, 1946.
6. ER, "Speech before the Women's Division of the United Jewish Appeal of Greater New York," February 20, 1946; *ER Papers*, vol. 1, 255–258.
7. My Day, November 7, 1945; My Day, December 18, 1945; *ER Papers*, vol. 1, 154.
8. ER to Clarence Pickett, December 17, 1946, and Pickett to ER, December 27, 1946; *ER Papers*, vol. 1, 427, 429n18.
9. My Day, November 7, 1945.
10. Michael J. Cohen, *Truman and Israel* (Berkeley: University of California Press, 1990), 127.
11. Leonard Dinnerstein, *America and the Survivors of the Holocaust* (New York: Columbia University Press, 1982), 90–92.

12. Editors' introduction to ER to James McDonald, April 28, 1946; *ER Papers*, vol. 1, 295;
13. My Day, June 22, 1946.
14. "Excerpts from Address by Bevin at the Labor Party's Conference," *NYT*, June 13, 1946, 4.
15. My Day, June 15, 1946.
16. My Day, June 22, 1946.
17. "President Orders Speedy Admission of More Refugees," *NYT*, December 23, 1945, 1.
18. Dinnerstein, *America and the Survivors of the Holocaust*, 113–16.
19. My Day, November 20, 1946.
20. Dinnerstein, *America and the Survivors of the Holocaust*, 6–7.
21. Alfred Perkins, *Edwin Rogers Embree: The Julius Rosenwald Fund, Foundation Philanthropy, and American Race Relations* (Bloomington: Indiana University Press, 2011), 81, 197. Marshall Field was also a trustee of the Rosenwald Fund from 1941 to 1948. See also Edwin R. Embree and Julia Waxman, *Investment in People: The Story of the Julius Rosenwald Fund* (New York: Harper & Brothers, 1949).
22. Dinnerstein, *America and the Survivors of the Holocaust*, 117–18, 135–36.
23. "The Text of Truman's Call on Congress to Meet the Country's Grave Problems," *NYT*, January 7, 1947, 16.
24. Dinnerstein, *America and the Survivors of the Holocaust*, 123–25.
25. "New Quota Sought for War Refugees," *NYT*, January 31, 1947, 15. Harrison was the dean of the University of Pennsylvania Law School and a former United States commissioner of immigration.
26. *ER Papers*, vol. 1, 600n2; Lessing Rosenwald to ER, February 21, 1947; Citizens Committee for Displaced Persons Correspondence; Box 52; Rosenwald Papers; Library of Congress.
27. My Day, March 5, 1947.
28. My Day, June 30, 1947.
29. Dinnerstein, *America and the Survivors of the Holocaust*, 132–33, 149–50.
30. My Day, July 23, 1947.
31. ER to Charl Williams, August 24, 1947; ER and Williams Correspondence; Box 3; Charl Williams Papers; Library of Congress.
32. Quoted in Dinnerstein, *America and the Survivors of the Holocaust*, 171.
33. Quoted in Dinnerstein, *America and the Survivors of the Holocaust*, 172.
34. My Day, June 5, 1948.
35. Blanche Wiesen Cook, *Eleanor Roosevelt, Vol. 3: The War Years and After, 1939–1962* (New York: Viking, 2016), 560.
36. My Day, June 12 and June 14, 1948.
37. "Truman's Statement on Refugee Bill," *NYT*, June 26, 1948, 7.
38. Quoted in Dinnerstein, *America and the Survivors of the Holocaust*, 176.

39. Dinnerstein, *America and the Survivors of the Holocaust*, 172–82, 249, 251–53, 271.
40. James McDonald to Felix Frankfurter, November 30, 1944; Folder: Felix Frankfurter; Box 2; McDonald Papers; Columbia. See also, James G. McDonald, *Palestine: The Primary Hope of the Post-War Era* (New York: United Palestine Appeal, November 1944) and *The Time for Discussion Is Past* (Washington, DC: Zionist Organization of America, 1948).
41. Sumner Welles, *Palestine's Rightful Destiny* (New York: American Christian Palestine Committee, 1946); Welles, *A Jewish Commonwealth Now* (New York: American Jewish Congress, 1947), an address delivered on May 19, 1947, to the American Jewish Congress in Boston.
42. Aline May Lewis Goldstone (Mrs. Lafayette A. Goldstone) to ER, January 13, 1946; quoted in *ER Papers*, vol. 1, 219.
43. Loy Henderson, head of the Bureau of Near Eastern and African Affairs at the State Department, sent a report to Secretary of State Byrnes in August 1945 stating that Palestine lacked the capacity to provide housing and jobs to a large number of new immigrants. The British White Paper of 1939 made the same assertion and argued that large-scale Jewish immigration and land purchases would deprive Arabs of their means of making a living. A royal commission of inquiry led by Lord Robert Peel, on the other hand, concluded that Jewish immigration did not degrade the Arab standard of living and advocated the establishment of a Jewish state. *ER Papers*, vol. 1, 220n5.
44. ER to Goldstone, January 18, 1946; *ER Papers*, vol. 1, 219–20.
45. My Day, August 19, 1946.
46. Sarah Siegel to ER, August 21, 1946; ER to Siegel, September 5, 1946; Folder: Sia–Sil; Correspondence 1945–52; Eleanor Roosevelt Papers (hereafter: ERP); FDR Library (hereafter: FDRL).
47. My Day, July 24, 1946.
48. My Day, April 26, 1947.
49. ER to Marshall, May 26, 1947; Marshall to ER, June 20, 1947, RG59, 501.BB Palestine/5-2647, NARA.
50. ER to Truman, August 21, 1947; Truman to ER, August 23, 1947; *ER Papers*, vol. 1, 609–10.
51. Quotation from Eva Warburg Unger to ER, August 17, 1947, in editors' commentary; ER to Truman, August 30, 1947; *ER Papers*, vol. 1, 610–11.
52. *ER Papers*, vol. 1, 611n3.
53. My Day, September 12, 1947.
54. Loy Henderson, Oral History Interview, Truman Library, 127. Quoted by H. W. Brands in *Inside the Cold War: Loy Henderson and the Rise of the American Empire, 1918–1961* (New York: Oxford University Press, 1991), 181.
55. The vote was 33 in favor, 13 against, 10 abstentions, and 1 absent. Cohen, *Truman and*

Israel, 150–72; Howard M. Sachar, *A History of Israel from the Rise of Zionism to Our Time,* 3rd ed. (New York: Knopf, 2007), 298–99.

CHAPTER 14

1. My Day, March 1, 1948; ER to Lydia Bacon, February 27, 1948 and notes; *ER Papers*, vol 1, 748–49.
2. My Day, February 13, 1948.
3. My Day, February 13, 1948.
4. "UNSCOP Report to the General Assembly," September 3, 1947; United Nations General Assembly, A/364; H. W. Brands, *Inside the Cold War: Loy Henderson and the Rise of the American Empire, 1918–1961* (New York: Oxford University Press 1991), 181–82.
5. James Reston, "Bipartisan Policy on Holy Land Seen," *New York Times* (*NYT*), January 27, 1948, 8.
6. ER to Marshall January 28, 1948; ER to Truman, January 29, 1948; and ER to Marshall, February 1948; *ER Papers*, vol 1, 722–26.
7. Truman to ER, February 2, 1948; *ER Papers*, vol 1, 726.
8. "U.N. Palestine Force Urged by Mrs. Roosevelt, Welles," *NYT*, February 24, 1948, 1, 4.
9. "United Nations Security Council Palestine Sessions, Report No. 34"; Folder: Organizations, UN, Security Council Reports; Box 2; Robison Family Papers, Ann Green Robison; American Jewish Historical Society (AJHS).
10. Benjamin V. Cohen, "The United Nations and Palestine," reprinted from the *New York Herald Tribune* (*NYHT*), March 16 and 17, 1948 by the American Association for the United Nations; Folder: Palestine/Israel 1948–74; Box 12; Benjamin V. Cohen Papers; Library of Congress.
11. Sumner Welles, "Elements of Security: Moral Leadership is Missing," *Washington Post*, March 30, 1948, 13.
12. ER to Marshall, March 22, 1948; George Marshall to ER, March 24, 1948; *ER Papers*, vol 1, 774–76.
13. Truman to ER, March 25, 1948; *ER Papers*, vol 1, 777.
14. My Day, March 26, 1948; *ER Papers*, vol 1, 777–78. There were those, even in the Jewish community, who continued to oppose partition. Lessing Rosenwald, president of the ACJ, said in a radio address that the UN vote for partition in November had been a mistake that could still be corrected. "The United States will emerge the stronger for having the courage to admit and correct its mistake." "Rosenwald Urges Trusteeship Plan," *NYT*, April 8, 1948, 8.
15. My Day, March 2, 1948.
16. Quoted in editor's commentary, *ER Papers*, vol 1, 779.
17. ER to Truman, March 26, 1948; *ER Papers*, vol 1, 780.
18. My Day, March 27, 1948.

19. My Day, April 7, 1948.
20. Howard M. Sachar, *A History of Israel from the Rise of Zionism to Our Time*, 3rd ed. (New York: Knopf, 2007), 304–11.
21. ER to Truman, May 11, 1948; ER to Marshall, May 11, 1948; *ER Papers*, vol 1, 804–05.
22. ER to Marshall, May 16, 1948; Truman to ER, May 20, 1948; *ER Papers*, vol 1, 823–25; Michael J. Cohen, *Truman and Israel* (Berkeley: University of California Press, 1990), 215–20.
23. ER, "The Declaration of Human Rights," 13; Speech and Article File; Eleanor Roosevelt Papers (hereafter: ERP); FDR Library (hereafter: FDRL).
24. James Loeffler, *Rooted Cosmopolitans: Jews and Human Rights in the Twentieth Century* (New Haven: Yale University Press, 2018), 96–97, 114, 121–23, 128, 172–73, 186-89. See also, Michael N. Barnett, *The Star and the Stripes: A History of the Foreign Policies of American Jews* (Princeton: Princeton University Press, 2016), 123–24, 135–36, 147–48. While the American Jewish Committee opposed the establishment of a Jewish state prior to the UN vote for partition, it supported it after the vote. The anti-Zionist American Council for Judaism continued to call for a UN trusteeship. See Cohen, *Truman and Israel*, 192.
25. "Russian Says U.S. Condones Slavery," *NYT*, December 9, 1947.
26. "Mrs. Roosevelt Urges a Drive to Make U.S. Democracy Work," text of "Humanistic Democracy and the American Ideal," address to the Forum on Current Problems, October 24, 1939, sponsored by the *New York Herald Tribune* (*NYHT*), October 25, 1939, 18.
27. ER, "For American Unity," in *American Unity: A Monthly Manual of Education*, Issued by Council Against Intolerance in America, 1942; Folder: Human Rights; Topical Files; ERP; FDRL.
28. Loeffler, *Rooted Cosmopolitans*, 179.
29. ER, Message to the National Conference of the Christian Committee of the United Jewish Appeal, Shoreham Hotel, Washington, DC, 1950, enclosed in ER reply to Meyer F. Steinglass, UJA, to ER, telegram, April 13, 1950; Folder: United Jewish Appeal; Correspondence 1945–1952; ERP; FDRL.
30. Wadad Dabbagh to ER, n.d., quoted in *ER Papers*, vol 1, 818.
31. Sachar, *A History of Israel*, 120–22; Ian J. Bickerton and Carla L. Klausner, *History of the Arab-Israeli Conflict* (Upper Saddle River, NJ: Prentice Hall, 2007), 40–41, 58–60.
32. ER to Dabbagh, May 13, 1948; *ER Papers*, vol 1, 818–19.
33. "Rights Plan Hailed by Mrs. Roosevelt," *NYT*, June 21, 1948, 9.
34. Dabbagh to ER June 30, 1948; ER to Dabbagh July 10, 1948, *ER Papers*, vol 1, 819–20.
35. Quoted in Dinnerstein, *America and the Survivors of the Holocaust* (New York: Columbia University Press, 1982), 92.
36. My Day, May 27, 1948.

37. My Day, June 25, 1948.
38. Quoted by ER in My Day, August 21, 1948.
39. My Day, August 21, 1948.
40. *ER Papers*, vol 1, 886n4.
41. My Day, September 22. 1948.
42. My Day, August 21, 1948.
43. "Progress Report of the United Nations Mediator on Palestine," September 16, 1948; General Assembly Official Records: Third Session, Supplement No. 11 (A/648). http://web.archive.org/web/20051210224540/http://domino.un.org/unispal.nsf/9a798adbf322aff38525617b006d88d7/ab14d4aafc4e1bb985256204004f55fa!OpenDocument.
44. ER to Baruch, October 15, 1948; *ER Papers*, vol 1, 911–17.
45. ER, Memorandum for the President, December 28, 1948; *ER Papers*, vol 1, 985n6.
46. ER to George Marshall, November 3, 1948; *ER Papers*, vol 1, 929–30.
47. "Extract from Speech by Aubrey S. Eban at Youth Aliyah Presentation to Mrs. Eleanor Roosevelt," February 10, 1949; Folder 248; Box 33; RG7; HA.
48. Sachar, *A History of Israel*, 350–51.
49. The idea that the struggle of the Jews for an independent state was an anticolonial uprising against the British was later greatly amplified by Uris's novel *Exodus* and the film made from it. See Amy Kaplan, "Zionism as Anticolonialism," in *Our American Israel: The Story of an Entangled Alliance* (Cambridge, MA: Harvard University Press, 2018), 80–87.
50. My Day, September 14, 1948.
51. Michelle Mart, *Eye on Israel: How America Came to View Israel as an Ally* (Albany, NY: State University of New York Press, 2006), 1–22. See also, Amy Kaplan, *Our American Israel: The Story of an Entangled Alliance* (Cambridge, MA: Harvard University Press, 2018), 58–93.
52. My Day, September 14, 1948.

CHAPTER 15

1. Ari Shavit, *My Promised Land: The Triumph and Tragedy of Israel* (New York: Spiegel & Grau, 2013), 148.
2. My Day, April 13, 1946; My Day, June 11, 1946.
3. "Morgenthau Gets Jewish Fund Post," *New York Times* (*NYT*), January 3, 1947, 44.
4. Raphael, *A History of the United Jewish Appeal, 1939–1982* (Providence, RI: Scholars Press, 1982), 29–30.
5. Emily Alice Katz, *Bringing Zion Home: Israel in American Jewish Culture, 1948–1967* (Albany, NY: State University of New York Press, 2015), 42.
6. Lessing J. Rosenwald to ER, February 28, 1949; ER to Rosenwald, March 21, 1949;

Folder: Rosena–Rosenw; Correspondence 1945–1952; Eleanor Roosevelt Papers (hereafter: ERP); FDR Library (hereafter: FDRL).

7. Lea R. (Mrs. Hal) Horne to ER, March 2, 1950; Folder: United Jewish Appeal; Correspondence 1945–1952; ERP; FDRL.
8. Statement attached to Harry Seeve to ER, December 12, 1952; Folder: United Jewish Appeal; Correspondence 1945–1952; ERP; FDRL.
9. "On Mrs. Eleanor Roosevelt, Recipient of Henrietta Szold Citation," February 20, 1949; "Mrs. Roosevelt Receives Henrietta Szold Award," news clip, *New York Herald Tribune* (*NYHT*), February 11, 1949; Folder: ER & Hadassah 76–2; Small Collections: Hadassah; FDRL.
10. Brownstone, PR Director, Youth Aliyah, to Thompson, January 26, 1949 with enclosed information: "Background Material on Youth Aliyah for Mrs. Eleanor Roosevelt"; "Our Answers to Your Questions"; Folder: Conventions/Szold Award, 1948; RG3; HA.
11. "The 40,000 Hitler Did Not Get," rpt of William L. Shirer, "Zionists Mark 15 Years' Migration: 40,000 Children Moved Since Hitler's Rise, Plus 35,000 in Next 2 Years, Will Give Israel the Youngest Population in the World," *NYHT*, February 6, 1949.
12. Moshe Kol, Remarks at the Memorial Meeting for Eleanor Roosevelt, Jerusalem, November 25, 1962; Folder: Eleanor Roosevelt & Hadassah; Memorials 76–2; Small Collections: Hadassah; FDRL.
13. ER, *India and the Awakening East* (New York: Harper & Brothers, 1953), 31–34.
14. See especially, Benny Morris, *The Birth of the Palestinian Refugee Problem, 1947–1949* (Cambridge: Cambridge University Press, 1988) and *1948: A History of the First Arab-Israeli War* (New Haven: Yale University Press, 2008), 91–97, 120–21, 132. See also, Shavit, *My Promised Land*. On Morris, see David Remnick's review of *1948*: "Blood and Sand: A Revisionist Israeli Historian Revisits His Country's Origins," *The New Yorker*, May 5, 2008.
15. ER to William T. Hillard, August 17, 1951; Folder: Hik–Hill; Correspondence 1945–52; ERP; FDRL.
16. Shira Robinson, *Citizen Strangers: Palestinians and the Birth of Israel's Liberal Settler State* (Stanford, CA: Stanford University Press, 2013), 35–36.
17. My Day, December 1, 1951; ER to Hillard, August 17, 1951.
18. Quoted in Hertzel Fishman, *American Protestantism and a Jewish State* (Detroit: Wayne State University Press, 1973), 132–35.
19. Charles Malik to ER, February 8, 1952 [misdated 1951]; Folder: Malik, Charles; Correspondence 1945–1952; ERP; FDRL.
20. ER, *India and the Awakening East*, 26–28.
21. William Eddy, who served as America's first minister to Saudi Arabia, and ER's cousin, Kermit Roosevelt Jr., a senior officer in the CIA's Middle Eastern division and one of

the founders of the American Friends of the Middle East, were two other important pro-Arabists. See Hugh Wilford, *America's Great Game: The CIA's Secret Arabists and the Shaping of the Modern Middle East* (New York: Basic Books, 2013).

22. Michael B. Oren, *Power, Faith, and Fantasy: America in the Middle East 1776 to the Present* (New York: W. W. Norton, 2007), 217–18.
23. Stephen B. L. Penrose, *The Palestine Problem: Retrospect and Prospect* (New York: American Friends of the Middle East, 1954), 6.
24. ER, *India and the Awakening East*, 25.
25. Penrose, *The Palestine Problem*, 6–8, 10–14.
26. Dispatch from Harold B. Minor, American minister to Lebanon, to U.S. Department of State, February 14, 1952. RG59, 032 Roosevelt, Eleanor D. (Mrs.) HH/2–1452, NARA.
27. Dispatch from Harold B. Minor, February 14, 1952.
28. ER, *India and the Awakening East*, 28–31.
29. "Speech before Women's Division of the United Jewish Appeal of Greater New York," February 20, 1946; *ER Papers*, vol. 1, 258.
30. "Mrs. Roosevelt Ends Tour," *Jerusalem Post*, February 20, 1952.
31. Headlines in the Arab Press on Feb. 21 included the following in Ad–Difa: "Obvious Zionist! Mrs. Roosevelt Refuses to Comment on Politics in Arab Countries! The Miserable Plight of the Refugees Did Not Touch Her In the Least," Quoted in S. Roger Tyler Jr., American consul, Jerusalem, "Arab Press Reaction to Mrs. Roosevelt's Visit," Dispatch #171, February 29, 1952. RG59, 811.41, 2952. Roosevelt, Eleanor, NARA.
32. The Nation Associates (now The Nation Builders) is the nonprofit organization that publishes *The Nation* and promotes a progressive agenda.
33. S. Roger Tyler Jr., "Arab Press Reaction to Mrs. Roosevelt's Visit," Dispatch #165, February 21, 1952, RG59, 032 Roosevelt, Eleanor 2–2152, NARA.
34. S. Roger Tyler Jr., "Arab Press Reaction to Mrs. Roosevelt's Visit," February 21, 1952, and enclosure: "My Lady . . . . Eleanor!" *Falasteen*, February 15, 1952; Dispatch #165; RG59, 032 Roosevelt, Eleanor 2–2152, NARA. *Falastin* is spelled *Falasteen* in Tyler's report. Originally published in Jaffa, the newspaper moved to East Jerusalem during the 1948 Arab-Israeli war.
35. ER, "First Need: Resettlement," *The Nation*, June 7, 1952, 556–57 (transcript of ER's speech at the Nation Associates conference).
36. Ali Ash Sheikh Said Al Qaderi to ER, February 13, 1952; Folder: Q; Correspondence 1945–52; ERP, FDRL. Original letter was in Arabic. Translator unknown.
37. ER, *India and the Awakening East*, 2–3, 17.
38. "Mrs. Roosevelt's Visit to Syria," William L. Eagleton, Third Secretary, American Consulate, Syria, Dispatch #481 to Department of State, February 19, 1952, RG59, 811.41 Roosevelt, Eleanor/2–1952, NARA.
39. ER, *India and the Awakening East*, 14–16; 19–20.
40. Joyce Antler, *The Journey Home: Jewish Women and the American Century* (New York:

41. Julia A. [Mrs. Alexander M.] Dushkin to ER, February 17, 1952; Folder: Israel Feb 14–20, 1952; Trip Files; ERP; FDRL.
42. "Mrs. Roosevelt Unwearied After 14-Hour Tour," *Jerusalem Post*, February 17, 1952.
43. "Mrs. Roosevelt Ends Tour," *Jerusalem Post*, February 20, 1952.
44. Deborah Dash Moore, "Bonding Images: Miami Jews and the Campaign for Israel Bonds," in *Envisioning Israel: The Changing Ideals and Images of North American Jews*, ed. Allon Gal (Detroit: Wayne State University Press, 1996), 255–56.
45. My Day, March 28, 1955.
46. Baratz to ER, October 17, 1955; Folder: Baratz, Joseph; Correspondence 1953–1956; ERP; FDRL.
47. Baratz to ER, December 10, 1956; Folder: Baratz, Joseph; Correspondence 1953–1956; ERP; FDRL.
48. Welcome by Yosef Sprinzak, Speaker of the Knesset, in receiving ER at his offices in the Knesset, March 23, 1955; Folder: England, France, Italy, Israel, Mar.–Apr., 1955; Trip Files; ERP; FDRL.
49. ER, Foreword to *A Village by the Jordan* (Press Department of Ichud Habonim, Tel Aviv, 1960). ER wrote her foreword for an earlier edition published in 1956.
50. Richard Funkhouser to ER, April 14, 1952; ER to Funkhouser, April 21, 1952; Folder: Fu–Fy; Correspondence 1945–52; ERP; FDRL. My Day, June 30, 1952. Funkhouser had heard ER speak to the Near Eastern, South Asian and African Bureau of the State Department on April 10, 1952.
51. ER, "Presentation by Mrs. Franklin D. Roosevelt," Youth Aliyah 25th Anniversary Conference, Plaza Hotel, NYC, February 4, 1959, 2; Folder 273: 25th anniversary of Youth Aliyah conference; Box 36; RG1; HA.
52. ER, *India and the Awakening East*, 31–34.
53. Quoted in Shavit, *My Promised Land*, 62.
54. ER, "First Need: Resettlement," 556–57.
55. My Day, March 2, 1962. In her foreword to Golda Meir's *Selected Papers*, ER quoted from Meir's 1957 speech in which she said: "This people is prepared to forgive and forget everything, for the sake of attaining an atmosphere of peace and tranquility in which to do creative work, and in the desire (which many people may not understand) to guide our neighbors beyond the frontiers toward creative work." Eleanor Roosevelt, Foreword to *This Is Our Strength: Selected Papers of Golda Meir*, ed. Henry M. Christman (New York: Macmillan, 1962).
56. Ruth Gruber, *Haven: The Dramatic Story of 1000 World War II Refugees* (New York: Three Rivers Press, 2000), 294.
57. See Amy Kaplan, *Our American Israel: The Story of an Entangled Alliance* (Cambridge, MA: Harvard University Press, 2018), 89.

CHAPTER 16

1. Moshe Kol, Remarks at ER memorial meeting, Jerusalem, November 25, 1962; Folder: ER and Hadassah Memorials 76–2; Small Collections: Hadassah; FDR Library (hereafter: FDRL).
2. Excerpt from minutes of meeting of Youth Aliyah committee of Hadassah on plans for trip by ER and Lash to Israel, March 3; Folder: 239; 1955; RG1/Box 33; HA.
3. Interview with Trude Lash conducted by Thomas F. Soapes, November 21, 1977, 20; Eleanor Roosevelt Oral History Transcripts; FDRL.
4. Erica B. Simmons, *Hadassah and the Zionist Project* (New York: Rowman & Littlefield, 2006), 171.
5. Summary of comments by Mrs. Hamerman regarding her visit to Cambous with ER, H.M.O—Med. Center Minutes, December 6, 1960; ER and Hadassah Memorials 76–2; Small Collections: Hadassah; FDRL; "Report on Mrs. Roosevelt's Visit to Cambous, Sunday, March 13, 1955"; Folder: 239; Box 33; RG1; HA.
6. ER, "Children of Israel," *Midstream: A Jewish Monthly Review* I (Fall 1955), 110–11.
7. Trude Lash to Miriam Freund, March 18, 1955; Folder: 239; Box 33; RG1; HA.
8. ER, "Children of Israel."
9. ER, "Promise Fulfilled," *Hadassah Newsletter*, November 1955, 5 (a condensation of ER's address to Hadassah Convention attended by 3,000 women); Periodical Collection; FDRL.
10. Rivka A. Eisikovits, "The Educational Experience and Performance of Immigrant and Minority Students in Israel," *Anthropology & Education Quarterly* 28 (September 1997): 398.
11. Ari Shavit, *My Promised Land: The Triumph and Tragedy of Israel* (New York: Spiegel & Grau, 2013), 283.
12. Simmons, *Hadassah*, 161.
13. There was a darker side to the process of assimilating children during Israel's early years, which was unknown at the time. A debate in Israel about the fate of a large number of Jewish children from Yemen and other Arab countries remains unresolved. The families of the children were told that their babies had died of illness after being taken to a hospital but weren't shown their bodies or provided with a death certificate. The families suspect that some of the children were kidnapped, then given or sold to childless Ashkenazi families in Israel or to American Jewish couples. Some may have been sent to be raised by couples in kibbutzim. See Ofer Aderet, "Israel Agrees to Open Graves of Missing Yemenite Children for DNA Testing," *Haaretz*, January 24, 2018. For the story of an Iraqi Jewish child kidnapped and sent to a kibbutz where he was assigned new parents, see Lifted Snap #908, http://snapjudgment.org.
14. Reuven Feuerstein, David Krasilowsky, and Yaacov Rand, "Innovative Educational Strategies for the Integration of High-Risk Adolescents in Israel," *Phi Delta Kappan* 55 (April 1974): 556.

15. ER, "Children of Israel."
16. My Day, March 25, 1955; Zev Weiss to Miriam Freund, Chairman, National Youth Aliyah Committee, August 18, 1955; Folder 311; Box 42; RG1; HA.
17. Lash, "Mrs. Roosevelt Revisits Israel," *Hadassah Newsletter*, May 1955; Folder: 311; Box 42; RG1; HA
18. Quoted in Howard M. Sachar, *A History of Israel from the Rise of Zionism to Our Time*, 3rd ed. (New York: Knopf, 2007), 478. See also, Simmons, *Hadassah*, 174.
19. "My Day," March 30, 1955.
20. Alexander Dushkin, a leading American expert on education, who was hired by Youth Aliyah to evaluate its programs in 1947, came away with a similar conclusion about the effectiveness of the organization's programs: "We saw these young people transformed; sturdier, healthier, with proud and secure experience as successful workers." Quoted in Simmons, *Hadassah*, 157.
21. Lash, "Mrs. Roosevelt Revisits Israel."
22. Feuerstein et al., "Innovative Educational Strategies," 557.
23. "Eleanor Roosevelt at Bet Mazmil," Hadassah report (typescript), May 18, 1955, 1; Folder: ER Visits to Israel, 1952, 1955; Small Collections: Hadassah; FDRL.
24. ER, "Promise Fulfilled."
25. "Visit of Mrs. Roosevelt to Mexico City, November 12–14, 1958," Dispatch from American Embassy, Mexico to Department of State, November 17, 1958; RG59, 032 Roosevelt, Eleanor/11-1758 HBS, NARA.
26. "The Roosevelt Story," *Youth Aliyah Review* (Autumn 1952); Folder: Youth Aliyah; Correspondence 1957–1962; Eleanor Roosevelt Papers (hereafter: ERP); FDRL.
27. Moshe Kol to Mrs. A. P. (Bertha) Schoolman, May 13, 1957; Folder: ER and Hadassah 76–2; Small Collections: Hadassah; FDRL.
28. "Mrs. Roosevelt's Visit," *Jewish Chronicle*, May 10, 1957; Folder: ER and Hadassah 76–2; Small Collections: Hadassah; FDRL.
29. Baratz to ER, December 10, 1956; Folder: Baratz, Joseph; Correspondence 1953–1956; ERP, FDRL.

CHAPTER 17

1. Hertzel Fishman, *American Protestantism and a Jewish State* (Detroit: Wayne State University Press, 1973), 98–101.
2. Susan Ware, *Letter to the World: Seven Women Who Shaped the American Century* (New York: Norton, 1998), 79. Thompson came to regard Zionism as an aggressive, expansionist ideology.
3. By 1954, the AFME's board of directors also included Rabbi Elmer Berger, executive director of the anti-Zionist American Council for Judaism.
4. Caitlin Carenen, *The Fervent Embrace: Liberal Protestants, Evangelicals, and Israel* (New York: New York University Press, 2012), 65.

5. Fishman, *American Protestantism and a Jewish State*, 101–104, 106. See also Hugh Wilford, "American Friends of the Middle East: The CIA, US Citizens, and the Secret Battle for American Public Opinion in the Arab-Israeli Conflict, 1947–1967," *Journal of American Studies* 51 (February 2017).
6. Rabbi Jerome Unger to Local Committees of the American Zionist Council, March 20, 1951; American Friends of the Middle East; 116/18–חץ; Israeli State Archives.
7. Memo from Karl Baehr to Abe Harman, Esther Herlitz, Rabbi Jacob Herzog, and Shmuel Bendor, January 8, 1951; American Christian Palestine Committee; 2464/13–חץ; Israeli State Archives.
8. Memo from Abe Harman to Shmuel Bendor, January 23, 1951; Memo from Bendor to Harman, February 5, 1951; American Christian Palestine Committee; 2464/13–חץ; Israeli State Archives. For an in-depth discussion of the competition between the ACPC and AFME in seeking to shape American public opinion toward Israel, see Carenen, *The Fervent Embrace*, 59–78, 95–105, 87–92, and 107–114.
9. Mossie (Mrs. James D.) Wyker to ER, May 16, 1955; ER's penciled reply on Wyker's May 16th letter; Wyker to ER, May 28, 1955; Folder: Wyker, Mrs. James D.; Correspondence 1953–56; Eleanor Roosevelt Papers (hereafter: ERP); FDR Library (hereafter: FDRL).

    Wyker asked ER for something to read about Israel. ER said the best book was *The Birth of Israel: The Drama as I Saw It* by Jorge Garcia Granados (1948). She also recommended James McDonald, *My Mission to Israel* and Bartley Crum, *Behind the Silken Curtain*. ER to Wyker, June 3, 1955; Folder: Wyker, Mrs. James D.; Correspondence 1953–56, ERP; FDRL.
10. ER to Wyker, June 3, 1955; Wyker to ER, June 19,1955; Folder: Wyker, Mrs. James D.; Correspondence 1953–56; ERP; FDRL.
11. Charl Ormond Williams to ER, December 12, 1955; Folder: Williams, Charl O.; Correspondence 1953–56; ERP; FDRL.
12. Gideon Tadmor to ER, January 12, 1956; ER to Tadmor, January 18, 1956; Folder: Tadmor, Gideon; Correspondence 1953–56; ERP; FDRL.
13. See Hugh Wilford, *America's Great Game: The CIA's Secret Arabists and the Shaping of the Modern Middle East* (New York: Basic Books, 2013), 177–88.
14. ER to Henry A. Byroade, Assistant Secretary of State for Near Eastern and South Asian Affairs, April 6, 1953; RG59; CDF 1950-54; 611.84A/4-653; NARII.
15. My Day, January 28, 1954.
16. Steven L. Spiegel, *The Other Arab-Israeli Conflict: Making America's Middle East Policy, from Truman to Reagan* (Chicago: University of Chicago Press, 1985), 65.
17. My Day, November 3, 1955.
18. Baratz to ER, October 17, 1955; Baratz to ER, November 21, 1955; Folder: Baratz, Joseph; Correspondence 1953–56; ERP; FDRL.
19. Wilford, *America's Great Game*, 181–83.

20. ER to Baratz, December 8, 1955; Folder: Baratz, Joseph; Correspondence 1953–56; ERP; FDRL.
21. Goldstein to ER, January 6, 1956 and enclosure, "The Crisis in the Middle East: A Statement to the American People;" Folder: Goldstein, Israel; Correspondence 1953–1956; ERP; FDRL.
22. Polier to ER, January 9, 1956; Folder: Polier, Justine; Correspondence 1953–1956; ERP; FDRL.
23. "Text of Statement on Arms for Israel: Achievements Are Noted Arms Races Deplored," *New York Times* (*NYT*), January 29, 1956, 4.
24. "Truman Urges U.S. to Send Israelis Defensive Arms," *NYT*, January 29, 1956, 1.
25. "Take the Middle East out of Domestic Politics," display ad, *NYT*, January 25, 1956, 20; Baratz to ER, February 8, 1956; Folder: Baratz, Joseph; Correspondence 1953–56; ERP; FDRL.
26. My Day, February 24, 1956.
27. Spiegel, *The Other Arab-Israeli Conflict*, 66.
28. Quoted in Howard M. Sachar, *A History of Israel from the Rise of Zionism to Our Time*, 3rd ed. (New York: Knopf, 2007), 488.
29. My Day, November 2, 1956. It is a measure of the influence attributed to ER at the time that ER's entire column was reprinted in the *New York Times* the following day as a display ad paid for by the New York Committee for Stevenson, Kefauver, Wagner. It was headlined: "do we have to side with . . . THE KREMLIN and the DICTATOR of EGYPT." *NYT*, November 3, 1956. The presidential election took place on November 6.
30. Thomas J. Hamilton, "U.S. Move Backed," *NYT*, November 2, 1956, 1.
31. "U.N. Votes Police Force to Keep Peace in Mideast," *NYT*, November 5, 1956, 1.
32. Spiegel, *The Other Arab-Israeli Conflict*, 74–76.
33. Statement from ER, Chairman, Board of Governors; Clark M. Eichelberger, Executive Director; Charles W. Mayo, President; and Oscar A. de Lima, Chairman, Board of Directors, AAUN, November 8, 1956; Folder: Cohen, Benjamin; Correspondence 1957–1962; ERP; FDRL.
34. My Day, November 26, 1956.
35. Spiegel, *The Other Arab-Israeli Conflict*, 77.
36. My Day, January 7, 1957. See Sachar, *A History of Israel*, 439–41.
37. My Day, February 21, 1957.
38. Spiegel, *The Other Arab-Israeli Conflict*, 78–81; W. H. Lawrence, "President Says U.N. Has No Choice But to Force Israel Out of Egypt," *NYT*, February 21, 1957, 1.
39. Baratz to ER, March 6, 1957; ER to Baratz, April 2, 1957; Folder: Baratz, Joseph; Correspondence 1957–1962; ERP; FDRL.
40. Spiegel, *The Other Arab-Israeli Conflict*, 85.

41. ER to Gus Ranis, February 16, 1957; Folder: Ranis, Gustav; Correspondence 1957–1962; ERP; FDRL. Ranis and ER became friends after they both spoke at his Brandeis graduation.
42. ER to Albert Epstein, February 28, 1957; Folder: Epstein, Albert; Correspondence 1957–1962; ERP; FDRL.
43. Abba Eban, *Personal Witness: Israel Through My Eyes* (New York: G. P. Putnam, 1992), 295.

CHAPTER 18

1. John F. Sears, "Eleanor Roosevelt, Morocco, and the Immigration of Jews to Israel" (unpublished manuscript). ER's masterly letter of July 31, 1956, to Sultan Mohammed V asking him to permit the Jews detained in a camp in Morocco to emigrate to Israel is reprinted in Joseph Lash, *Eleanor: The Years Alone* (New York: W. W. Norton, 1972), 338–39.
2. Moshe Kol to ER, September 30, 1958; Folder: ER and Hadassah 76-2 folder; Small Collections: Hadassah; FDR Library (hereafter: FDRL).
3. Kol to ER, February 26, 1959; Folder: Youth Aliyah; Correspondence 1957–1962; Eleanor Roosevelt Papers (hereafter: ERP); FDRL.
4. My Day, March 26, 1959.
5. ER's itinerary for March 18–20, 1959, prepared by the American embassy; Folder: Israel March 22–29, 1959; Trip Files; ERP; FDRL.
6. My Day, April 2, 1959.
7. My Day, April 4, 1959.
8. My Day, April 6, 1959.
9. K. J. Mann to ER, March 8, 1959; Folder: Israel March 22–29, 1959; Trip Files; ERP; FDRL.
10. My Day, April 7, 1959.
11. Albert B. Franklin, American consul general, Jerusalem, to Acting Secretary of State Herter, telegram, March 13, 1959; RG59, 032 Roosevelt, Eleanor/3-1359, NARA; Franklin to Secretary of State, telegram, March 24, 1959; RG59, 032 Roosevelt, Eleanor/3-2459; NARA; Franklin to Secretary of State, telegram, March 26, 1959, RG59, 032 Roosevelt, Eleanor/3-2659, NARA.
12. Franklin to Secretary of State, March 30, 1959; RG59, 032 Roosevelt, Eleanor/3-3059, NARA.
13. My Day, April 9, 1959.
14. My Day, March 27, 1959.
15. My Day, April 10, 1959. See also My Day, March 27, 1959, in which she quotes an Iranian as saying, "Persians look after ourselves."
16. Gideon Tadmor to ER, February 9, 1959; Folder: Tadmor, Gideon; Correspondence 1957–62; ERP; FDRL.

17. My Day, April 2, 1959; My Day, April 3, 1959.
18. Shira Robinson, *Citizen Strangers: Palestinians and the Birth of Israel's Liberal Settler State* (Stanford, CA: Stanford University Press, 2013), 38–40, 59–60, 188–93, 194–98.
19. ER to Henry Morgenthau III, April 1. 1959; Folder: Morgenthau, Henry III; Correspondence 1957–62; ERP; FDRL.
20. ER to Ben-Gurion, April 2, 1959; Folder: Israel March 22–29, 1959; Trip Files; ERP; FDRL.
21. ER to Meir, April 2, 1959; Folder: Meir, Golda; Correspondence 1957–1962; ERP; FDRL.
22. Meir to ER, telegram, October 17, 1962; Folder: Meir, Golda; Correspondence 1957–1962; ERP; FDRL.
23. ER to Meir, April 2, 1959.
24. My Day, April 8, 1959.
25. My Day, April 17, 1959.
26. Baratz to ER, August 6, 1958; Baratz to ER, December 10, 1958; Folder: Baratz, Joseph; Correspondence 1957–1962; ERP; FDRL.
27. Baratz to ER, February 23, 1959; Folder: Baratz, Joseph; Correspondence 1957–1962; ERP; FDRL.
28. ER to Meir, January 30, 1962; Folder: Meir, Golda; Correspondence 1957–1962; ERP; FDRL.
29. ER to Yitzhak Ben-Zvi, March 1, 1962; Folder: Beno–Berd; Correspondence 1957–62; ERP; FDRL.
30. Tadmor to ER, December 8, 1959; Folder: Tadmor, Gideon; Correspondence 1957–62; ERP; FDRL.
31. ER to Meir, January 30, 1962; Folder: Meir, Golda; Correspondence 1957–1962; ERP; FDRL.
32. ER to Meir, March 1, 1962; Folder: Meir, Golda; Correspondence 1957–1962; ERP; FDRL.
33. My Day, February 28, 1962.
34. Eleanor Roosevelt, "My Day at Beersheba," *Hadassah Magazine* 42, no. 8 (April 1962).
35. Trude Lash to Miriam Freund, March 19, 1955; Folder 239: Youth Aliyah–France; Box 33; RG1; HA.
36. My Day, February 28, 1962.
37. Charles M. Segal to ER, January 29, 1959; Folder 273: 25th anniversary of Youth Aliyah conference; Box 36; RG1; HA.
38. ER, "Presentation by Mrs. Franklin D. Roosevelt," Youth Aliyah 25th Anniversary Conference, Plaza Hotel, NYC, February 4, 1959, 2; Folder 273: 25th anniversary of Youth Aliyah conference; Box 36; RG1; HA.
39. Quoted by Moshe Kol in remarks at a memorial meeting for ER at the International Cultural Center for Youth in Jerusalem, November 25, 1962; Folder: ER and Hadassah Memorials 76–2; Small Collections: Hadassah; FDRL.

CONCLUSION

1. *My Day*, December 7, 1956.
2. ER, "Children of Israel," *Midstream: A Jewish Monthly Review* 1 *(Fall 1955), 110–11.*
3. Michelle Mart, *Eyes on Israel: How America Came to View Israel as an Ally* (Albany, NY: State University of New York Press, 2006), 91–92.
4. For a harsh assessment of ER's views on Israel and the Arabs, see Geraldine Kidd, *Eleanor Roosevelt: Palestine, Israel and Human Rights* (London: Routledge, 2018). Kidd regards the role of the United States in the establishment of Israel as a disastrous mistake that contradicted American values, undermined American interests, unjustly deprived Palestinian Arabs of the right to self-determination, and dispossessed the Arabs of their lands. She holds ER partly responsible for the outcome.
5. Joseph P. Lash, *Eleanor Roosevelt: The Years Alone* (New York: W. W. Norton, 1972), 122; Lash, Notes on an interview with Durward Sandifer, May 5, 1970; Joseph Lash Papers, FDR Library (hereafter: FDRL).
6. Article 21(3) of the Universal Declaration of Human Rights.
7. ER to Charl Williams, April 1, 1958; Folder: Williams, Charl O.; Correspondence 1957–62; Eleanor Roosevelt Papers (ERP); FDRL.
8. Eleanor Roosevelt, *Tomorrow Is Now* (New York: Harper & Row, 1963), 88.

BIBLIOGRAPHY

Antler, Joyce. *The Journey Home: Jewish Women and the American Century*. New York: Free Press, 1997.

Baratz, Joseph. *A Village by the Jordan.* Tel Aviv: Ichud Habonim, 1960.

Barnett, Michael N. *The Star and the Stripes: A History of the Foreign Policies of American Jews.* Princeton: Princeton University Press, 2016.

Becker, Stephen. *Marshall Field III: A Biography.* New York: Simon and Schuster, 1964.

Bickerton, Ian J., and Carla L. Klausner. *History of the Arab-Israeli Conflict.* Upper Saddle River, NJ: Prentice Hall, 2007.

Black, Allida M. *Casting Her Own Shadow.* New York: Columbia University Press, 1996.

Black, Allida M. *Courage in a Dangerous World: The Political Writings of Eleanor Roosevelt.* New York: Columbia University Press, 2000.

Black, Allida M., John F. Sears, and Mary Jo Binker, et al., eds. *The Eleanor Roosevelt Papers, Vol. 1: The Human Rights Years, 1945–1948.* Thomson Gale, 2007; rpt. University of Virginia Press, 2009. Citations refer to the Thomson Gale edition.

Black, Allida, Mary Jo Binker, Christopher Brick, Robert P. Frankel, Jr., and Christy Regenhardt, et al., eds. *The Eleanor Roosevelt Papers, Vol. 2: The Human Rights Years, 1949–1952.* Charlottesville, VA: University of Virginia Press, 2012.

Brands, H. W. *Inside the Cold War: Loy Henderson and the Rise of the American Empire, 1918–1961.* New York: Oxford University Press, 1991.

Breitman, Richard, and Alan M. Kraut. *American Refugee Policy and European Jewry, 1933–1945.* Bloomington: Indiana University Press, 1987.

Breitman, Richard, and Allan J. Lichtman. *FDR and the Jews.* Cambridge, MA: Harvard University Press, 2013.

Breitman, Richard, Barbara McDonald Stewart, and Severin Hochberg, eds. *Refugees and Rescue: The Diaries and Papers of James G. McDonald, 1935–1945*. Bloomington: Indiana University Press, 2009.

Breitman, Richard, Barbara McDonald Stewart, and Severin Hochberg, eds. *Advocate for the Doomed: The Diaries and Papers of James G. McDonald, 1932–1935*. Bloomington: Indiana University Press, 2007.

Carenen, Caitlin. *The Fervent Embrace: Liberal Protestants, Evangelicals, and Israel*. New York: New York University Press, 2012.

Chadacoff, Rochelle, ed. *Eleanor Roosevelt's My Day: Her Acclaimed Columns 1936–1945*. New York: Pharos Books, 1989.

Close, Kathryn. *Transplanted Children: A History*. New York: United States Committee for the Care of European Children, 1953.

Cohen, Michael J. *Truman and Israel*. Berkeley: University of California Press, 1990.

Cook, Blanche Wiesen. *Eleanor Roosevelt, Vol. 1: The Early Years, 1884–1933*. New York: Viking, 1992.

Cook, Blanche Wiesen. *Eleanor Roosevelt, Vol. 2: The Defining Years, 1933–1938*. New York: Viking, 1999.

Cook, Blanche Wiesen. *Eleanor Roosevelt, Vol. 3: The War Years and After, 1939–1962*. New York: Viking, 2016.

Davie, Maurice R. *Refugees in America: Report of the Committee for the Study of Recent Immigration from Europe*. New York: Harper & Brothers, 1947.

Dinnerstein, Leonard. *America and the Survivors of the Holocaust*. New York: Columbia University Press, 1982.

Dinnerstein, Leonard. *Antisemitism in America*. New York: Oxford University Press, 1994.

Dwork, Debórah. *Children with a Star: Jewish Youth in Nazi Europe*. New Haven: Yale University Press, 1991.

Dwork, Debórah, and Robert Jan Van Pelt. *Flight from the Reich: Refugee Jews, 1933–1946*. New York: W. W. Norton, 2009.

Eban, Abba. *Personal Witness: Israel Through My Eyes*. New York: G. P. Putnam, 1992.

Embree, Edwin R., and Julia Waxman. *Investment in People: The Story of the Julius Rosenwald Fund*. New York: Harper & Brothers, 1949.

Erbelding, Rebecca. *Rescue Board: The Untold Story of America's Efforts to Save the Jews of Europe*. New York: Doubleday, 2018.

Feingold, Henry L. *The Politics of Rescue: The Roosevelt Administration and the Holocaust, 1938–1945*. New York: Holocaust Library, 1970.

Fishman, Hertzel. *American Protestantism and a Jewish State*. Detroit: Wayne State University Press, 1973.

Fry, Varian. *Assignment: Rescue*. New York: Four Winds Press, 1968. First published as *Surrender on Demand*. New York: Random House, 1945. Citations refer to Four Winds Press edition.

Gal, Allon, ed. *Envisioning Israel: The Changing Ideals and Images of North American Jews*. Detroit: Wayne State University Press, 1996.

Gellman, Irwin F. *Secret Affairs: Franklin Roosevelt, Cordell Hull, and Sumner Welles*. Baltimore: Johns Hopkins University Press, 1995.

Goodwin, Doris Kearns. *No Ordinary Time: Franklin and Eleanor Roosevelt: The Home Front and World War II*. New York: Simon & Schuster, 1994.

Gruber, Ruth. *Haven: The Dramatic Story of 1,000 World War II Refugees*. New York: Three Rivers Press, 2000. First published as *Haven: The Unknown Story of 1,000 World War II Refugees*. New York: Coward-McCann, 1983. Citations refer to the revised Three Rivers Press edition.

Gruber, Ruth. *Inside of Time: My Journey from Alaska to Israel*. New York: Carroll & Graf, 2003.

Gutman, Israel, ed. *The Encyclopedia of the Righteous Among the Nations*. Jerusalem: Yad Vashem, 2007.

Hett, Benjamin Carter. *Crossing Hitler: The Man Who Put the Nazis on the Witness Stand*. New York: Oxford University Press, 2008.

Hickok, Lorena. *Empty Without You: The Intimate Letters of Eleanor Roosevelt and Lorena Hickok*, ed. Rodger Streitmatter. New York: Free Press, 1998.

Isenberg, Sheila. *A Hero of Our Own: The Story of Varian Fry*. New York: Random House, 2001.

Kaplan, Amy. "Zionism as Anticolonialism." In *Our American Israel: The Story of an Entangled Alliance*. Cambridge, MA: Harvard University Press, 2018.

Katz, Emily Alice. *Bringing Zion Home: Israel in American Jewish Culture, 1948–1967*. Albany: State University of New York Press, 2015.

Katzburg-Yungman, Mira. *Hadassah: American Women Zionists and the Rebirth of Israel*. Oxford: Littman Library of Jewish Civilization, 2002.

Kelly, Jon. "Hans Litten: The Man Who Annoyed Adolf Hitler." *BBC News Magazine*, August 19, 2011. https://www.bbc.com/news/magazine-14572578.

Kidd, Geraldine. *Eleanor Roosevelt: Palestine, Israel and Human Rights*. London: Routledge, 2018.

Klapper, Melissa R. "'Those by Whose Side We Have Labored': American Jewish Women and the Peace Movement between the Wars." *Journal of American History* 97, no. 3 (December 2010): 636–658.

Koster, Henry, and Irene Kahn Atkins. *Henry Koster*. Metuchen, NY: Scarecrow Press, 1987.

Kraut, Benny. "Towards the Establishment of the National Conference of Christians and Jews: The Tenuous Road to Religious Goodwill in the 1920s." *American Jewish History* 77, no. 3 (March 1988): 388–412.

Kurth, Peter. *American Cassandra: The Life of Dorothy Thompson*. Boston: Little, Brown, 1990.

Lash, Joseph. *Eleanor Roosevelt: A Friend's Memoir*. New York: Doubleday, 1964.

Lash, Joseph P. *Eleanor and Franklin*. New York: W. W. Norton, 1971.

Lash, Joseph P. *Eleanor Roosevelt: The Years Alone*. New York: W. W. Norton, 1972.

Lipstadt, Deborah E. *Beyond Belief: The American Press and the Coming of the Holocaust*. New York: Free Press, 1986.

Loeffler, James. *Rooted Cosmopolitans: Jews and Human Rights in the Twentieth Century*. New Haven: Yale University Press, 2018.

Lowenstein, Sharon R. *Token Refuge: The Story of the Jewish Refugee Shelter at Oswego, 1944–1946*. Bloomington: Indiana University Press, 1986.

Mart, Michelle. "Eleanor Roosevelt, Liberalism, and Israel." *Shofar* 24, no. 3 (Spring 2006): 58–89.

Mart, Michelle. *Eye on Israel: How America Came to View Israel as an Ally*. Albany: State University of New York Press, 2006.

McDonald, James G. *Palestine: The Primary Hope of the Post-War Era*. New York: United Palestine Appeal, November 1944.

McDonald, James G. *The Time for Discussion Is Past*. Washington, DC: Zionist Organization of America, 1948.

McDonald, James G., and Harry Emerson Fosdick. *Addresses on Modern Christian German Martyrs*. New York: American Christian Committee for German Refugees, 1937.

Moorehead, Caroline. *Gellhorn: A Twentieth-Century Life*. New York: Henry Holt, 2003.

Morgenthau, Henry, III. *Mostly Morgenthaus*. New York: Ticknor & Fields, 1991.

Morris, Benny. *The Birth of the Palestinian Refugee Problem, 1947–1949*. Cambridge: Cambridge University Press, 1988.

Morris, Benny. *1948: A History of the First Arab-Israeli War*. New Haven: Yale University Press, 2008.

Nasaw, David. *The Last Million: Europe's Displaced Persons from World War to Cold War*. New York: Penguin Press, 2020.

Newton, Verne, ed. *FDR and the Holocaust*. New York: St. Martin's Press, 1996.

Oren, Michael B. *Power, Faith, and Fantasy: America in the Middle East 1776 to the Present*. New York: W. W. Norton, 2007.

Ostrovsky, Michal. "'We Are Standing By': Rescue Operations of the United States Committee for the Care of European Children." *Holocaust and Genocide Studies* 29 (Fall 2015): 230–50.

Paldiel, Mordecai. *Diplomatic Heroes of the Holocaust*. Jersey City, NJ: KTAV Publishing House, 2007.

Papanek, Ernst (with Edward Linn). *Out of the Fire*. New York: William Morrow, 1975.

Penkower, Monty Noam. *The Holocaust and Israel Reborn*. Urbana: University of Illinois Press, 1994.

Penrose, Stephen B. L. *The Palestine Problem: Retrospect and Prospect*. New York: American Friends of the Middle East, 1954.

Perkins, Alfred. *Edwin Rogers Embree. The Julius Rosenwald Fund, Foundation Philanthropy, and American Race Relations*. Bloomington: Indiana University Press, 2011.

Pfister, Tom, Peter, and Kathy. *Eva and Otto. America's Vetting and Rescue of Political Refugees during World War II*. Los Angeles: Pfisters, 2017.

Pfister, Tom, Peter, and Kathy. *Eva & Otto: Resistance, Refugees, and Love in the Time of Hitler*. West Lafayette, IN: Purdue University Press, 2020.

Pickett, Clarence. *For More Than Bread*. Boston: Little, Brown, 1953.

Pleasants, Julian M. *Buncombe Bob: The Life and Times of Robert Rice Reynolds*. Chapel Hill: University of North Carolina Press, 2000.

Raphael, Marc Lee. *A History of the United Jewish Appeal, 1939–1982*. Providence, RI: Scholars Press, 1982.

Renaud, Terence. "The German Resistance in New York: Karl B. Frank and the New Beginning Group, 1935–45." Undergraduate thesis, Boston University, 2007. http://terencerenaud.com/german_resistance.htm.

Renaud, Terence. "'This Is Our Dunkirk': Karl B. Frank and the Politics of the Emergency Rescue Committee." Student essay, Boston University, 2009. http://terencerenaud.com/The_Politics_of_the_ERC_FINAL.htm.

Robinson, Shira. *Citizen Strangers: Palestinians and the Birth of Israel's Liberal Settler State*. Stanford, CA: Stanford University Press, 2013.

Roosevelt, Eleanor. "Children of Israel." *Midstream: A Jewish Monthly Review* 1 (Fall 1955): 110–11.

Roosevelt, Eleanor. "First Need: Resettlement." *The Nation* (June 7, 1952): 556–57.

Roosevelt, Eleanor. "For American Unity." In *American Unity: A Monthly Manual of Education*. Council Against Intolerance in America, 1942.

Roosevelt, Eleanor. Foreword to *This Is Our Strength: Selected Papers of Golda Meir*, ed. Henry M. Christman. New York: Macmillan, 1962.

Roosevelt, Eleanor. "Mrs. Roosevelt Answers Mr. Wells on the Future of the Jews." *Liberty* 15 (December 31, 1938): 4–5.

Roosevelt, Eleanor. My Day, The Eleanor Roosevelt Papers Digital Edition (2017). https://erpapers.columbian.gwu.edu/browse-my-day-columns.

Roosevelt, Eleanor. "My Day at Beersheba." *Hadassah Magazine* 42, no. 8 (April 1962): 5.

Roosevelt, Eleanor. *The Autobiography of Eleanor Roosevelt*. New York: Da Capo Press, 1992.

Roosevelt, Eleanor. *India and the Awakening East*. New York: Harper & Brothers, 1953.

Roosevelt, Eleanor. *The Moral Basis of Democracy*. New York: Howell, Soskin, 1940.

Roosevelt, Eleanor. *This Troubled World*. New York: H. C. Kinsey, 1938.

Roosevelt, Eleanor. *Tomorrow Is Now*. New York: Harper & Row, 1963.

Rubinstein, William D. *The Myth of Rescue*. London: Routledge, 1997.

Sachar, Howard M. *A History of Israel from the Rise of Zionism to Our Time*, 3rd ed. New York: Knopf, 2007.

Saenger, Gerhart. *Today's Refugees, Tomorrow's Citizens: A Study of Americanization.* New York: Harper & Brothers, 1941.

Sauvage, Pierre. *Varian Fry in Marseille.* http://www.varianfry.org/sauvage_fry_oxford_en.htm.

Shavit, Ari. *My Promised Land: The Triumph and Tragedy of Israel.* New York: Spiegel & Grau, 2013.

Simmons, Erica B. *Hadassah and the Zionist Project.* New York: Rowman & Littlefield, 2006.

Sitkoff, Harvard. *New Deal for Blacks: The Emergence of Civil Rights as a National Issue. Volume 1: The Depression Decade.* New York: Oxford University Press, 1978.

Smith, Neil. *American Empire: Roosevelt's Geographer and the Prelude to Globalization.* Berkeley: University of California Press, 2003.

Spiegel, Steven L. *The Other Arab-Israeli Conflict: Making America's Middle East Policy, from Truman to Reagan.* Chicago: University of Chicago Press, 1985.

Ware, Susan. *Letter to the World: Seven Women Who Shaped the American Century.* New York: Norton, 1998.

Weber, Ronald. *The Lisbon Route.* Lanham, MD: Ivan R. Dee, 2011.

Welles, Benjamin. *Sumner Welles: FDR's Global Strategist.* New York: St. Martin's Press, 1997.

Welles, Sumner. *Palestine's Rightful Destiny.* New York: American Christian Palestine Committee, 1946.

Wells, H. G. "The Future of the Jews." *Liberty 15* (December 24, 1938): 6–7.

Wentling, Sonja Schoepf, and Rafael Medoff. *Herbert Hoover and the Jews: The Origins of the "Jewish Vote" and Bipartisan Support for Israel.* Washington, DC: David S. Wyman Institute for Holocaust Studies, 2012.

Wilford, Hugh. *America's Great Game: The CIA's Secret Arabists and the Shaping of the Modern Middle East.* New York: Basic Books, 2013.

Wyman, David S. *Abandonment of the Jews: America and the Holocaust, 1941–1945.* New York: Pantheon Books, 1984; rpt. New Press, 2007. Citations refer to the New Press edition.

Wyman, David S. *Paper Walls: America and the Refugee Crisis, 1938–1941.* New York: Pantheon Books, 1968, rpt. 1985.

Wyman, David S., and Rafael Medoff. *A Race Against Death: Peter Bergson, America, and the Holocaust.* New York: New Press, 2002.

INDEX

Note: Photo gallery pages are indicated by *g1p1* (gallery 1, p. 1), *g2p3* (gallery 2, p. 3), and so forth.

A

A. D. Gordon Agriculture and Nature Study Institute, 209–10
AAUN (American Association for the United Nations), 227, 232
ACCGR (American Christian Committee for German Refugees), 25–28
ACLU (American Civil Liberties Union), 11
ACPC (American Christian Palestine Committee), 223, 225
Adams, Mildred, 77
Addams, Jane, *g1p1*, 10–11, 28, 145
AFL. *See* American Federation of Labor
AFME. *See* American Friends of the Middle East
African Americans, 46, 49–51, 113, 119, 134, 163, 184, 247
AFSC. *See* American Friends Service Committee
AJC. *See* American Jewish Congress
Ali Ash Sheikh Said Al Qaderi, 204
Alien Registration Act (Smith Act), 111
Allen, Jay, 90–91, 101
Alling, Paul, 153
Alonei Yitzhak Children's Village, *g2p9*, 236–37
Alsop, Joseph, 62–64, 66, 89, 267n8
America First Committee, 112
American Association for the United Nations (AAUN), 227, 232
American Christian Committee for German Refugees (ACCGR), 25–28
American Christian Palestine Committee (ACPC), 223, 225
American Christians, 2, 9–10, 26–28, 44–45, 108, 113–14, 127, 194, 208, 223–26. *See also* "non-Aryan" Christian refugees
American Civil Liberties Union (ACLU), 11
American Committee for the Evacuation of British Children, 67
American Council for Judaism, 163, 195–96, 227, 229

American Federation of Labor (AFL), 11–12, 53, 229
American Financial and Development Corporation for Israel, 196
American Friends of the Middle East (AFME), 224, 227, 229–30
American Friends Service Committee (AFSC), 160; and American Jewish Joint Distribution Committee (JDC), 68–70; approach to rehabilitation, 2, 21–22, 141–42, 146, 159, 207, 247; and coal miners in West Virginia, 19–21; and Israel's Arab citizens, 239; and "non-Aryan" Christians, 22–23, 26, 36, 48; and *Refugee Facts* pamphlet, 108–10, 111, 167; and relief programs in Germany and France, 22–25, 29, 36–37, 55, 74, 119–20; and subsistence homestead programs, 20, 23–25, 142, 207. *See also* Pickett, Clarence E.
American Hebrew Medal, 10
American Jewish Committee, 10, 109, 163, 184
American Jewish Congress (AJC), 10–12, 108–9, 129
American Jewish Joint Distribution Committee (JDC), 68–70, 99, 116, 120, 144, 235–36
American Jews: effect of persecution of Jews abroad on, 17, 35, 37; FDR's inclusion in his administration, 16; and funding for settlements in Palestine, 141, 206; response to extermination camps by, 127–29; response to establishment of Israel by, 247
American League for a Free Palestine, 153–54, 169
American Legion, 55
Americans for Democratic Action, 223
American Unity, 114, 185

American Zionist Council (AZC), 225
Anglo-American Committee of Inquiry, 160–61, 170–72, 176
Anschluss, 32, 34, 51, 122, 142
anti-immigration sentiment, 2, 55–57, 59, 72, 107–12, 162, 165–66, 277n2
antilynching bill, 49–51
anti-Nazi groups and refugees, 11, 73–78, 86, 93, 98
antisemitism: and aid to European Jews, 133; and Isaiah Bowman, 35; in Congress, 97, 113; and ER, 3–6, 41, 43, 46, 113–15, 133–34; and failed rescue of 5,000 Jewish children, 121; and FDR, 4, 16; and Henry Ford, 4; and Charles Lindbergh, 112; and the National Conference of Christians and Jews, 44–45; and the Wagner-Rogers bill, 56; and H. G. Wells, 41; and wider distribution of Jews, 42. *See also* anti-immigration sentiment
Arab-Israeli war of 1948, 187–93
Arab refugees, 188–89, 202–4, 228, 230, 249. *See also* Palestinian Arabs
Arabs: and American Christians, 224–25; and Arab Christians, 223–24, 238; and Arab-Israeli conflict, 187–88, 190–91, 233; and defiance of the United Nations (UN), 175–76, 187, 204, 249; and disparity between Arabs and Israelis, 210–13; and the Eisenhower administration, 227–28; as residents of Israel, 239–40; and military assistance to Arab nations, 228; and nationalism, 40; and oil, 177; propaganda in U.S. by, 229; and Universal Declaration of Human Rights (UDHR), 185–87. *See also* American Friends of the Middle East; Palestinian Arabs
Armstrong, Hamilton Fish, *91p2*, 102–3

Arthurdale, 19–21, 138, 142, 207, 209. *See also* subsistence homestead program
assimilation. *See under* immigration (Israel); Roosevelt, Eleanor
Attlee, Clement, 160
Austin, Warren, 178, 182, 190, 204
Austria, 25, 32, 34–35, 51–52, 54, 72, 142
AZC (American Zionist Council), 225

B
Baehr, Karl, 225
Baldwin, Joseph C., 134
Balfour, Arthur, 140, 202
Balfour, Robert, 222
Balfour Declaration, 140–41, 170, 173, 178–79, 186–87, 201–2, 223, 226
Baqa-al-Garbya, 239
Baratz, Joseph, *g2p5*, 208–10, 222, 229–30, 233, 241–42
Bar-David, Molly Lyons, 195
Baruch, Bernard, 4, 21, 44, 189–90
Beersheba, 149, 207–8, 237, 243
Begin, Menachem, 171
Ben-Gurion, David, *g2p11*, 181–82, 212, 219, 227, 232, 240–41
Benjamin, Paul C., 94–98, 274n4
Ben-Zvi, Yitzhak, 212, 242
Bergson, Peter (Hillel Kook), 130, 132, 153, 169
Berle, A. A. Jr., 73
Bernadotte, Folke, and peace plan for Palestine, 188–91
Bernard, Viola W., 53, 68
Bet Mazmil Community Health Center, 219–20
Bevin, Ernest, 160–62, 172
Beyond Tears (Litten), 97–99
Biddle, Eric, 68–69, 84
Biddle, Francis, 62–64, 83
Bill of Rights (U.S.), 184–85. *See also* Universal Declaration of Human Rights
Bingham, Hiram IV, 78–79, 91
"The Black Book of Polish Jewry," 131
Blaustein, Jacob, 118–19, 184–85
Blitzer, Max, 25
Bohlen, Charles "Chip," 179–80, 190
Bohn, Frank, 76, 79, 81–82
"The Bombers Are Coming," 67
Bowman, Isaiah, *g2p2*, 35, 148–51, 154, 155, 169–70, 249
Breckinridge, Sophonisba, 63–64
Breitman, Richard, 126
Brodie, Israel, 222
Brodsky, Berta, 17–18, 21
"Brotherhood Day," 45
Buck, F. W., 56
Buck, Pearl, 118
Bullitt, William, 124–26
Bunche, Ralph, 191
Byrnes, James, 157
Byroade, Henry A., 227–28

C
Cadman, S. Parkes, 44
Cambous, France, 215–16, 219, 235
Campbell, Beth, 47
Carlin, George, 43
Cassin, René, 183–85
Catt, Carrie Chapman, 9–12, 15, 28, 108
CCDP (Citizens Committee on Displaced Persons), 163–65
Cecil, John, 56
Centre Américain de Secours (American Assistance Center), 77–79
The Christian Century, 224
Christianity. *See* American Christian Committee for German Refugees; American Christians; Roosevelt, Eleanor: and Christianity; National

Christianity (*continued*)
  Conference of Christians and Jews; Nazi Germany: and Christianity; "non-Aryan" Christian refugees
"Christianity in Action: Experiments in Social Regeneration" (Pickett), 47–48
Christians. *See* American Christians; "non-Aryan" Christian refugees
Citizens Committee for Children of New York, 214–15
Citizens Committee on Displaced Persons (CCDP), 163–65
City of Benares, 67
civil rights, 9, 14, 49–51, 114–15, 163, 184–87, 201, 247
Clifford, Clark, 175, 181, 227
Clinchy, Everett R., 44–45
Close, Kathryn, 123–24
Cohen, Benjamin, 53, 178, 183, 190
Cold War, 204–5, 227, 249
colonialism, 191, 211, 231, 248
colonization, 35–36, 143, 212
Colony Club, 6
Committee for a Jewish Army of Stateless and Palestinian Jews, 130
Communism, 45, 110, 164, 196, 204–5, 210–11, 227, 234, 244–45, 249
community building, 20–22, 136–38, 141–44, 239
Conference on the Cause and Cure of War, 12, 28–30, 183
Congress. *See* antisemitism: in congress; Costigan-Wagner antilynching bill; Emergency Committee to Save the Jews of Europe; immigration (U.S.); Roosevelt, Eleanor: DP immigration bills; Suez Crisis; Wagner-Rogers Bill
Congress House, 108–9
Congress Weekly, 129

Connally, Tom, 157
Cook, Blanche Wiesen, 29
Corr, Maureen, 243
Costigan-Wagner antilynching bill, 49–51
Coulter, Eliot, 85
Cox, E. E, 167
cultural integration. *See* immigration (Israel): assimilation of children
Cyprus, British detention camps on, 170, 172–74, 180
Czechoslovakia, 32–33, 36–37, 105, 181, 228–29
Czech student refugees, 104–6

D
Dabbagh, Wadad, 186–87
Davis, Norman, 70
Declaration of the Rights of Man, 184–85. *See also* Universal Declaration of Human Rights
Degania, 208–10, 222, 241–42. *See also* Baratz, Joseph
Deri, Aryeh, 216–17
de Sola Pool, Tamar, 148, 153
Dewey, Thomas E., 137, 144, 154, 194
Dickstein, Samuel, 56
Dinnerstein, Leonard, 168
displaced persons (DPs): and the Anglo-American Committee of Inquiry, 161; DP camps, 157–67, 174, 180, 191, 220–21, 245; and the International Refugee Organization (IRO), 159; and the Truman administration, 162–64, 168. *See also* Citizens Committee on Displaced Persons; Stratton bill; Wiley-Revercomb DP bill
Displaced Persons Act, 168
Dominican Republic, 35
Doony, Catherine, 59

INDEX

Dubinsky, David, *g1p9*, 137
DuBois, Josiah E. Jr., 134–35
Dulles, John Foster, 157–58, 190, 227, 229–31
Dushkin, Julia (Mrs. Alexander M.), *g2p6*, 207

E

Eban, Abba, 191, 241
Egypt, 190–91, 212, 228–33
Eilat, 236–37
Ein Kerem Medical Center, 237
Einstein, Albert, 103–4, 137
Eisenhower administration, 227–35, 240
Eisenhower Doctrine, 233–34
Elath, Eliahu, 222
Eleanor Roosevelt Youth Aliyah Day Centre, 237, 243
Elliott, John, 108
Elman, Mischa, 109
el-Rifai, Samir, 238
Emergency Committee to Save the Jews of Europe, 131–32, 134
Emergency Refugee Shelter at Fort Ontario, Oswego, NY, *g1p10*, 136–38
Emergency Rescue Committee (ERC), 3, 72–106. *See also* Fry, Varian; immigration (U.S.); President's Advisory Committee on Political Refugees; visa policy (U.S.)
Entr'aide Européenne, 22–23
ERC. *See* Emergency Rescue Committee
Ernst, Arthur, 137
Eshkol, Levi, 218
Évian Conference, Évian-les-Bains, France, 34–35
Exodus (ship), 173–74
Exodus (Uris), 192, 195
Eye on Israel (Mart), 192

F

Falastin, 204, 238
fedayeen, 191
Federal Council of Churches, 25, 45, 164
Federal Emergency Relief Administration (FERA), 19–20, 33
Feisal, Emir, 186
FERA (Federal Emergency Relief Administration), 19–20, 33
Ferguson, Homer, 165
Field, Marshall III, 3, 53, 61, 68–71, 80, 84, 120–22, 265n10
Fischer, Erna, 85
Fleeson, Doris, 2
Flournoy, Richard, 64
Ford, Henry, and "The International Jew: The World's Problem" (article), 4
Foreign Affairs, 38
Foreign Policy Association (FPA), 7–8, 12, 73
Forrestal, James, 177
Fort Ontario (Emergency Refugee Shelter, Oswego), 136–38
Fosdick, Harry Emerson, 26
Four Freedoms, 114
FPA. *See* Foreign Policy Association
France: exit permits from, 71, 77–78, 90, 94, 100, 124–25; fall of, 61, 72, 83, 89; and Fry, 77–79, 102–3, 106; and German refugees, 22, 73–77; and Gurs camp, 93; refugee children, evacuation from, 67–71, 116–17, 119–24; and Suez Crisis, 231–32. *See also* Emergency Rescue Committee; Fry, Varian; Vichy government of France; visa policy (U.S.)
Franco, Francisco, 32
Frank, Karl B., 73–74, 76, 80–81
Frankfurter, Felix, 10, 11, 44, 83, 168

Freier, Bill (Bill Spira), 78
Friedman, Joseph, 135
Friendship Houses (refugee hostels), 108
Fry, Eileen, 102–3
Fry, Varian, *g1p5*, 73–79, 80–82, 90–92, 100–101, 102–3, 106, 116–17, 270n4
Fullerton, Hugh, 78–79
Funkhouser, Richard, 210
Fushan, Louis, 42
"The Future of the Jews" (Wells), 40–43

G
Gannett, Taylor, 86–87, 90
Gaon, Solomon, 222
Garner, John Nance, 34
Gellhorn, Martha, *g1p7*, 33–34, 36–37, 88
Gellman, Irwin, 126
General Federation of Women's Clubs, 165
German Jewish Children's Aid, 69
Germany. *See* Nazi Germany
Goebbels, Joseph, 98
Goldstein, Israel, 229
Goldstone, Aline, 169
Good Neighbor League Committee on the Émigré and the Community, 108
Gordon, A. D., 209–10
Granoff, Abraham, 175
Great Britain: and Anglo-American Committee of Inquiry, 160–61, 170–72; and Balfour Declaration, 140–41; and Blitz, 83; ER as critical of, 172–73, 188, 191, 248; ER's 1957 visit to, 222; and evacuation of children to the United States, 61–67, 89; and the *Exodus*, 173–74; and internment camps on Cyprus, 173–74; Jewish immigration to Palestine, prevention of, 126, 140–41, 149, 151–53, 159–61, 170–74, 248; and King David Hotel attack, 171–72; and Mandate for Palestine, 41, 140–41, 161, 178–79, 181–82, 191; and the Suez Crisis, 231–32; and Youth Aliyah, 148, 222
Great Depression, 4, 11, 33, 49, 52, 107
Green, William, 53
Greenberg, Marian, 147–48
Greenwald, Morton, 113
Gruber, Ruth, 138–39, 195, 212
Grynszpan, Herschel, 37, 39
Gurewitsch, David, 198
Gurewitsch, Edna, 243
Gurs camp, 70, 93, 116

H
Haber, William, 168
Hadassah: and absorptive capacity of Palestine, 148–49; annual conventions of, 17, 146, 216, 221; founding of, 146; and Jewish child refugees in Teheran, 153; medical centers and services in Israel of, 146, 206–8, 219–20, 236–37; membership of, 206; and Henrietta Szold, 145–48, 197, 207. *See also* Youth Aliyah
Hadassah Magazine, 243
Hadassah Newsletter, 195, 215, 218
Haganah, 188, 199
Haifa, 221, 236
Hall, George Henry, 172
Halprin, Rose, 149–51, 170
Halsted, James A., 236
Hamilton, Alice, 10–11, 29
Hanfstaengl, Ernst "Putzi," 8
Harman, Abe, 225
Harrison, Earl, 160, 164, 167
Hart, Henry, 83–84

Hart, Moss, 130
Hasan-El-Kaatib, 237–38
Hecht, Ben, 130
Henderson, Loy, 174–75, 177
Henry Street Settlement, 5, 146. *See also* settlement house movement
Hickok, Lorena ("Hick"), 19
High Commission for Refugees (Jewish and Other) Coming from Germany, 12–15
Hill, Dorothy, 93–94, 274n2
Hitler, Adolph, 23, 24, 32, 36–37, 49, 51, 61, 75, 78, 93, 110, 141, 144, 165, 171, 183, 224; and Hans Litten, 98; and McDonald, 7–9; and National Conference of Christians and Jews (NCCJ), 44–45; and Nuremberg Laws, 14; and protests against in U.S., 9–12, 15–16, 38, 117, 128–30, 133
Holocaust, 1–3, 115, 123, 183, 215; and survivors of, 139, 158, 168, 173–74, 177, 194–95, 198, 221, 244–45, 247. *See also* Nazi Germany
Hoover, Herbert, 52–53
Hoovervilles (homeless encampments), 20
Hopkins, Garland Evans, 224
Hopkins, Harry, 19, 33
Horne, Lea, 196
HRC. *See* United Nations Human Rights Commission
Hull, Cordell, 12, 34, 58, 63–66, 96, 124–26
human rights, 9–10, 114–15, 134, 158, 176, 183–87, 203, 247–50; and genocide, 183; and economic and social rights, 114, 184–85. *See also* Universal Declaration of Human Rights
Human Rights Commission. *See* United Nations Human Rights Commission

Hutchins, Robert, 76
Hyman, Joseph, 35, 68

I

ICASR (Intercollegiate Committee to Aid Student Refugees), 57–59, 105
Ickes, Harold, 20, 138
IGCR. *See* Intergovernmental Committee on Refugees
immigration (Israel): assimilation of children, 216–19, 236–37, 243–45, 296n13; Israel's open immigration policy, 194, 199, 200, 206; North African and Middle Eastern immigrant children, 215, 218–19, 228, 243–42. *See also* Youth Aliyah
immigration (Palestine): and Balfour Declaration, 141, 186; Bowman's assessment of absorptive capacity, 148–51; British efforts to restrict Jewish immigration to Palestine, 126, 140–41, 149, 151–53, 159, 160–61, 170–74, 248; and ER's attitude toward immigration to Palestine, 149, 160–61, 170–71; and Palestine as a possible haven for Jewish refugees, 168–72
immigration (U.S.): and anti-immigration sentiment, 2, 55–57, 59, 61, 72, 107–12, 162, 165–66; and barriers of American immigration laws, 51–52, 83, 162, 164–66; and British children endangered by Blitz, 61–67; and concerns about subversion, 103–4; and DP bills, 166–68; and efforts to liberalize immigration policy, 11–12, 96, 112; and LPC rule, 51–52; and *Quanza*, 79–80; and quotas, 4, 34, 43, 51–52, 54–57, 60, 77, 79, 68, 120, 141, 162, 164, 167, 277n4; and restrictionist refugee policies,

immigration (U.S.) (*continued*)
125–26, 138; and *St. Louis* refugees,
79–80; and temporary havens, 136–38;
and Wagner-Rogers bill, 54–57. *See
also* antisemitism; refugees; visa policy
(U.S.)
Immigration Act of 1924, 83
Immigration and Naturalization Service
(INS), 62, 80, 84, 111
India and the Awakening East (Roosevelt),
210–11, 226
Inglis, Agnes, 61, 111–12
INS. *See* Immigration and Naturalization
Service
Intercollegiate Committee to Aid Student
Refugees (ICASR), 57–59, 105
Intergovernmental Committee on
Refugees (IGCR), 35–36, 126, 152–53
International Court of Justice, 211–12
"The International Jew: The World's
Problem," 4
Internationaler Sozialistischer
Kampfbund (ISK), 93–95, 98
international police force, 30–31, 176–78,
228, 231–32
International Refugee Organization
(IRO), 159–60, 194
International Socialist Fighting Alliance,
93–95, 98
International Student Service (ISS), 59,
104–5
intolerance, *See* prejudice
"Intolerance" (Roosevelt), 46
Iran, 236, 239–40
Iraq, 150, 153, 200, 218, 225, 228
Irgun, 151, 171–72, 199
IRO (International Refugee
Organization), 159–60, 194
ISK (Internationaler Sozialistischer
Kampfbund), 93–95, 98

isolationism, 28, 33, 112
Israel: agricultural settlements, 197,
208–10, 242; and American Jews,
195–96, 208, 229, 232; and American
social reformers, 207; American
support for, 223–27; Arab-Israeli
conflict, 187–88, 190–92, 210–13,
225, 229–30, 234; Arab-Israeli war
of 1948, 191, 203, 208, 226, 241, 248;
Arabs living in, 239–40; defensive
weapons to, 229–30; and Eisenhower
administration, 227–34; founding
of, 185, 194–95, 248–50; and human
rights, 185, 248; invasion of the Sinai,
231–33; and Moroccan Jews, 215–16,
235; U.S. recognition of, 181–83. *See
also* Hadassah; immigration (Israel);
Roosevelt, Eleanor, trips to Israel;
Youth Aliyah
Israel Without Tears (Gruber), 195
ISS (International Student Service), 59,
104–5

J
Jacobson, Eddie, 138, 175, 227
Jacobson, Gunther, 98
JDC. *See* American Jewish Joint
Distribution Committee
Jerusalem, 146, 171, 181, 189, 204, 206–8,
234, 236–38
Jerusalem Post, 207–8
Jessup, Philip, 190
Jewish Labor Committee (JLC), 76, 94
Jewish National Fund, National Women's
Committee of, 142–43
"The Jew's Lot in Germany" (Cadman),
44
JLC (Jewish Labor Committee), 76, 94
Johnson, Lyndon, 233
Jordan, 191, 203, 206, 226, 238

Junior Hadassah, 147
Justice Department (U.S.), 62–63, 66, 69, 76, 78, 80, 83–85, 89. *See also* visa policy (U.S.)

K
"Keepers of Democracy" (Roosevelt), 45
Kennedy, Joseph, 65–66
Kenworthy, Marion, 53, 68
Khoury, Bechara el, 200
kibbutzim, 22, 138, 207–9, 237, 239, 241. *See also* Degania
King David Hotel, bombing of, 171
Kingdon, Frank, 61, 76, 85–86, 88, 94, 102, 106
Kirchwey, Freda, 76, 154
Kiryat Gat, 243–44
Kiryat Hayovel, 219–20
Knesset, 209
Knowland, William, 233
Kol, Moshe, *g2p11*, 138–39, 198, 214–15, 222, 227, 235–36, 245–46
Kook, Hillel. *See* Bergson, Peter
Kristallnacht (the "night of broken glass"), 37–40, 44, 50, 52, 57, 108, 118, 139, 147
Kurth, Peter, 38

L
LaGuardia, Fiorello, 12
Landman, Isaac, 10
Landsberg, Clara, 10–11
Lang, Robert, 122
Lape, Esther, 28
Lash, Joseph, 59, 73, 104–6, 158, 248
Lash, Trude, *g2p7–8*, 104–5, 214–19, 244
Lauterpacht, Hersch Zvi, 183–85
Laval, Pierre, 67, 117, 121–22
League of Nations, 12–13, 15, 30, 140, 156, 177
League of Women Voters, 9

Lebanon, 191, 200–201, 203–5, 226
LeHand, Marguerite ("Missy"), 12–14
Lehi, 172, 189, 199
Lehman, Edith, 99
Lehman, Herbert H., 5, 44, 50, 60, 99, 137, 178, 195
Leiper, Henry Smith, 45
Lemkin, Raphael, 183
Leon Blum Colony, 142–44
Lerner, Max, 131–32
Levi, Juda, 137
Levin, Maier M., 42
Levy, Adele Rosenwald, 53, 68, 70, 145, 163–64
Lewinski, Eva, *g1p8*, 93–98, 103
Lewis, John L., 53, 137
Liberty, 40–43
Lichtman, Allan, 126
Lindbergh, Charles, 112
Lisbon, Portugal, 67–70, 78, 80, 86, 88, 90, 99, 120
Lithuania, 162
Litten, Hans, 97–98
Litten, Irmgard, 97–100
Litten, Rainer, 97–100, 275n24
Loeffler, James, 183
London Times, 15
Long, Breckinridge, *g1p8*; advice on blocking visas, 88; conflict with ER, 72, 87–89, 90, 94, 96, 100–102, 125, 135; and emergency visas to political refugees, 76–77, 81–84, 87–89, 94; and FDR, relationship with, 87–89, 96; and Eileen and Varian Fry, 102; and Litten case, 100; and Lustig case, 87–88; obstruction of visa process, 64, 89–90, 125, 134–35; and *Quanza* refugees, 80; and tightening of visa regulations, 80–81, 103–4
Lovett, Robert, 177

Lowdermilk, Walter S., 149
Lubitsch, Ernst, 92
Luce, Clare Booth, 118
Lustig, Hans, 85–90, 99, 107, 272n41
lynching, 49–51

M

ma'abarah (camp for absorbing refugees), 218
MacArthur, Douglas II, 86
MacLeish, Archibald, 117–18
Malik, Charles, 198–200
Malin, Patrick, 68
Mann, K. J., *g2p6*, 207–8, 237
Manning, William T., 195
Marseille, France, 67, 77–81, 95, 105, 120
Marshall, George, 173, 176–79, 181–82, 188–90
Marshall Plan, 177
Mart, Michelle, 192, 248, 256n6
McClay, John, 153
McDonald, James G., *g1p2*; as chairman of President's Advisory Committee on Political Refugees (PACPR), 35, 76, 82–85, 101, 104, 120; ER, relationship with, 3, 7–9, 12–13, 25, 161, 169; as High Commissioner for Refugees Coming from Germany, 12–15, 23, 34; meeting with Hitler, 8; and FDR, 7–8, 12–17, 24–25, 34–35, 82–84, 101, 104, 120–21, 135; Palestine as solution to the Jewish refugee problem, 168–71; and subsistence homestead program, 23–24, 25; advice regarding Wagner-Rogers bill, 55.
McGrath, J. Howard, 167
McPherson, Flora, 117
Meier Shfeyah youth village, 147
Meir, Golda, *g2p12*, 233, 240–42

Mercer, Lucy, 5
Messersmith, George, 57–58
Mexico, 79, 221
Miller, Louis, 219
Moffat, Jay Pierrepont, 12, 54, 58
The Moral Basis of Democracy (Roosevelt), 48
Morgenthau, Elinor, *g1p1*, 5–6, 10, 16–17, 136, 146, 148, 153, 196
Morgenthau, Henry Jr., 5–6, 34, 112, 134–35, 195–96; and "Personal Report to the President" on the State Department's subversion of rescue efforts, 134–35
Morgenthau, Henry III, 5–6, 240
Moroccan Jews, 215–16, 235, 242, 244
Morris, Benny, 199
Moskowitz, Belle, 5
Mouzinho, 69–71
"Mrs. Roosevelt Answers Mr. Wells on the Future of the Jews" (Roosevelt), 40–44, 115, 133
"Mrs. Roosevelt Is on Stump for New Brand of Citizenship" (Campbell), 47
Muslims, 199, 223–24, 236, 248
My Promised Land (Bar-David), 195
My Promised Land: The Triumph and Tragedy of Israel (Shavit), 216

N

Nasser, Gamal Abdel, 228–29, 231, 233–34
National Committee on the Cause and Cure of War, 12, 28–30, 183
National Conference of Christians and Jews (NCCJ), *g1p9*, 44–47, 113–14; Brotherhood Day and Week, 45; Round Tables, 45, 114; Ten Commandments of Good Will, 45, 263n19

National Coordinating Committee for Aid to Refugees and Emigrants Coming from Germany, 25, 108, 144. *See also* National Refugee Service
National Council of Jewish Women, 178
National Refugee Service (NRS), 68, 138, 144
Nazi Germany: Allies' condemnation of, 129; American Friends Service Committee (AFSC) in, 22–25, 29, 36–37, 55; and American policy of noninterference, 14–16, 26–28; and antilynching bill, 49–51; and anti-Nazi groups, 11, 93, 98; and anti-Nazi refugees, 73–78, 136; armistice agreement with the Vichy government, 78, 122; and Christianity, 25, 59, 97; FDR's response to, 10, 15–16, 37, 135; Kristallnacht, 37–39; and James McDonald, 7–8, 12–15; and National Conference of Christians and Jews (NCCJ), 44–45; Nuremberg Laws, 14; and *Pastor Hall*, 98; program to exterminate the Jews, 127–30, 163; program of forcing Jews from Germany, 13–14; protests against in U.S., 9–12, 15, 117, 128–30, 133; and Ravensbrück Women's Preventive Detention Camp, 117–19; and subsistence homestead programs for refugees from, 23–25. *See also* Holocaust
NCCJ. *See* National Conference of Christians and Jews
Neal, Claude, 50
Negev, 189–93, 207, 237
Neutrality Act, 60, 67
New Deal, 19, 33, 49–50, 149, 183, 185, 207, 244. *See also* subsistence homestead program

New York Herald Tribune Forum on Current Problems, 110
New York Herald Tribune, 44, 106, 112, 198
New York Times, 8–9, 15, 95–96, 121, 127, 177, 189, 230
New York World-Telegram, 179
New Zionist Organization, 151
Niebuhr, Reinhold, 76, 137, 223
Niles, David, 175, 227
"non-Aryan" Christian refugees, 13–14, 22–23, 25–28, 34, 36, 48, 51, 54, 67, 197
Non-Sectarian Committee for German Refugee Children, 55–56, 60–61
Non-Sectarian Foundation for Refugee Children, 60–61
Nuremberg Laws, 14

O

O'Day, Caroline, 61
O'Dwyer, William, 195
Oeuvre de Secours aux Enfants (OSE), 68–69
ORT (organization), *g2p6*, 141–46, 247, 284n5
Oswego, NY (Emergency Refugee Shelter at Fort Ontario), 136–38

P

PACPR. *See* President's Advisory Committee on Political Refugees
Palestine: absorptive capacity of, 149, 154, 170–71, 192–93, 289n43; and American Jewish organizations, 163; American League for a Free Palestine, 153–54; Anglo-American Committee of Inquiry, 160–61, 170; and Balfour Declaration, 140–41, 178, 186–87, 226; Bernadotte peace plan, 189–90;

Palestine (*continued*)
and Isaiah Bowman's analysis of, 148–51, 249; British efforts to restrict Jewish immigration to, 126, 140–41, 149, 151–53, 159, 160–61, 170–74, 248; Committee for a Jewish Army of Stateless and Palestinian Jews, 130; FDR's position on future of, 154–55; and Hadassah, origins of, 146; and Haganah, 188; as homeland for the Jewish people, 40, 140–41, 147, 150, 155, 163, 169, 178, 186, 201–2, 204, 211, 223, 247; and Jewish refugees, 126, 168–69; Jewish settlements in, 140–41, 146–47, 150, 169, 178–79, 180, 194, 248; and nationalism, 40–41; and United Jewish Appeal (UJA), 194; and United Palestine Appeal (UPA), 144; and Universal Declaration of Human Rights, 186–87, 249; UN Special Committee on Palestine (UNSCOP), 172–75, 177; and Youth Aliyah, 145, 147–48. *See also* Palestinian Arabs; partition plan for Palestine

Palestine, 145

Palestinian Arabs: and American Friends of the Middle East (AFME), 224; conflict with Israelis, 199–203; and Malik, 198; and Penrose, 200–203; pro-Arab viewpoints in America, 224–25; as refugees, 188, 199, 202–3, 204; and Universal Declaration of Human Rights, 186–87; and UN Special Committee on Palestine, 174–75, 177, 180; and UN trusteeship for Palestine, 178–80, 190–91, 204. *See also* Palestine; partition plan for Palestine

Papanek, Ernst, 68, 268n32

Pappé, Ilan, 199

Pardesiya, 218

partition plan for Palestine, *g2p4*; and American Christians, 223–24; and Arab-Israeli conflict, 187–88, 190–91; and international police force, 176–78; Negev, assignment of, 188–91; and Penrose, 200–202; and principle of self-determination, 174, 177, 202; and strategic importance of oil, 177; and Truman administration, 175, 176–79, 190; and UDHR, 185–87; and UNSCOP report, 174–75, 176–78; and UN trusteeship as alternative to partition, 126, 178–80, 190–91, 204; and Welles, 169. *See also* Palestine; Palestinian Arabs

Pastor Hall, 98, 275n21

Paul, Randolph, 134–35

Pearson, Drew, and Washington Merry-Go-Round column, 64

Peck, William L., 79

Pehle, John, 134–35

Pell, Herbert C., 80–81

Penrose, Stephen B. L., Jr., *g2p5*, 200–203, 224

Perkins, Frances, 58

Pfister, Otto, 95, 98

Phillips, William, 12, 15

Pickett, Clarence E., *g1p2*; access to ER and FDR, 23–24; and citizenship in a democracy, 48; and *Refugee Facts*, 109, 111; and Christianity in action, 47–48; and subsistence homestead programs, 20, 23–25; visits to AFSC centers in Europe ("To Our Friends" letters), 24–25, 29, 36. *See also* American Friends Service Committee

Pickett, Lilly, *g1p2*, 24–25, 29, 36

The Plot Against America (Roth), 42

Point 4 program, 205–6, 236

Poland, 128, 133, 141, 148, 162; and Ravensbrück Women's Preventive Detention Camp, 117–19; and Wiley-Revercomb DP bill, 167–68
Polier, Justine, *g2p3*, 60–61, 68; Arab-Israeli conflict, statement on, 229–30; and British policies re Palestine, 151–52; and ER, 47, 53, 55, 96, 140, 163, 184–85; on Cardinal Spellman, 56; and Wagner-Rogers Bill, 53, 56
Portugal, 67–71, 73, 78, 86, 88, 90, 94, 97, 99, 120, 122–23
Prague, 26, 36–37, 85
Pratt, Trude. *See* Lash, Trude
prejudice, 3, 16, 38–39, 41, 44–46, 56, 90, 97, 108–9, 111–15, 131, 133–34, 167–68, 171
President's Advisory Committee on Political Refugees (PACPR), 35, 76–78, 80–85, 87, 92–95, 100–105, 120, 125
Pritchard, Edward F. Jr., 68
Progressive reform movement, 145–46, 207
Protest Committee of Non-Jewish Women Against the Persecution of Jews in Germany, 9–10
The Protocols of the Elders of Zion, 4
public health, 5, 17, 146, 207, 217

Q

Quakers. *See* American Friends Service Committee; Pickett, Clarence E.
Quanza, *g1p6*, 79–80

R

Ramat Hadassah Szold, 197
Rankin, John Elliott, 113
Rath, Ernst vom, 37
Ravensbrück Women's Preventive Detention Camp, 117–19, 139
Razovsky, Cecilia, 25
Read, Elizabeth, 28
Reading, Stella, 222
Rees, Elfan, 199–200
Refugee Facts, *g1p4*, 109–11, 165, 167
refugees: resettlement of European refugees in undeveloped areas, 35–36; temporary havens for, 132, 134, 136–38. *See also* Arab refugees; displaced persons; *immigration entries*
Reston, James, 177
Reuther, Walter, 229
Reynolds, Robert, 109
Rhoads, Grace Jr., 23
Riegner, Gerhart, 127
Ritchie, Frank, 26–28
Rivington Street Settlement, 4, 108, 146
Roberts, Kenneth, 4
Robinson, Joseph, 10
Rockefeller, Nelson, 195
Rogers, Edith Nourse, *g1p3*, 54–55
Rogers, Will Jr., 130, 134, 153–54
Roosevelt, Eleanor (ER): and African Americans, 46, 49–51, 113, 134, 247; and American Friends Service Committee (AFC), 19–22, 47–48; and American Jews, 16–18, 147, 195–96, 198, 247; and antilynching bill, 49–51; and antisemitism, 3–6, 41, 43, 46, 113–15, 133–34, 262n6, 282n17; and Arab citizens of Israel, *g2p9*, 239–40; and Arab point of view, 198–204, 247–48; and Arab refugees, 199, 202, 249; and assimilation, 41–44, 108–10, 215–20, 243–45; and Balfour Declaration, 140, 186–87; and Baratz, 208–10, 229–30, 233, 241–42; and charity versus self-help, 21, 146,

Roosevelt, Eleanor (ER) (*continued*) 159, 203, 245; and Christianity, 46–48, 159, 203; and citizenship in a democracy, 47–48, 114–15; and Cold War, 204–5, 249; and colonialism, 191, 211, 231, 248, 292n49; and commitment to rescuing Jews, 138–39; and constraints as wife of the president, 1, 12, 16, 28, 37–39, 109, 129–30, 139, 142–44, 154, 156; and contrast between Arabs and Iranians versus Israelis, 206, 210–13, 239–40; and contributions of immigrants to America, 16, 87, 92, 106, 108, 111–12; and cooperative communities, 19–22, 136–38, 141–44, 207, 239; and criticism of Great Britain, 151–53, 160, 170, 172–74, 248; and criticism of lack of government action to rescue Jews, 129–31; and Eisenhower administration, 227–30, 233–34; and DP camps in Germany, *g2p1*, 158–59; and DP immigration bills, 164–68; on fear distorting reality, 43, 45–46, 97, 104, 110, 166, 180; and Varian Fry, 79, 91, 102–3, 106; and fundraising for Hadassah and Youth Aliyah, 221–22; and growth, capacity for, 3, 6, 248; as idealist and pragmatist, 169–72, 212–13, 249; influence of, 1, 26–27, 44–45, 63–66, 92, 95, 99, 108–9, 129, 121, 136, 144, 146–48, 156, 176, 192, 194–95, 197, 204, 225, 242, 299n29; and interventions to alter American refugee policy, 63–66, 120–21; and Israeli leaders, 240–42; and Kristallnacht response, 37–39; and Joseph Lash, 59, 73, 104–6, 158, 214–16, 218–19, 248, 255–56; and Trude Lash (Pratt), 104–6, 214–19, 224; and Adele Levy, 163; and Breckinridge Long, 72–73, 87–89, 96, 100, 274n13; and James McDonald, 7–8, 12–14, 15–16, 24, 35, 101; My Day column (*see* Roosevelt, Eleanor, My Day column); and naïveté, 29, 63, 118–19, 139, 175, 211–12; and obstruction of visas, deliberate nature of, 85–89, 124–25; and Palestine, future of, 141, 154–55, 169–72; Palestine partition plan, support for, 174–75, 176–83, 185–87, 189–91, 203, 226, 248–49, 302n4; prejudice and intolerance, efforts to combat, 41, 44–46, 111–15, 133–34; publications of (*see* Roosevelt, Eleanor, publications); and Quaker approach to conflict, 21–22, 29–31; and Quaker approach to rehabilitation, 2, 21–22, 141–42, 146, 159, 207, 247; and religious beliefs, 46–48; and response to Nazi plans to exterminate the Jews, 128–32; and "sermons on citizenship," 47–48, 110, 111, 166; and silence about Nazi persecution of the Jews, 6, 7, 15–17, 19, 26–28, 30, 129–30, 270n13; speeches of (*see* Roosevelt, Eleanor, speeches); and stereotypes of Jews, 3, 115, 133–34, 192, 208; and subsistence homestead programs, 20–22, 25, 207; and trips to Israel (*see* Roosevelt, Eleanor, trips to Israel); and Universal Declaration of Human Rights (UDHR), 183–87; and vision of Israeli-Arab cooperation, 211–13, 295n20; and Sumner Welles, 73, 94–95, 100–101, 124–25; and Suez Crisis, 231–34, 240.

Roosevelt, Eleanor, My Day column: and avoidance of controversial foreign policy matters, 27, 39, 117–19, 127–33,

144; British children, effort to alter policy on, 63–66; and Dorothy Thompson's On the Record, comparison to, 38–39; and outspokenness after leaving White House, 160–62, 165–67, 170–74, 179–81, 189, 199, 228, 232–33; as a PR resource for Israel, 242; indirect yet pointed style of, 1, 22, 27, 39, 41, 118–19, 127–28, 132, 139

Roosevelt, Eleanor, publications: "For American Unity," 114, 185; If You Ask Me column, 156; *India and the Awakening East*, 210–11; "Intolerance," 46; "Keepers of Democracy," 45; *The Moral Basis of Democracy*, 48; "Mrs. Roosevelt Answers Mr. Wells on the Future of the Jews," 40–43, 45–46, 115; *This Troubled World*, 30; *Tomorrow Is Now*, 250; "What Religion Means to Me," 46–47

Roosevelt, Eleanor, speeches: Chautauqua speech (July 1933), 46; "Humanistic Democracy and the American Ideal," 185; "The Outlook for Peace" (Tenth Conference on the Cause and Cure of War, January, 1935), 29–30; "Promise Fulfilled" (Hadassah convention, 1955), 221; speech at twentieth annual convention of Hadassah (October 1934), 17

Roosevelt, Eleanor, trips to Israel: 1952 visit, 139, 198, 206–7; 1955 visit, 214–21, 244; 1959 visit, 235–38; 1962 visit, 242–45

Roosevelt, Franklin D. (FDR), 5, 8, 11, 20, 26–27, 34–36, 52–53, 64–67, 73, 75, 81–89, 91, 101, 104, 110, 120–21, 144, 150, 156; and antilynching bill, 49–51; and antisemitism, 4, 16; inclusion of Jews in administration, 16; and Jewish voters, 154–55; and Kristallnacht, 37; and Breckinridge Long, 87–89, 96; and James McDonald, 8, 12–13, 15–16; and Clarence Pickett, 23–24, 25, 36; and plan to rescue 5,000 Jewish children, 120–21; response to Nazi persecution of the Jews, 10, 15–16, 28, 129, 135, 257n25; response to pressure to rescue European Jews, 128–30, 134–35; and subsistence homestead programs, 20, 23–24, 25; United Nations Commission for the Investigation of War Crimes, his call for, 128; visa policy and procedure, handling of, 52, 79–89, 91, 96, 108; and Wagner-Rogers bill, 55

Roosevelt, Nina, 236–37, 240

Rooted Cosmopolitans: Jews and Human Rights in the Twentieth Century (Loeffler), 183

Rosenstein, Emily, 142

Rosenwald, Lessing, 163, 165, 195–96

Rosenwald, William, 68

Roth, Philip, 42

Rothschild, Florence, 16–17

Rusk, Dean, 182

S

Sandifer, Durward, 248

Schneiderman, Rose, *g1p9*, 5, 35, 37, 141–43

Segal, Charles, 244

Serpa Pinta, 71

settlement house movement, 4–5, 108–9, 145–47, 247

Sharp, Martha, 69

Shavit, Ari, 216–17

Sheil, Bernard, 53

Shirer, William L., 198

Shlaim, Avi, 199
Shulman, Herman, 129
Siegel, Sarah, 170–71
Silver, Abba Hillel, 163
Silverman, Sidney, 127
Simmons, Erica, 217
Smart, Joseph, 136–37
Smilansky, Moshe, 211
Smith, Al, 12
Souvestre, Marie, 46
Soviet Union, 157–58, 167, 177–78, 181, 184, 204–5, 227–29, 231–32, 234, 244, 249
Spain, 32–33, 78, 94, 99, 122–23, 158
Spanish Civil War, 30, 32–33
Spellman, Frances Joseph (Cardinal, Archbishop of New York), 56
Sprinzak, Yosef, 209–10
St. Louis, 79–80
State Department, 14–16, 26–28, 76–77, 81–84, 86–91, 94–95, 99–101, 105, 122–23, 141, 152–53, 162, 164; and the American Friends of the Middle East (AFME), 224; and ER's criticism of, 85, 95–97; and Varian Fry, 78–79, 102–3, 106; and obstruction of immigration and rescue efforts, 12, 65, 80–89, 134–35; and opposition to partition of Palestine, 174–78, 182–83, 223; and *Quanza* refugees, 80. *See also* Emergency Rescue Committee; United States Committee for the Care of European Children; visa policy (U.S.); Welles, Sumner
State of Israel bonds, 196
Stein, Anna, 93–94
Steinhardt, Laurence, 82–83, 89, 152
Stettinius, Edward, 135, 157
Stratton, William G., 164

Stratton bill, 164–66
Struma, sinking of, 151–53
Sturmabteilung (SA), 97–98
subsistence homestead program, 20, 23–25, 29, 142, 207. *See also* Arthurdale
Suez Crisis, 191, 231–34, 240
Sulzberger, Arthur Hays, 163
Summerlin, George, 143–44
Swichkow, Louis, 43
Syria, 191, 200, 205–6, 241
Szold, Henrietta, *g2p8,* 145–48, 207, 247, 285n21; and Henrietta Szold Award, 197

T
Tadmor, Gideon, 226–27, 239–40, 242–43
Talmadge, Julius V., 162
Teheran child refugees, 153
Tel Aviv, Israel, 172, 236
Tennessee Valley Authority (TVA), 149
This Troubled World (Roosevelt), 30, 32, 213
Thomas, Elbert, 178
Thompson, Dorothy, *g1p3;* advocate for refugees, 38–39; and American Friends of the Middle East (AFME), 229–30; criticism of Israel, 224; ER's admiration for, 39, 119; and Kristallnacht, 38–39; On the Record column, 38–39, 225; "To a Jewish Friend," 38; testimony on Wagner-Rogers bill, 56
Thompson, Malvina ("Tommy"), 13, 23
Tiberias, 236
"To a Jewish Friend" (Thompson), 38
Toller, Ernst, 98
Troper, Morris, 70, 99
Truman, Harry S., 231; and admittance of Jews to Palestine, 159–61; and Bernadotte peace plan, 189–91; and

defensive weapons for Israel, 229; and legislation to admit DPs to U.S., 162–64, 168; Eisenhower, contrasted to, 227, 234; and ER's appointment to the American delegation to the UN, 155–58; ER's influence on, 204; and *Exodus* refugees, 173–74; and Fort Ontario refugee camp, 138; and partition plan for Palestine, 176–79, 189–90; Point 4 program, 204–5; State of Israel, establishment of, 181–83

Tuck, S. Pinckney, 121–22

TVA (Tennessee Valley Authority), 149

Tydings, Millard, 11–12

Tyler, S. Roger, 204

U

UDHR. *See* Universal Declaration of Human Rights

Ufa film studio, 86

UJA. *See* United Jewish Appeal

Unger, Eva Warburg, 173–74

Unger, Jerome, 225

UNICEF (United Nations International Children's Emergency Fund), 160

Unitarian Service Committee, 69

United Jewish Appeal (UJA), 144–45, 158, 185, 192, 194–96, 247; and National Christian Committee, 185, 195

United Jewish Service, 138

United Nations (UN), 156–58, 174–75, 177–91, 205–6, 227, 231; and displaced persons in 1946, 157–58; and international police force, 176–78, 228, 231–32; and Palestine, future of, 169, 172–80, 188–91; and Suez Crisis, 232–33. *See also* International Refugee Organization; partition plan for Palestine; United Nations Special Committee on Palestine; Universal Declaration of Human Rights

United Nations Commission on Palestine, 178

United Nations Emergency Force, 232

United Nations Human Rights Commission (HRC), 10, 176, 179, 181, 183–84, 227

United Nations International Children's Emergency Fund (UNICEF), 160

United Nations Relief and Rehabilitation Administration (UNRRA), 159

United Nations Relief and Works Agency for Palestine Refugees, 203

United Nations Special Committee on Palestine (UNSCOP), 172–75, 176–77, 180

United Palestine Appeal (UPA), 144

United States Committee for the Care of European Children (USCCEC), *gips*, 3; and evacuation of refugee children from Britain, 61–67; and evacuation of refugee children from France, 67–71, 119–22; formation of, 61; fundraising efforts of, 70–71; and *Our Job Goes On: Rescue* and *Refuge* (pamphlet), *gips*, 70; and *Quanza* refugees, 80; and State Department policies, 61–66, 68–69, 84, 120–23

Universal Declaration of Human Rights (UDHR), 9–10, 114, 183–87, 198, 224, 249

UNRRA (United Nations Relief and Rehabilitation Administration), 159

UNSCOP. *See* United Nations Special Committee on Palestine

Uris, Leon, 192, 195

USCCEC. *See* United States Committee for the Care of European Children

V

Vandenberg, Arthur, 157
Vichy government of France, 67–68, 78–79, 116–17, 121–22, 125; deportations of Jews to Eastern Europe, 117, 120
A Village by the Jordan (Baratz), 210
visa policy (U.S.), 78–79, 93–95; and affidavits, 52, 62, 66, 69, 103, 120, 125, 138, 162; and British endangered children, 61–68; and Czech student refugees, 105; and emergency visas for political refugees, 73–77, 80–91, 94–97, 103–4; and ER's private views on State Department obstruction, 95–97; and Intercollegiate Committee to Aid Student Refugees (ICASR), 57–59; and Interdepartmental Committee, 84–85, 95, 104; Jewish children from France, failed rescue of, 120–21, 123; and Justice Department, 62–63, 66, 69, 76, 78, 80, 83–85, 89, 137–38; Litten case, 98–100; and Long's deliberate delays, 89–90; LPC rule, 51–52; Lustig case, 85–87; and President's Advisory Committee on Political Refugees role (PACPR), 76–77, 81–84; process of obtaining an American visa, 51–52, 103–4; State Department's tightening of regulations, 80–85, 103–4; and Vogls, 85. *See also* immigration (U.S.); Welles, Sumner
Vishinsky, Andrei, 157–58, 176
Vogl, Rosa, 85, 99, 272n39
Volksdeutsche, 167
Von Halle, Oscar, 124

W

Wagner, Robert, 54, 57
Wagner-Rogers bill, 52–57, 60, 164, 197, 246
Wald, Lillian, 5, 10–11, 28, 145–46
Warburg, Gisela, 148, 153
Warburg, Ingrid, 76, 89–91, 99–100, 102, 173
Warburg, Max, 42
Waren, Helen, 173
War Refugee Board, 34, 135–36
Warren, Avra, 64, 90–91, 101, 105, 124–25
Warren, George L., g1p2, 68, 76, 82–85, 96, 104, 120
Washington Jewish Review, 16, 46–47
Watson, Thomas, 195
Weill, Kurt, 130
Weiss, Louis, 60, 68–69, 84
Weizmann, Chaim, 186, 202
Weizmann, Vera, 208, 237
Welles, Sumner, g1p2, 34–36, 54, 55, 57–58, 74, 80–85, 89–92, 94–95, 98–102, 104–6, 117, 123–26; ER, relationship with, 3, 73, 124–28, 152, 281n33; and failed rescue of Jewish children, 120–21; and fear of subversives among refugees, 82, 126, 287n42; and Varian Fry, 91, 106; and international police force for Palestine, 178; Palestine, future of, 169; puzzling response to refugee crisis, 73, 100–101, 123–25; and resettlement of refugees in Latin America and elsewhere, 36; Riegner's report on Nazi extermination camps, 127; and sinking of *Struma*, 152–53; others attesting his sympathy for Jewish refugees, 58, 64, 69, 126, 282n34–35
Wells, H. G., 40–43
"We Shall Never Die," 130–32
"What Religion Means to Me" (Roosevelt), 46–47
White, Walter, 49–51
Wiley-Revercomb DP bill, 166–68

Williams, Charl Ormond, 166, 225–27
Wilson, Hugh, 37
Wilson, M. L., 20
Wilson, Woodrow, 140–41, 202
Wiltwyck School, 68
Winchell, Walter, 113
Wisconsin Jewish Chronicle, 16–17
Wise, James Waterman, 114
Wise, Louise, 108
Wise, Rabbi Stephen, 10, 11–12, 80, 127–30, 132, 141, 154, 163
Wolf, Willi, 77
Women's Division of the American Jewish Congress, 108–9
Women's Division of the Democratic Party, 5
Women's Division of the United Jewish Appeal of Greater New York, 158–59
Women's International League for Peace and Freedom, 11, 28–29
Women's Zionist Organization of America. *See* Hadassah
Woolf, S. J., 157
World Court, 28, 30
World Jewish Congress, 127, 134–35, 184
World War I, 22, 28, 187
Wyker, Mossie, 225–26

Y
Youth Aliyah, 2, 3; accomplishments of, 220–21, 245, 297n20; approach to social problems, 207; and assimilation of young immigrants, 217–19, 243–45; ER as World Patron of, 197–98, 206, 214–15, 222, 235, 242–43; history of, 145; its meaning to ER, 145, 241–42, 247, 250; mission of, 147–48; and Henrietta Szold, 145–46. *See also* Baratz, Joseph; Hadassah; Kol, Moshe; Moroccan Jews
Youth Aliyah Review, 222

Z
Zeilsheim Jewish DP camp, *g2p1*, 158
Ziff, Nell, 147
Zionism: and anti-Zionists, 163, 184, 196, 227, 290n14, 291n24; and Cohen, 178; definition of, 283n1; and ER 41, 140, 143, 163, 169–71, 186, 226, 294n31; and Gordon, 209; argument for a Jewish state, 171; and Penrose, 201–2; and Polier, 184; and Schneiderman, 142; and Szold, 145–46; and Thompson, 224–26, 229; H. G. Wells's attack on, 41; and Youth Aliyah, 217. *See also* Hadassah; Wise, Rabbi Stephen
Zionist Organization of America, 154

ABOUT THE AUTHOR

John F. Sears served as executive director of the Franklin and Eleanor Roosevelt Institute from 1986 until 1999 and as associate editor at the Eleanor Roosevelt Papers Project from 2000 until 2007. *The Eleanor Roosevelt Papers, Vol. 1*, appeared in 2007. He is also the author of *Sacred Places: American Tourist Attractions in the Nineteenth Century*. He has taught at Tufts University, Boston University, and Vassar College.

www.ingramcontent.com/pod-product-compliance
Lightning Source LLC
Chambersburg PA
CBHW061424300426
44114CB00014B/1525